PEOPLE, MARKETS, GOODS:
ECONOMIES AND SOCIETIES IN HISTORY

Volume 19

The Great Famine in Ireland and Britain's Financial Crisis

T0366405

PEOPLE, MARKETS, GOODS:
ECONOMIES AND SOCIETIES IN HISTORY

ISSN: 2051-7467

Series editors
Steve Hindle – Washington University, St Louis
Jane Humphries – University of Oxford, London School of Economics
Willem M. Jongman – University of Groningen
John Turner – Queen's University Belfast
Jane Whittle – University of Exeter
Nuala Zahedieh – University of Cambridge

The interactions of economy and society, people and goods, transactions and actions are at the root of most human behaviours. Economic and social historians are participants in the same conversation about how markets have developed historically and how they have been constituted by economic actors and agencies in various social, institutional and geographical contexts. New debates now underpin much research in economic and social, cultural, demographic, urban and political history. Their themes have enduring resonance – financial stability and instability, the costs of health and welfare, the implications of poverty and riches, flows of trade and the centrality of communications. This paperback series aims to attract historians interested in economics and economists with an interest in history by publishing high quality, cutting edge academic research in the broad field of economic and social history from the late medieval/ early modern period to the present day. It encourages the interaction of qualitative and quantitative methods through both excellent monographs and collections offering path-breaking overviews of key research concerns. Taking as its benchmark international relevance and excellence it is open to scholars and subjects of any geographical areas from the case study to the multi-nation comparison.

PREVIOUSLY PUBLISHED TITLES IN THE SERIES ARE
LISTED AT THE BACK OF THIS VOLUME

The Great Famine in Ireland and Britain's Financial Crisis

Charles Read

THE BOYDELL PRESS

First published 2022
The Boydell Press, Woodbridge

ISBN 978-1-78327-727-8

The Boydell Press is an imprint of Boydell & Brewer Ltd
PO Box 9, Woodbridge, Suffolk IP12 3DF, UK
and of Boydell & Brewer Inc.
668 Mt Hope Avenue, Rochester, NY 14620–2731, USA
website: www.boydellandbrewer.com

A catalogue record for this book is available
from the British Library

Contents

Illustrations

Figures

Charts

Tables

The author and publisher are grateful to all the institutions and individuals listed for permission to reproduce the materials in which they hold copyright. Every effort has been made to trace the copyright holders; apologies are offered for any omission, and the publisher will be pleased to add any necessary acknowledgement in subsequent editions.

Preface

A gigantic economic and humanitarian tragedy caused by disease. A crisis that required, in response, an unprecedented programme of government intervention that drove the Treasury to the brink of fiscal meltdown. A crisis that put the constituent countries of the United Kingdom further down the path towards separation. This may sound like a description of Great Britain in the age of the covid-19 pandemic in the 2020s. Yet it could also very easily be a description of the United Kingdom of Great Britain and Ireland in the age of the Irish famine of the 1840s. In the late summer of 1845 *phytophthora infestans*, a potato blight rapidly spreading around the world, was detected in Ireland for the first time. In Britain, within two years, exactly 175 years before the publication of this book, the fiscal demands of this crisis triggered a series of severe financial crises, which threw the funding for the relief effort in Ireland off course. In Ireland, within five years or so of the blight's appearance, a quarter of its population had either unexpectedly died or emigrated. The sense that the British government's response to the famine was inadequate inspired generations of Irish nationalists and fuelled their demands for separation, culminating in the independence of the Irish Free State in 1922, a century to the year before the publication of this book.

Why was excess mortality during the famine so high, and who or what should we blame for it? This is a question that has consumed the thoughts of many polemicists, historians and economists since the 1840s. Many point the finger of blame at the British government. Ireland was a constituent part of the United Kingdom, the richest country in the world at the time, so why were its poor left to starve? Those of a nationalist persuasion claim that the inadequate relief effort amounts to 'genocide' by Britain against Ireland. Most scholars, in recent decades, have preferred to emphasise the influence of *laissez-faire* ideas on policymakers. This book excavates from the archives a hitherto ignored narrative, which links the famine to the United Kingdom's transition onto the 'classic' gold standard policies and the political and financial crises they caused in the 1840s. The narrative this book unveils is not of *laissez-faire*, but of unprecedented government intervention to save lives that went disastrously off course due to political and financial instability in Britain.

The research for this book took place over the course of a decade bookended by two economic disasters. My interest in the Irish famine first began as a PhD student at the University of Cambridge in the wake of the global financial crisis of 2007–09. I finished the first manuscript of this book as a fellow at Corpus Christi College, Cambridge, during the first lockdown of 2020 resulting from the covid-19 pandemic. At the start of this project, 'excess mortality' was not a commonly used phrase, and the idea that a disease spreading around the world – potato or human – could lay waste to the British and Irish economies seemed to most people something that belonged to the distant past. Covid-19 changed all that. The year 2020 was a reminder of the power of pandemics to shape history. Across the world excess deaths soared as health systems collapsed. A disease, a virus just 0.1 microns wide, triggered panic in financial markets everywhere on Earth. Governments, in Britain and elsewhere, struggled to get the situation under control.

The covid-19 pandemic was also a reminder that the reactions of governments to such disasters is what comes to shape most of the discussion about them in their aftermath. Many commentators have already framed the debate over the British government's reaction to covid-19 in remarkably similar terms as historians do the Irish famine. Did Britain's initially *laissez-faire* reaction to the pandemic in March 2020 cost 20,000 lives as a result of delaying the country's first lockdown by a week? Or were the 20,000 excess deaths in British care homes in March and April 2020 the result of the government's ham-fisted intervention that cleared elderly patients from hospitals into them, along with the virus? The British government's decision in this period to advise its citizens to wash their hands to protect themselves from the virus, rather than take the more effective measure of wearing masks, can similarly be seen as a cack-handed intervention resulting from a lack of accurate scientific knowledge. The debate among scholars between *laissez-faire* versus misguided-intervention interpretations of the covid-19 pandemic in Britain will surely continue, as it has about the Irish famine since the 1840s.

This book argues that to understand why the British government failed to save more lives in Ireland, it is necessary to understand why the interventions it designed to attempt to do this failed so badly. This is an area surprisingly neglected by most historians in favour of ideological explanations of the crisis. The inspiration and justification for this book is firmly based in the archives of correspondence and publications available to historians. During my initial explorations into the Russell papers at the National Archives at Kew, the overwhelming impression that economic circumstances were the main determinant of Irish relief policy leapt out at me. I had initially approached the subject with a different thesis in mind, namely that the mistake the government made was an overfocus on supply-side policies when the famine was more of an economic crisis triggered by a deficiency of demand. My first few days reading the Russell papers disabused me of that notion. The government after 1846 was focused on the demand-side issue of how to pay for the relief effort; the problem was that two severe financial crises in 1847 got in the way of their plans. I followed where the source material led me, abandoning my preconceptions. My research became a much more disruptive and controversial intervention in the literature on the Irish famine than I was planning, but one that has been necessary to produce a thesis as close to the original sources as possible. In the ten years since my initial research on the subject, sifting through a wealth of relevant material has only confirmed my revised argument that financial circumstances, combined with the Russell government's Parliamentary weakness, were the major factors.

Such a conclusion is radical and new in the historiography of the Irish famine. Even so, it is a literature sorely in need of disruption. It is still a literature framed by either echoing the conclusions of early Irish nationalists writing about the famine, such as John Mitchel, or by reacting against them (revisionists), or by reacting against the reactions (post-revisionists and anti-revisionists). Should Mitchel's ideas still dominate debate on the famine in the twenty-first century? John Mitchel was an anti-Semitic conspiracy theorist, a racist campaigner for slavery in America and a hypocrite who during the famine attacked the British government for feeding the Irish poor (later reversing this position in his best-known writings about the event). Given the trend to decolonise history curriculums around the world, it should be quite a surprise that his ideas have done so much to shape the scholarly debate on the subject, as well as still being repeated so scandalously often in popular histories of the famine.

This book seeks to stimulate debate in new directions and to move the literature on from Mitchel's old interpretations, in three main ways. First, this volume goes beyond arguments about whether the famine was a genocide to look at why relief policy failed in spite of good intentions towards Ireland from senior politicians. As Peter Gray recently pointed out in the *Cambridge History of Ireland*, there is nothing in the archives to back up a charge of 'intentional genocide'. Cormac Ó Gráda has emphasised that policymakers wanted to save lives during the famine: '*Nobody* wanted the extirpation of the Irish'. As a person of Armenian and Ethiopian descent whose family has more recent experience of genocide and famine in the twentieth century, I believe that such accusations of genocide should always be investigated seriously. Nevertheless, the problem is that there is no evidence to back up such a claim when it comes to the Irish famine. To water down the meaning of genocide to include Ireland would weaken the word's power to shock in the modern world when describing deliberate and intended mass murder.

Second, this book unveils the role that Irish politicians played in the crisis, rather than telling the story purely in terms of British colonialism. British politicians had an incentive to treat Ireland well: the fear of the revival of the Repeal movement and of revolution in 1848, if nothing was done to help Ireland, was a real worry among policymakers. Even so, approaching the Irish famine with a colonial paradigm has become increasingly fashionable among some scholars in recent years. However, Irish MPs held the balance of power in the House of Commons after 1847 and there were Irish Catholic Treasury Lords throughout the Whigs' period of office (1846–52), including supporters of Repeal of the Act of Union. In short, Irish representatives held significant political influence during the famine and their failure to wield this to achieve a better outcome is one of the more puzzling features of the crisis.

Third, this book argues that it is impossible to understand why British policy went wrong in Ireland in parochial terms without an understanding of what was happening elsewhere in the world. To understand why the government's relief efforts in Ireland were so inadequate after 1847 requires an understanding of London's financial markets. To understand those, in turn, requires an understanding of the politics and economics of America and continental Europe. To understand what went wrong with Ireland's relief effort requires an understanding of what went right with more successful rescue efforts in other places suffering famine and financial crisis, such as Mauritius. I hope this book, therefore, helps to take the study of the Irish famine in a global direction.

In short, this book hopes to redirect discussion of the policy errors made during the Irish famine off the dangerous academic ground over which it has travelled in recent years. The nationalist and colonialist paradigms that have returned to fashion do not fully explain why policymakers both British and Irish made the decisions they did, nor why those decisions failed to save as many lives in Ireland as intended. More dangerously, they offer a false reassurance that many of the errors made belong in a distant era, long past, of national and colonial prejudice that Irish independence in 1922 brought to an end, with the implicit suggestion they could not happen again in a more modern, enlightened world. Perhaps the most worrisome takeaway from this book is that many of the problems faced by policymakers during the famine still trouble their counterparts in the world today. As the covid-19 pandemic has shown, governments are still overwhelmed when new diseases sweep over their borders. Their capacity to respond to them is still limited by the gyrations of financial markets and by the amount of political capital they possess. And still surprisingly few people are willing to pay more in tax to subsidise the most vulnerable members of their communities. Some 175 years on from the worst period of the Irish famine, the world has changed less than many might think.

Acknowledgements

The completion of this book would have not been possible without the help of a large number of people, for which I am immensely grateful. First of all, I would like to thank my doctoral supervisors at the University of Cambridge, Eugenio Biagini and Martin Daunton, for all their advice, encouragement and support during the development and completion of my PhD thesis entitled 'British Economic Policy and Ireland, c.1841–53' (2016), which contains my earliest research about the Irish famine. Their sage comments and advice on my doctoral and postdoctoral research has resulted in a much better book. I would also like to thank Kevin O'Rourke and Harold James, who examined my doctoral work, for their useful and very generous suggestions about how to develop my ideas about the famine further. I would also like to thank Caoimhe Nic Dháibhéid, my supervisor in Irish history as an undergraduate, who was the first to suggest that I should undertake academic research into the Irish famine.

I would like to thank all those who read sections of this book (in its current or previous forms) or listened to and gave feedback on presentations based on parts of it at conferences, seminars and workshops, in particular: Frank Barry, Victoria Bateman, Andy Bielenberg, Richard Bourke, Stephen Broadberry, Graham Brownlow, D'Maris Coffman, Chris Colvin, Vincent Comerford, Neil Cummins, Alan de Bromhead, Enda Delaney, Sean Eddie, Alan Fernihough, Roy Foster, Frank Geary, Peter Gray, David Higgins, Boyd Hilton, Sara Horrell, Aiden Kane, Christine Kinealy, Peter Mandler, Eoin McLaughlin, Renaud Morieux, Conor Morrissey, Duncan Needham, Cormac Ó Gráda, David Ormrod, George Peden, Peter Solar, Solomos Solomou, Sam Watling, Philip Yorath and Nuala Zahedieh (and my apologies to anyone who I have accidentally left out). Eugenio Biagini, Martin Daunton and Liam Kennedy read the entire manuscript, and the final version of this book is much improved as a result. All remaining errors and omissions are my own. I would also particularly like to thank Doug Kanter for bringing my attention to quotations from the archives that did much to bolster my arguments in several places in this book.

I am grateful to the Economic History Society for its unprecedented support for this project. The society has awarded earlier versions of the research presented in this book its New Researcher Prize (2014), T. S. Ashton Prize for the best *Economic History Review* article (2017) and Thirsk-Feinstein PhD

Dissertation Prize (2017), as well as bursaries to present my early findings at its annual conferences. I would also like to thank its presidents and publication committees past and present for their enthusiastic support for publishing this volume in the Society's 'People, Markets, Goods: Economies and Societies in History' monograph series. I would like to thank my editors Michael Middeke and Elizabeth Howard at Boydell & Brewer for producing such a finely assembled volume and Joshua Hey for his close attention to detail in the copy-editing. My thanks also go to anonymous reviewers at Boydell & Brewer, the *Economic History Review*, the *Historical Journal*, *Irish Economic and Social History*, *History* and *History & Policy* for their useful comments, which have all helped to produce a much-improved book. I would also like to thank the International Economic History Association for the award of their prize in 2018 for the best dissertation in nineteenth-century economic history completed at any university in the world in 2015, 2016 or 2017, an important vote of moral support that helped spur me to continue my research on the Irish famine.

I am also aware of the debt owed to those unnamed staff of libraries and archives who made access to the source material not only possible but efficient. In particular, I would like to thank James Collett-White of the Bedfordshire and Luton Archives and Record Service for alerting me to the Irish Diary of the Second Earl de Grey, which had hitherto been overlooked by historians. I would also like to thank the Earl of Clarendon for permission to quote from the Clarendon Papers in the Bodleian Library at the University of Oxford.

In addition, I would like to acknowledge the institutions that funded the research presented in this book and that have helped to sustain my academic career. The Arts and Humanities Research Council of the United Kingdom, the University of Cambridge and Christ's College all helped to fund the MPhil and PhD theses in which I first began to explore the 1840s. I would also like to thank the Master and Fellows of Peterhouse, Cambridge, for electing me to dining rights during my doctoral research. I have appreciated my affiliations since this period to the Faculty of Economics at Cambridge, where I am now an Affiliated Lecturer, and the Centre for Financial History at Darwin College, where I am now a Research Associate. I would also like to thank Roy Foster and the Principal and Fellows of Hertford College, Oxford, for electing me to the Government of Ireland Senior Scholarship there; the Master and Fellows of Fitzwilliam College, Cambridge, for electing me for a year as a bye-fellow; and the Master and Fellows of Corpus Christi College, Cambridge, for electing me to a fellowship and college lectureship in history. At Corpus I would like to particularly thank the current and former masters of the College, Christopher Kelly and Stuart Laing, for their unceasing support for this project, as well as all my other colleagues who have made life at Corpus so enjoyable, particularly: Christopher Andrew, Marina Frasca-Spada, Andrew Harvey, John Hatcher, Philippa Hoskin, Shruti Kapila, Peter Martland, Amar Sohal, Emma Spary, Michael Sutherland and Samuel Zeitlin. Finally, I would like to thank the British

Academy for the award of a postdoctoral fellowship that has enabled me to conduct more research on the financial crisis of 1847 and on the Mauritian crisis for this book.

My thanks also go to all those too numerous to mention who acted as a sounding board for my ideas about economics, history and Ireland over the past decade and provided stimulating conversation. However, I would like to particularly highlight Robin Adams, Niamh Gallagher, Eriko Padron-Regalado, Brian Varian and Lewis Willcocks for their camaraderie as fellow early-career scholars during the long process of turning the PhD thesis into a book. Their contribution to this project is invaluable.

Most of all, I would like to thank my parents for their love and support, without whom this project would never have been started or completed. This book is dedicated to them, as well as all those who died in Ireland as a result of the famine between 1845 and 1853.

Dr Charles Read
Corpus Christi College, Cambridge

Abbreviations

BoE.A.	Bank of England Archive
B.L.	London, British Library
B.L.A.R.S.	Bedfordshire and Luton Archives and Record Service
c. (cc.)	column (columns)
C.U.L.	Cambridge University Library
CUP	Cambridge University Press
D.U.L.	Durham, University Library
LSE	London School of Economics
JSSISI	Journal of the Statistical and Social Inquiry Society of Ireland
MUP	Manchester University Press
N.A.	Kew, National Archive
NBER	New York, National Bureau of Economic Research
N.L.I.	Dublin, National Library Ireland
O.B.L.	Oxford, Bodleian Library
OUP	Oxford University Press
PP	Parliamentary papers
PRONI	Belfast, Public Record Office of Northern Ireland
S.U. H.L.	Southampton University, Hartley Library

Introduction

The Almighty, indeed, sent the potato blight, but the English created the famine.[1]

J. Mitchel, *The Last Conquest of Ireland (Perhaps)* [1861].

Everything in Ireland resolves itself into a money question.[2]

Charles Wood (chancellor of the exchequer) to Lord Clarendon
(as lord-lieutenant of Ireland), 25 September 1847.

Prologue: the quiet before the storm

When the Second Earl de Grey boarded the train home from Dublin for the final time, at a quarter past eleven on 16 July 1844, the retiring lord-lieutenant of Ireland was exhausted – but relieved.[3] The 43-year-old Union between Great Britain and Ireland – tied together to form the United Kingdom in 1801 – looked safer than it had for decades. Just a year earlier the situation had looked very different. Daniel O'Connell's Loyal National Repeal Association was at the height of its popularity. Its demand for Repeal of the Act of Union and the restoration of an Irish Parliament in Dublin had caught the imagination of the Irish masses. The size of O'Connell's rallies – dubbed 'Monster meetings' by the press – grew larger and larger.[4] In August 1843 at the Hill of Tara, by tradition the seat of the High Kings of Ireland, up to 750,000 people – approximately a tenth of the Irish population – reportedly turned out to hear

---

1   J. Mitchel, *The Last Conquest of Ireland (Perhaps)* [1861], P. Maume (ed.), (Dublin: University College Dublin Press, 2005), p. 219.
2   Wood to Clarendon, 25 September 1847, C.U.L., Hickleton papers, MS. MF A4.57 reel 1495.
3   'Earl de Grey's Irish Diary' 1844 vol., B.L.A.R.S., Lucas archive, L31/114/17–21 (1841–44 with 2 vols. for 1843), loose front page; idem., p. 143. Thomas Philip de Grey, Second Earl de Grey, Third Baron Grantham, Sixth Baron Lucas (1781–1859) born Thomas Philip Robinson, Weddell after 1803, Lord Grantham from 1786 to 1833.
4   For a full list of 'Monster meetings' see D. O'Connell, *The Life and Times of Daniel O'Connell, M.P.: With the Beauties of His Principal Speeches* (Dublin: James McCormick, 1846), pp. 137–38.

O'Connell speak.[5] A meeting at Clontarf in October was going to be greater still. However, O'Connell – whose movement had often used the threat of force (though never fully followed through) to achieve its political objectives – had overplayed his hand.[6]

Banners appeared promising the deployment of 'Repeal Cavalry' at the meeting.[7] De Grey chose his moment to strike, issuing a proclamation banning the meeting the night before. De Grey called O'Connell's bluff; the nationalist leader lacked the time to protest the decision using the legal system, forcing him to call off the meeting to avoid imminent violence.[8] British troops steamed into Dublin's harbour and Ireland's main nationalist newspaper, the *Freeman's Journal*, alleged that the troops had been summoned to, 'cut the people down' and 'run riot in the blood of the innocent'.[9] But the more enthusiastic Repealers who ignored O'Connell and turned up at the fields of Clontarf found there was no fight to be had. De Grey, it turned out, had bluffed them too. He had given the troops orders to stay away from Clontarf. Repeal supporters itching for a fight were left milling around with nothing to do.[10]

British officials were shocked at how quiet Ireland became in the months after Clontarf, no doubt helped by economic recovery after a good harvest in the autumn of 1843.[11] Crime abated, and the threat of civil unrest subsided. Ireland's murder rate fell sharply in 1844, as well.[12] O'Connell spent three months in prison for sedition in 1844, before his year-long sentence was overturned by an appeal court.[13] With O'Connell's martyrdom over, donations to the Repeal Association collapsed.[14] By then, Young Ireland, a rising new

5   J. Mitchel, *The History of Ireland: From the Treaty of Limerick to the Present Time*, vol. 2 (London: James Duffy, 1869), p. 357.
6   For threats of force see quotes from Protestant landowners' letters in 'Extracts from very recent private letters on the state of the country and the policy of the Government', 18 July 1843, B.L.A.R.S., Lucas archive, L29/700/36/11; D. Connor, J. Gillman, W. L. Shouldham & T. Gillman to De Grey, 24 November 1843, B.L., Graham papers, Add. MS. 79641, f. 35; De Grey to Graham, 7 August 1843, B.L., Graham papers, Add. MS. 79623, f. 157; De Grey to Peel, 3 November 1841, B.L., Peel papers, Add. MS. 40477, f. 65. See also A. MacIntyre, *The Liberator: Daniel O'Connell and the Irish Party 1830–1847* (London: Hamish Hamilton, 1965), p. 269.
7   'Earl De Grey's Irish Diary' 1843 vol. 2, pp. 51–52.
8   De Grey did not believe O'Connell would 'put his neck into a halter'; see 'Earl De Grey's Irish Diary' 1843 vol. 1, p. 127; 'Earl De Grey's Irish Diary' 1843 vol. 2, p. 48.
9   *Freeman's Journal*, 7 October 1843.
10   'Earl De Grey's Irish Diary' 1843 vol. 2, pp. 51–52.
11   'Earl de Grey's Irish Diary' 1844 vol., pp. 21, 28.
12   R. McMahon, *Homicide in Pre-famine and Famine Ireland* (Oxford: OUP, 2013), p. 20.
13   L. J. McCaffrey, *Daniel O'Connell and the Repeal Year* (Lexington: University of Kentucky Press, 1966), pp. 211–12.
14   C. Read, 'The Repeal Year in Ireland: An Economic Reassessment', *Historical Journal*, 58:1 (2015), 111–35, at p. 133, citing Repeal rent data collected from *The Nation*.

group of nationalists, had fallen out with O'Connell's loyalists over whether to use violence to achieve their goals. O'Connell was unable to reunite his movement as his charismatic authority drained along with his health.[15] He died in early 1847 on a pilgrimage to Rome.[16]

Many constitutional nationalists today mourn O'Connell's failure.[17] If Repeal had been achieved, Ireland could have gained independence without Young Ireland and the physical-force nationalism it inspired.[18] Nevertheless this should not take away from De Grey's achievement of politically defusing Irish separatism without a drop of blood being spilled or a single shot fired. Compared with the scale of violence seen during the Peterloo massacre of 1819, the Chartists' Newport Rising of 1839 and the revolutions in continental Europe of 1848, the peaceful disintegration of the Repeal movement is a notable exception to the bloody norm in this period.

This was the job Sir Robert Peel, the British prime minister, appointed De Grey as lord-lieutenant of Ireland to achieve in 1841. De Grey, one of the richest landowners in Britain, had already gained a reputation for restoring public order during periods of civil unrest without resorting to violence. As lord-lieutenant of Bedfordshire and a Major in the Yorkshire Yeomanry, he had used similar tactics to the ones he deployed at Clontarf to halt riots without bloodshed.[19] Later, in his memoirs, he claimed that if he had led the yeomanry at Peterloo in 1819, 'we should never have heard of the "Manchester Massacres"'.[20] In the 1820s he had replaced the guns of his gamekeepers on his estates with 'long sticks' – an experiment that was the model for London's new unarmed Metropolitan Police Force that Peel had established as home secretary.[21] Later, in Ireland, he introduced the country's first gun-control laws – an issue which became a particular interest of his.[22]

Peel had hoped to consolidate De Grey's achievements in 1843 with a set of targeted policies to bind moderate Catholics in Ireland closer to the Union. 'Now if ever', Peel wrote to the Cabinet on 11 February 1844, 'there is the

---

15   McCaffrey, *Daniel O'Connell and the Repeal Year*, pp. 211–12; MacIntyre, *The Liberator: Daniel O'Connell and the Irish Party 1830–1847*, pp. 277–78.

16   R. V. Comerford, 'O'Connell, Daniel (1775–1847)', *Oxford Dictionary of National Biography* (Oxford: OUP, 2009), online at <http://www.oxforddnb.com/view/article/20501> [accessed 17 July 2010].

17   *The Irish Examiner*, 22 August 2019.

18   Ibid.

19   Peel to De Grey, 14 January 1823, B.L.A.R.S., Lucas archive, L30/18/41/6; *Transcript of the 'Memoirs of the Earl de Grey'* [1859] B.L.A.R.S., CRT/190/45/2, p. 35.

20   De Grey is referring to the Peterloo Massacres of 16 August 1819 by the phrase 'Manchester Massacres'. See *Transcript of the 'Memoirs of the Earl de Grey'* [1859], p. 36.

21   See *The Times*, 20 November 1832, p. 6 on gamekeepers' batons.

22   For Irish Arms Act 1843 see 'Earl De Grey's Irish Diary' 1842 vol., pp. 44–45 and 'Earl De Grey's Irish Diary' 1842 vol., p. 27 and 1843 vol. 1, p. 46 on gun control.

prospect of detaching from the ranks of agitation and Repeal a considerable portion of the moderate Roman Catholics and of doing this consistently with the honour of the Government'.[23] The Charitable Bequests Act of 1844 allowed Catholics to donate money to their church in their wills for the first time since the Reformation.[24] New non-denominational universities, the Queen's Colleges of Belfast, Cork and Galway, were founded to allow middle-class Catholics access to higher education.[25] And Peel tripled the government's grant to Maynooth College for the training of Catholic priests in 1845.[26] Moreover, export prices for Irish agricultural products also rose, helping the economy of rural Ireland recover from the slump of 1842–43.

His policies initially looked like they were working. Later the prime minister looked back at this period remembering the 'happy lot' of Ireland with 'agriculturalists looking forward with hope, Ireland in a state of comparative prosperity, the greatest export trade that was ever known'.[27] Then an economic and humanitarian catastrophe struck Ireland that derailed the British government's plans. In October 1845 a letter arrived for Peel from Lord Heytesbury, De Grey's successor as lord-lieutenant, in Dublin. It informed him of the seriousness of a new potato disease that was threatening to wipe out the season's crop.[28] The consequences of that news, and the way the government handled it, were to change the history of Ireland and its relationship to the United Kingdom forever.

The biggest economic disaster in modern British history

Ireland in the nineteenth century was no stranger to harvest failure and famine. In the words of Cecil Woodham-Smith, a British historian, 'the unreliability of the potato was an accepted fact in Ireland, ranking with the vagaries of the weather'.[29] Subsistence crises – either on an Ireland-wide or regional level – had already struck that century in 1799–1802, 1816–18, 1822, 1831, 1835–37 and 1839.[30] There was also a severe but short-lived economic downturn in 1842–43,

---

23   Cited in McCaffrey, *Daniel O'Connell and the Repeal Year*, p. 214.
24   MacIntyre, *The Liberator: Daniel O'Connell and the Irish Party 1830–1847*, p. 281.
25   Ibid.
26   See C. Read, 'Peel, De Grey and Irish Policy 1841–44', *History*, 99:334 (2014), 1–18, at p. 2 for a summary of these policies.
27   *Hansard*, CVI, 6 July 1849, c. 1432.
28   P. Gray, *Famine, Land and Politics: British Government and Irish Society 1843–1850* (Dublin: Irish Academic Press, 1999), p. 99.
29   C. Woodham-Smith, *The Great Hunger: Ireland 1845–49* (London: Penguin Books, 1991), p. 38.
30   See L. Kennedy, P. M. Solar, 'The Famine that Wasn't? 1799–1801 in Ireland', QUCEH Working Paper Series 2019-06 (2019), 1–33; C. Ó Gráda, 'Famine in Ireland, 1300–1900', UCD Centre for Economic Research Working Paper Series WP15/13 (2015), 1–34, at pp.

at first thought to be a food shortage, but it was probably caused by the falling prices of agricultural produce triggered by tariff reductions in the budget of 1842.[31] Economic historians have noted that the years 1872 and 1879, decades after the Great Famine, also saw harvest failures that reduced potato yields to levels roughly equivalent to the catastrophic harvest of 1846.[32] Nonetheless, the demographic consequences of all these other crises were limited. So initially, as Woodham-Smith has rightly commented, 'the possibility of yet another failure caused no particular alarm' in Ireland in 1845.[33] However, it turned out to be the first of a series of catastrophically failed harvests. As calculations by Peter Solar have shown, no other European country, in the 1840s, suffered so many successive years of persistent harvest failure, and no other comparable European country suffered as great a deficit in food as Ireland.[34] The result was an economic disaster that was on a greater scale than any other in nineteenth- or twentieth-century Britain or Ireland.

The Great Irish famine or *an Gorta Mór* ('The Great Hunger' in Irish), as historians in Great Britain and Ireland came to call it, ranks among the worst demographic, economic and humanitarian disasters in the history of both countries since the Black Death. That is true measured by both its immediate effects and long-run consequences. The famine began with the appearance of two potato diseases in 1845, dry rot, an old one, and *phytophora infestans*, a new one imported from the Americas.[35] These blights reduced potato yields in Ireland by between a third and a quarter in 1845, and between 75% and 97% in the following year, 1846.[36] Reduced yields persisted into the 1850s. In the

10–11; E. M. Crawford, 'Dearth, Diet, and Disease in Ireland, 1850: A Case Study of Nutritional Deficiency', *Medical History*, 28:2 (1984), 151–61, at p. 151.

31 See, for instance, Read, 'The Repeal Year in Ireland: An Economic Reassessment', 111–35, at pp. 123–35.

32 P. M. A. Bourke, 'The Extent of the Potato Crop in Ireland at the Time of the Famine', *JSSISI*, 10:3 (1959/60), 1–35, at p. 11.

33 Woodham-Smith, *The Great Hunger*, p. 38.

34 P. M. Solar, 'The Great Famine Was no Ordinary Subsistence Crisis', in E. M. Crawford (ed.), *Famine: The Irish Experience 900–1900* (Edinburgh: John Donald, 1989), 112–31, at pp. 127–9.

35 A 'dry' and a 'wet' form of rot were reported in the United Kingdom and the United States; see: 'Report of Royal Dublin Society', B.L., Peel papers, Add. MS. 40577, ff. 21–24; 'Report of Agricultural Chemistry Association, Edinburgh', B.L., Peel papers, Add. MS. 40577, f. 141.

36 *Correspondence explanatory of the measures adopted by Her Majesty's government for the relief of distress arising from the failure of the potato crop in Ireland*, PP 1846 (735) XXXVII.41, p. 5; for low estimate of loss in 1846 see Bourke, 'The Extent of the Potato Crop', p. 11; for high estimate of loss in 1846 see *Correspondence from July 1846 to January 1847 relating to the measures adopted for the relief of distress in Ireland*, PP 1847 (761) LI.1, p. 57.

longer term still, economically, demographically, and politically, the disease was
to change the course of Irish history.

The arrival of the blight, unsurprisingly, caused a severe negative economic
shock. Just before *phytophora infestans* arrived in 1845, potatoes grew on almost
a third of Ireland's tilled acreage, according to Cormac Ó Gráda, providing
food for around three million people.[37] By the early 1840s two-fifths of the Irish
population ate little else, according to estimates produced by Austin Bourke,
and a further two-fifths depended on the potato for at least half of their diet.[38]
The collapse in potato yields accordingly reduced economic activity sharply.
Economic historians estimate that, from peak to trough, Ireland's GDP fell by
around a fifth to a quarter during the crisis.[39]

The demographic impact of the crisis can clearly be seen in the dramatic
fall in Ireland's population, starting in the late 1840s. Various scholars have
estimated excess mortality between 1845 and 1851 to range from as low as
207,000 to as high as 1.5 million people. The current consensus among post-
revisionist scholars sits between those two figures and assumes that around a
million people died and a further million or more emigrated.[40] Many towns
in western Ireland shrank to the size of villages and some villages disappeared completely. Worse, the end of the famine did not stop Ireland's loss of
population. The famine is, with some justification, seen by many scholars as
initiating the great flood of emigration which became an important feature of

37   C. Ó Gráda, *Ireland before and after the Famine* (Manchester: MUP, 1993), p. 10.
38   P. M. A. Bourke, *'The Visitation of God'? The Potato and the Great Irish Famine*
(Dublin: Lilliput Press, 1993), p. 99, cited in Kennedy, Solar, 'The Famine that Wasn't?
1799–1801 in Ireland', p. 2.
39   K. H. O'Rourke, 'Monetary Data and Proxy GDP Estimates: Ireland 1840–1921', *Irish
Economic and Social History* 25 (1998), 22–51, at pp. 47–48; see also more recently F. N. G.
Andersson, J. Lennard, 'Irish GDP between the Famine and the First World War: Estimates
Based on a Dynamic Factor Model', *European Review of Economic History* 23:1 (2019),
50–71 at p. 70.
40   See summary of the scholarly debate in P. P. Boyle, C. Ó Gráda, 'Fertility Trends, Excess
Mortality, and the Great Irish Famine', *Demography*, 23:4 (1986), 543–62, at p. 543, in
particular citing S. H. Cousens, 'Regional Death Rates in Ireland during the Great Famine,
from 1846 to 1851', *Population Studies*, 14:1 (1960), 55–74, at p. 64 (c. 860,000 deaths)
and J. Mokyr, 'The Deadly Fungus: An Econometric Investigation into the Short Term
Demographic Impact of the Irish Famine', *Discussion Paper Northwestern University*, no.
333 (1978), 1–75, at p. 18 (c.1,069,000 deaths); 207,000 is the lower estimate calculated in
H. P. H. Nusteling, 'How Many Irish Potato Famine Deaths?: Towards Coherence of the
Evidence', *Historical Methods*, 42:2 (2009), 57–80, at p. 74; around 500,000 is the figure given
in E. R. R. Green, 'Agriculture', in R. D. Edwards, T. D. Williams (eds.), *The Great Famine:
Studies in Irish History 1845–52* (Dublin: Browne and Nolan, 1956), 89–128, at p. 126; 1.5
million is the upper estimate provided in M. W. Flinn (ed.), *Scottish Population History from
the 17th Century to the 1930s* (Cambridge: CUP, 1977), p. 421.

Irish social and economic life in the late nineteenth and twentieth centuries.[41] As the research of Kevin O'Rourke has shown, the blight triggered lower agricultural yields that persisted throughout the rest of the nineteenth century.[42] Lower yields meant lower demand for agricultural labour, nudging or forcing many in rural Ireland to move overseas to find new opportunities.

The fall in population continued into the twentieth century. An island-wide population of over eight million in the 1841 Census declined to a trough of just over four million maintained between the 1920s and the 1960s.[43] Since then there has been some increase in population, thanks to a revival in economic growth and a new flow of inward migration after both the Republic of Ireland and Northern Ireland (as part of the United Kingdom) joined the European Economic Community in 1973. Even so, the gains since the 1970s have not been enough to replace what had been lost since the 1840s. Even today the island of Ireland is the only country-level area in Europe which has a smaller population than it had in the mid-1840s. Roughly 1.7 million (a fifth) fewer people live on the island of Ireland today than did on the eve of the famine. This stands in stark contrast to other countries in Europe that have suffered from famines more recently, such as Poland and Ukraine, which have seen their populations more than recover since.

Politically, the memory of the famine had an important role in permanently altering the course of the history of the United Kingdom of Great Britain and Ireland. The Repeal movement, which had demanded the restoration of Irish legislative independence, split and collapsed in the 1840s. However, over the following couple of decades, a series of publications authored by Irish nationalists accused British politicians of exacerbating the famine's death toll as a matter of policy. The most memorable of these, John Mitchel's *The Last Conquest of Ireland (Perhaps)* [1861], argued that the British government deliberately used a policy of *laissez-faire*, or non-interference, during the famine period to reduce the Irish population and destroy their native culture.[44] 'The Almighty, indeed, sent the potato blight', Mitchel famously thundered in that book, 'but the English created the famine'.[45]

41   G. O'Brien, *An Economic History of Ireland from the Union to the Famine* (London: Longmans, Green & Co., 1921), p. 3, cited in K. H. O'Rourke, 'Did the Great Irish Famine Matter?', *Journal of Economic History*, 51:1 (1991), 1–22, at p. 1.
42   Bourke, 'The Extent of the Potato Crop in Ireland', p. 11; O'Rourke, 'Did the Great Irish Famine Matter?', pp. 19–20.
43   See Figure 1 in A. S. Fotheringham, M. H. Kelly, M. Charlton, 'The Demographic Impacts of the Irish Famine: Towards a Greater Geographical Understanding', *Transactions of the Institute of British Geographers*, 38:2 (2013), 221–37, at p. 222.
44   Mitchel, *The Last Conquest of Ireland (Perhaps)*, p. 219.
45   Ibid.

Helped by Mitchel's book as well as by other polemicists, the perception that relief-efforts were mismanaged by the British government during the famine fuelled the fire of resentful and violent Irish nationalism.[46] As Richard English has noted, 'the Famine ... produced a newly large and angry transatlantic Irish nationalism, and provided a basis for lastingly rage-filled revanchism'.[47] The famine itself triggered only a small rebellion in Ireland in 1848.[48] Yet the famine was clearly on the minds of physical-force nationalists later in the century. The Irish Republican Brotherhood (often referred to as the Fenians), one such revolutionary nationalist organisation dedicated to the establishment of an independent Irish republic, developed in the aftermath of the famine and staged its own bigger but similarly unsuccessful revolt in 1867, now known to historians as the 'Fenian Rising'.[49] Growing resentment among the Irish electorate against rule from London later in the nineteenth century resulted in the formation of the constitutionalist and electorally successful Home Rule movement, as well as other more violent forms of Irish separatism, which culminated in the Easter Rising of 1916 and the departure of the Irish Free State from the United Kingdom in 1922.[50]

Innovative research over the past decade suggests a direct link. Most striking was a recent paper by Gaia Narciso of Trinity College Dublin and Battista Severgnini of the Copenhagen Business School, which showed that the areas of Ireland hit most heavily by the famine in the 1840s produced disproportionately higher numbers of rebels that took part in the Irish Revolution of 1913–21.[51] Moreover, the famine's shadow continued long beyond independence. The Republic of Ireland's enthusiastic embrace of membership of the European Union since 1973, and of the euro currency since 2002, has been interpreted as motivated in part by a rejection of its past as part of the United Kingdom, including its use of the pound sterling under the Act of Union.[52] In short, the Irish famine should be seen as a seminal moment for both the history of Ireland as well as that of the United Kingdom more generally.

---

46   See B. Jenkins, *Irish Nationalism and the British State* (Montreal: McGill-Queen's University Press, 2006), pp. 255–86.
47   R. English, *Irish Freedom: The History of Nationalism in Ireland* (London: Macmillan, 2006), p. 169.
48   See C. Kinealy, *Repeal and Revolution: 1848 in Ireland* (Manchester: MUP, 2009), especially pp. 234–75.
49   See R. Kee, *The Green Flag: A History of Irish Nationalism* (London: Penguin, 2000), pp. 301–32.
50   Ó Gráda, *Ireland before and after the Famine*, p. 99.
51   G. Narciso, B. Severgnini, 'The Deep Roots of Rebellion: Evidence from the Irish Revolution', *Trinity Economics Papers* 2216 (2017), online at <http://eh.net/eha/wp-content/uploads/2018/06/Narciso.pdf> [accessed 30 January 2020].
52   See C. Read, 'Ireland and the Perils of Fixed-Exchange Rates', History & Policy paper, 20 February 2015, online at <http://www.historyandpolicy.org/policy-papers/papers/ireland-and-the-perils-of-fixed-exchange-rates> [accessed 25 Mar 2016].

Polemicists and the famine

Recently, the notion that the famine amounted to a genocide perpetrated by the British government against the Irish people has been revived among the general public by Tim Pat Coogan, a journalist and polemicist.[53] In 2012 he published a book entitled *The Famine Plot*, accusing British officials of genocide according to the official United Nations definition formulated in 1948, 'intent to destroy, in whole or in part, a national, ethical, racial or religious group'.[54] He polemically accused academic historians and the modern Irish establishment of covering up Britain's culpability for the disaster. The book was savaged by academics in learned journals and was attacked by one respected historian of the famine as a 'polemic without plausibility' in *The Irish Times*.[55] Nevertheless, his book received a surprisingly warm welcome from the international media, which gave its conclusions disproportionate air time.[56] A movie called *Black '47*, an Irish box-office success released in October 2018, further popularised the genocide argument by telling the fictional story of an Irish soldier returning to Ireland to get revenge against the British for killing his family in the famine.[57]

Coogan's book does little more than rehearse the sorts of arguments about the famine developed by Mitchel, himself a polemical nationalist, in the 1860s. The academic and popular debate on the famine is still shaped by his general arguments, whether in support or in reaction to them. In the 1861 edition of *The Last Conquest of Ireland (Perhaps)*, Mitchel put forcefully the accusation of purposeful murder against the English government: 'a million and a half men women and children were carefully, prudently, and peacefully slain by the English government'.[58] Commonly repeated arguments – including the idea that *laissez-faire* policies were deliberately used to kill the Irish, that there was enough food in Ireland during the famine but the British deliberately encouraged exports to cost more Irish lives, and that racism was the prime motivator of British policy towards Ireland – all have their origins in Mitchel's polemic.

---

53   T. P. Coogan, *The Famine Plot* (London: Palgrave Macmillan, 2012), pp. 31, 229–31.
54   Idem., p. 230.
55   P. Gray, 'Polemic without Plausibility', *The Irish Times*, 19 January 2013, online at <https://www.irishtimes.com/culture/books/polemic-without-plausibility-1.963743> [accessed 29 March 2021].
56   See, for instance, *The Boston Globe*, 3 December 2012, online at <https://www.bostonglobe.com/arts/books/2012/12/03/book-review-the-famine-plot-england-role-ireland-greatest-tragedy-tim-pat-coogan/6eP6yaKm16wIw8qx3xEDkK/story.html> [accessed 7 March 2020]; *The Economist*, 12 December 2012, online at <https://www.economist.com/prospero/2012/12/12/opening-old-wounds> [accessed 7 March 2020].
57   'Black '47: Brain-Twitching Great Irish Famine Revenge Thriller', *The Irish Times*, 5 September 2018.
58   Mitchel, *The Last Conquest of Ireland (Perhaps)*, p. 219.

Most academic historians now reject Mitchel's and Coogan's arguments as not history, but advocacy for the nationalist and separatist causes. Neither used the personal papers of politicians to determine what their intentions were really, even though proving intention is a necessary prerequisite for legally sustaining any accusation of genocide. As the American political scientist Guenter Lewy has stated, 'Proof of specific intent is necessary to find an individual guilty of genocide, and the role of intent is similarly crucial when the historian assesses an episode of mass death that occurred in the past'.[59] A large loss of life 'by itself ... should never be sufficient for a finding of genocide'.[60] There is little real evidence showing malign intent. As a recent survey of the literature on the famine in the *Cambridge History of Ireland* put it, 'there is no evidence in the archive' to back up a charge of 'intentional genocide'.[61] Furthermore, as Ó Gráda pointed out, the pre-occupation of politicians during the famine was to save lives and not destroy them; 'food availability *was* a problem; *nobody* wanted the extirpation of the Irish'.[62] Furthermore, both Coogan and Mitchel lack the evidence to sustain their arguments. As Peter Gray astutely noted of Coogan's book, 'source references, the touchstone of historical professional practice, are sparse, often vague and in some cases of dubious reliability', lacking page references in most of the footnotes, and noting that the text was marred by 'numerous mistakes, misspellings, anachronisms and repetitions'.[63]

Worse still is Mitchel's hypocrisy. In the 1860s he accused the British of racism and of starving the Irish people, but in the 1840s his take on the famine was deeply anti-Semitic. He also criticised the government for taxing wealthier people (like himself) to feed the poor, particularly hypocritical since he later accused the British of purposefully not feeding them. 'The ruling powers in our country ... have undertaken the duty of *feeding the Irish people* ...', he thundered in *The Nation* in December 1846, 'the effect of their administration in this matter will be that starvation will be averted for this season at the cost of an excessive outlay in money, a vital injury to that class or interest most in need of being cherished'.[64] After he left *The Nation*, he founded his own newspaper, the *United Irishman*, where he could really let rip. 'Lord John Russell is bringing his Jew Masters into Parliament – the gold mongering bullionist and Israelitish interest cannot be stronger in the councils of "our rulers" than it is already ...', he raged on the leader page of its first edition.[65] After escaping to America, he

59   G. Lewy, 'Can there Be Genocide without the Intent to Commit Genocide?', *Journal of Genocide Research* 9:4 (2007), 661–74, at p. 671.
60   Ibid.
61   P. Gray, 'The Great Famine, 1845–50' in T. Bartlett, J. Kelly (eds.), *The Cambridge History of Ireland*, vol. 3 (Cambridge: CUP, 2018), 639–65, at p. 658.
62   Ó Gráda, *Ireland before and after the Famine*, p. 138.
63   Gray, 'Polemic without Plausibility', *The Irish Times*, 19 January 2013.
64   *The Nation*, 12 December 1846, p. 7.
65   *United Irishman*, 2 February 1848, p. 2.

set up another paper, *The Citizen*, from which his words in support of slavery ('we deny it is a crime or a wrong, or even a peccadillo, to hold slaves … we wish we had a good plantation well stocked with healthy negroes in Alabama') were spread around the world.[66] Some commentators, including Peter O'Neill, have called for a 'nuanced' understanding of this outburst, claiming it was to emphasise Mitchel's assertion that the Irish were treated worse than slaves.[67] It should be noted, though, that this position is now associated with attempts by white supremacists to undermine the struggle for black civil rights in contemporary American politics.[68]

Turning away from racist mythmaking towards real historical analysis, there was a common public-policy issue facing both Ireland and the formal British colonies that had seen their slave populations emancipated in the 1830s under the Slavery Abolition Act. The subsistence farming of the rural poor in Ireland and the slave plantations in the mainly sugar-producing colonies had kept both populations (more or less) fed in previous decades. However, the blight in Ireland, the abolition of slavery and Britain's move towards free trade helped to wipe away these economic systems and increased the exposure of the affected populations to the vagaries of global markets into which their produce was sold. The issue facing British policymakers was how to ensure that these populations remained employed and fed. Given the dominance of liberal political economy in this era, the answer invariably meant some kind of reform of capitalism. Should these reforms be seen as helping or hindering the Irish population during the famine? This is a question that has polarised historical opinion to the present day.

Historians and the famine

It has often been stated by historians that the nationalist interpretation of the famine story grew up because of a lack of scholarly interest in or public discussion of the famine during the nineteenth century. However, this is not

---

66 Quotations spread widely across the world: *The Spectator*, 5 April 1854, p. 15; *Punch*, 11 February 1854, p. 51; *The Morning Chronicle*, 3 February 1854, p. 3; *Liberator* (Boston, MSS), 17 February 1854, p. 1; *Geelong Advertiser and Intelligencer* (Australia), 25 May 1854, quoting *The Citizen*, second edition; *The Citizen*, 14 January 1854, p. 25.
67 P. D. O'Neill, 'Memory and John Mitchel's Appropriation of the Slave Narrative', *Atlantic Studies*, 11:3 (2014), 321–43. For Mitchel's 'Celtic Supremacist' views, 'the Celtic is the superior breed', see J. Quinn, 'Southern Citizen: John Mitchel, the Confederacy and Slavery', *History Ireland*, 15:3 (2007), 30–35, at p. 31.
68 Debunking the imagery of the 'Irish slaves' meme, online at <https://limerick1914. medium.com/the-imagery-of-the-irish-slaves-myth-dissected-143e70aa6e74> [accessed 29 November 2021].

an entirely fair assessment of the older historical literature about the event.[69] Charles Trevelyan, the assistant secretary of the Treasury, began the debate on the famine with a defence of government policy in *The Irish Crisis*, which was published in 1848 first as an article in the *Edinburgh Review* and then as a book.[70] Several lengthy critiques of the arguments presented in these publications soon appeared, most notably George Poulett Scrope's *The Irish Relief Measures, Past and Future*, published in early 1848, in the preface of which he accused Trevelyan of excessive optimism: 'a stranger to the real events of the last two years might read through the whole hundred pages without even finding out that during the "Irish Crisis" several hundred thousand souls perished in Ireland of want, through the inefficiency of those "colossal" relief measures'.[71]

The first quasi-scholarly critique of Trevelyan's arguments came in 1874 when John O'Rourke, who had been a student at Maynooth College during the famine and was now a Catholic parish priest, published *The History of the Great Irish Famine of 1847*.[72] Dedicated to 'my fellow countrymen', and based on numerous interviews, reports and official sources, the book is a balanced critique of the British response to the famine.[73] He criticised the Russell government for its 'lack of promptness and decision' in delivering assistance and as for the 'Gregory Clause', he considered that 'a more complete engine for the slaughter and expatriation of a people was never designed'.[74] This provision was a particularly controversial amendment to one of the Poor Relief (Ireland) Acts of 1847 proposed by William Gregory, an Irish Conservative MP and landlord, compelling occupiers of a quarter of an acre of land or more to surrender their plots if they wished to obtain public relief.

Even so, some features of O'Rourke's interpretation of the famine have striking similarities to the writings produced by revisionists in the twentieth century. As Christophe Gillissen has recently noted, O'Rourke stood back from terming it as 'genocide', or whatever the Victorian equivalent of that term

69   N. Ó Cioséin, 'Was there "Silence" about the Famine?', *Irish Studies Review*, 4:13 (1995), 7–10.

70   C. E. Trevelyan, 'The Irish Crisis', *Edinburgh Review*, 87:175 (January 1848), 229–320; C. E. Trevelyan, *The Irish Crisis* (London: Longman, 1848).

71   G. P. Scrope, *The Irish Relief Measures, Past and Future* (London: James Ridgway, 1848), p. iii.

72   C. Gillissen, 'Charles Trevelyan, John Mitchel and the Historiography of the Great Famine', *Revue française de civilisation britannique*, 19:2 (2014), 195–212, at pp. 200–01.

73   J. O'Rourke, *The History of the Great Irish Famine of 1847* (London: James Duffy, 1875), p. vi.

74   J. O'Rourke, *The History of the Great Irish Famine of 1847 with Notices of Earlier Irish Famines*, third edition (Dublin: James Duffy, 1902), p. 331, cited in Gillissen, 'Charles Trevelyan, John Mitchel and the Historiography of the Great Famine', p. 201.

would have been.[75] The government's response was inadequate, O'Rourke argued. However, he also argued that criticism of British policymakers should be put in the context of the immense and unexpected scale of the problems that they faced:

> to have met the Potato Famine with anything like complete success, would have been a Herculean task for any government. The total failure of the food of a nation was ... a fact new in history; such being the case, no machinery existed extensive enough to neutralize its effects, nor was there extant any plan upon which such machinery could be modelled. ... Great allowance must be therefore made for the shortcomings of the Government, in a crisis so new and so terrible.[76]

In short, O'Rourke argued, 'it must be admitted that Lord John Russell and his colleagues were painfully unequal to the situation'.[77]

This book remained in print until the turn of the twentieth century, when other proto-revisionist accounts followed. William Patrick O'Brien's *The Great Famine in Ireland*, published in 1896, attempted to rebut some of the wilder claims of nationalist polemicists. As a retired civil servant who 'had commenced work in 1847 under Burgoyne's Relief Committee and had later served as a Poor Law inspector', he has been accused by some historians of deferring too much to Trevelyan's *The Irish Crisis*.[78] In 1921, at the time of the Anglo-Irish War, George O'Brien, an economics professor at University College Dublin, published *The Economic History of Ireland from the Union to the Famine*. The chapters on the famine reiterated O'Rourke's main points of criticism of the British government.[79] Together, these works helped to establish the main lines of scholarly debate about the famine in the early twentieth century, between a moderate critique and a moderate defence of the British relief effort.

In contrast, later in the twentieth century, scholarly interpretations of the famine became more divided and extreme. Three loose groups of thinking about the famine have dominated the field since the middle of that century. All position themselves in reaction to the nationalist polemics of the nineteenth

75   Gillissen, 'Charles Trevelyan, John Mitchel and the Historiography of the Great Famine', p. 201.
76   O'Rourke, *The History of the Great Irish Famine of 1847* (1875), pp. 196–97.
77   Idem., p. 197.
78   W. P. O'Brien, *The Great Famine in Ireland: And a Retrospect of the Fifty Years 1845–95; with a Sketch of the Present Condition and Future Prospects of the Congested Districts* (London: Downey and Company, 1896); for O'Brien's biographical details and the historical reception of his book, see 'The Great Famine Revisited: General Introduction', in C. Kinealy (ed.), *The History of the Irish Famine: Volume I: The Great Irish Famine* (Abingdon: Routledge, 2019).
79   O'Brien, *An Economic History of Ireland from the Union to the Famine*, pp. 222–80.

century, or are reactions to those reactions, and side-line the rest of the older historiography on the famine.[80] The first is a group of historians, often called the 'revisionists', who sought to professionalise the study of history in Ireland and to develop a new narrative of the famine as 'a self-conscious reaction against an earlier nationalist tradition of historical interpretation'.[81] In particular, they sought to downplay the importance of the crisis and to stress long-term structural trends instead of British policy decisions as the primary force driving change in Irish history. Many also emphasised Malthusian interpretations of the famine that saw it as something which was inevitable and which policymakers could do little to avoid.[82]

Most prominent among the revisionists were Robert Dudley Edwards and Desmond Williams, two history professors at University College Dublin who wanted the Irish historical profession to develop non-nationalist narratives of events.[83] In 1938 they had founded *Irish Historical Studies*, a new academic journal, which they hoped would make the writing of Irish history more professional and objective. They helped to spread revisionist ideas relating to the famine through their editing of the Irish government's official history of the famine, the only multi-author history book commissioned by the Irish government between the 1930s and the 1970s.[84]

The resulting book was late in coming to print and the chaotic way in which it was assembled left much room for other interpretations of the famine to develop. Ó Gráda in the 1990s revealed the full story, using recently released government files and interviews with surviving contributors. The book took 12 years to produce, missed all the centenaries of the famine with which its publication was supposed to coincide and undershot the expectations of those who had commissioned it.[85] First proposed by Taoiseach Éamon de Valera in 1944, this book proved to be a disappointment to him when it was finally published in

---

80   As noted in R. Haines, *Charles Trevelyan and the Great Irish Famine* (Dublin: Four Courts Press, 2004), p. 9.
81   B. Bradshaw, 'Nationalism in Historical Scholarship in Modern Ireland', *Irish Historical Studies*, 26:104 (1994), 329–51, at p. 329.
82   See, for instance, K. Connell, *The Population of Ireland 1700–1845* (Oxford: OUP, 1975); T. W. Freeman, *Pre-famine Ireland: A Study in Historical Geography* (Manchester: MUP, 1957); D. Grigg, *Population Growth and Agrarian Change: An Historical Perspective* (Cambridge: CUP, 1980).
83   A. Clarke, 'Edwards, Robert Walter Dudley (1909–1988), Historian', *Oxford Dictionary of National Biography* (Oxford: OUP, 2004), online at <https://www.oxforddnb.com/view/10.1093/ref:odnb/9780198614128.001.0001/odnb-9780198614128-e-54049> [accessed 8 March 2020]; J. McGuire, 'T. Desmond Williams (1921-87)', *Irish Historical Studies*, 26:101 (1988), 3–7.
84   Ó Cioséin, 'Was there "Silence" about the Famine?', p. 8.
85   C. Ó Gráda, 'Making History in Ireland in the 1940s and 1950s: The Saga of the Great Famine', *The Irish Review (Cork)*, 12 (Spring–Summer 1992), 87–107.

1956 after a decade of delays, including the loss of the footnotes for the chapter about medical history 'allegedly in a London taxi-cab'.[86] De Valera, it is said, had expected the first single-volume scholarly history about the Irish famine to be about 1,000 pages long and to be imbued with nationalist fervour.[87] If that was the Taoiseach's aim, Edwards and Williams were not the scholars for the job. What De Valera got was a 436-page administrative history written from the perspective of politicians, poor-law officials, medical practitioners and so on.[88] Ó Gráda has commented that although the book contained 'some excellent material that is of enduring value', it did not provide a unified narrative of the crisis that De Valera and most casual readers were looking for.[89] The title had changed from the originally proposed 'History of the Great Famine' to 'Studies in the History of the Irish Famine' – an admission of the volume's more limited scope.[90] A lack of co-ordination between the authors of the chapters is particularly evident, with conflicting guestimates of the death toll given in different chapters.[91]

Nevertheless, the book was generally reviewed favourably at the time and a generation of revisionist scholarship followed in its wake.[92] Louis Cullen, for instance, attempted to set the Irish famine in the long run development of the Irish economy, while stressing economic factors instead of political ones, culminating in the 1972 publication of *An Economic History of Ireland since 1660*.[93] 'Irish economic development' in the long run, Cullen suggested, 'is more independent of non-economic factors than has generally been believed'.[94] With or without a famine, 'a decline in population was inevitable' in Ireland.[95] To Raymond Crotty, a historian of Irish agriculture writing in 1966, the Irish famine was 'not, as has been frequently claimed, a watershed – at least in any meaningful sense'.[96] In 1974 the journal *Irish Economic and Social History* was

86   Haines, *Charles Trevelyan and the Great Irish Famine*, p. 10; C. Brady (ed.), *Interpreting Irish History: The Debate on Historical Revisionism, 1938–1994* (Dublin: Irish Academic Press, 1994), p. 279; Ó Gráda, 'Making History in Ireland in the 1940s and 1950s', pp. 95–96.
87   C. Tóibín, 'Colm Tóibín on the Great Irish Famine', *London Review of Books*, 20:15 (30 July 1998); Edwards, Williams (eds.), *The Great Famine: Studies in Irish History 1845–52*.
88   Tóibín, 'Colm Tóibín on the Great Irish Famine'; Edwards, Williams (eds.), *The Great Famine: Studies in Irish History 1845–52*
89   Ó Gráda, 'Making History in Ireland in the 1940s and 1950', p. 96.
90   Idem., p. 92.
91   Idem., p. 95.
92   Idem., p. 96.
93   L. M. Cullen, *An Economic History of Ireland since 1660* (London: B. T. Batsford, 1972).
94   L. M. Cullen, 'Irish Economic History: Fact and Myth', in L. M. Cullen (ed.), *The Formation of the Irish Economy* (Cork: Mercier Press, 1969), 113–24, at p. 113.
95   L. M. Cullen, 'Irish History without the Potato', *Past & Present*, 40:1 (1968), 72–83, at p. 83.
96   R. D. Crotty, *Irish Agricultural Production: Its Volume and Structure* (Cork: Cork University Press, 1966), p. 132.

established with the aim of encouraging quantitative study as well as a more scientific and impartial approach to the subject.[97] Roy Foster, whose reputation has become associated with revisionism, hoped it would turn out to oppose what he called 'moralising generalisation' by looking at impartial facts.[98] The conclusions reached by revisionist historians were brought to a popular audience by Foster's *Modern Ireland* (1988), which argued that differences between 'before and after the famine' were not so great, and Mary Daly's *The Famine in Ireland* (1986) which suggested that 'given the degree of disruption caused by the potato failure of 1846, the role of the British government as a relief agent should perhaps be seen in a more sympathetic light than it is generally regarded'.[99] Most revisionist literature was also accused by its critics of being 'reductivist' in that it sought to minimise the importance of the famine.

In response to the perceived 'generosity and restraint' of revisionist historians there arose a second group of historians, loosely called the 'post-revisionists' who sought to connect with the human horror experienced during the Irish famine.[100] This group attacked the revisionists' 'dispassionate, sanitized approach to the Great Irish famine' and lampooned 'the inability of practitioners of value-free history to cope with the catastrophic dimensions of the Irish past'.[101] They provoked post-revisionist writers to produce detailed accounts of the undoubted suffering of the Irish poor, while senior politicians, influenced by *laissez-faire* ideology, cut relief, a genre started by Cecil Woodham-Smith's *The Great Hunger* (1962).[102] They were influenced by the discovery and presentation of Trevelyan's so-called 'semi-official' papers by Jenifer Hart, a historian at Oxford University. Woodham-Smith, using Hart's research, argued that the assistant secretary of the Treasury was the official responsible for the formulation and implementation of policies that, in her view, deliberately exacerbated the effects of the famine on the poor in Ireland.[103]

97   D. Dickson, P. Roebuck, 'Editorial', *Irish Economic and Social History* 1:1 (1974), 5; L. A. Clarkson, 'The Writing of Irish Economic and Social History since 1968', *Economic History Review*, 33:1 (1980), 100–11, at pp. 100–01.

98   R. F. Foster, 'The Problems of Writing Irish History', *History Today*, 34:1 (1984), 27–30, at p. 28.

99   R. F. Foster, *Modern Ireland 1600–1972* (London: Penguin, 1988), p. 318; M. E. Daly, *The Famine in Ireland* (Dundalk: Dundalgan Press for the Dublin Historical Association, 1986), p. 113.

100   Haines, *Charles Trevelyan and the Great Irish Famine*, p. 10; C. Ó Gráda, *The Great Irish Famine* (Cambridge: CUP, 1995), p. 3, citing Woodham-Smith, *The Great Hunger*, pp. 75–76.

101   Ó Gráda, *The Great Irish Famine*, p. 34 n. 31; Bradshaw, 'Nationalism in Historical Scholarship in Modern Ireland', p. 340.

102   Woodham-Smith, *The Great Hunger*.

103   Haines, *Charles Trevelyan and the Great Irish Famine*, p. 10; J. Hart, 'Sir Charles Trevelyan at the Treasury', *English Historical Review*, 75:294 (1960), 92–110.

Though the book was popular among the public, it was initially derided by academic historians in Ireland. However, the graphic descriptions of the horrors of the famine that it revealed prompted another Oxford historian, A. J. P. Taylor, in a book review, to label the event a 'genocide', and compare it with the Holocaust, suggesting 'all Ireland was a Belsen'.[104] In contrast, such was the low opinion of Woodham-Smith's book among Irish historians at University College Dublin that they set an exam question for their final-year students in 1963 asking whether '*The Great Hunger* is a great novel?'[105] More recently in 2004, Robin Haines forcefully debunked Hart and Woodham-Smith's interpretation of Trevelyan's letters. She had discovered that Hart had cited just 27 letters of the 6,000 pages available in his letter books; in the words of Haines she 'paraphrased an unrepresentative handful guaranteed to ridicule – and demonize – her subject'.[106]

Even so, since the 1980s the post-revisionist interpretation that Hart and Woodham-Smith inspired has increasingly dominated the literature on the famine. Economic historians have undermined revisionist arguments downplaying the importance of the famine, by collecting and crunching economic and demographic data. Joel Mokyr attacked Cullen's underlying assumption that the famine was an inevitable Malthusian disaster by applying cliometric methods to the issue in his quantitative study of the famine published in 1983. Instead, he blamed the starvation on the perception amongst English and Scottish investors that Ireland was a 'hostile country'.[107] Kevin O'Rourke's study, 'Did the Great Irish Famine Matter?', published in 1991, also re-established the famine as a 'major watershed' in Irish agricultural history.[108]

Post-revisionists also emphasise the role of ideologies such as providentialism in explaining why British policy failed in Ireland, a trend begun by Hart and Woodham-Smith.[109] As Ó Gráda summarised the state of academic opinion in 1999, the main cause of inadequate relief efforts was 'doctrinaire neglect'.[110] Gray, a leading scholar of the impact of ideology on politicians during the famine, emphasised the influence of 'Christian providentialism'

---

104   Haines, *Charles Trevelyan and the Great Irish Famine*, p. 11; A. J. P. Taylor, 'Genocide: A Review of *The Great Hunger* by Cecil Woodham-Smith (1962)', *New Statesman*, 23 November 1962, p. 741, republished in A. J. P. Taylor, *Essays in English History* (Harmondsworth: Penguin, 1976), 73–79.
105   Ó Gráda, *The Great Irish Famine*, p. 3.
106   Haines, *Charles Trevelyan and the Great Irish Famine*, pp. 3–9, 547–54.
107   J. Mokyr, *Why Ireland Starved: A Quantitative and Analytical History of the Irish Economy, 1800–1850* (London: George Allen & Unwin, 1983), pp. 291–93.
108   O'Rourke, 'Did the Great Irish Famine Matter?', p. 20.
109   Haines, *Charles Trevelyan and the Great Irish Famine*, p. 10.
110   C. Ó Gráda, *Black '47 and Beyond: The Great Irish Famine in History, Economy and Memory* (Chichester: Princeton University Press, 1999), p. 10.

and 'commitment to *laissez-faire*' on the formation of relief policy.[111] Both he and Ó Gráda contrasted 'the harsh policies of Russell and Charles Wood [his chancellor of the exchequer]', based on *laissez-faire*, with 'Peel's determined action'.[112] The harvest failures turned into a famine, they argue, not because British politicians deliberately wanted to reduce or hurt the Irish population – on this point they strongly oppose the nationalist interpretation – but because the contemporary dominance of *laissez-faire* ideas and political economy persuaded policymakers that less government intervention was for the best.

Over the past 20 years a third group of historians has emerged, the 'anti-revisionists', who argue that the post-revisionists have not unpicked the tapestry of historiography back far enough to 'ground formerly held by the traditional nationalist school'.[113] Christine Kinealy has been a pioneer in this historio-graphical shift and has published extensively on traditional nationalist themes such as the famine's 'impact', the role of providential ideology in worsening the crisis and the animating force it gave to rebellion, physical-force nationalism and the Irish diaspora.[114] Her work has come under sustained criticism from revisionists such as Daly, who have pointed out that, 'far from presenting a new and more nuanced interpretation of the Famine, many of her arguments echo John Mitchel'.[115] Following Kinealy's lead, the recent work of Ciarán Ó Murchadha cites racism and the 'deliberate systematic use of an environmental

111   Gray, *Famine, Land and Politics*, pp. 95, 124; idem., 'Potatoes and Providence', *Bullán*, 1:1 (1994), 75–90, at pp. 76–78; idem., 'National Humiliation and the Great Hunger: Fast and Famine in 1847', *Irish Historical Studies*, 32:126 (2000), 193–216, at pp. 215–16.
112   Gray, *Famine, Land and Politics*, pp. 95, 124; Ó Gráda, *The Great Irish Famine*, pp. 43, 45.
113   Haines, *Charles Trevelyan and the Great Irish Famine*, p. 11.
114   See, in particular, C. Kinealy, *The Great Irish Famine: Impact, Ideology and Rebellion* (New York: Palgrave, 2002); C. Kinealy, *A Death-Dealing Famine: The Great Hunger in Ireland* (London: Pluto Press, 1997); C. Kinealy, *This Great Calamity: The Irish Famine, 1845–52* (Dublin: Gill and Macmillan, 1994); C. Kinealy, 'Beyond Revisionism: Reassessing the Irish Famine', *History Ireland*, 3:4 (1995), 28–34; C. Kinealy, 'Peel, Rotten Potatoes and Providence', in A. Marrison (ed.), *Free Trade and its Reception 1815–1960: Freedom and Trade: vol. 1* (London: Routledge, 1998), 50–62; C. Kinealy, 'Food Exports from Ireland 1846–47', *History Ireland*, 5:1 (1997), 32–36; C. Kinealy, 'Potatoes, Providence and Philanthropy: The Role of Private Charity during the Irish Famine', in P. O'Sullivan (ed.), *The Irish Worldwide. Vol. 6: The Meaning of the Famine* (London: Leicester University Press, 1997), 140–71; C. Kinealy, '"Brethren in Bondage": Chartists, O'Connellites, Young Irelanders and the 1848 Uprising', in F. Lane, D. Ó Drisceoil (eds.), *Politics and the Irish Working Class, 1830–1945* (London: Palgrave Macmillan, 2005), 87–111; C. Kinealy, *Charity and the Great Hunger in Ireland: The Kindness of Strangers* (London: Bloomsbury Academic Press, 2013).
115   M. E. Daly, 'Historians and the Famine: A Beleaguered Species?', *Irish Historical Studies*, 30:120 (1997), 591–601, at p. 595.

catastrophe to destroy a people' in explaining why the British relief effort was so inadequate.[116]

Kinealy also contributed to the recent shift towards re-emphasising what anti-revisionists argue to be the colonial dimension of the crisis.[117] This theme has been particularly emphasised by historical geographers over the past decade.[118] 'Relief strategies became increasingly bio-political in nature and intent', David Nally, one such historical geographer, argued in 2011, and were shaped by Ireland's colonial relationship to Britain, which he argued encouraged policy to become 'faminogenic'.[119] The high levels of excess mortality and emigration present in Ireland during the famine, he argued, were largely orchestrated by policies for social reform and structural reform drawn up by the British government in London. His chapter in the *Atlas of the Great Irish Famine* (2012) portrayed the British response to the famine as driven by imperial and colonial prejudice towards the Irish; the chief imperative was the maintenance of British economic interests in Ireland rather than saving lives.[120] William Smyth, another historical geographer, writing in the same book, has gone further, to argue that relief policy during the famine continued a pattern of British imperial domination over Ireland that played out over the *longue durée*.[121]

There has also been an upsurge in new books declaring the Great Famine to be a genocide perpetrated by the British government. These not only include Coogan's *The Famine Plot* (2012), but also several others including *United Ireland, Human Rights and International Law*, by Francis Boyle, an American law professor.[122] On the back of these publications, several American states have added the Irish famine as an example of genocide through mass starvation to their school curriculum. Despite this, few of these books provide much evidence that the famine was a genocide beyond secondary quotations taken out of context principally from Woodham-Smith and Kinealy. This is but one political agenda that the memory of the famine is now used to

---

116   C. Ó Murchadha, *The Great Famine: Ireland's Agony 1845–52* (London: Continuum Books, 2011), pp. 197–98.

117   C. Kinealy, 'Was Ireland a Colony?', in T. McDonough (ed.), *Was Ireland a Colony? Economics, Politics and Culture in Nineteenth Century Ireland* (Dublin: Irish Academic Press, 2005), 48–65.

118   Gray, 'The Great Famine, 1845–1850', p. 640.

119   D. P. Nally, *Human Encumbrances: Political Violence and the Great Irish Famine* (Notre Dame: University of Notre Dame Press, 2011), p. 227.

120   D. P. Nally, 'The Colonial Dimensions of the Great Irish Famine' in J. Crowley, W. J. Smyth, M. Murphy (eds.), *Atlas of the Great Famine, 1845–52* (Cork: Cork University Press, 2012), 64–74.

121   W. J. Smyth, 'The Longue Durée – Imperial Britain and Colonial Ireland', in J. Crowley et al. (eds.), *Atlas of the Great Irish Famine, 1845–52* (Cork: Cork University Press, 2012), 46–63.

122   Coogan, *The Famine Plot*; F. Boyle, *United Ireland, Human Rights and International Law* (Atlanta: Clarity Press, 2012).

justify. Anti-revisionist interpretations of the crisis have been used to support a wide diversity of modern-day political and economic viewpoints in recent years, including opposition to British rule in Ireland, '*laissez-faire* economics', 'neo-liberalism', and free-market Thatcherism, and, more recently and perhaps most absurdly, as a way of overcoming environmentalist opposition to the use of genetically modified seed crops in the developing world.[123] This politicking has helped to widen the divide between the popular memory and discussion of the Irish famine and the historical questions of what actually happened in the past, and why.

There have been several attempts by historians to push back against the rising tide of anti-revisionism about the famine. The first notable sally, already mentioned, was Haines' *Charles Trevelyan and the Great Irish Famine*, published in 2004.[124] Richly and deeply researched, the book attempted to skewer the impression given by Hart and Woodham-Smith in the foundational texts of the post-revisionism that Trevelyan was the villain of the famine, driven by providentialism and *laissez-faire* ideology; 'on the evidence of a few selected passages their authors have convinced themselves and others that Trevelyan *was* the fiend he was held to be'.[125] '*Phytophtora infestans*, not Trevelyan', she argued, 'was the tyrant who brought death and suffering to Ireland on a scale never before witnessed'.[126]

The second was a journal article published in 2009 by Hubert Nusteling, a historian of demography at Radboud University in the Netherlands, which countered the attempts of some nationalist commentators to maximise and exaggerate the death toll of the famine.[127] By re-examining English, Irish, and American demographic statistics to produce new estimates of the extent of mortality during the Irish famine, he found that 'there was much more emigration and significantly less mortality in Ireland than is commonly believed'.[128] He concluded that, once figures for Irish migration out of Britain were taken away from the number of Irish people who disappeared between the 1841 and 1851 Censuses, excess mortality from the famine was probably only around 207,000. That is more in the ballpark of the official estimate of deaths due to famine-related causes and diseases in the 1851 Census (360,871) than it is of most post-revisionist estimates (Mokyr, in 1983, calculated 1.08m to 1.50m).

123   See Kinealy, *The Great Irish Famine*, pp. 25–29, 103, 116; K. A. McComas, J. C. Besley, J. Steinhardt, 'Factors Influencing U.S. Consumer Support for Genetic Modification to Prevent Crop Disease', *Appetite*, 78 (2014), 8–14.
124   Haines, *Charles Trevelyan and the Great Irish Famine*.
125   Idem., p. xii.
126   Idem., p. 546.
127   Nusteling, 'How Many Irish Potato Famine Deaths?: Towards Coherence of the Evidence'.
128   Idem., pp. 76–77.

Nusteling's estimates produce a lower death rate in Ireland in 1846–51 than Amsterdam had between 1751 and 1835.[129] The bulk of 'victims' of the famine, he suggested, were the famine emigrants who became the working classes of industrial Britain: 'many more inhabitants permanently emigrated from Ireland than starved in their homeland, and industrial England is more Irish than is generally assumed'.[130] Attempts by revisionist historians to downplay the death toll during the famine, he concludes, were 'not unfounded'.[131] However, unlike many of those interpretations, Nusteling accepts the demographic importance of the famine for both British and Irish history, and acknowledges that it remains 'a terrible period' for Ireland, in which approximately 4m out of its population of around 8m in 1841 unexpectedly emigrated or died within a decade.[132]

The third attempt at moderation is Liam Kennedy's *Unhappy the Land: The Most Oppressed People Ever, the Irish?*, a critique of nationalist interpretations of Irish history published in 2015.[133] Kennedy since the 1990s has rejected the sort of colonial paradigm for Irish history that anti-revisionist scholars of the famine have increasingly tried to place that event into.[134] Particularly interesting is Kennedy's personal account of how difficult it is to escape from the doctrinaire history taught to children in Ireland.[135]

This difficulty may explain why, although these scholars acknowledge the enormity and scale of the famine, their work has generally not broken through into the public consciousness as much as, for instance, Coogan's *The Famine Plot* has. Some nationalists, *à la* Brendan Bradshaw, a Cambridge historian, might chide that this is the result of trying to write 'value-free' history which lacks 'access to the kind of moral and emotional register necessary to respond to human tragedy'.[136] Those criticisms miss the point. First, modern historical method has values: objectivity and fidelity to the archival evidence are necessary to find out how events actually happened, or to quote Leopold von Ranke, its pioneer, 'how it essentially was' (*'wie es eigentlich gewesen'*).[137] Second, emotion can and should fuel demands for historical rigour. If the Irish famine

129   Idem., p. 72.
130   Idem., p. 76.
131   Idem., p. 74.
132   Ibid.
133   L. Kennedy, *Unhappy the Land: The Most Oppressed People Ever, the Irish?* (Sallins: Merrion Press, 2015), pp. 81–126.
134   L. Kennedy, *Colonialism, Religion and Nationalism in Ireland* (Belfast: The Institute of Irish Studies, 1997), especially chapter 7.
135   Kennedy, *Unhappy the Land: The Most Oppressed People Ever, the Irish?*, pp. 187–89, 194.
136   Bradshaw, 'Nationalism in Historical Scholarship in Modern Ireland', p. 341.
137   The two interpretations of Leopold von Ranke's dictum of *'wie es eigentlich gewesen'* can be found in L. von Ranke, *The Theory and Practice of History: Edited with an Introduction by Georg G. Iggers* (Abingdon: Routledge, 2010), p. xiv.

is a terrible human disaster, from which lessons should be learnt by modern policymakers, then objectively finding out what actually happened and went wrong during the disaster should be prioritised over Bradshaw's obsession with the history of identity politics.[138] What were the intentions of policymakers during the famine? What was the impact of their policies on the ground? Why did their policies not work in the way they had intended them to? Only with the answers to these questions, obtained through the archives, is it possible to explain what went wrong in Ireland in the late 1840s and what public-policy lessons, if any, should be learnt from the experience.

Ireland and the economics of famine

In addition to the debate in the historical literature that echoes or responds to the nationalists' interpretation of events, many economists have attempted to link the Irish example to their theories about modern famines. Most of the existing literature on the Irish famine seeks to respond to either the Malthusian concept of famine, with its emphasis on overpopulation, or the interpretation of famine by classical economists, who emphasise the effectiveness of efficient markets and *laissez-faire* solutions as policy tools during food shortages. Some of the literature has discussed the more recent idea of food 'entitlements' as defined by Amartya Sen and other scholars in the 1980s, but there has been little research on the political and fiscal difficulties associated with entitlement transfers during periods of economic history such as the Irish famine.[139]

Famines, Thomas Malthus believed, were sudden, acute adjustments caused by a long-run demographic crisis. It is well known that Malthus argued 'population, when unchecked, increases in a geometrical ratio; subsistence, increases only in an arithmetical ratio', and that disequilibrium in the trend of population and food production growth will be corrected when 'famine, with one mighty blow, levels the population with the food of the world'.[140] His initial solution to the problem of famine was for governments to withdraw welfare and relief, such as the Poor Law, and promote moral restraint to reduce the rate of growth of the population through a 'preventative check' to prevent 'premature death' afflicting the population.[141]

Malthus eventually revised his view of famine by emphasising preventative checks, in particular to 'diminish ... proportions of births and marriages' by

138   Bradshaw, 'Nationalism in Historical Scholarship in Modern Ireland', pp. 350–51.
139   A. Sen, *Poverty and Famines: An Essay on Entitlement and Deprivation* (Oxford: OUP, 1981), pp. 45–51.
140   T. Malthus, *An Essay on the Principle of Population* (Cambridge: CUP, 1992), p. 43.
141   T. Malthus, *An Essay on the Principle of Population* (1798 edition), chapter VII, para. 19.

marriage later in life.[142] Furthermore, he distanced himself from Smith and Ricardo concerning ideas on open trade.[143] This revision has not stopped some economists, including Barbara Solow, describing pre-famine and famine Ireland as 'a case study in Ricardian and Malthusian economics … and … classical remedies'.[144] Malthusian interpretations of population growth and famine have subsequently been attacked by many modern economists including Susan Watkins and Jane Menken, John and Pat Caldwell, and Robert Fogel.[145] In the Irish context, Mokyr has challenged the notion that the Irish famine was a Malthusian disaster in his quantitative study of the event, blaming poverty, inequality, and underdevelopment instead of overpopulation. However, the quality of his data and his methods of econometric analysis have come under severe attack by Dudley Baines and Peter Solar, who have argued that they were based more on 'guestimates' than hard evidence.[146] Nevertheless, recent quantitative work by Áine Doran has also failed to find evidence of increasing poverty or famine severity being a result of overpopulation, underlining how far modern scholarship has stepped away from Malthusian views of the crisis.[147]

In contrast to Malthus' emphasis on the role of government to constrain population growth to prevent famine, Smith and Ricardo described the effect of misguided government intervention in markets worsening famines. In *The Wealth of Nations*, Smith directly blamed government intervention, and not merchants or the hoarding of food, for famine.[148] The best preventative against famine, in Smith's view, was a free-trade system within the British Empire that allowed market forces to allocate food to where it was needed.[149] Ricardo echoed both the Malthusian view, blaming overpopulation for famines, and Smith's

---

142   T. Malthus, *An Essay on the Principle of Population: The Sixth Edition*, vol. 2 (London: John Murray, 1826), p. 266.

143   Idem., pp. 208–09.

144   B. L. Solow, *The Land Question and the Irish Economy, 1870–1903* (Cambridge, MA: Harvard University Press, 1971), p. 196.

145   S. C. Watkins, J. Menken, 'Famine in Historical Perspective', *Population Development Review*, 11:4 (1985), 647–75; J. C. Caldwell, P. Caldwell, 'Famine in Africa: A Global Perspective', in E. Van De Walle, G. Pison, M. Sala-Diakandam (eds.), *Mortality and Society in Sub-Saharan Africa* (Oxford: OUP, 1992), 361–83; R. W. Fogel, 'Second Thoughts on the European Escape from Hunger: Famine, Chronic Malnutrition and Mortality Rates', in S. R. Osmani (ed.), *Nutrition and Poverty* (Oxford: OUP, 1992), 243–86.

146   See Mokyr, *Why Ireland Starved*, pp. 291–94; D. Baines, 'Review: *Why Ireland Starved* by J. Mokyr', *Economica* (1985), 524–26; J. Mokyr, 'Reply to Peter Solar', *Irish Economic and Social History*, 11:1 (1984), 116–21; P. M. Solar, 'Why Ireland Starved: A Critical Review of the Econometric Results', *Irish Economic and Social History*, 11:1 (1984), 107–15.

147   Á. Doran, 'A Poor Inquiry: Poverty and Living Standards in Pre-Famine Ireland', *Queens' University Centre for Economic History Working Paper*, 21-01 (2021).

148   A. Smith, *An Inquiry into the Causes of the Wealth of Nations* (Oxford: OUP, 1993), p. 324.

149   Idem., p. 335.

view, blaming government intervention for famines: 'the evil proceeds from bad government, from the insecurity of property, and from a want of education in all ranks of the people'.[150] He believed that shortages could always be made up by imports.[151]

Many scholars, including Woodham-Smith, have argued that policy-makers and administrators increased the mortality rate during the famine by adopting such policies: 'almost without exception, the high officials and politicians responsible for Ireland were fervent believers in non-interference by Government'.[152] The policy they adopted, according to Woodham-Smith, was strict *laissez-faire*: 'the loss of the potato crop was therefore to be made good … by the operations of private enterprise and private firms, using the normal channels of commerce'.[153] Woodham-Smith argued that this plan was faulty because 'where relief would be most needed, the means by which it was to be supplied seldom existed'.[154] Anti-revisionist scholars have developed this line of argument. Nally, a historical geographer, has attempted to transpose back to the period of the Irish famine the type of theory propounded by Jlateh Jappah and Danielle Smith, who have developed the idea that a lack of government action during crises should be seen as 'faminogenic policies' and 'state-sponsored famine', and that political leaders who follow such policies should be charged with crimes against humanity.[155]

However, applying this idea to the 1840s is highly anachronistic. Academic historians argue that the same moral standards cannot be applied in the context of mid-nineteenth century Ireland as in the modern politics of humanitari-anism; to do so is the scholarly definition of anachronism.[156] Furthermore, given that Nally, Lebow, and other recent anti-revisionist studies do not use the private papers of politicians at all in their research, they ultimately fail to determine what the real intentions of policymakers were, or distinguish them from actual outcomes.[157]

150   D. Ricardo, *On the Principles of Political Economy and Taxation* (London: John Murray, 1821), Chapter 5.
151   D. Ricardo, *An Essay on the Influence of a Low Price of Corn on the Profits of Stock* (London: Murray, 1815), p. 35.
152   C. Woodham-Smith, *The Great Hunger: Ireland 1845–49* (London: Hamish Hamilton, 1962), p. 54.
153   Idem., p. 54.
154   Idem., p. 55.
155   Nally, *Human Encumbrances: Political Violence and the Great Irish Famine*, p. 227; J. V. Jappah, D. T. Smith, 'State Sponsored Famine: Conceptualizing Politically Induced Famine as a Crime against Humanity', *Journal of International and Global Studies*, 4:1 (2012), 17–31.
156   C. Read, 'Review: David P. Nally, *Human Encumbrances: Political Violence and the Great Famine*', *Irish Economic and Social History*, 39:1 (2012), 155–57.
157   R. N. Lebow, *White Britain and Black Ireland: The Influence of Stereotypes on Colonial Policy* (Philadelphia: Institute for the Study of Human Issues, 1976); Nally, *Human*

Neither do these scholars' interpretations fit with other historians' narratives. Rather than seeing the Russell government as an opponent of humanitarianism, some academics see it as having played an important role in the creation of international human-rights law.[158] In 1851 Russell told Lord Palmerston, his foreign secretary, that they could 'wink at [M. de] Vattel', an eighteenth-century legal scholar famous for his defence of the Westphalian idea that nations should have full sovereignty over their own affairs.[159] De Vattel's principles could be helpfully ignored – or 'winked' at – in order to assist Britain's Royal Navy in completing its mission to suppress the Atlantic slave trade, an undertaking that legal scholars see as the foundation upon which the modern edifice of international human-rights law was built.[160] There is some evidence that Russell personally (but ineffectively) opposed Peel and his own chancellor's 'fiscal puritanism'; he was frequently keen for his government to do more to help Ireland even after the severe financial crises of 1847; some historians describe his ministry's legislative achievements in Great Britain as 'a high-water mark of State intervention'.[161] As Haines has pointed out, 'in the mid-1840s, Whig leaders railed against the abstract political economy of the Conservative government', which, they believed, did not treat factory operatives as *citizens* with rights.[162] The anti-revisionist turn in the literature has not fully answered the question of why a government so ideologically attached to the politics of humanitarianism and intervention failed so badly in Ireland, against its avowed best intentions.

In contrast to classical ideas about the economics of famine, modern discussions around Amartya Sen's 'entitlement approach', and the supply- or demand-side nature of food crises, have only been applied in very specific situations to debates over the Irish famine.[163] His theory challenged the food availability decline (FAD) theory which became popular among British civil

Encumbrances: Political Violence and the Great Irish Famine, pp. 302–35.

158 R. Huzzey, 'Review: *The Slave Trade and the Origin of International Human Rights Law*', *Journal for Maritime Research*, 14:2 (2012), 139–41; R. Huzzey, *Freedom Burning: Anti-Slavery and Empire in Victorian Britain* (New York: Cornell University Press, 2012), p. 145.

159 Russell to Palmerston, 24 September 1851, S.U. H.L., Palmerston papers, GC/RU/424, cited in Huzzey, 'Review: *The Slave Trade and the Origin of International Human Rights Law*', p. 139.

160 Ibid.; J. S. Martinez, *The Slave Trade and the Origins of International Human Rights Law* (Oxford: OUP, 2012).

161 P. Mandler, *Aristocratic Government in the Age of Reform: Whig and Liberal 1830–52* (Oxford: OUP, 1990), pp. 217, 252.

162 Haines, *Charles Trevelyan and the Great Irish Famine*, p. 543; Mandler, *Aristocratic Government in the Age of Reform*, p. 221.

163 P. M. A. Bourke, 'The Irish Grain Trade, 1839–48', *Irish Historical Studies*, 20:78 (1976), 156–69, at pp. 165–66; Ó Gráda, *Ireland before and after the Famine*, pp. 121–25.

servants in India in the twentieth century. The Famine Inquiry Commission in India, for instance, concluded that the Bengal famine of 1943 was due to 'the serious shortage in the total supply of rice available for consumption in Bengal as compared with the total supply normally available'.[164] Carl Eicher, an agricultural economist, has argued that famines, particularly in Africa, are caused by 'a food production gap and hunger', in absolute terms.[165] However, since the publication of Sen's *Poverty and Famines* in the early-1980s, 'the FAD approach' has been replaced with Sen's idea that famine mortality is driven by the inequitable distribution of food entitlements, which, in a market economy, shows itself as a lack of monetary demand for food.[166] When Sen investigated the Bengali famine of the 1940s and other modern famines in Ethiopia, the Sahel, and Bangladesh, he criticised Adam Smith's vision that markets could relieve famines.[167] Smith is 'concerned with efficiency in meeting a market demand', but there is 'nothing on meeting a need that has not been translated into effective demand because of lack of market-based entitlement and shortage of purchasing power'.[168]

In spite of the widespread recognition of Sen's work on famines, there has been very little interest among economic historians in applying a demand-side entitlements approach to analysing the situation in 1840s Ireland. Ó Gráda has questioned whether Sen's observations apply to the Irish famine. Although he asked 'was there still enough, suitably divided out, to feed everybody?', he did not attempt a full economic analysis of whether this criticism was empirically true or not.[169] Sen himself does not directly study Ireland in detail, but he quotes it as an example of a 'slump famine'. Crises with 'food being *exported* from famine-stricken areas', as was the case in 1840s Ireland, 'may be a natural characteristic of the market which respects entitlements rather than needs', he argued.[170]

Contemporary accounts in Ireland agree that entitlements were often the key issue in the famines of the nineteenth century. In the 1816–18 famine, the *Irish Farmers Journal* emphasised 'the want of employment as the chief cause of stress', and that the famine was caused 'not from absolute want of food but from the want of means to purchase it'.[171] A Parliamentary committee investi-

164   *Report on Bengal*, Famine Inquiry Commission, India (New Delhi: Government of India, 1945), p. 77.
165   See C. K. Eicher, 'Facing up to Africa's Food Crisis', *Foreign Affairs*, 61:1 (1982), 151–74.
166   Sen, *Poverty and Famines: An Essay on Entitlements and Deprivation*, p. 154.
167   Idem., p. 161.
168   Ibid.
169   Ó Gráda, *Ireland before and after the Famine*, p. 122.
170   Sen, *Poverty and Famines: An Essay on Entitlements and Deprivation*, pp. 161–62.
171   *Irish Farmers' Journal*, 9 August 1817.

gating the Irish famine of 1822 concluded that the problem was due less to a lack of food than to 'the want of means of purchasing it'.[172] During the Irish famine itself, in 1845, the Countess de Grey, on whose Irish family's estates the first sighting of the potato blight was recorded, noted in her diary that 'there is plenty of food there now, but no means of purchasing it for most of the people now see money scarcely'.[173] These contemporary comments anticipate Sen's entitlements thesis almost two centuries later.

Yet, scholars have been more interested in applying the entitlements approach in a political rather than economic sense. Nally has recently tried to apply Sen's ideas about entitlements to the Irish famine but focused entirely on political entitlements in order to link this to his arguments about the culpability of British politicians.[174] A full assessment of how macroeconomic and micro-economic forces from both within the United Kingdom and abroad may have affected entitlements has not yet been carried out. Whether the sort of redistri-bution of entitlements between different classes that Sen theoretically proposes would have actually been possible or worked as intended given the real-world constraints, economic, financial, and political, facing the British government during the famine will therefore be dealt with in this book.[175]

Alex de Waal responded to Sen's work by introducing the factor of nutrition, and pointing out that the success of famine relief relied on not just providing entitlement to food but to food of good nutritional quality.[176] Leslie Clarkson and Margaret Crawford followed this up with specific suggestions that nutritional diseases such as pellagra might have been present during the Irish famine.[177] These ailments are serious and may have been linked to the inadequacy of the replacement staple food, Indian corn, which was imported during the famine from the United States. Specific cases illustrating nutritional disease have been confirmed by recent archaeological excavations that have taken place since Clarkson and Crawford's study.[178] Tantalisingly, some of the resulting information shows that teenagers in workhouses suffered

---

172   Cited in Ó Gráda, *Ireland before and after the Famine*, p. 122.

173   'Lady de Grey's Diary' c. 1845, B.L.A.R.S., Lucas archive, L30/18/70. Although Henrietta (formerly Lady Grantham) became Countess de Grey in 1833, she was also commonly known as 'Lady de Grey' and much material relating to her is referenced under that name. See C. Read, 'De Grey [née Cole], Henrietta Frances, Countess de Grey (1784–1848)', *Dictionary of Irish Biography* (January 2014).

174   Nally, *Human Encumbrances: Political Violence and the Great Irish Famine*, p. xi.

175   Sen, *Poverty and Famines: An Essay on Entitlements and Deprivation*, pp. 179–84.

176   A. de Waal, 'A Re-assessment of Entitlement Theory in the Light of the Recent Famines in Africa', *Development and Change*, 21:3 (1990), 469–90.

177   L. Clarkson, M. Crawford, *Feast and Famine: Food and Nutrition in Ireland 1500–1920* (Oxford: OUP, 2001), p. 146.

178   J. Geber, E. Murphy, 'Scurvy in the Great Irish Famine', *American Journal of Physical Anthropology*, 148:4 (2012), 512–24. 'Indian corn' refers to a variety of maize now commonly

under-feeding, and then recovered by eating a maize diet, but then died after a further two to three years.[179] This is consistent with maize providing calories but not sufficient nutrients on its own for the long-term health of famine survivors. How widespread such nutritional problems were during the famine, and what role they played in frustrating the attempts by policymakers to redistribute entitlements, are questions yet to be fully investigated by historians, but they will also be addressed in this book.

British economic policy and the Irish famine

Commentators on the famine have frequently wondered why the British government did not raise more loans to fund relief for Ireland. For instance, William Smith O'Brien, leader of the Young Ireland movement, believed that 'loans' for public works and mines in combination with emigration might have saved more Irish people from starvation.[180] The general idea that deficit-financed public works could have saved more people from starvation gained popular credence after the publication of John Maynard Keynes' *The General Theory* in 1936. Yet there has been no study using the type of international-macroeconomic analysis pioneered by his followers in the 1960s to assess what problems there were which may have limited the United Kingdom's ability to raise loans for relief policies.[181] Nor has the general economic background to the famine in Britain been fully explored. What were the budgetary and tax implications of funding relief in Ireland? Was the cash available; if not how was it to be raised and what effect did this have on financial markets? Whether economic and financial issues were the real motive behind the speed and severity of cuts in the government funding of relief policies which were suddenly fully implemented in the spring of 1847 will be investigated in this book.

Post-revisionist and anti-revisionist historians have preferred to blame British '*laissez-faire*' (or let-it-be) policies, including Britain's move towards unilateral free trade, as the tools with which Ireland was damaged in the 1840s. But not all historians have agreed with this analysis. In the 1940s Bartlett Brebner pointed

---

referred to as 'flint corn'. Its scientific name is *Zea mays* var. *indurate*. In the 1840s 'Indian corn' was the commonly used name, and is the term used throughout this book.

179   J. Beaumont, J. Montgomery, 'The Great Irish Famine: Identifying Starvation in the Tissues of Victims Using Stable Isotope Analysis of Bone and Incremental Dentine Collagen', *PLoS ONE*, 11:8 (2016), 469–90.

180   W. S. O'Brien, *Principles of Government*, vol. 2 (Boston: P. Donahoe, 1856), p. 230.

181   For a history of international macroeconomics, and of the role economists such as James Meade, Robert Mundell and Marcus Fleming had in its development, see M. Obstfeld, 'International Macroeconomics: Beyond the Mundell-Fleming Model', *NBER Working Paper* no. 8369 (2001), 1–56, at pp. 3–12.

out that British governments in the nineteenth century were very interventionist, particularly in legislation, while publicly espousing *laissez-faire* ideas. He claimed 'it is possible to tabulate the parallel developments of *laissez-faire* and state intervention year by year', as if the rhetoric about the former was used to draw attention away from the reality of the latter.[182] George Bernstein, writing in 1995, believed *laissez-faire* amounted to 'Irish mythology' and pointed to the 'onset of a financial crisis during 1847' as the incentive 'for placing more of the relief burden on the Irish'.[183] Moreover, he claimed, after the apparent failure of British government intervention between 1846 and 1848 to avert mass mortality in Ireland, British liberals needed *laissez-faire* as a rhetorical excuse to give them 'a clear conscience' that the famine was 'beyond the ability of human ingenuity to avert or mitigate'.[184]

He was by no means the first historian to be left unimpressed by the notion that *laissez-faire* ideas dominated policy decisions on relief. A particular mystery arose over the major cutback of the previously generous Treasury funding of relief in May 1847 and the subsequent cancellation of any Treasury support for funding through the Poor Law system and local taxes. In the 1970s Robert Montague's research about relief policy during the Irish famine had led him to query whether political economy was responsible for triggering the Russell government's relief policy U-turn.[185] He concluded that 'most economists shared a general set of notions about the British economy – notions that they did not believe appropriate in an Irish context'.[186] He found the 'Whig *volte-face*' in relief policy in 1847 to be 'one of the most surprising aspects of the Whig programme for Ireland' and put it down to the public-works schemes being seen to have failed in their purpose.[187] Even so, the question still remained to be satisfactorily answered. Peter Mandler, writing in 1990, found the hiatus in policy puzzling as well. He thought that the changes were certainly a 'high water-mark of *laissez-faire*', but perversely were right in the middle of a session which otherwise was very redolent of state intervention; he suspected Treasury involvement in forcing the U-turn.[188]

'*Laissez-faire*' policies have since been fully explored by Gray and they are an important theme of his book *Famine, Land and Politics* (1999).[189]

---

182 J. B. Brebner, 'Laissez Faire and State Intervention in Nineteenth-Century Britain', *Journal of Economic History*, 8:S1 (1948), 59–73, at p. 65.

183 G. L. Bernstein, 'Liberals, the Irish Famine and the Role of the State', *Irish Historical Studies*, 29:116 (1995), 513–36, at p. 525.

184 Idem., p. 536.

185 R. J. Montague, 'Relief and Reconstruction in Ireland 1845–49', University of Oxford, unpublished DPhil dissertation (1977), p. ii.

186 Ibid.

187 Idem., p. 142.

188 Mandler, *Aristocratic Government in the Age of Reform*, pp. 251–52.

189 Gray, *Famine, Land and Politics*.

However, it is difficult to see how even the large number of references to 'laissez-faire' and 'political economy' given throughout that book supply the *entire* answer to the question of the change in policy. Gray's approach has resulted in some important archival discoveries, but the neglect of alternative economic and financial influences on policy decisions, even though they abound in the original sources, mean that the entire story is yet to be told. This book presents some of the missing mechanisms and detailed explanations for how the events of 1847 arose, other than simply linking the ideas of policymakers to *laissez-faire* ideology.

A further problem is that the '*laissez-faire*' approach does not reveal the full complexity of the ideologies at play.[190] Some scholars, for instance, suggest that Trevelyan, Wood and the war and colonial secretary, Henry George (the Third Earl) Grey, were 'like-minded men', a '"moralist" ideological grouping'.[191] This ignores the serious and important disagreements that existed between them in this period on economic theory and policy. In reality, as this book exposes, this was a period when civil war broke out between Wood and Grey inside the Cabinet, and more widely in 'political economy' outside it, over monetary policy. Much of the contemporary debate over how to respond to the Irish famine in Great Britain was just one battle in a long war over political economy between the ideas of the Currency School, that Wood followed at the Treasury, and those of the Banking School, which influenced Grey at the Colonial Office.[192] Wood and Grey had very different policy prescriptions about how to deal with the financial panics of 1847, which had made it more difficult to raise loans for financing famine relief in Ireland, and they spectacularly fell out over the issue.[193] As Ireland came under the Treasury's authority – because it was not legally a colony – it was the ideas of the Currency School that prevailed over Britain's official and charitable responses to the Irish famine.

An added complication is that, frequently, the intention of economic policy was not the same as the outcome – a fact that should be unsurprising considering the lack of economic data and knowledge politicians then had about how to run the world's first industrialised economy in its earliest days. So both intention and outcome need to be analysed in order to gain a full understanding

190   Idem., p. 14; Some contradictions and complexities are discussed in B. Hilton, *The Age of Atonement: The Influence of Evangelicalism on Social and Economic Thought, 1795–1865* (Oxford: OUP, 1988), pp. 109–10, 249–50.
191   For example, Gray, *Famine, Land and Politics*, p. 231.
192   A. J. Schwartz, 'Banking School, Currency School, Free Banking School', in *The New Palgrave Dictionary of Economics*, 1 (London: Palgrave Macmillan, 2008), 353–58.
193   Note Wood's increasingly rude tone in his letters to Grey, who was his brother-in-law, e.g. 'I prefer the appearance of your book to your own appearance in Parliament': Wood to Grey, 7 March 1853, 8–14 March 1853, 3 April 1853, D.U.L., Earl Grey papers, GRE/B105/7/24–32.

about the relationship between British policy and the Irish economy. The presentation of economic influences in this book should be regarded as complementary to Gray's work, filling in the gaps left by the rigorous pursuit of his theme and the academic methods he used in his book. It is not intended to replace his work but to extend it. The public arena in the 1840s was full of the 'political economy' he describes, but the main policymakers often disavowed it, particularly in connection with Ireland. 'You must not think that I am insensible to the state of Ireland or the necessity of Government interference to an extraordinary degree', Wood wrote to Russell on being challenged on the issue.[194] Peel declared, in 1845, 'he … was not prepared to apply to the rural population of this country those principles of political economy which many hon. Gentlemen were disposed to do'.[195] Frequently, *laissez-faire* was used as a means to persuade members of Parliament or the general public to agree with policy decisions made for other reasons, not as a policy tool itself.[196] This book will look at the background to the famine in Britain and reveal that financial and political instability and discord were more important influences than have hitherto been recognised.

Scholars such as Michael Davis have developed the concept of *laissez-faire* government policy in the context of British colonies. They suggest Britain's whole colonial 'public finance strategy' was purposefully used to subjugate other countries and have adopted the emotive term 'Late Victorian Holocausts' to describe the effect.[197] However, much of this research assumes that British officials were fully in control of events at the time, an assumption that is not entirely sound for the Irish famine. Numerous other problems were distracting policymakers, particularly the financial crisis enveloping the City of London in 1847, and the difficulties of a minority government trying to pass legislation through the British Parliament. In short, the British state behaved more like a beached whale than the mighty, purposeful leviathan of nationalist folklore.

These constraints on state action are increasingly emphasised by the most recent generation of economic historians responding to Sen's and Davis's conclusions on Victorian famines. Tirthankar Roy, for instance, has pointed out that famines did not disappear with colonialism. He has emphasised the natural causes of famine and suggested that the limitations of knowledge available and the 'fiscal capacity of the state' shaped official responses to famine in late-Victorian India.[198] Yet was Ireland really treated as a colony during the famine? This study will look at one of Britain's colonies which also suffered a severe harvest failure and catastrophic banking crisis in 1847, Mauritius, and

194 Wood to Russell, 16 October 1846, N.A., Russell papers, PRO 30/22/5D, ff. 214–15.
195 *Hansard*, XXCI, 2 July 1845, c. 1427.
196 Idem., CIV, 2 April 1849, c. 215.
197 M. Davis, *Late Victorian Holocausts* (Brooklyn, NY: Verso, 2000), pp. 116, 234–35, 316.
198 T. Roy, 'Were Indian Famines "Natural" or "Manmade"?', *LSE Economic History Working Papers* 243/2016 (2016), 1–24, at p. 5.

compare the more successful British response there with that seen in Ireland. Mauritius had similar problems to Ireland, but the main difference between the two appears to be the financial system deployed to rescue the economy rather than the varying influence of *laissez-faire*.

The answer proposed in this book as to why Irish relief policy was changed in 1847, at the height of the famine, is to an extent still one of ideology. It is one of unreasoned allegiance to the principles of the Bank Charter Act of 1844, which was based on the theories of the banker Samuel Jones-Loyd (Lord Overstone from 1850). This is what appears to have been the issue, not the influence of *laissez-faire* ideology. The Bank Charter Act was jointly supported by Peel (Conservative prime minister from 1841 until the end of June 1846) and Wood (Whig chancellor of the exchequer from 1846 to 1852).[199] In renewing the Bank of England's Charter to act as banker to the government and to issue currency, Peel made a number of changes which he believed would aid the stability of prices, or to put it another way, of the value of the currency.[200] Wood 'warmly supported' the Bank Charter Act and defended Peel's legislation firmly thereafter.[201] The Act made the Bank restrict the number of its notes in circulation (above a certain fiduciary limit) according to the gold bullion which it held in its vaults.[202] However, not all that gold belonged to the Bank. Bullion tended to exit the Bank's coffers (called a bullion drain) and return as trade and investment flows required it to do so. This arrangement could mean that at certain times, as occurred in 1847, bullion would leave the Bank and the notes in circulation would be limited, leading to a financial 'panic' and difficulty in obtaining credit, or loans.[203]

The principle of squeezing credit in times of bullion drains was a policy of the Currency School of economists and bankers and dates back to David Ricardo.[204] The opposing Banking School, based on the ideas of Thomas Tooke, thought that restrictions on banknote circulation should be far looser.[205] The *Punch* cartoon on the cover of this book, dated 29 May 1847, shows what

199   R. J. Moore, *Sir Charles Wood's Indian Policy 1853–66* (Manchester: MUP, 1966), p. 5.
200   See C. Read, 'The Political Economy of Sir Robert Peel', in J. Hoppit, A.B. Leonard, D.J. Needham (eds.), *Money and Markets: Essays in Honour of Martin Daunton* (Woodbridge: Boydell Press, 2019), 71–89, at pp. 78–83.
201   Moore, *Sir Charles Wood's Indian Policy 1853–66*, p. 5.
202   Bank Charter Act 1844, 7 & 8 Vict. c.32.
203   C. Goodhart, 'The Bank of England, 1694–2017', in R. Edvinsson, T. Jacobson, D. Waldenström (eds.), *Sveriges Riksbank and the History of Central Banking Studies in Macroeconomic History* (Cambridge: CUP, 2018), 143–71, at p. 147.
204   See D. Ricardo, *High Price of Bullion, a Proof of the Depreciation of Banknotes* (London: Murray, 1811); D. Ricardo, *Plan for the Establishment of a National Bank* (London: Murray, 1824).
205   Schwartz, 'Banking School, Currency School, Free Banking School'; M. Smith, *Thomas Tooke and the Monetary Thought of Classical Economics* (Abingdon: Routledge, 2011), especially pp. 189–91.

general contemporary opinion believed happened in April 1847: England (John Bull) was economically paralysed and financially embarrassed because of the provisions of the Bank Charter Act of 1844.[206] This circumstance wrecked a large £8m loan taken out by the Russell government for Irish relief by making it impossible to spend the money quickly and prevented further loans from being taken out for the same purpose. There followed the rapid shut-down of relief works and transfer of costs to local taxes in Ireland.

The Currency and Banking Schools were loose groupings of individuals, and even more loosely they are the ancestors of the modern schools of thought within macroeconomics: Monetarism and Keynesianism.[207] Like the Currency School, Monetarists still believe in controlling the economy by controlling the money supply (equivalent to the circulation of banknotes in Peel's Act), reducing it in a crisis if necessary to avoid inflation. Meanwhile Keynesians, just like the Banking School, often suggest that public spending and credit should be increased in a crisis, boosting the money supply for investment. The growing influence of Monetarism in recent decades may explain why Irish economic historians have neglected financial aspects of the famine. Ó Gráda has described in his economic history of modern Ireland how, after a rapid increase in public debt caused by the use of policies which were labelled 'Keynesian' in the 1970s, Monetarism was seen by economic historians generally as a saviour of the Irish economy, until the banking crisis in the first decade of the twenty-first century.[208] Economic historians in recent decades, therefore, had a strong incentive to turn a blind eye to the possibility that an intellectual ancestor of the policies that appeared to work so well in the modern period may have exacerbated the Irish famine and killed so many. The general reading public, in any case, may have not appreciated the intricacies between the views of the Currency School and the Banking School, nor their impact in Ireland and Mauritius, so it is hardly surprising that this angle has been neglected. As Charles Kindleberger and Robert Aliber have noted, the tendency of individuals to 'suppress information that does not conform to the model they have implicitly adopted' is a common human reaction, and the neglect of monetary policy as an issue during the famine is merely a further example.[209]

This apparent 'silence' on the issue continued that of British officials on the Irish loan crisis of 1847 at the time. They did not wish for discussion of it to precipitate another crisis, and so the Parliamentary inquiries into the

206 *Punch*, 29 May 1847, pp. 221–22.
207 Schwartz, 'Banking School, Currency School, Free Banking School'; G. R. Steele, *Monetarism and the Demise of Keynesian Economics* (London: Palgrave Macmillan, 1989), pp. 78–80.
208 C. Ó Gráda, *A Rocky Road: The Irish Economy since the 1920s* (Manchester: MUP, 1997), p. 71.
209 C. P. Kindleberger, R. Z. Aliber, *Manias, Panics and Crashes: A History of Financial Crises* (New York: Wiley, 2005), p. 42.

financial panics that year took place in secret.[210] However, the continued feeling of resentment towards British policymakers expressed by some nationalist commentators today, such as Coogan, can be seen as a reaction of disbelief at the obviously limp explanation of *laissez-faire*. That appearance has produced their suspicion that something is being hidden. They are right, and the best way to satisfy that protest is to give a full explanation of what drove economic policy during the famine – even though it may not be the answer they were hoping for.

Summary of chapters

The first chapter sketches the political and economic background against which the tragedy of the famine unfolded. It opens with a comparison between the historical reputations of Trevelyan and Overstone and queries whether traditional interpretations have portrayed these individuals' influence on policy accurately in comparison with each other. To fully understand how policy was formulated it is important to look beyond the 'great men' who supposedly made it, at how institutional constraints came to shape it. The influence of civil servants and ideologues was weakened by the power of politicians. The power of politicians, in turn, was limited by what they could get passed into law by Parliament, a matter not helped by the disintegration of the Conservative Party in 1846 over the Corn Laws and the fact that the subsequent Whig government did not hold a majority in Parliament for the next six years. Britain in the 1840s had become prone to political and financial instability, which limited the ability of policymakers to respond exactly how they wished to the harvest failure in Ireland. The chapter explains how this instability came about and how it weakened Britain's most important political and financial institutions during a crucial period for Irish history.

The second chapter answers a long-standing historiographical puzzle about what Peel's economic-policy goals really were in the 1840s. Historians have long argued over why Peel repealed the Corn Laws. Was Peel, in 1846 and in his memoirs, telling the truth when he said he needed to repeal them in order to help Ireland during the famine? Some academic opinion tends to regard this reasoning as insincere, and sees Peel as cynically exploiting the crisis to impose his long-held 'doctrinaire approach' to free trade.[211] This chapter argues that much of that historical debate about 1846 and the Corn Laws is a

---

210   See, for instance, *Report from the Secret Committee of the House of Lords on Commercial Distress*, PP 1847–48 (565 & 565-II) VIII Pt. III.1; *Report from the Secret Committee of the House of Commons on Commercial Distress*, 1847–48 (395) VIII Pt.I.1.
211   B. Hilton, 'Peel: A Reappraisal', *Historical Journal*, 22:3 (1979), 585–614, at p. 587; B. Hilton, *A Mad, Bad, and Dangerous People? England 1783–1846* (Oxford: OUP, 2006), p. 507.

red herring, and has ignored Peel's more important contribution to economic policy in the age of the Irish famine. Peel's tariff reductions in 1842 had a much greater impact on food markets than those in 1846, which only lowered – rather than eliminated – wheat tariffs, at least initially. Peel's significant influence was in developing the wider economic-policy regime of the 1840s: a fixed-exchange rate with a controlled banknote supply (the Banking Acts of 1844 and 1845), freer trade and capital flows (achieved with tariff reductions in 1842 and 1846), and low interest rates and balanced budgets to help pay off the debts incurred during the Napoleonic Wars. The chapter explains Peel's economic intentions behind these policies, and why he did not see himself as a *laissez-faire* ideologue. Instead, he (and other informed commentators including the Royal Family) thought he was following a middle course between *laissez-faire*, free trade and free banking on the one side and intervention, protection, and banknote regulation on the other. The last part of this chapter investigates Peel's set of policies in the context of modern economic theory and concludes that he did not see the trade-off inherent in them, as modelled in Robert Mundell and Robert Fleming's macroeconomic-policy trilemma of the 1960s. He leaned towards the Currency School, which, as some monetarists do today, refused to countenance such ideas. Peel's political achievement was that his policies were then adopted by Charles Wood, the Whig chancellor of the exchequer, after his government collapsed in 1846.[212] However, rather than providing economic and financial stability during the Irish famine, Peel's policies can be argued to have destabilised the banking system at precisely the time policymakers needed it to fund Irish relief efforts. Weakened financial institutions limited the ability of policymakers to respond exactly how they wished to the harvest failure in Ireland.

The third and fourth chapters look at how the combination of Peel's and Wood's economic-policy choices constrained the ability of the British government to fund relief efforts after 1845. The literature on the Irish famine contrasts Peel's generous relief policies until the fall of his government in 1846 with the parsimony of the subsequent Whig government under Lord John Russell.[213] In contrast, these chapters will first show the extent to which the economic and famine-relief efforts of the Peel government between 1845 and 1846 were continued by the Russell government between 1846 and 1847.[214] This fact should not come as a surprise: the Whigs did not have a majority in Parliament and relied on Peel and his supporters to get their financial legislation through after 1846. A new examination of how events unfolded given here

212   Peel's and Wood's overall agreement on economic policy has been previously noted by Robin Moore; see Moore, *Sir Charles Wood's Indian Policy 1853–66*, pp. 5–6.
213   For instance, Ó Gráda, *The Great Irish Famine*, pp. 43, 45.
214   A similar point has been made by Robin Haines; see Haines, *Charles Trevelyan and the Great Irish Famine*, pp. 542–43.

uses a combination of economic theory and empirical evidence to show that it was not political change and the influence of *laissez-faire* ideologues that caused famine-relief spending to be cut at the height of the famine, but a set of severe financial crises in 1847 caused by Peel's economic-policy reforms.[215] The financial crises match the changes in policy over Irish relief spending to the day in 1847, unlike other explanations for the policy change, which do not correlate closely at all. Chapter 4 concludes by explaining how and why alternative ways of raising the funds to continue Peel's original policies – such as by raising the income tax or restricting convertibility to enable more borrowing – failed in 1847–48. Not only did Wood's Plan A fail, but Plan B and Plan C did as well. The events of 1847 left policymakers unable to respond exactly as they originally intended to the harvest failure in Ireland.

The fifth chapter examines the intention and outcome of the redistributive policies the government imposed on Ireland, in the context of a growing shortage of Treasury advances. No longer able to fund grants and loans for Irish relief efforts through central government borrowing, Lord John Russell's minority government was forced to find a different source of funds. They did so by placing it fully onto the shoulders of the Irish Poor Law Unions, funding it from redistributive taxation on Irish property owners. This policy, loosely, has some similarities to Amatyr Sen's theories about redistributing entitlements during famines. The chapter investigates how successful these policies were, as well as why they failed to save as many lives as policymakers originally intended. It will conclude that Ireland's tax base was too small and its economy too underdeveloped to fund the levels of relief needed to avoid excess mortality. Even if the desired outcome had been achieved, there were nutritional problems with Indian corn as a replacement staple food that would have undermined any relief effort that included this strategy. In short, this chapter shows how wide the implementation gap was between how policy-makers intended to intervene to help the Irish poor during the famine and what actually happened on the ground.

The sixth chapter examines the ideological fight within the British government between supporters of the Bank Charter Act and its opponents and their influence on relief policies during harvest failures in Ireland and Mauritius in 1847. It lays out the argument that the disagreement was not solely between *laissez-faire* ideas and intervention, but more importantly, between supporters of the Currency School's Bank Charter Act and its heterodox opponents. In the Whig Cabinet, followers of the Currency School – who held the interventionist view that the government should regulate the quantity of banknotes issued as well as the value of the currency – were ideologically wed to Peel's

---

215   C. Read, 'Laissez-faire, the Irish Famine and British Financial Crisis', *Economic History Review*, 69:2 (2016), 411–34.

policies on banking. They sought to maintain them during the crises of 1847 even at the cost of cutting spending on Irish famine relief. Meanwhile, those with heterodox economic views – including the Banking School which held the *laissez-faire* idea that governments should not regulate the issue of banknotes – argued within the Cabinet to loosen Peel's policies in order to allow more borrowing to pay for Irish famine relief and for assisted emigration. The Currency School won in the case of Ireland. But in Mauritius – the other part of the British Empire to suffer harvest failure and banking crisis in 1847 (which was partly non-English speaking and Catholic too) – the Bank Charter Act's opponents won. Mauritius received a different set of relief policies than Ireland, designed by the Colonial Office, which were a success in comparison to Ireland. Mass starvation was averted and the crisis left no long-term demographic mark. This chapter lays out what happened in Mauritius during its crisis and why British relief policy – particularly the world's first currency board – was so successful in comparison to relief efforts in Ireland. The conclusion challenges the drift in the anti-revisionist literature towards the idea that British colonialism was responsible for the severity of the famine. The reality was much more complex than that and was more tied up with the weakness of the United Kingdom's political and financial institutions in the 1840s.

The main conclusions are as follows. First, the causes and outcomes of the Irish famine can only be fully understood within the context of the fiscal and monetary union Ireland was part of – the United Kingdom. Second, British relief policy during the famine was affected by an economic downturn in 1846 and financial crises in Britain in 1847 to an extent that historians have hitherto not fully recognised. This includes the decision to cut centrally funded relief efforts and move the financing of them to local control and funding that ultimately raised the excess mortality rate during the worst of the famine by the failure of some of the relief arrangements. Third, fiscal and financial crisis in Britain was contributed to by the Currency School's interventionist macroeconomic policies, in spite of Peel's original intention that they would help Ireland and all working people and agricultural communities within the United Kingdom. This outcome was the result of Sir Robert Peel, Lord John Russell and Sir Charles Wood not understanding the policy choices contained in what has become known as the macroeconomic-policy trilemma. Free flows of capital and a fixed-exchange rate left interest rates at the mercy of bullion flows, and a shortage of credit occurred just as a loan was being raised to fund relief. Fourth, this same set of policies prevented the government from using fiscal and monetary policy tools to raise and redistribute aggregate demand across Britain and Ireland that could have reduced mortality rates. Other redistributive and interventionist government policies aimed at boosting food supplies, that were adopted in 1847 after the failure of Peel's economic policies, had unintended consequences and further damaged Ireland's economy. Fifth, the debate between the government at the time was less between *laissez-faire* ideologues and supporters of intervention and more between advocates of Peelite sound finance, buttressed by Overstone and the Currency School, and their opponents including the Third Earl Grey, James Wilson and the Banking School. The Currency School controlled relief policy in Ireland, where their attachment to the gold standard hindered its effectiveness. Its opponents' ideas, which were implemented in Mauritius, proved to be relatively more successful. It was less *laissez-faire*, and more the Currency School and its Bank Charter Act which caused Ireland's harvest failures in 1840s to trigger the biggest economic-policy failure in the history of the United Kingdom.

I

The sources of financial and political instability

I acted as Chairman of the great London Committee in connection with the
Irish Famine ... And when afterwards we looked back ... more harm than
good had resulted from our interference.

> Overstone to Merivale (civil servant at India
> Office) January 1874(?) (copy).[1]

The background in Ireland to the Irish famine has been copiously described
by many able historians.[2] However, the political and economic background to
the decisions made by politicians in Britain in relation to the famine has been
neglected, in favour of religious and cultural explanations, in particular those
relating to the grip of providentialism on policymakers.[3] This approach – which
has provided many interesting and valuable insights in recent decades – has
nevertheless obscured the role that political and financial instability played
in determining events. This chapter introduces the background to how these
insecurities arose in the 1840s and explains why they need to be understood by
historians to create a more complete picture of public policy during the famine.

During the famine, the Parliamentary system reached a stalemate position
in which theoretically, on a party basis, Irish MPs held the balance of power
in deciding what legislation was passed.[4] Therefore, in theory, no legislation
should have been passed that harmed Ireland where there was discord between
the parties. Of course, in practice, the position was far more complex because
of the extent to which parties were divided between and within themselves.

1   D. P. O'Brien, *The Correspondence of Lord Overstone* (Cambridge: CUP, 1971), vol. 3,
pp. 1260–61.
2   See particularly: C. Ó Gráda, *Ireland: A New Economic History 1780–1939* (Oxford:
OUP, 1994); idem., *Ireland before and after the Famine* (Manchester: MUP, 1993); P. Gray,
Famine, Land and Politics: British Government and Irish Society, 1843–50 (Dublin: Irish
Academic Press, 1999).
3   B. M. Walker, 'Politicians, Elections and Catastrophe: The General Election of 1847',
Irish Political Studies, 22:1 (2007), 1–34, has discussed some of the Parliamentary-political
context for Ireland, but the focus of research in recent decades in relation to Great Britain and
the famine has been substantially on cultural and religious factors such as providentialism.
4   See Chart 1.1.

Figure 1.1. A caricature of the 'hard calculator' based on Lord Overstone (Samuel Jones-Loyd), *The Money Bag* (London: D. F. Oakey, 1858), vol. 1, cover. Both *The Money Bag* and the Banking School blamed Lord Overstone for the provisions in the Bank Charter Act of 1844, which they claimed caused periodic financial crises such as those in 1847, which are shown in Chapters 3 and 4 to have damaged the British government's ability to raise loans for relief during the Irish famine.

Political instability had reached its summit in the 1840s from its roots in the 1830s. The Reform Act of 1832 still had not brought the vote to most working men (let alone women). Although it may seem by today's standards modest in its consequences, in its own period the Act 'could scarcely have caused a more drastic alteration in England's political fabric', in the words of John A. Phillips and Charles Wetherell.[5] The old party system was quickly destroyed and reshaped. Politicians became more partisan, and the articulation of ideas became more important in their campaigning.

The new party system that arose in stages between the 1830s and the 1850s was thus not a more stable one. Parties split into factions, and their members of Parliament often refused to vote along party lines. A rising impression of

5   J. A. Phillips, C. Wetherell, 'The Great Reform Act of 1832 and the Political Modernisation of England', *American Historical Review*, 100:2 (1995), 411–36, at p. 412.

violence and threats to senior politicians made them aware of the 'mob' and its potential political ambitions, acting as another constraint on what British governments could do during this period. The result was an era of frequent Parliamentary defeats for government legislation, sharp policy U-turns by ministers, and governmental instability. As the next chapters go on to explain, the consequence of all this was that Lord John Russell's government found itself unable to raise taxation or reform Britain's currency legislation to help Ireland. It was unable to help fund further famine relief in the late 1840s as there simply was not a stable majority in Parliament for it to rely upon to pass its bills.

Disagreement in Parliament over currency regulation was not helped by stalemate within political economy over this issue. Today it is often popularly assumed that 'political economy' was a cohesive set of views built around *laissez-faire* ideology which counselled against government interference, particularly in famines. In fact, in the 1840s, it was deeply divided between the so-called Banking School's and Currency School's views of monetary policy. The next few chapters will describe how Britain's institutional regime of currency regulation made it harder to raise government loans for Irish relief in the economic context of 1847. With financial instability preventing a loan and political instability blocking off national taxation as a source of funds, the government was left with few other options to raise funding.

The reaction of many historians to the messy complexity of the various forms of instability in Britain in the 1840s has been to blame the more constant Charles Edward Trevelyan (1807–86). He was the permanent civil servant who was in charge of implementing the government's attempts at famine relief in Ireland. He has long been the British official Irish nationalists love to hate. Since Jenifer Hart's and Cecil Woodham-Smith's work in 1960s, he has been described as a Whig ideologue, an austere political economist obsessed with *laissez-faire* and the person who was not simply director, but architect and dictator, of the government's mean-fisted relief policy.[6] He is often presented as fully culpable for the government's policy errors during the disaster. He has become a household name and folk villain in Ireland, not least thanks to 'The Fields of Athenry', a popular Irish folk ballad written by Pete St. John in 1979, but addressed to a fictional young man sentenced to penal transportation during the famine:

> ... you stole Trevelyan's corn,
> So the young might see the morn,
> Now a prison ship lies, waiting in the bay.[7]

6   R. Haines, *Charles Trevelyan and the Great Irish Famine* (Dublin: Four Courts Press, 2004), pp. 2–3.
7   *The Irish Times*, 24 December 2010, online at <https://www.irishtimes.com/sport/celebrating-a-song-for-the-people-1.689195> [accessed 5 January 2020].

However, how responsible was Trevelyan really for creating the government's policy? This book is not the first to argue that blaming Trevelyan for the worst of the famine is a red herring that distracts from others; his role at best was subservient to the politicians. Relief was cut sharply at the beginning of May 1847. The burden of paying for it was transferred from the Treasury in London to local taxes in Ireland. As the assistant secretary to the Treasury, Trevelyan led the implementation of all of these decisions, but the decisions were made by politicians, not him. His job was to put their commands into practice and to expend government money effectively and with accountability, rather than to make policy. Responsibility for raising funds from taxation or loans, for making decisions about overall priorities for spending and for formulating legislation, lay with the government and with Parliament. Up to mid-1846, Sir Robert Peel was in control as prime minister and first lord of the Treasury of a Conservative government. He was fiercely interested in the practicalities of economic theory and was the main driving force in policy. After the change from a Conservative to Whig government in summer 1846, the chancellor of the exchequer, Sir Charles Wood, and the Lords of the Treasury, were in the driving seat when it came to the question of how Irish relief should be paid for. They all operated, in theory, under the oversight of the first lord of the Treasury, Lord John Russell, as the Whig's prime minister after mid-1846, who was in turn accountable to Parliament.

If Trevelyan was controlled by politicians, did anyone in turn control or influence them? The focus on Trevelyan in previous accounts of the famine ignores a more important ideological influence on the Peel and Russell governments' economic policies. This is the pressure from Samuel Jones-Loyd, 1st Baron Overstone from 1850 (1796–1883), a wealthy banker who was the intellectual leader of the Currency School and architect of Peel's Bank Charter Act of 1844. It is under his advice that the rules under which Britain's gold standard operated were set up in 1844 by Peel's government. The Russell government, or more specifically, Wood as chancellor, then decided to maintain this system at almost any cost in spite of the problems that it caused for raising loans for Irish relief in 1847.

Overstone's views included a far more extreme version of *laissez-faire* than those of the other politicians or civil servants discussed in this book. In dealing with famines, Overstone warned of:

> The danger, the derangement, and the mischief sure to arise from any interference with the regular processes of supply and demand – The competition of private traders (if not interfered with) will meet a demand, from whatever cause arising, with more certainty and regularity than can be secured by Government interference.[8]

---

8   O'Brien, *The Correspondence of Lord Overstone*, vol. 3, pp. 1260-61.

This book explores the idea that it was Overstone's currency policies that were behind Britain's inadequate policy response to famine in Ireland. Politicians during the famine, both Conservative and Whig, and their civil servants, such as Trevelyan, may have been caught up in the economic policies which he recommended and promoted based on his reputation of a superior understanding of financial affairs. Overstone's ideas were not defined by *laissez-faire*, however: he supported the freedoms of free trade but also the restrictions of limiting banknote circulation. His main purpose, as a banker, was the stability of Britain's currency, and he thought that both these positions would help his overall aim. Peel borrowed many of his ideas, as Chapter 2 will describe, to encourage stability in food prices and to appease the labouring classes. The contest to be the villain of the famine should be between Overstone as the author of one of the main principles behind the United Kingdom's financial policies and Peel as the politician who implemented them.

The portrayal of Trevelyan as villain and Overstone as a hero of the famine – because of his involvement in charitable relief efforts – is just one common myth about the period that must be challenged in order to fully understand the shortcomings of policy. This chapter reveals quite the opposite: that Overtone is the fiend Trevelyan is often held up to be in popular histories of the famine. Ideas other than providentialism, the belief that God ordered events, were important in explaining the behaviour of key politicians. These ideas related to economic theory but not in a straightforward way. A civil war had broken out in liberal 'political economy' between Overstone's Currency School and its critics, the Banking School. There simply was no single 'political-economy' view of financial crises, nor of how to raise finance for famine-relief efforts. This chapter will first compare Trevelyan and Overstone as candidates for the 'villain' of the famine, despite neither being a minister in charge of policy. The chapter will then lay out in more detail the roots of financial instability and political instability that hobbled the government's famine-relief efforts for Ireland so catastrophically throughout the rest of the 1840s.

Trevelyan: villain or red herring?

Trevelyan was the civil servant in charge of administrating the relief programme on behalf of the government. He came to this responsibility as a Treasury official with experience of keeping account of money, but not of major relief schemes. He had a limited number of staff working from a run-down building in London with only Victorian methods of communication on which to rely. Politicians were frequently obstructive of his work. Under the Peel government, he was rebuked for acting on his own initiative.[9] Under the subsequent Russell government, his

9   Peel to Goulburn, 15 April 1846, B.L., Peel papers, Add. MS. 40445, f. 335.

correspondence often appears to have been based on instructions or drafts by Wood.[10] He is frequently seen by his critics as an enthusiast of *laissez-faire* and providentialist ideas towards Ireland during the famine. Yet these characterisations are far from unquestionable proofs of the case against him.

Trevelyan's promotion of *laissez-faire* economic theory to his junior officials has been taken by historians from a specific period when there was an intense shortage of food. This has incorrectly been applied to his whole career in some narratives of the famine. The period was the autumn of 1846, when storms in France damaged its wheat harvest, resulting in a shortage of bread in that country at an earlier stage than elsewhere in Europe. Of this there was full awareness in Ireland through the local newspapers.[11] Trevelyan became aware of a heavy demand for wheat from the continent in September 1846, writing to Routh 'It is also little known what, from reliable sources, we are suffering from our continental neighbours'.[12] He believed that France and Belgium had placed large orders for grain in America, as well as buying up the new wheat harvest in England.[13] The more serious matter was that this demand occurred at the same time as imports were unavailable from America, owing to the harvest cycle. Trevelyan's response to this was to insist that prices were allowed to rise in order to discourage exports to the continent, and he sent quotations from the eighteenth-century economist Adam Smith to the Treasury's Commissariat officers and clerks to back up the idea. Peter Gray has cited this correspondence as an example of a constant adhesion to an ideology of political economy that historians often paint for Trevelyan.[14] However, as the main sources of food threatened to run out over October and November, it could alternatively be considered a practical exigency, designed to ensure that there was a price incentive for imports to continue to enter the country during that specific period. As Trevelyan explained, 'high prices are necessary to attract from abroad the supplies required to fill up the void', but that was a comment specific to this precise period of shortage only.[15] In this, as in nearly all his actions, Trevelyan acted under Wood's instructions. An alternative policy could have been to ban exports of grain – but that was a matter that politicians needed to decide and legislate for in Parliament, which would have taken time,

10 Cover note, 9 September 1848, N.A., Treasury papers, T64/370B/1.
11 *Freeman's Journal*, 8 August 1846, 31 August 1846, 5 September 1846, 9 September 1846, 10 October 1846.
12 Trevelyan to Routh, 29 September 1846, O.B.L., Trevelyan letter books, vol. 8, pp. 112–13.
13 Ibid.
14 Gray, *Famine, Land and Politics*, pp. 252–54.
15 Trevelyan to Kennedy, 17 September 1846, O.B.L., Trevelyan letter books, vol. 8, pp. 74–76 (original underline).

while the matter of Treasury officials allowing food prices to rise according to market forces clearly sat within Trevelyan's remit.

The other letter often used to prove Trevelyan's malign influence on policy during the famine is one addressed to Thomas Spring Rice, 1st Baron Monteagle of Brandon (1790–1866), dated 9 October 1846.[16] Spring Rice came from the Anglo-Irish aristocracy, but had a relatively unusual background. His ancestors were Jacobite, Scottish Catholics who had remained loyal to King James II after he was deposed in 1688. His grandfather had converted to Protestantism, but there was still an air of distrust between many Whigs and Monteagle. It was made far worse by Monteagle's performance as chancellor of the exchequer between 1835 and 1839, which was remembered unfavourably by many Whigs (including, most notably, Wood) as he had left a growing budget deficit.[17] In 1839, when he stepped down from the Cabinet, he took up the position of comptroller general of the exchequer, an overpaid sinecure that was abolished when he relinquished it.[18]

During the famine, Monteagle bombarded Trevelyan and the Whigs with requests for more government funding, in particular to support schemes for emigration.[19] This has often been viewed favourably in modern times as representing the impoverished Irish, but at the time, the reaction of Wood as chancellor and Russell as prime minister was that Monteagle was out to save himself money on the expenses of his Irish estate: 'as you will see he has only one object in mind, namely the relief of the Irish landlords from the pressure of their tenantry'.[20]

Trevelyan was left in the middle of this controversy, having to deflect Monteagle's approaches. The letter used against Trevelyan, in judging his reputation, is a rebuff to Monteagle's petitioning for more cash. The private letter tells the Irish landlord that officialdom is working very hard on the relief effort, that few landowners in Ireland have given any actual assistance to the relief effort and then ridicules him (Trevelyan was known for his cheek) by quoting what was generally taken to be the landlord's attitude back at him:

> I think I see a bright light shining in the distance through the dark cloud which at present hangs over Ireland … The deep and inveterate root of social evil remains, and I hope I am not guilty of irreverence in thinking that, this being altogether beyond the power of man, the cure has been applied by the direct

16   Trevelyan to Monteagle, 9 October 1846, N.L.I., Monteagle papers, NLI.MS. 13,397/11.

17   J. Parry, *The Rise and Fall of Liberal Government in Victorian Britain* (New Haven: Yale University Press, 1993), p. 332.

18   *Hansard*, CXI, 27 May 1850, c. 407: 'By Lord Monteagle's appointment to the office of Comptroller General the noble got what he (Col. Sibthorp) called "something comfortable to pop into"'.

19   Grey to Russell, 16 October 1846, N.A., Russell papers, PRO 30/22/5D, ff. 216–17.

20   Wood to Grey, 19 October 1846, D.U.L., Earl Grey papers, GRE/B122/3/14.

stroke of an all-wise Providence in a manner as unexpected and unthought as it is likely to be effectual.[21]

The words Trevelyan uses are very similar to those used just a few months later by James Lalor, a member of Young Ireland, again to provoke landowners.[22] Both Trevelyan and Lalor talk about light and shade and refer to 'Providence' and the inevitable demise of the way in which a certain section of society exists. Trevelyan would have been aware of the nationalists' description of the attitudes of landlords, which is caricatured here by him, as a keen collector of nationalist ballads and leaflets.[23] In using similar rhetorical devices to repulse Monteagle, he appears closer to the nationalists than to the Irish landlords. Historians should therefore tread carefully with Trevelyan's use of providentialist language, which was often merely a rhetorical device to defend policy decisions made by others, or even to lampoon his correspondents. What is clear is that it was seldom the real reason why a decision had been made in the first place.

The most recent exposition of the Irish folk myth that Trevelyan was a dominating figure who developed famine relief policy, was a racist and purposefully exterminated Irish paupers has been given by Tim Pat Coogan, who has made it into a main plank of his argument that genocide was committed.[24] Coogan's argument springs from two letters from Trevelyan addressed to the editor of the *Morning Chronicle* in 1843.[25] They followed Trevelyan's trip to Ireland in which he picked up the widely spread propaganda-rumours of violent rebellion in the period of the 'Monster' meetings to press for Repeal of the Union. Coogan presents the letters as critical of Daniel O'Connell, but in both the versions from *The Morning Chronicle* and *The Standard* they are supportive because the letters were an appeal against a possible uprising and violent methods of protest:

> O'Connell, although the author of all this mischief, is, nevertheless, now our chief ground of reliance for the preservation of the peace. As an English gentleman was lately driving in the neighbourhood of Dublin his attention was attracted by G. P. O. (from the *General Post-office*) on all the mile stones and he asked his car driver what it meant. 'Oh, sir, don't you know what that means? *God Preserve O'Connell* to be sure,' a prayer in which I heartily join.[26]

21   Trevelyan to Monteagle, 9 October 1846, N.L.I., Monteagle papers, NLI.MS. 13,397/11.
22   J. F. Lalor, *To the Landowners of Ireland, Tenakill, Abbeyleix, April 19th, 1847*, cited in Gray, *Famine, Land and Politics*, p.174.
23   See, for instance, Treasury note, 2 April 1850, N.A., Treasury papers, T64/370C/1.
24   T. P. Coogan, *The Famine Plot* (London: Palgrave Macmillan, 2012), pp. 60–63, 236–46.
25   *Morning Chronicle*, 14 and 16 October 1843, p. 3, signed 'Philalethes' = Lover of truth.
26   Idem., 16 October 1843, p. 3; *The Standard*, 16 October 1843, p.1.

On the inside page of *The Standard*, on the front of which Trevelyan's second letter was published, was an article detailing O'Connell's arrest.[27] Trevelyan's words highlighting O'Connell's role in keeping the peace would have appeared as almost a criticism of the government's legal action taking place against the nationalist leader. In the *Morning Chronicle* the letter and a similar article were on the same page.[28] Coogan claims Trevelyan was a racist, but Trevelyan presents the southern Irish as 'naturally an amiable, good humoured and contented people ... systematically plied with misrepresentations' and he had 'great respect' for Father Mathew, a Catholic priest who led Ireland's mass temperance movement.[29] Later Trevelyan in fact took offence at anti-Catholic and racist characterisations of the Irish; he had one relief officer during the famine cautioned for the 'excess of his Protestant zeal' and threatened another who used a racist expression about the Irish in a report with being dealt with 'according to Nadir Shah's code'.[30]

Most damaging to an understanding of how economic policy was formulated is Coogan's inaccurate claim that Trevelyan's arrogance in sending the letters to the *Morning Chronicle* in 1843 without the prior approval of Sir James Graham, the home secretary, and Peel as prime minister continued unchallenged and enabled him to create and impose his own policies.[31] In reality, Trevelyan received an immediate rebuke from Graham about the first letter, 'you have committed a serious mistake', and that was the beginning of him being kept on a short leash.[32] When Graham reorganised the Relief Commission in February 1846, there was no doubt he, as home secretary, was in charge.[33] This was reiterated early on in the famine when, in April 1846, Peel reminded Goulburn, his chancellor of the exchequer, that Trevelyan 'was not to give instructions in private letters' and should be rebuked for acting on his own initiative.[34] Instructions to Trevelyan were given by the Lords of the Treasury and noted as 'Treasury minutes'.[35] When replying to letters in the post-1846 period, Trevelyan always made it very clear that the incoming letter had been 'laid before the

27 *The Standard*, 16 October 1843, p. 2.

28 *Morning Chronicle*, 16 October 1843, p. 3.

29 Idem., 14 October 1843, p. 3; Trevelyan to Clark, 9 June 1846, Trevelyan letter books, vol. 7, pp. 30–32.

30 Trevelyan to Routh, 25 June 1847, Trevelyan letter books, vol. 15, p. 246 and Trevelyan to T.F. Kennedy, 25 January 1847, Trevelyan letter books, vol. 11, pp. 221–22, both cited in Haines, *Charles Trevelyan and the Great Irish Famine*, p. 8.

31 Coogan, *The Famine Plot*, pp. 60–64.

32 Graham to Trevelyan, 14 October 1843, B.L., Graham papers, Add. MS. 79729, f. 33.

33 Trevelyan to Routh, 5 February 1846, Newcastle University Library, Trevelyan papers, outward letter book GB 186 CET/1/6.

34 Peel to Goulburn, 15 April 1846, Peel papers, B.L., Peel papers, Add. MS. 40445, f. 335.

35 Trevelyan to Pennefather, 3 July 1848, N.L.I., Relief Commission papers, RLFC3/1/4068; 'Treasury minute' dated 29 June 1847, Hickleton Papers, C.U.L. MS MF A4.59 reel 1498.

Lords T. ...' and in giving instructions he was always 'commanded by the Lords T. to transmit to you...'.[36] 'Treasury Minutes', albeit often written in Trevelyan's hand, and later published under his name, were generally referred to by civil servants as 'their Lordships' Minutes' – not Trevelyan's personal directions.[37] He was always aware of 'others higher than I am', and in October 1847, Trevelyan was still showing a subservient attitude by asking Russell 'whether your Lordship has any Commands for me'.[38]

Letters quoted as showing his personal opinions – in what is often called by historians his 'semi-official correspondence' – can, more correctly, be interpreted as his use of the government line to refuse funding to wealthy landowners, particularly Monteagle, to conserve relief funds for areas that were in greater need of government support.[39] Monteagle was troublesome to the government, and Trevelyan, in an attempt to shame Monteagle with the Irish peer's own providentialist views, has been accused by historians of having them himself. The inconsistency of Trevelyan's responses to different correspondents is the clue that he did not necessarily share Monteagle's views. It is clear from his official papers that he worked steadily to prioritise the limited amount of Treasury funds to the areas where landlords and Poor Law Union were least able to employ or support starving labourers.[40]

When Trevelyan had the opportunity to act within his own discretion, he tended to act on behalf of the underdogs, not against them. This was as true in Ireland as it was in India. As the beginning of the financial crisis built up in 1847, Trevelyan suggested to the Provincial Bank of Ireland that letters of credit be made available for charitable donations for famine relief, free of administration charges, to enable money to be transferred from London to places in Ireland. Because of a shortage of credit, the usual bills of exchange would not have been available, and so the Bank took up his idea.[41] He also devised a way of loaning money to Irish Poor Law Unions to spend on famine relief without it being declared part of the government's deficit in order to please financial markets while ensuring finance for relief was still available (the same accounting ruse was used more recently in the United Kingdom to move student loans out of the deficit until the Office for National Statistics put a final stop to it in

---

36   Treasury Blue Books, N.A., Treasury papers, T/14/30, e.g. p. 112, 23 November 1846; p. 227, 20 November 1846; p. 237, 3 December 1847.

37   Treasury Blue Books, 26 June 1846, N.A., Treasury papers, T/14/30, p. 67.

38   Trevelyan to Clark, 9 June 1846, O.B.L., microfilm, Trevelyan letter books, vol. 7, p. 32; Trevelyan to Creed, 30 December 1846, O.B.L., microfilm, Trevelyan letter books, vol. 10, p. 279; Trevelyan to Russell, 9 October 1847, N.A., Russell papers, PRO 30/22/6F, ff. 170–71.

39   J. Hart, 'Sir Charles Trevelyan at the Treasury', English Historical Review, 75:294 (1960), 92–110, at p. 92; e.g. Trevelyan to Monteagle, 9 October 1846, N.L.I., Monteagle papers, MS. 13,397/11.

40   For instance, see Figures 4.2 and 4.3; N.A., Treasury papers, T64/370 C/3.

41   Provincial Bank of Ireland to Trevelyan 4 March 1847, N.A., Treasury papers, T64/362A.

2019).[42] After 1846 Trevelyan tried to water down Wood's more extreme draft letters and instructions, not surge ahead of them.[43] When the most stringent cuts came, Trevelyan, then visiting Ireland and away from British government influence, showed his real opinions differed from pure *laissez-faire* policy and were not anti-Irish. He joined John Burgoyne (Chief of the Royal Engineers, assisting in organising relief) in trying to provoke more private charitable giving with public letters because they thought government relief efforts would prove inadequate after October 1847. Trevelyan warned that now 'no assistance whatever will be given from national funds' because of fiscal problems and admitted that the fall-back plan to bind 'together employer and employed in mutually beneficial circumstances' could only proceed 'as fast as can reasonably be expected under the circumstances'.[44]

Trevelyan's oscillation between obedience and rebellion over his advocacy of a more generous fiscal approach to local populations around the British Empire is a feature throughout his career. For instance, Trevelyan had been writing since the 1830s to *The Times* as 'Indophilus' arguing that Britain should do more to help the native population of India.[45] Later, he advocated equal rights for Hindus, Muslims, and Christians and favoured the appointment of Indians to senior positions.[46] As Governor of Madras in 1860, he was reprimanded in India for trying to use leaks to the press to undermine James Wilson's stringent fiscal restrictions, as India's finance minister, which were threatening Trevelyan's more generous policies.[47] When Trevelyan took over as finance minister in 1862, he used creative accounting tricks and the issuance of new loans to start extensive public-works schemes, including irrigation and transport, a practice that ended in him being denounced by *The Times*.[48]

---

42 Irish advances counted neither as expenditure nor income in Britain's national accounts; see *Hansard*, XCVI, 28 February 1848, cc. 1393, 1414–15. Office for National Statistics, *Student Loans in the Public Sector*, 21 June 2019.

43 Compare Trevelyan's letter of 14 September 1848 to the Poor Law Commission, quoted in C. Kinealy, *A Death-Dealing Famine: The Great Hunger in Ireland* (London: Pluto Press, 1997), p. 148, with Wood's original instructions to Trevelyan in cover note, Wood to Trevelyan, 9 September 1848, N.A., Treasury papers, T64/370B/1.

44 Both letters were published together, *The Times*, 12 October 1847, p. 5.

45 L. Trevelyan, *A Very British Family: The Trevelyans and Their World* (London: I.B. Tauris, 2006), p. 54. 'Indophilus' = Friend of India.

46 R. Haines, 'Trevelyan, Sir Charles Edward (1807–86)', *Dictionary of Irish Biography* (October 2009), online at < https://www.dib.ie/biography/trevelyan-sir-charles-edward-a8647> [accessed 21 January 2021].

47 *Hansard*, CLVIII, 11 May 1860, cc. 1130–61; C. E. Trevelyan, *Statement of Sir C. E. Trevelyan of the Circumstances connected with his Recall from India* (London: Longman, 1860). James Wilson was the first editor of *The Economist* and became a Whig politician. His economic views were non-mainstream.

48 *The Times*, 1 July 1865, p. 9.

Trevelyan did not, as is often claimed, devise the Russell government's famine policies. He merely facilitated the feedback from officers and organised the discussions of ministers and implemented measures when they had been decided.[49] It is quite possible that if he had devised them, without the financial crisis, they may well have ended up more generous towards Ireland than they actually were, as his biographer Haines has claimed.[50] In April 1848, after government funding for relief had ceased, one of his letters to Lord Clarendon, the viceroy in Ireland, shows an emotional breakdown, as the mask of the hardened civil servant slips. He begins, as usual, by emphasising the 'strong necessity for economy', and goes on 'although we are unable to give the same practical proof of sympathy, as formerly, – the only one that will be acceptable from the Treasury – I can assure your Lordship that Ireland is as much in our minds – and I think I may add for others as I am sure I can for myself in our <u>hearts</u>, as ever'. He continues describing the amounts spent including an expenditure of £800 per week, but the physical handwriting changes after the word 'hearts' and is very erratic indicating intense emotion.[51] Trevelyan was upset the Treasury could help no more.

It is clear that the important historical questions of who made the overall decisions about economic policy and Ireland have been overwhelmed by Irish folk traditions about Trevelyan's role in the famine. In Ireland, Trevelyan seemed to be the source of most instructions and explanations about Irish relief, thanks to his name being printed on Treasury circulars and official proclamations, as well as his authorship of *The Irish Crisis*, a pamphlet explaining and defending the government's relief policies against its critics. In contrast, from the evidence in British archives, he was a civil servant employed by and firmly expected to carry out the instructions of his political masters. They had overall control of all his communications, including *The Irish Crisis*.[52] The first version, published in the *Edinburgh Review*, appeared anonymously, and was heavily revised, edited and vetted by various members of the Cabinet including Wood, Russell, Sir George Grey the home secretary and the Third Earl Grey the colonial secretary.[53] Much of the last paragraph, often cited by many historians as evidence of Trevelyan's 'savage providentialism', seems to have been written by Russell as prime minister.[54] The editor of the *Edinburgh Review* had originally

---

49   Haines also comes to a similar conclusion; see Haines, *Charles Trevelyan and the Great Irish Famine*, p. 544.

50   Ibid.

51   Trevelyan to Clarendon, 24 April 1848, O.B.L., Clarendon papers, Ms. Clar. dep. Irish box 60 (original underline).

52   C. E. Trevelyan, *The Irish Crisis* (London: Longman, 1848).

53   Haines, *Charles Trevelyan and the Great Irish Famine*, p. 400.

54   Trevelyan to Burgoyne, 11 November 1847, Trevelyan letter books vol. 17, p. 264, cited in Haines, *Charles Trevelyan and the Great Irish Famine*, pp. 400–01.

targeted Overstone as the author, and Trevelyan was required to ghost-write what the banker had been anticipated to produce.[55] As a result, as Haines has shown, the publication was 'in effect, a joint enterprise, although as usual the politicians expected anonymity'.[56] The later book emphasised the positive effect of the Treasury's relief schemes, no doubt under Trevelyan's influence. The ideology it contained, however, was unquestionably Overstone's.

Overstone: hero or villain?

So who was the principal ideological influence on the British governments of the 1840s? This book will argue it was Overstone. The first government of the famine period, that of Peel from 1841–46, introduced the final legislation to a series of Peel's policies on currency and finance, the Bank Charter Act of 1844. In this legislation, which was part of an attempt to limit food-price inflation and bring stability to commodity markets, Peel adopted the recommendations of Overstone. Denis Patrick O'Brien, who has edited his correspondence, describes Overstone as the inspiration behind the development of Britain's monetary system in the nineteenth century and therefore a contributor to its wealth and commercial success.[57] However, others nearer the time interpreted him as the instigator of a monetary system that brought regular periods of financial crisis and high interest rates in the mid-nineteenth century.[58]

Overstone often appears in a favourable light in histories of the famine, thanks to his chairmanship of the British Association for the Relief of the Extreme Distress of the Remote Parishes in Ireland and Scotland.[59] However, his role was not as beneficial to Ireland as might be assumed from first glance.[60] His organisation only raised in the order of £270,000 for Ireland and Scotland combined, excluding the Queen's letters, whereas Overstone's currency theories were blamed, at the time by his critics, for amplifying the effects of the famine,

55   Haines, *Charles Trevelyan and the Great Irish Famine*, pp. 406, 326.
56   Idem., p. 400.
57   O'Brien, *The Correspondence of Lord Overstone*, vol. 1, p. 144.
58   *The Money Bag*, pp. 111–15. For background on *The Money Bag* which ruthlessly criticised the Currency School (Figure 1.1) see *Sheffield Independent*, 8 May 1858, p. 9; D. F. Oakey, the publisher, was listed as bankrupt in the *London Gazette*, 16 November 1858, and his criticism of the consequences of Overstone's policies can therefore be linked with his personal experience of the aftermath of the financial crisis of 1857. Those contributing were Edward Stillingfleet Cayley, an MP on the Parliamentary Select Committee after the 1857 crisis, and his son George John Cayley.
59   O'Brien, *The Correspondence of Lord Overstone*, vol. 1, p. 392.
60   Idem., pp. 392–94.

rendering ineffective an £8m loan and destroying the prospect of further loans to fund relief.[61]

The committee of the Association contained many members who acted in earnest, because they foresaw or appreciated the great problems which the developing famine presented. However, the appointment of Overstone as chair – due to his standing as an influential figure in the financial centre of the City of London – resulted in the Association being disproportionately influenced by banking interests.[62] The Association was used primarily to reduce the monies that might be needed to be raised by government loans to purchase abroad food for Ireland, fearing that the resulting expenditure would increase the danger of a bullion drain and financial panic. When this danger had emerged and passed, the Association was run down, well before the humanitarian disaster in Ireland had ended.

Even at the time Overstone and his ideas were portrayed by the press as mean-spirited. He was referred to by *The Times*, admiringly, as the 'hard calculator', and lampooned by opponents of the Currency School for this reputation (see Figure 1.1).[63] Historians looking closely at Overstone's life have sensed 'a certain feeling of inhumanity' and an 'impression of hardness'.[64] His motives were widely portrayed as self-serving rather than humanitarian in mission. At the time, critics of the Bank Charter Act of 1844, including Lord Bentinck, a leading Conservative critic of Peel's government, suggested that its provisions were designed to create periods of high interest rates from which experienced investors, including Overstone himself, could make large profits. In a letter to John Croker, he described how Overstone had discounted debentures for £25,000 from a manufacturer desperate for credit in the period of high rates when they could have been discounted for £2,000 shortly afterwards. 'Is not usury like this enough to make one's blood boil?'[65] Later the Banking School,

---

61   *Report of the British Association for the Relief of the Extreme Distress in Ireland and Scotland* (London: Richard Clay, 1849), p. 50; 'The famine was the primary cause of our distress ... Then comes the Bill of 1844 ... We want a vessel that can breast the storm and ride out a gale of wind in safety; but the Bill of 1844 foundered [in] the very first sea that struck it': Mr William Brown, MP for South Lancashire, merchant and banker, *Hansard*, XCVI, 17 February 1848, cc. 834–35.

62   C. Kinealy, 'The British Relief Association and the Great Famine in Ireland', *Revue Française de Civilisation Britannique*, 19:2 (2014), 49–66, at p. 50.

63   *The Times*, 24 November 1857, p. 5; Overstone communicated with corrupt City editor Marmaduke Sampson, *Rubery v. Grant and Sampson*, *Daily News*, 19 January 1875, pp. 3–4; O'Brien, *The Correspondence of Lord Overstone*, numerous references – see index 'Sampson', vol. 3, p. 1542.

64   O'Brien, *The Correspondence of Lord Overstone*, vol. 1, p. 3; quoting T. E. Gregory, A. Henderson, *The Westminster Bank through a Century* (London: OUP, 1936), pp. 158–59.

65   Bentinck to Croker, 3 November 1847, in L. Jennings (ed.), *The Croker Papers: The Correspondence and Diaries of the Late Right Honourable John Wilson Croker* (Cambridge: CUP, 2012), pp. 151–52.

in *The Money Bag*, claimed that in the heat of examination at the secret 1857 Enquiry 'Lord Overstone ... roundly stated that the main bulk of his fortune was made by charging high rates of interest, which was, of course, a direct infraction of the then existing usury laws', but that this admission was deleted from proofs of the report before publication.[66] Chapter 4 will show evidence that the 1847 financial crisis, shortly following the 1844 Act, damaged the prospect of raising loans for Irish relief as interest rates rose.

Neither does Overstone's role in the British Association redeem him in this characterisation. He was surprisingly critical of humanitarian intervention in Ireland, even at the worst of the famine. The report on the Association's activities, signed by Overstone as chairman, frequently refers to the 'evils' which were caused or could be caused by their operations: 'assuredly, evils of a greater or lesser degree must attend every system of gratuitous relief'.[67] It projects no confidence, or zeal to give benefit, as driving Overstone's leadership of the Association. A similar lack of enthusiasm cannot be attributed to some of the voluntary agents that served the organisation. For instance, Count Paul Edmund de Strzelecki, a Polish geologist and philanthropist, gave his services as an agent on a voluntary basis. After the initial period of relief, Strzelecki stayed on and by February 1848 arranged the feeding of around 146,500 schoolchildren with rye bread, a nutritious alternative to Indian corn.[68] He had clothes made for some children with military-surplus clothing arranged by Trevelyan and stitched by the Ladies Societies in Dublin – an example of the co-operation that Trevelyan gave to the Association.[69] However, on 21 July 1848, Strzelecki was summarily dismissed by Overstone, even though the Association still had funds.[70] The remaining monies were transferred to the government Poor Law scheme to be given as grants or loaned to the Unions from December 1847.[71] No attempt was made to raise further funds on the basis of Count Strzelecki's work, and the feeding of children did not continue.

In Overstone's correspondence there are other examples of him declining to help Ireland during the famine. In 1847 he refused to invest in a scheme for drainage and land reclamation in Ireland when requested to do so by Clarendon, even when offered an interest rate of 5% on his money.[72] His reluctance to

66   *The Money Bag*, p. 244.
67   *Report of the British Association for the Relief of the Extreme Distress in Ireland and Scotland*, pp. 45, 47, 48, 90, 92, 100.
68   Idem., p. 167.
69   Idem., p. 133.
70   Idem., pp. 188, 49–52.
71   W. Stanley, Secretary Poor Law Commission, to Strzelecki, 20 December 1847, in *Papers relating to proceedings for the relief of distress and state of the Unions and Workhouses in Ireland*, fifth series (Dublin: Poor Law Commission Office, 1848), p. 5.
72   O'Brien, *The Correspondence of Lord Overstone*, vol. 1, p. 386; R. D. C. Black, *Economic Thought and the Irish Question* (Cambridge: CUP, 1960), pp. 36, 178–86, 386 n. 5.

invest in Ireland – an attitude which he may have helped to propagate in the City of London as the result of his intellectual and financial influence – is but one explanation for why capital inflows from Great Britain to Ireland remained low throughout the rest of the nineteenth century.

In short, Trevelyan gets too much of the blame, and Overstone not enough, for the government's cuts to Irish famine relief in 1847. Not only Overstone personally, but also the financial system that he had helped to design should share much of the blame for the inability of the government to raise further loans for famine relief after 1847 without panicking markets. Trevelyan, in contrast, was left with the operational details of how to deal with the mess that the consequent lack of Treasury funds at the worst period of the famine caused. Their wider economic ideas were not cut from the same cloth as may, at first, be assumed. Trevelyan's family were recognised opponents of slavery – his father-in-law was the well-known abolitionist campaigner, Zachary Macaulay – and throughout his career he was sympathetic towards the people whose lands Britain had colonialised, as has been described.[73] Overstone, in contrast, was accused, rightly or wrongly, throughout his career of supporting slavery, an impression not helped by his vote in Parliament against the condemnation of the conviction of the Methodist missionary John Smith for supposedly exciting insurrection among slaves in Demerara in 1823.[74]

Overstone's Currency School and its critics

'Political economy' is often blamed for the defunding of famine relief in 1847. Yet there was no unified and generally accepted school of thought that can be reliably linked with this policy. Rather, it was a consequence of a conflict in ideas within 'political economy' that was exposed before the Bank Charter Act of 1844 was passed and which was reignited by the famine.

The two schools of thought involved were the Currency School, which became dominant, and the Banking School, which was less successful at the time, but provides insights today into what happened in the financial crises of 1847.[75] They were both concerned with producing a stable paper note currency that would maintain its value against commodities and enable commerce to

---

73   Trevelyan, *A Very British Family*, p. 54. Indophilus = Friend of India.
74   D. R. Fisher, 'Loyd, Samuel Jones (1796–1883), of 22 New Norfolk Street, Park Lane, Mdx.', in D. R. Fisher (ed.), *The History of Parliament: The House of Commons 1820–32* (2009), online at <https://www.historyofparliamentonline.org/volume/1820-1832/member/loyd-samuel-1796-1883> [accessed 27 June 2021].
75   O'Brien, *The Correspondence of Lord Overstone*, vol. 1, pp. 70–144; D. Kynaston, *Till Times Last Sand: A History of the Bank of England* (London: Bloomsbury, 2020), pp. 138–39.

take place. Each School had its own theory about financial crises, how they arose and how they related to the currency system. From the beginning of the 1840s, controversy raged over Overstone's plans for control of currency. 'Political economy' split into a 'Currency School', supported by Overstone's theories and followed by Peel and Wood, and a 'Banking School', followed more by the Third Earl Grey, the Whig war and colonial secretary, which sought to understand crises and avoid them.[76]

There is a profusion of Greys in politics around this period who should not be confused with one another. In the Whig government of 1847 to 1852, Henry George Grey, the Third Earl Grey (1802–94), ran the Colonial Office, a department whose oversight included much of the Empire, but not Ireland. He was also known as Viscount Howick and was the son of Charles Grey, the Second Earl Grey (1764–1845), who had been the prime minister between 1830 and 1834 and championed the Reform Act of 1832. The Third Earl Grey's cousin was Sir George Grey (1799–1882), the home secretary from 1846 to 1852, whose department did include oversight of Irish policy. Charles Wood, the Whig chancellor, was the Third Earl Grey's brother-in-law through his marriage to Lady Mary Grey, who was a daughter of the Second Earl Grey. It should be noted that none of them were related to the Second Earl de Grey (1781–1859), originally Thomas Robinson, a Peelite with a similar name who served as the Conservative prime minister's lord-lieutenant of Ireland between 1841 and 1844.[77]

At the heart of the family feud between Wood and the Third Earl Grey over currency was the relationship of paper currency to gold. Following Peel's recommendation, the British pound was linked to gold after 1819 by making it 'convertible'. Each note holder could exchange his notes for gold coin or bullion (bars) on demand at the issuing bank. The idea was that this would link the value of notes to that of gold, making it stable in value against gold and also against commodities. To run this system banks that issued notes had to retain a stock of bullion, the 'bullion reserve'. Just as banks took in deposits and then lent the money out, only keeping a proportion back to cover demands for withdrawals, 'the bullion reserve' was considerably less than the total value of notes issued. The hope was that all note holders would not want gold at the same time, just as not all depositors at a bank would want to withdraw their money at the same time. This practice made banking a risky business. If conditions arose which caused a high demand for withdrawals or notes at the same time the bank might have to 'stop' payments and, if insolvent, might cease operations altogether.

76 Idem., p. 138.
77 See C. Read, *Earl de Grey* (London: Willow, 2007) for more biographical details about the Second Earl de Grey.

In 1844 Peel introduced new legislation concerning the 'Charter' of the Bank of England. The Bank's Charter allowed it to be constituted as a joint-stock bank and gave it note-issuing rights and the role of managing the government debt. Each Charter only lasted a specified period and often there were break clauses. In the early 1840s, Peel took advantage of one in the 1833 Bank Charter Act to update the legislation, as was expected. He wanted to improve price stability and found the Currency School theory as presented by Overstone the most convincing method of achieving this. It was based on the quantity theory of money, which claims that prices will rise as the amount of money increases if the amount of goods available remains the same. Overstone therefore proposed limiting the amount of notes issued in proportion to the amount of gold held in its reserve.[78] The principle was incorporated into the Bank Charter Act of 1844 by Peel. In addition, the Bank was divided into two parts – the Issue Department to issue notes and the Banking Department to carry out commercial business – in an attempt to keep apart the two types of business. It was arranged that in England other banks would stop issuing notes and gradually be phased out as banks of issue.

The Banking School's opposition to these measures made itself apparent at the 1840 and 1841 Enquiries and at the secret Enquiry into the financial crisis of 1847.[79] It was always a collection of heterodox alternative opinions, and not entirely coherent in its views. Even so, what tended to unite them was their worry about what would happen when bullion flowed out of the country, taking some of the Bank's bullion reserve with it, a situation known as a 'bullion drain'. Under the Act, it was anticipated that the notes in circulation would be decreased in proportion to the decreasing bullion reserve causing a shortage of notes. The note issue that was not required to be backed by the bullion reserve was to be invested in various forms of secure debt. This debt would be sold off in a crisis as no longer required which would decrease its price, thereby increasing its yield and interest rates in general. These circumstances would therefore lead to a credit squeeze in what, in view of the bullion drain, would already be adverse financial circumstances. The Banking School viewed a credit squeeze as detrimental to commerce but the Currency School thought it would help by attracting back bullion from abroad. The Banking School believed that more than this was needed: the Bank of England Bank Rate would have to be increased to raise market interest rates by the amount required to attract back bullion. In later decades the Currency School belatedly came to agree with the Banking School that credit squeezes would not automatically

78   *Report from the Select Committee on Banks of Issue; with the minutes of evidence, appendix, and index*, PP 1840 (602) IV.1, pp. iv–v.
79   Idem., PP 1840 (602) IV.1; *First report of the Select Committee on banks of issue*, PP 1841 Session 1 (366) V.1; *Report from the Secret Committee of the House of Commons on Commercial Distress*, PP 1847–48 (395) VIII.1, VIII.379.

bring back bullion, and policy intervention in form of raising the Bank Rate was necessary.[80]

The Currency School theory of why bullion flowed internationally, ascribed to by Overstone, was based on David Hume's price-specie flow mechanism, which proposed that under a gold standard (constant exchange rate) between two countries trade imbalances would adjust automatically. When a country had higher imports and prices than another, it had to pay the net trade balance to the other country with a net flow of gold, putting up the prices in the other country and reversing the net flow of goods and gold. It was believed that bullion flows were principally associated with trade and prices. The Banking School agreed that the mechanism existed but pointed to bullion flows that took place for other reasons, such as those associated with foreign investment, as more important because they were associated with crises.[81] If another country had a higher interest rate, gold would be sent out from lower interest-rate countries for investment or for funding short-term debt, and then repatriated with the profit. A fixed-exchange rate made the process less risky, but it was assumed that eventually the interest rates would draw together, stopping or reversing the flows promptly and causing commercial disruption. The lower interest rate country would have had to raise its rates to stop or reverse the bullion drain. So interest rates would tend to draw together in periods of financial crisis.

A sleight of hand, used when the Bank of England was set up, increased the tendency for bullion drains. If the Bank had truly been divided into Issue and Banking Departments, their funds should have been separate. However, in reality the bullion reserve against which the circulation of notes was measured included not only bullion owned by the Bank, but the bullion held on behalf of depositors in the Banking Department. This meant that depositors could withdraw the bullion as well as note holders. Worse, notes could be restricted in issue, but depositors could not be denied the withdrawal of their money without stopping the Bank. The table published each week in the *London Gazette* gave the impression the bullion to back circulation was held solely within the Issue Department, and many were under the illusion that there was an additional stock of bullion within the Banking Department.[82] In contrast,

---

80 O'Brien, *The Correspondence of Lord Overstone*, vol. 2, pp. 667–74, 626; Lord Overstone, *Tracts and Other Publications on Metallic and Paper Currency* [1857], ed. J. R. McCulloch (London: published privately by Lord Overstone, 1857), pp. 355–57

81 T. Tooke, *On the Bank Charter Act of 1844* (London: Longman, 1856), pp. 85–87; Adam Smith also noted that it took very long periods for prices to adjust to changes in the availability of precious metals; see Wood to Peel, 26 September 1849, B.L., Graham papers, Add. MS. 79713, f. 36.

82 Wood contributed to this illusion by referring to 'a reserve of notes and bullion which did not exceed £3,800,000' when explaining what had happened in October 1847: but this was mainly a note reserve together with coins to pay change. It was not a bullion reserve. *Hansard*, XCV, 13 November 1847, c. 461.

the currency board scheme that the Third Earl Grey developed in 1847 for Mauritius included Commissioners who held all the specie against which the currency was issued, so that drains were not such a problem.

The financial crises of 1847 and the failure to successfully raise enough loans to pay for famine relief in Ireland provoked the Third Earl to demand an Enquiry on the commercial distress and the 1844 Act from Russell as prime minister.[83] Peel and Wood, as chancellor, who supported the former prime minister's main economic policies, dominated the Commons enquiries. Although the Enquiry held by the House of Lords concluded 'that the Panic was materially aggravated by the operation of that Statute [the Act of 1844]', this opinion was ignored by the government, as it was entitled to do in the absence of the agreement of the House of Commons, where the same motion was defeated by just two votes.[84] Thus, by the narrowest of margins in Parliament, the Currency School view and Bank Charter Act of 1844 survived. Even if the Russell government had pressed ahead with reform, Parliamentary approval would have been unlikely; neither school of thought controlled a clear majority in Parliament, and the Peelites would have done their best to block any changes. So, with the passage of time, the ideas embodied in the 1844 Act eventually became the orthodox view on how the pound should be administered – with the exception of a few short periods of suspension during crises – until Britain left the gold standard in 1931.

The Currency School's ideas remain influential into the twenty-first century. The Bank of England is required by law to primarily consider price inflation when setting interest rates.[85] The Banking School's ideas remain relevant, however, because the 'carry trade' has demonstrated that capital flows for investment do take place from a low to a high interest rate country and they are believed to have been significant in the run up to the global financial crisis of 2007–09.[86] Furthermore, with investment flows it is comparative nominal rates, adjusted only by risk and transaction costs, that are important because the investment is viewed from one country only, by comparing absolute returns. The third and fourth chapters of this book will investigate these issues of financial instability in relation to the crises of 1847 in more detail.

83   Russell to Grey, 26 November 1847, D.U.L., Earl Grey papers, GRE/B122/3/103.
84   *Reports from the Secret Committee of the House of Lords on the causes of distress*, PP 1847–48 (565, 565-II), p. xlv.
85   Bank of England Act 1998, c. 11.
86   T. Chuffart, C. Dell'Eva, 'Did Carry Trades Hamper Quantitative Easing Effectiveness in Japan?', *International Symposium on Money, Banking and Finance*, paper (France, 2018); T. Chuffart, C. Dell'Eva, 'The Role of Carry Trades on the Effectiveness of Japan's Quantitative Easing,' *International Economics*, 161:C (2020), 30–40.

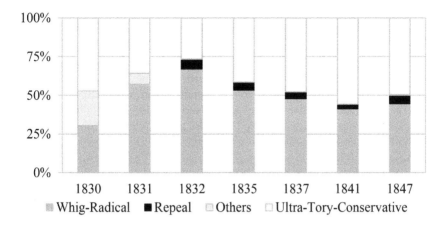

Chart 1.1. Share of MPs elected at each general election by party allegiance. *Sources*: *Return of the name of every member of the lower house of Parliament*, PP 1878 (69-I) microfiche no 84.478-85 Pt. II; B. M. Walker, *Parliamentary Election Results in Ireland 1801–1922* (Dublin: Royal Irish Academy, 1978); F. W. S. Craig, C. Railings, M. Thrasher, *British Electoral Facts 1832–1999* (Abingdon: Routledge, 2018).

Political instability

Financial instability was worsened by political instability, which, in particular, limited the British government's ability to raise taxation and alter the Bank Charter Act to aid relief efforts during the famine in Ireland. Political instability, as defined by frequently changing governments and prime ministers, and the inability of governments to pass their preferred legislation, was particularly characteristic of the 1830s and 1840s. During the famine, it made both the raising of taxes and the reform of banking legislation, to allow for greater Treasury spending on Irish relief, more difficult, if not seemingly impossible. Problems had arisen at the end of the 1820s, but in the 1831 and 1832 elections there were clear majorities in Parliament for the ruling party, as can be seen from Chart 1.1. However, this was due to conflict over reform of the electoral system. From 1837 onwards the dividing line between numbers of MPs for each party was close to the 50% mark and governments became unstable and found it difficult to get their Bills passed in Parliament. To add to the problems, some MPs held strong personal opinions and changed parties, as individuals and groups, making matters more difficult for government whips trying to get legislation passed.

Uncertainty arose at the end of the 1820s when Lord Liverpool's long-lasting Tory government came to an end after the general election of 1826. It was followed by a short spell with George Canning as a Tory prime minister, who led a coalition with the Whigs under Lord Lansdowne, and an even shorter period with Frederick John Robinson (brother of the Second Earl de Grey; became Viscount Goderich and then the Earl of Ripon, 1782–1859) notionally in charge. Robinson, a liberal Tory and a well-meaning man, allegedly burst into tears, in front of King George IV, at the disarray of factions into which MPs had split and his inability to gain sufficient loyalty to pass legislation, including proposals for improvements in Ireland.[87] The Duke of Wellington (1769–1852), who is most famous for winning the Battle of Waterloo, took over as Tory prime minister in January 1828, and there was disagreement within his government in 1829 over the issue of the emancipation of Catholics.[88] The issue arose when O'Connell, a popular leader in Ireland, won the 1828 by-election in County Clare and he was legally barred from taking his seat in the House of Commons because he was a Catholic.

Wellington, it was said, as a hard-line military man, was inclined to give his Cabinet orders rather than discuss matters.[89] Those Tories who had been loyal to Canning (known as Canningites) left the Cabinet in May, just before another election in July 1830, called on the death of King William IV, and joined the Whigs. The Canningites were moderate Tories who were in favour of free trade and Catholic emancipation. Peel would not join with them at first, but now, in 1829, with Wellington he implemented Catholic emancipation and later in 1846 amended the Corn Laws, making him well-known for two of the biggest U-turns in modern British political history. In reaction to Catholic emancipation in 1829, the 'Ultra Tory' group of MPs led by Edward Knatchbull was created and supported by some Tory peers in the House of Lords.[90] When the law on voting was changed, the eligibility requirement by value of land was updated from forty shillings to ten pounds, which led to a whole new campaign championed by the Second Earl Grey for 'Reform' to reduce this requirement.

Wellington reacted badly to the demand for Reform and on 2 November 1830 declared in the House of Lords that 'he was not only not prepared to bring forward any measure of this nature, but he would at once declare that as far as he was concerned, as long as he held any station in the government of the country, he should always feel it his duty to resist such measures when proposed

87   W. D. Jones, *Prosperity Robinson: The Life of Viscount Goderich 1782–1859* (London: Macmillan, 1967), pp. 203, 175.
88   Parry, *The Rise and Fall of Liberal Government in Victorian Britain*, pp. 51–53.
89   P. Hennessy, *Whitehall* (London: Secker & Warburg, 1989), p. 309.
90   Idem., p. 55.

by others'.[91] There followed a period of threatened and actual violence that can be argued to have made the Tories, especially Peel, more mindful of the mob and open to conciliation. A letter dated 4 November 1830 to Wellington from 'Captain Swing', the fictitious gang leader of the Swing rioters who protested against rural poverty, read:

> Sir. Your base vile conduct to and treatment of your fellow subjects, your determination to turn a deaf ear to their remonstrances, has made you an object of popular vengeance and of popular hatred. Take my advice, act openly and nobly as becomes a Briton: reform that vile nest of corruption which is bred in Downing Street, destroy those vultures that prey on the public liver or beware! I say beware! Beware! Beware! Yours, Swing.[92]

The Radical wing of the Whigs were equally riotous and sent threatening letters to the new William IV.[93] Chart 1.1 shows that the 1830 election results, at which electoral reform was a big issue, left the balance of power in the hands of a large group of undecided MPs. British governments were formed at the request of the Monarch on the basis of the leaders' support in Parliament, and party allegiance might be a guide to this, but there was little discipline or organisation that bound parties together. Governments could not be sure of winning a vote in the House just on party arithmetic. Wellington was concerned about the security situation and thought it best that he should withdraw as prime minister despite having the largest following. So, Charles Grey (Second Earl Grey) found himself at the head of a cabinet which contained a motley group of Canningites and some Radicals as well as Whigs, and he pursued Radical policies including a Reform Bill that would extend the ability to vote to a greater number of the population.[94]

After his success with Catholic emancipation, O'Connell took the opportunity to commence a campaign of the Repeal of the Union, which he saw as linked with Reform.[95] He 'was thoroughly convinced, that if the Union were not repealed, Ireland would indeed soon cease to be a constituent part of the British empire'. Ireland needed a domestic legislature. 'If anything could retard the Repeal of the Union, by remedying existing evils, it would be the beneficial

91 *Hansard*, I, 2 November 1830, c. 53.
92 Displayed in 'Wellington and his papers' exhibition in the Special Collections Gallery in the S.U. H.L., 13 October to 5 December 2008, 'Swing' to Wellington, 4 November 1830, S.U. H.L., Wellington papers, WP 1/1159/93.
93 H. Arbuthnot, *The Journal of Mrs. Arbuthnot, 1820–1832*, vol. 2, F. Bamford, G. Wellesley (eds.), (London: Macmillan, 1950), 7 November 1830.
94 Parry, *The Rise and Fall of Liberal Government in Victorian Britain*, pp. 50–70.
95 A. Macintyre, *The Liberator* (London: Hamish Hamilton, 1965), p. 13.

measure of Reform now under discussion'. He emphasised that the 'friends of the Repeal of the Union' did not want complete political separation.[96]

The Whigs and many others celebrated triumphantly when a Reform Bill was passed. Thomas Macaulay wrote that 'Such a scene as the division of last Tuesday I never saw, and never expect to see again'.[97] The Bill was passed by only one vote, and Charles Wood, who was nearest the tellers, stood on the benches and shouted out the result. The Tories were disappointed but particularly incensed over the proposed reduction in the proportion of seats in England in favour of Wales, Scotland and Ireland. The Whigs lost an amendment to the Bill on this issue, in committee on 19 April 1831. The Whigs resigned and another election was held. Further violence erupted and 'the mob' attacked Apsley House, Wellington's residence. His apparent fall from war hero to villain offended the Duke, who wrote to his friend Harriet Arbuthnot, 'I learn from John [his servant] that the mob attacked my House and broke about thirty windows'.[98] After a second attack, he wrote 'John saved my house ... they certainly intended to destroy [it] and did not care one pin for the poor Duchess being dead in the house [Catherine 'Kitty' Wellesley died on 24 April, three days before the first attack]'.[99] 'It may be relied upon we shall have a revolution' he concluded.[100]

The 1831 election was held starting in June and the Whigs returned with a much higher number of MPs. A renewed attempt at a Reform Bill was made but was turned down by the predominantly Tory House of Lords in October. Further violence and protests followed. The Second Earl Grey resigned again but Wellington, Peel and the Tories refused to take office. Instead, they allowed the Bill to pass in the Lords showing some deference to the protests of the mob. In addition, in a public mood when the king was hissed in public and mud thrown at his carriage, Grey had intimidated William IV into agreeing that additional Whig Lords would be appointed to support the Bill if it were not allowed through. The Reform Act was given Royal Assent on 7 June 1832.[101]

96 *Hansard*, III, 4 March 1831, c. 21.
97 Macaulay to Thomas Ellis, 30 March 1831, on the vote in the House of Commons on the Reform Act, in T. Pinney (ed.), *Letters of Thomas Babington Macaulay*, vol. 2 (Cambridge: CUP, 1974–81), pp. 9–11; E. A. Smith, *Reform or Revolution? A Diary of Reform in England, 1830–32* (Stroud: Sutton, 1992), pp. 58–59.
98 G. Wellesley (ed.), *Wellington and His Friends* (London: Macmillan, 1965), Wellington to Harriet Arbuthnot, 28 April 1831, pp. 94–95.
99 Idem., Wellington to Harriet Arbuthnot, 29 April 1831, p. 95. Iron shutters were fitted over the windows of Apsley House, and it has been said Wellington acquired the nickname of the 'Iron Duke' partly because of them. Much annoyed, Wellington wanted to apply for compensation from the parish for the broken windows (£59 12s), Messrs. Farrers and Company to Wellington, S.U. H.L., Wellington papers, WP 1/1182/29.
100 Wellesley (ed.), *Wellington and His Friends*, Wellington to Harriet Arbuthnot, 1 May 1831, p. 95.
101 1832 2 & 3 Will. IV c. 45; Parry, *The Rise and Fall of Liberal Government in Victorian Britain*, p. 97.

The legislation removed the representation from 56 'rotten boroughs' and 30 more MPs were taken from counties with low populations. In return, new seats were distributed over highly populated counties and towns. In addition, Scotland was given eight extra seats and Ireland was given five more. Owners of land worth 10 pounds or more were granted the right to vote, as well as leaseholders and tenants who paid an annual rent of 50 pounds or more. The Act thus gave more middle-class men the right to vote.

Another election followed in December 1832 according to the provisions of the Reform Act. The Second Earl Grey again became prime minister of the government that followed. He supported the idea of Lord Anglesey, the lord-lieutenant of Ireland, to appropriate the funds of the Protestant Church of Ireland to support the Irish Catholic Church (who were not necessarily in agreement with this idea). Edward Smith-Stanley, the chief secretary for Ireland at this point and later the 14th Earl of Derby, left the Whig Cabinet in May 1834 after a disagreement over such proposals. He took with him Graham, who had resigned as first lord of the Admiralty, Lord Ripon (Frederick Robinson), who had resigned as lord privy seal, and the Duke of Richmond, who had resigned as postmaster general. O'Connell, representing Catholic interests, called them the 'Derby Dilly' disparagingly, but they represented the middle ground of politics and were to join with Peel and the Tories to form a more widely electable Conservative Party for the 1841 election, frustrating O'Connell's access to power via deals with the Whigs.[102]

The Second Earl Grey resigned as prime minister in July 1834 because of the dispute over church funding after Lord John Russell exposed the political schism in the Commons.[103] William IV asked William Lamb, Second Viscount Melbourne, to form a government in July 1834, but then the king sacked him on 14 November because the prime minister had intended to bring Russell into the Cabinet. This action shook the foundations of Britain's Parliamentary system through the dismissal of a leader with a majority in the House of Commons. It brought further instability in a period when there were three general elections and four prime ministers in four years. The king wanted Peel to form a government, but Wellington had to fill in because Peel was on holiday. Peel set out the principles of what now became known as the Conservatives in his 'Tamworth Manifesto' and formed a government after the 1835 election, but Peel resigned on 8 April 1835 because he had been unable to gather together a majority in the House of Commons.[104]

Melbourne returned to be prime minister, overseeing a comparatively stable period until 1841 because of an alliance, the so-called Lichfield House

102 Parry, *The Rise and Fall of Liberal Government in Victorian Britain*, p. 109.
103 *Hansard*, XXIV, 2 June 1834, cc. 29–34.
104 R. Peel, *The Manifesto by Robert Peel MP, British Prime Minister, addressed to the electors of the borough of Tamworth but intended for a national readership*, published on 18 December 1834.

Compact, with O'Connell.[105] In the period that followed the Irish Poor Law 1838, the Irish National Education system and the appointment of Catholics to positions of authority were seen as key Whig achievements in Ireland, but the House of Lords and Anglican landowners became resentful of O'Connell and his supporters 'controlling' the government.[106]

The Second Earl Grey had overseen the passing of the Slavery Abolition Act on 28 August 1833 but left the problems of implementing it to his successors.[107] Melbourne was unequal to this task, having limited reforming zeal in this area. He saw everyone as slaves of some kind and believed that the abolition of slavery could never be fully implemented globally because of the risk of war against slaving nations and the imperative of economic forces.[108] O'Connell, by contrast, always campaigned against slavery in America, because he believed the Irish subsistence economy could be seen as the equivalent of slavery.

Unsurprisingly, this issue contributed to the next outbreak of instability in government. In May 1839 Melbourne resigned after a close vote on a Bill to suspend the Jamaican Assembly for not implementing the abolition of slavery properly. Peel tried to form a government, but Queen Victoria, who had recently ascended the throne, refused to accept Peel's proposed changes to the Queen's ladies-in-waiting, who were mostly Whig and were normally a political appointment. The so-called 'Bedchamber Crisis' meant that Melbourne returned, but two years later he lost a no confidence motion by one vote and dissolved Parliament. The resulting 1841 election gave the Conservatives a majority provided that the liberal and Ultra wings of the party stayed united. However, as Peel moved towards reducing tariffs in his 1842 budget and reducing farmers' profits, Peel gradually lost the support of rural Conservatives. His religious reforms – particularly the tripling of the Maynooth grant – worsened tensions between Peel's loyal frontbenchers and increasingly critical backbenchers further.

Peel's changes favoured the workers in the industrial towns of the north because they promised cheap imported food, particularly meat. In Ireland pig prices dropped sharply after the tariff changes of the 1842 budget took effect, and this correlated with an increase in financial support for the Repeal of the Union movement and ushered in the period of vast Monster meetings of protest.[109] In

---

105   A. H. Graham, 'The Lichfield House Compact', *Irish Historical Studies*, 12:47 (1961), 209–25.

106   Parry, *The Rise and Fall of Liberal Government in Victorian Britain*, p. 139.

107   Slavery Abolition Act 1833 (3 & 4 Will. IV c. 73).

108   Melbourne to Russell, 3 September 1838 in *Lord Melbourne's Papers* (London: Longmans, 1889), pp. 376–77. See p. 376 for Melbourne's comment to Archbishop Whately, 'the abolition of slavery was great folly'.

109   C. Read, 'Taxation and the Economics of Nationalism in 1840s Ireland', in D. Kanter, P. Walsh (eds.), *Taxation, Politics, and Protest in Ireland, 1662–2016* (Basingstoke: Macmillan, 2019), 199–225, at pp. 214–19.

London, Peel's private secretary, Edward Drummond, was assassinated, probably in mistake for Peel in early 1843, by the mentally unstable Daniel M'Naghten.[110] Although there appeared to be no direct motive related to policy, the event contributed to a general atmosphere of unease, especially when Richard Cobden, a radical MP and free-trade campaigner, used it to make a threat to Peel.[111]

When the potato blight ruined the potato crop in Ireland in 1845, bringing about the destitution of tenant farmers and threatening widespread famine, Peel discussed with his Cabinet the suspension of the duties on imported corn. Everyone suspected that this was a one-way process and abolition would follow, because cheap food had become a necessity in both Ireland and Britain. Most of the Cabinet had problems with the idea, and Peel decided not to introduce a measure which appeared to be going back on the promises he had previously given. Instead, he resigned, intending to leave the issue to the Whigs who were ideologically committed to the principle.[112] The Queen turned to Russell on 8 December 1845, but two days after telling Queen Victoria that he could form a government Russell had to inform her he had failed. This about-turn was because the Third Earl Grey had refused to serve if Lord Palmerston was made foreign secretary.[113] The Queen sent for Peel who seized the moment and promised to resume office and to introduce a Bill for the gradual repeal of the Corn Laws that he hoped would benefit all classes within the United Kingdom and satisfy both ends of the political spectrum within his party.

However, when the Bill passed, the Ultras were after Peel's political blood, and he was defeated on an Irish Coercion Bill and resigned as prime minister. Russell took over with Wood as his chancellor of the exchequer running a minority government. Political instability was back with a vengeance. After the 1847 election, there were 292 Whig and Radical MPs, 325 Conservatives and Ultras and 36 followers of O'Connell. In this position, the government had to co-operate with either the Repealers or with Peel and his remaining Conservative followers in order to get its budgets and financial proposals passed into law. If there was a Whig backbench rebellion on an issue, the new government needed both groups on side. Therefore, the position remained politically unstable, and Parliamentary arithmetic became an increasing restraint on government action after 1847.

In short, Peel's government left a poisoned chalice for the Whigs in 1846. The Bank Charter Act of 1844 had left a fragile financial system that came to grief when the economic pressures of 1847 were placed upon it. The repeal of the

110   The spelling of this name is uncertain with several versions from different sources.
111   J. R. Thursfield, *Peel* (London: Macmillan, 1891), p. 225; *Hansard*, LXVI, 17 February 1843, cc. 838–39.
112   R. A. Gaunt, *Sir Robert Peel: The Life and Legacy* (London: I. B. Tauris & Co., 2010), pp. 123–24.
113   Russell to Grey, 21 December 1845, N.A., Russell papers, PRO 30/22/4 E, ff. 257–58.

Corn Laws, meanwhile, had split the Conservative Party. The fragmentation of the political system that this caused made it difficult for the subsequent Whig government to get its legislation passed during the famine, or to resolve the problems caused by Peel's banking legislation.

So why did Peel pursue these two policies when their results were so worrisome? The next chapter examines the motives and intentions behind Peel's complete economic policy. It was an overarching macroeconomic policy with three main strands combining currency, fiscal and commercial considerations, and was borrowed from a number of campaigners. In selecting his economic policies, Peel had to choose between ideas from the Currency School and the Banking School about what caused financial instability, and he felt that he had to satisfy politically all sections of society: those who could vote as well as the unrepresented 'mob'. Then he had to get his legislation passed by an unpredictable and unstable Parliament. It was a tall order – and the results were mixed, at best.

2

The economic-policy reforms of Sir Robert Peel

… I have no hesitation in saying, that unless the existence of the Corn Law can be shown to be consistent not only with the prosperity of agriculture and the maintenance of the landlord's interest but also with the protection and the maintenance of the general interest of this country and especially with the improvement of the condition of the labouring classes, the Corn Law is practically at an end.

> Sir Robert Peel, Debate on Corn Laws, 15 March 1839.[1]

Sir Robert has *an immense scheme in view*; he thinks he shall be able to remove the contest [over repeal of the Corn Laws] entirely from the dangerous ground upon which it has got – that of a war between the manufacturers, the hungry and the poor against the landed proprietors, the aristocracy, which can only end in the ruin of the latter; he will not bring forward a measure upon the Corn Laws, but a much more comprehensive one. He will deal with the whole commercial system of the country. He will adopt the principle of the League, *that of removing all protection and abolishing all monopoly*, but not in favour of one class and as a triumph over another, but to the benefit of the nation, farmers as well as manufacturers.

> Memorandum, Prince Albert, 25 December 1845.[2]

I have not sought in my place in Parliament to obstruct the course of the Government by a factious opposition. (Cheers.) I have never entered into an unnatural coalition with men of extreme opinions in politics, nor sought to court the popular favour by giving a popular vote against my conviction. (Cheers.) I have never sought to exasperate the public mind by exaggerating that distress, which, in all civil societies, a portion of the people most unhappily ever endure.

> Sir Robert Peel, 'Tamworth Manifesto' of 1841, 28 June 1841.[3]

1 *Hansard*, XLVI, 15 March 1839, c. 757.
2 Prince Albert memorandum, 25 December 1845, Royal archives, microfilm 95709/5; A. C. Benson, Viscount Esher, *Letters of Queen Victoria, 1861*, vol. 2 (London: John Murray, 1908), p. 66 (italics in Benson and Esher).
3 R. Peel, *Tamworth election: speech of Sir Robert Peel, June 28, 1841* (London: John Ollivier, 1841), p. 5.

Figure 2.1. The quack betwixt two stools; and, as a matter of course, he'll come to the ground. *The Penny Satirist*, 3 June 1843, p. 1. The cartoon highlights the conflict between the political demands upon Sir Robert Peel from rural Ireland, represented by Daniel O'Connell, leader of the Repeal Association, and from industrialised England, represented by Richard Cobden, a free-trade campaigner.

The split of the Conservative Party over the repeal of the Corn Laws in 1846 stands among the most traumatic moments in British political history. Sir Robert Peel and the Duke of Wellington forced the measure through both Houses of Parliament successfully with the help of votes from the Whig opposition. In revenge, protectionist Conservatives voted with the opposition to defeat the government's important Irish Coercion Bill, which had become 'merely a test case for the survival of the government'.[4] The government's heavy loss forced Peel to resign, as he had promised to do if it was defeated.[5] The division between Peel's supporters and opponents became permanent. Most of Peel's Parliamentary supporters within the old Conservative Party became known as the 'liberal' Conservatives, or Peelites, evolving into the modern Liberal Party in 1859. The rebels formed a new Conservative Party, the direct institutional

4   N. Gash, *Sir Robert Peel: The Life of Sir Robert Peel after 1830* (London: Longman, 1972), p. 614.
5   R. Haines, *Charles Trevelyan and the Great Irish Famine* (Dublin: Four Courts Press, 2004), p. 108.

ancestor of the organisation of that name today. That rump had to wait until 1874 to win another majority in Parliament.

Although the repeal of the Corn Laws in 1846 clearly reshaped the party system in Britain, historians have been unable to agree on the nature of its relationship to the Irish famine. Was Peel sincere when he stated that repeal was necessary to help Ireland after the potato harvest failures began there in 1845? Or was this a convenient pretext that he leapt upon to finally implement a premeditated commitment to free trade? Did Peel deliberately intend to divide the Conservative Party to further his career, or was he trying to find a compromise over economic policy to avoid a split? This chapter argues that historians have sought to answer these questions by looking at too narrow a period, just around 1846. By looking further, it can be seen that Peel implemented a consistent set of economic policies between the 1820s and 1840s, which he thought would improve the condition of the labouring classes in both Great Britain and Ireland. The policy regime of 'sound finance' he introduced has been attributed by historians to Gladstone, but Peel initiated it, and his combination of policies remained the dominant economic framework in the United Kingdom until 1931.[6] This chapter explains what the intention behind these policies was, and the following chapters will describe how they did not work as intended, contributing to the inadequacy of relief efforts in Ireland during the famine.

Peel had won the election of 1841 and come into government pledging to preserve the Corn Laws. Unsurprisingly, therefore, Peel's subsequent decision to cut import duties in 1842 and then to repeal the Corn Laws in 1845–46 aroused a great amount of debate and made Peel the butt of jokes at the time (see Figure 2.4), as well as becoming a topic of much discussion by historians subsequently. The editors of Peel's *Memoirs* started off the debate about the intentions behind his policies by constructing chapters around his most controversial 'U-turns', including the repeal of the Corn Laws.[7] However, they tended to focus on policies as beliefs rather than tools to obtain intended outcomes. This has muddied the waters of historical analysis. The greatest weight in the section of the *Memoirs* on repeal is given over to the argument justifying it as a response to the Irish famine. Peel openly stated that he presented it in that way 'to interpose the only safeguard which it [wa]s in his power to interpose against lasting injury from unjust accusation'; or, in other words, because he thought to emphasise this reason would be most persuasive.[8]

Contrary to his expectations, many historians have since found this explanation unconvincing. Richard Gaunt has recently summarised the resulting

6   See, for instance, H. C. G. Matthew, 'Disraeli, Gladstone, and the Politics of Mid-Victorian Budgets', *Historical Journal*, 22:3 (1979), 615–43, at pp. 615, 638.

7   R. Peel, *Memoirs by the Right Honourable Sir Robert Peel*, ed. Earl Stanhope, E. Cardwell, vols. 2/3 (London: John Murray, 1857), pp. 97–325.

8   Idem., p. 107.

debate among historians as a contrast between an acceptance that policy was 'the outcome of immediate stimuli such as the failure of the Irish potato crop' and a belief in 'Peel's long term and premeditated commitment to the repeal of the Corn Laws'.[9] Norman Gash has maintained that there was a 'fundamental connection between the Irish potato disease and the abandonment of the corn laws'.[10] Gash defended Peel's sudden U-turn over the Corn Laws in 1845 by pointing out his 'instinct was always to the practical measure rather than the political gesture', what Robert Stewart referred to as his 'pragmatic temperament'.[11] This position has come in for substantial criticism in recent years. Robert Blake has argued that 'the repeal of Corn Laws did not make – and could not have made – much difference to the famine' and that 'Peel was already converted to free trade'. Blake asked: 'why did he do it with such alacrity and glee' when, at the end of 1845, he could have left it to the Whigs and their leader, Lord John Russell, who had at that time supported full free trade?[12] David Eastwood has gone further, arguing that Peel 'deliberately engineered' the destruction of the Conservative Party, so that he would gain credibility as a potential leader of a subsequent Whig-Liberal government.[13] Meanwhile, Cheryl Schonhardt-Bailey has argued that the decision of Peel and his supporters to break with their party was driven by the economic interests of their constituents, a conclusion she backs up by an impressive array of quantitative analysis.[14]

In forming these viewpoints, historians have tended to limit the consideration of policy to the particular decision to repeal the Corn Laws. There has been less analysis of how repeal fitted into his wider economic-policy agenda, which controlled and dominated British governments, Conservative and Whig, throughout the rest of the famine. In particular, his role in establishing a new economic-policy paradigm – that lasted for almost a century – has been downplayed. Although Gash has praised Peel as the 'chief architect' of the mid-Victorian 'age of stability', historians generally see William Gladstone and Benjamin Disraeli as more pivotal in establishing a political consensus around 'sound finance'.[15] However, as Martin Daunton has already pointed

---

9   R. Gaunt, *Sir Robert Peel: The Life and Legacy* (London: I. B. Tauris & Co., 2010), pp. 104–05.

10   Gash, *Sir Robert Peel: The Life of Sir Robert Peel after 1830*, p. 565.

11   Idem., p. 297; R. Stewart, *The Politics of Protection: Lord Derby and the Protectionist Party 1841–52* (Cambridge: CUP, 1971), p. 34.

12   R. Blake, *The Conservative Party from Peel to Churchill* (London: Eyre & Spottiswoode, 1970), p. 53.

13   D. Eastwood, 'Peel and the Tory Party Reconsidered', *History Today*, 42:3 (1992), 27–33, at p. 33.

14   See C. Schonhardt-Bailey, *From the Corn Laws to Free Trade: Interests, Ideas, and Institutions in Historical Perspective* (London: MIT Press, 2006).

15   Gash, *Sir Robert Peel: The Life of Sir Robert Peel after 1830*, p. 714; Matthew, 'Disraeli, Gladstone, and the Politics of Mid-Victorian Budgets', p. 642.

out, the historiographical veneration of Gladstone has downplayed Peel's role in establishing the policies his protégé continued.[16] Peel, as chairman of the currency commission in 1819, as a Cabinet minister in the 1820s, and as prime minister in the 1840s, drove the adoption of a set of four economic policies of which free trade was just one:

1. The value of British currency should be firmly fixed to a gold standard, with the pound freely convertible to gold by the Bank of England.
2. There should be a limited banknote supply, based on a fixed relationship to gold reserves.
3. Free movement of bullion from 1819 and free trade, or more accurately, lower tariffs on food and raw materials, from 1842.
4. Control of interest rates and a balanced budget in order to reduce the national debt.

All these policies were aimed at stability and affordable prices for the working man. The confusion in the literature over Peel's various 'for' and 'against' stances on the Corn Laws can be resolved by understanding this coherent plan. The policies pursued by Peel throughout his lifetime appear remarkably consistent if his overall economic aim of benefitting the labouring classes by ensuring low and stable prices, without lowering wages or hurting the agricultural sector, is taken into consideration. Such an aim is referred to in Peel's *Memoirs*, and it was his consistently declared preoccupation from c. 1830 to 1850. The variation in his support for free trade, in fact, was due to uncertainty about whether it would produce his desired aim of stable prices and whether the conditions were correct for it to do so. Peel was therefore consistent in aim – if not in policy – and he acted principally 'pro bono publico' rather than politically in the way Eastwood alleged.[17]

The literature on the repeal of the Corn Laws views the episode as a single event, but Peel saw it as a process. What historians have hitherto missed is that he explicitly developed the idea of slowly and partially implementing repeal of the Corn Laws in his legislation of 1846 to ensure that it would achieve his overall economic aim of helping the labouring classes through low and stable prices. He was in a rush to implement the idea in 1846 because Peel believed that Russell had indicated that the Whigs would bring in full free trade immediately. That would result in economic and political disaster, he thought. In Peel's view, doing it before Russell could do so meant it would be brought in gradually for the most benefit for all classes.[18] This would preserve political stability by

---

16 M. Daunton, *Trusting Leviathan: The Politics of Taxation in Britain, 1799–1914* (Cambridge: CUP, 2001), p. 81.
17 Eastwood, 'Peel and the Tory Party Reconsidered', p. 27.
18 Prince Albert memorandum, 25 December 1845; Benson, *Letters of Queen Victoria*, vol. 2, pp. 65–66.

alleviating the growing social unrest caused by the middle-class Anti-Corn Law League and the working-class Chartist movement in urban areas, while allowing the agricultural interest time to adapt, thereby reducing the likelihood of an agrarian backlash.[19] He hoped that a compromise would also help to resolve the economic tensions within his own party.

Although his Corn Law legislation was passed, and the anti-Corn Law agitation subsided, much of the rest of what he planned for his party did not turn out as planned. His government collapsed, in part because, as contemporaries noted, he was not very good at communicating his 'moderation' to his MPs.[20] The rest of this chapter uncovers what the intentions of Peel's economic reforms really were and why his reforms are crucial in any understanding of why British relief policy failed so spectacularly during the famine. The first section chronologically lays out the substantial archival evidence that suggests Peel's main reason for moving towards free trade was to achieve low but stable food prices out of concern for the welfare of the labouring classes. The second section explains how his banking and currency policies were also designed to help deliver the same aim. The third section shows why Peel's gradualism and moderation in economic legislation were important parts of these policies and how this explains his seemingly erratic support for Russell's government, including during the remainder of the famine after 1846. The final section introduces why, in economic theory, Peel's economic policies could not fully achieve all the outcomes that he hoped they would – and why they came to interfere with the financing of famine relief in Ireland after he left office.

Peel, free trade and the labouring classes

Many historians have touched upon Peel's aim of benefitting the labouring classes, although they have not always made it the main force of their argument. Derek Beales noted Peel's prioritisation of 'the comforts of the labouring classes' and Gash thought 'concern for the masses was never far away from his economic philosophy'.[21] Daunton, in considering the history of tax policy, has seen the lowering of tariffs and introduction of an income tax in Peel's 1842 budget as aimed at 'integrating classes and defusing social unrest'.[22] While pointing out that Peel's intellectual relationship with free trade went back to

---

19 *Hansard*, LXXXIII, 16 February 1846, cc. 1031–32.
20 Lady de Grey to Peel, 19 June 1844, Peel papers, B.L., Add. MS. 40547, ff. 130–35; see also Lord Sandon to Peel, 15 June 1844, and Peel to Sandon, 17 June 1844, cited in T. A. Jenkins, *Sir Robert Peel* (Basingstoke: Macmillan, 1999), pp. 116–17.
21 D. Beales, *From Castlereagh to Gladstone 1815–1885* (London: Sphere Books, 1971), p. 135; Gash, *Sir Robert Peel: The Life of Sir Robert Peel after 1830*, p. 565.
22 Daunton, *Trusting Leviathan*, p. 81.

1828, Boyd Hilton has identified the 'overriding' motive at that time as 'the need to safeguard food supply', and Daniel Verdier has put Peel's actions down to 'scarcity of foodstuffs'.[23] Uniquely, Douglas Irwin recognised that Peel's thinking was not dominated by political economy as well as noting his 'long' concern with 'the welfare of labour'.[24]

At the time Peel was 'elected Chairman of the Committee on the Currency and operation of the Bank Restriction Act' (currency commission) in 1819 he was in constant contact with his former tutor at Oxford University, Charles Lloyd.[25] From the record of their letters, we can understand how a pamphlet issued at the time encouraged Peel to focus on the welfare of the poor. It was published anonymously but written, as seemed to be generally known at the time, by Edward Copleston, Provost of Oriel College Oxford and later the Bishop of Llandaff. The full title of the pamphlet was *A letter to the Right Hon. Robert Peel on the Pernicious effects of a variable standard of value especially as it regards the condition of the lower orders and Poor Laws*. Copleston was a defender of the Arminian position against the Calvinist doctrine that predestination was an issue in everyday life. He wrote that 'Christ died for all men, that predestination relates only to the plan of redemption through Christ, that we have no concern with purpose or decree of the Almighty, except as far as Christ is the subject of it'.[26] That attitude was the basis of his *Letter to ... Peel*. If the fate of the poor was not predestined it followed that matters of currency and trade could be arranged to improve their lot because such matters had 'an intimate connexion ... with every constituent of social welfare and happiness'.[27] As this chapter demonstrates, that aim became Peel's guiding light connecting all his policies together.

Even so, Peel's initial reaction towards Copleston's pamphlet was dismissive. As he told Lloyd, Peel thought it derivative and misinterpreted the meaning of the motto on the front page 'Laissez-nous faire', as implying inaction similar to 'laissez-faire' (let it be against government interference) rather than the action (allow us to get on with it against restrictive legislation) intended.[28] He

---

23   B. Hilton, *A Mad, Bad, and Dangerous People? England 1783–1846* (Oxford: OUP, 2006), p. 268; D. Verdier, 'Between Party and Faction', in C. Schonhardt-Bailey (ed.), *The Rise of Free Trade*, vol. 4 (London: Routledge, 1997), 309–38, at p. 309.

24   D. Irwin, 'Political Economy and Peel's Repeal of the Corn Laws', *Economics and Politics*, 1:1 (1989), 41–59, at pp. 53–55.

25   Not to be confused with the Overstone Loyds; correspondence is in B.L., Peel papers, Add. MS. 40342.

26   E. Copleston, *An Enquiry into the doctrines of necessity and predestination: in four discourses preached before the University of Oxford* (Oxford: John Murray, 1821), p. 183.

27   E. Copleston, *A letter to the Right Hon. Robert Peel on the Pernicious effects of a variable standard of value* (London: John Murray, 1819), p. 9.

28   Peel to Lloyd, undated (1819?), B.L., Peel papers, Add. MS. 40342, ff. 20–25; 'Laissez-nous faire' was mentioned by the chancellor, Vansittart, as an alternative to his continued policy

changed his mind as others expressed their approval. 'Ripon' (Earl de Grey's brother, both of whom were Arminian inclined) 'commend[ed] the argument strongly' and Peel also told Lloyd that 'Canning spoke of it in high terms'.[29] Concern for the poor can be seen clearly in Peel's writings and speeches from this time and can be traced throughout Peel's career. Peel was home secretary when John Charles Herries produced his report supporting lower tariffs (even though Herries later sided with the protectionist Conservatives after 1846). The resulting Importation of Corn Act 1828 replaced a fixed duty on corn with a sliding scale.[30] However, Peel's first real policy initiative on free trade, with Herries and Henry Goulburn, was trying to remove the tax on beer and reduce the duties on hops and sugar, while replacing the government revenue using a property tax. Its stated aim was to reduce the weight of indirect taxation, and increased prices, placed 'on the shoulders of the middling and labouring classes'.[31] In 1834, when he spoke against free trade proposals, he considered the Corn Laws protected the 'moral and social interests of the whole community' because of the Poor Law contributions paid by landowners.[32] Again in 1839, when he still spoke supposedly in support of the Corn Laws, the same concern for the poor showed through, saying that the Corn Laws could only be maintained if they are 'shown to be consistent not only with the prosperity of agriculture and the maintenance of the landlord's interest' but also with the 'improvement of the condition of the labouring classes'.[33]

In 1839 his practical hope was for a better Corn Bill that would help the working classes. Later, in 1842, describing his plans for reducing a range of tariffs that year, Peel was more focused still: 'the great object ... is the welfare and benefit of the great body of people'.[34] With regard to 1846, in his *Memoirs*, before presenting a case based on famine, Peel cited the interests of 'the whole community' and his 'serious doubts whether ... cheapness and plenty are not ensured for the future' more effectively by free trade than by protection.[35] His emphasis in his *Memoirs* on the role of the famine in his decision making may well have been because the wider aim of low prices seemed weak and unsubstantiated, by comparison. Yet, even in 1850, he argued that the 'condition

of the Bank Restriction Act 37 Geo III c. 45 that suspended convertibility (*Hansard*, XX, 13 May 1811, c. 63) and Copleston is arguing against the chancellor's policy. 'Laissez-faire' by contrast became associated with the removal of restrictions on issue, consequent on convertibility, thereby referring to the opposite policy.

29   Peel to Lloyd undated (1819?), B.L., Peel papers, Add. MS. 40342, ff. 26–29.
30   Importation of Corn Act 1828, 9 Geo. IV c. 60.
31   Memorandum by Herries on free trade, n.d., c. 1830, S.U. H.L., Wellington papers, WP1/1164/11.
32   *Hansard*, XXII, 19 March 1834, c. 443.
33   *Hansard*, XLVI, 15 March 1839, c. 757.
34   *Hansard*, LX, 16 February 1842, c. 592.
35   Peel, *Memoirs*, vols. 2/3, p. 102.

of the working classes' was still 'the test by which the merits of the question [commercial policy] must be decided'.[36]

Peel's views were strengthened by a fear of revolution, one which was common among politicians of his generation. Eastwood has highlighted Peel's belief in 1842 'that if prices and unemployment continued at the current levels the security of property would be imperilled'.[37] Cobden claimed that Peel, on hearing of the overthrow of the French government in the 1848 revolution, had declared that 'this comes of trying to govern the country through a narrow representation in Parliament, without regarding the wishes of those outside'.[38] It vindicated his decision to repeal the Corn Laws against the wishes of his backbenchers: 'it is what this party behind me [the protectionist Conservatives] wanted me to do in the matter of the Corn Laws [in 1846], and I would not do it'.[39] He also expressed in 1848 his apprehension for the economic system if the ordinary people were ignored and turned to socialism, based on the French example of the consequences, warning that it would in effect 'burn the works of Turgot, of Say, and of Adam Smith'.[40]

Both the working classes and middle-class industrialists were included in his reference to 'those outside' Parliament, but Peel's enquiries for evidence were focused on labourers, particularly those living in small industrial towns similar to his constituency of Tamworth.[41] These enquiries led Peel to believe lower food prices tended to benefit the working classes and would not necessarily lower industrial or agricultural wages.

Although Hilton has pointed out 'the "danger of civil war" argument' was mainly highlighted 'by those historians who wish to label Peel first and foremost as a pragmatist', a gentler version of the concern also fits into the long-term aim of pre-empting the demands of the mob, as Stewart has put it, and taking care not to 'excite the feelings and inflame the passions of the people'.[42] Peter Ghosh has emphasised that Peel's 'oddity' in attending to the needs of the impoverished

---

36   Peel, *Memoirs*, vols. 2/3, p. 102. *Robert Peel, Bart.*, vol. 4 1842–50 (London: Routledge, 1853), p. 835, Taxation of the Country debate, 12 March 1850; see also p. 833.

37   D. Eastwood, '"Recasting Our Lot": Peel, the Nation, and the Politics of Interest', in L. Brockliss, D. Eastwood (eds.), *A Union of Multiple Identities: The British Isles c.1750–c.1850* (Manchester: MUP, 1977), 29–43, at p. 35.

38   J. Bright, J. E. Thorold Rogers (eds.), *Speeches on Questions of Public Policy by Richard Cobden, M.P.*, vol. 2 (London: T. Fisher Unwin, 1908), pp. 580–81.

39   Ibid.

40   *Hansard*, XCVIII, 18 April 1848, c. 469.

41   For example, 'Workers' wages in Barnstable Union', B.L., Peel papers, Add. MS. 40566, ff. 64–377b *passim*.

42   B. Hilton, 'The Ripening of Robert Peel', in M. Bentley (ed.), *Public and Private Doctrine: Essays in British History Presented to Maurice Cowling* (Cambridge: CUP, 1993), 63–84, at p. 71; Stewart, *The Politics of Protection*, p. 35; *Hansard*, XIII, 5 June 1832, c. 426.

addressed 'a serious danger to the aristocracy' and Peel's apprehension at the direction of the development of the electoral system.[43]

Therefore, Peel's attitude to the policy of free trade varied according to whether or not he understood it would produce the outcome he believed the masses wanted. The policy was not an end in its own right, but a means to achieve an underlying goal. He had defined their demand in his Tamworth Manifesto of 1841, sympathising with 'the poor manufacturers of Nuneaton' and their hope for 'increased employment, and a reduction in the price of bread'.[44] However, he went on to explain that great care has to be exercised in alterations to the Corn Laws in order to achieve the results wished for because even the experts did not agree.[45] Peel was wary of taking action that would cause increased fluctuations in prices which would outweigh any price reduction. Fluctuations in food prices, he argued, were greater than the fluctuations in the supply which was supposed to cause them. In 1840 he looked to the sliding scale to stabilise prices:

> Now neither upon this point would he pretend to deny that there had been great fluctuation in the price of corn, greater fluctuation than he wished to see in an article of such general consumption, but at the same time he doubted whether it would not be found upon examination that there had been a great or greater steadiness under the sliding scale, as it was called, than could be hoped for under any other system.[46]

He did not believe that full blown free trade would stabilise prices ('comparatively fixed price'), which he thought was 'the main object to be attained'.[47] His research suggested that 'with respect to the fluctuations in price I confess, having paid my best attention to this subject, that I have great doubts whether your expectations, that free trade in corn will produce a great fixity in price will be realised'.[48] As late as 1842, he still followed the belief that '... prices are more peculiarly affected by influences which fluctuate, and must of necessity be uncertain' and was still critical of moving towards full free trade; 'it appears to me that the strict principles of free trade cannot be applied without danger to the interests of the community'.[49]

---

43   P. Ghosh, 'Gladstone and Peel', in P. Ghosh, L. Goldman (eds.), *Politics and Culture in Victorian Britain: Essays in Memory of Colin Matthew* (Oxford: OUP, 2006), 43–73, at pp. 47–51.
44   Peel, *Tamworth election: speech of Sir Robert Peel, June 28, 1841*, p. 12.
45   See Irwin, 'Political Economy and Peel's Repeal of the Corn Laws', p. 45 for more examples of Peel's opinion of political economists as disagreeing.
46   *Hansard*, LIII, 3 April 1840, c. 523.
47   *Hansard*, LIX, 27 August 1841, c. 419.
48   Ibid.
49   *Hansard*, LX, 16 February 1842, c. 604.

Initially he was influenced by his President of the Board of Trade, Lord Ripon, the brother of the Earl de Grey, the then lord-lieutenant of Ireland. Ripon was a believer in 'reciprocity' rather than full free trade.[50] He advised Peel against unilateral reductions in tariffs. Most notably, on 7 October 1841, he wrote to Peel advising against reform of the Corn Laws as 'it would not be liked by our friends either in or out of Parliament' and that 'it would be most dangerous, if not fatal, to take any course that would make us habitually dependent on foreign countries for our supply of bread and corn'.[51] In a letter dated 29 November 1841, Ripon stated that previous experience showed that reciprocity was the only policy that worked to persuade other countries to reduce their tariffs on British goods:

> We have tried ineffectually to induce them [foreign governments] to open their doors by the partial openings from time to time we have made: mere example has not operated but offers of conditional advantages may have a very different effect and if we can get some one important state to come to an understanding with us, others will be obliged to follow.[52]

By contrast, as Colin Matthew has pointed out, Gladstone was ideologically driven. Once convinced of the case for unilaterally reducing tariffs, he even attempted to challenge Peel on 'corn law revision' and then threatened resignation when he did not get his way.[53] Ripon tended to avoid conflict within the Board of Trade by deferring arguments with Gladstone to the prime minister, which gave Gladstone an opportunity to persuade Peel of the correctness of his views.[54] Perhaps, as a result of this access, Gladstone was increasingly successful in persuading Peel of the case for unilateral tariff reductions and that free trade would help further the prime minister's goals. Peel came to be convinced that his principal aim, to lower prices, was not put at risk by slight imbalances of trade, which Ripon's slow progress through bilateral agreements to free trade was intended to guard against.

In the 1842 budget, the reduction by Sir Robert Peel's new government of 750 out of 1200 import duties was not aimed particularly at Ireland in its effects, but motivated by a United-Kingdom-wide agenda which included Ireland.[55] Peel's 1842 reforms were influenced by a Whig experiment in 1840–41 that had intended to reduce the budget deficit by raising tariffs, but had instead

50   W. D. Jones, *Prosperity Robinson: The Life of Viscount Goderich 1782–1859* (London: Macmillan, 1967), pp. 249–51.

51   Ripon to Peel, 7 October 1841, B.L., Peel papers, Add. MS. 40464, f. 28.

52   Ripon to Peel, 29 November 1841, B.L., Ripon papers, Add. MS. 40863, f. 254.

53   H. C. G. Matthew, *Gladstone 1809–1874* (Oxford: OUP, 1991), p. 66.

54   Ripon to Gladstone, October 1842, B.L., Gladstone papers, Add. MS. 44731, f. 5.

55   Gash, *Sir Robert Peel*, p. 319; A. Howe, *Free Trade and Liberal England 1846–1946* (Oxford: OUP, 1998), p. 4.

failed to produce sufficient revenue. Peel used this experience to justify reducing tariffs instead, but with the same aim of deficit reduction.[56] His rhetoric during 1840–41 attacked the size of the deficit, caused in his view by Whig mismanagement.[57] In an attempt to silence such criticisms, in May 1840, Francis Baring, the Whig chancellor of the exchequer, introduced a 5% increase in Customs and Excise Duties and 10% in Assessed Taxes to reduce an estimated deficit of £1,851,000. This was the first budget in decades to increase import duties.[58] These reforms benefitted rural areas including Ireland, where the Repeal of the Union movement enjoyed little support, and west Wales, where the economically driven Rebecca riots abated.[59] However, a manufacturing recession that disproportionately affected urban areas and government subsidies for the new universal Penny Post system meant that the budget deficit was not closed. As a result, Baring's reforms in the budget of 1840 were widely seen as a failure. Peel lost no opportunity in weaponising the issue of the growing budget deficit, charging the Whigs with 'the most flagrant and heinous mismanagement of the finances that had ever taken place under any Government'. 'Can there be a more lamentable picture than that of a Chancellor of the Exchequer seated on an empty chest – by the pool of bottomless deficiency – fishing for a Budget?', Peel roared at the government frontbench in the House of Commons just weeks before the Conservatives romped home with a sizeable Parliamentary majority in the general election of 1841.[60]

By the time Peel came to power it had already become clear that British manufacturing interests were suffering under higher tariffs, and that marginal increases in excise duties were much less effective in boosting revenues than increasing assessed taxes. Peel leapt on this opportunity to both eliminate the budget deficit and reduce tariffs, quoting the 1840 debacle in Parliament as important evidence to support the tariff-reducing and income-tax raising

56   1841 budget: *Hansard*, LVII, 30 April 1841, cc. 1295–372; for tax changes see B. Hilton, 'Peel: A Reappraisal', *Historical Journal*, 22:3 (1979), 585–614, at p. 597; Peel cutting tariffs to produce 'cheapness', B. Hilton, *Cash, Corn, Commerce: The Economic Policies of the Tory Governments 1815–1830* (Oxford: OUP, 1977), pp. 257–58, fiscal aim of balanced budget, p. 267.

57   *Hansard*, LIV, 15 May 1840, c. 156.

58   D. Steele, 'Baring, Francis Thornhill, First Baron Northbrook (1796–1866)', *Oxford Dictionary of National Biography* (Oxford: OUP, 2004), online edition., Jan 2008, online at <http://www.oxforddnb.com/view/article/1383> [accessed 4 December 2011]; L. Brown, *The Board of Trade and the Free-Trade Movement 1830–42* (Oxford: OUP, 1958), p. 219.

59   W. J. O'Neill Daunt, *Ireland and Her Agitators* (Dublin: J. Browne, 1845), p. 215, cited in P. M. Geoghegan, *Liberator: The Life and Death of Daniel O'Connell 1830–1847* (Dublin: Gill & Macmillan, 2010), p. 115; D. Williams, *The Rebecca Riots: A Study in Agrarian Discontent* (Cardiff: University of Wales Press, 1955), pp. vii, 189; A. Odlyzk, 'Collective Hallucinations and Inefficient Markets: The British Railway Mania of the 1840s' (2010), online at <http://www.dtc.umn.edu/~odlyzko> [accessed 23 November 2011], p. 32.

60   *Hansard*, LVIII, 18 May 1841, c. 639.

strategies of the 1842 budget.[61] The 5% increase in excise duties only increased revenues by £206,715 – 'but a little more than half per cent' – and not the £1,895,575, or 5% extra, that Baring had originally hoped for.[62] Conversely, the 10% increase in Assessed Taxes increased revenues by 11.75%.[63] Marginal cuts in rates of duties would impact less on revenues than the headline percentage, and thus, in revenue terms, import duties were the most efficient to reduce.[64]

An important driving force behind the desire to balance the budget was to stop adding to and if possible reduce the national debt. Peel berated the Whigs for adding to the enormous debt which regularly took more than half of annual government expenditure in interest payments:

> when I present to you a deficit of £3,000,000 in your expenditure at home and show you that you have a deficit of £2,500,000 in addition in another hemisphere, you tell me that I am over-rating the difficulties of the country. And I tell you that that is the natural consequences of conniving at such a state of things as you have for some time past been enduring. And then you tell me in turn, that after having incurred an enormous national debt to the amount of £800,000,000 there is no great harm in making to that debt the small addition of £2,000,000 more.[65]

When faced with a list of the 'comparative advantages and disadvantages of an Income Tax' prepared by Goulburn, in spite of the letter's bias towards its disadvantages, Peel was already firmly decided in favour of an income tax, to pay for reduced import duties, 'in point of reason and sound policy'. Peel's hope was that the result of this policy change was that lower food prices would be 'a great public advantage' without increasing the national debt.[66]

At the beginning of 1844, Peel believed that his economic policies to date were working, and that the benefits were being equally shared by Ireland. His considered opinion was that the only problem remaining was Irish attitudes, which required primarily the type of religious conciliation that he had been implementing since mid-1843 with his pro-Catholic patronage policy, Charitable Bequests Act, and policy of enlargement of the Maynooth Endowment.[67] In February 1844, he told the House of Commons in a speech on Ireland:

---

61   *Hansard*, LXI, 11 March 1842, c. 432; mistakenly referenced by Brown, The Board of Trade, p. 220, as vol. LX, c. 432.
62   *Hansard*, LXI, 11 March 1842, c. 470.
63   Ibid.
64   Ibid.
65   *Hansard*, LXII, 8 April 1842, c. 156.
66   Peel to Goulburn, 28 July 1841, Guildford, Surrey History Centre, Goulburn papers, 304/A1/1/2/548/1; Peel to Ripon, 1 April 1842, B.L., Ripon papers, Add. MS. 40863, f. 323; Howe, *Free Trade and Liberal England 1846–1946*, p. 7; Gash, *Sir Robert Peel*, p. 321.
67   See C. Read, 'Peel, De Grey and Irish policy 1841–44', *History*, 99:1 (2014), 1–18, at p. 2.

Our policy has been to maintain peace, to restore friendly relations with great powers, and to increase commerce. We have succeeded in improving the revenue, in restoring the balance between income and expenditure. We have witnessed with the highest satisfaction the gradual improvement of trade, and we trust the revival of prosperity in the commercial and manufacturing districts will be permanent. But at the same time, we cannot but confess, that with this *intestinum ac domesticum malum* [internal and domestic evil] – this unfortunate condition of Ireland – we cannot look upon the picture with unmingled satisfaction.[68]

The situation confirmed to him that he was correct in the way he thought the economy functioned. This included David Ricardo's belief that high food prices only benefitted the landlords. Peel had studied Ricardo's work in 1819–20 when he was chairman of the currency commission, and in particular Ricardo's arguments that landowners retained an unfair amount of the high food prices caused by the Corn Laws in the form of rent, or profit, and that the poorer tenants did not benefit from the higher prices: '… the interest of the landlord is always opposed to the interest of every other class in the community'.[69] Only landowners benefitted from high prices, while everyone else benefitted most from low ones. 'His situation is never so prosperous, as when food is scarce and dear: whereas, all other persons are greatly benefited by procuring food cheap'.[70] The assumption was that, if tariffs were reduced, it was the landowner rather than tenant or farmer who would suffer: 'as the revenue of the farmer is realized in raw produce, or in the value of raw produce, he is interested, as well as the landlord, in its high exchangeable value, but a low price of produce may be compensated to him by a great additional quantity'.[71]

Ricardo's arguments struck a chord with Peel, who privately considered the Irish landowners arrogant in that they believed themselves to be 'a superior and privileged class' who have 'the exclusive possession of favours of the Crown'.[72] However, Peel took this economic theory on board with care, aiming for moderate price reductions and stabilisation of prices which he hoped would not affect and antagonise the agricultural interest but would benefit the working

68   *Hansard*, LXXIII, 23 February 1844, c. 253.
69   D. Ricardo, *An essay on the influence of a low price of corn on the profits of stock: showing the inexpediency of restrictions on importation; with remarks on Mr Malthus's two last publications, 'An inquiry into the nature and progress of rent' and 'The grounds of an opinion on the policy of restricting the importation of foreign corn'*, [1815] published in J. R. Murray (ed.), *The Works of David Ricardo* (London: J. Murray, 1888), p. 378.
70   Ibid.
71   Ibid.
72   Draft, Peel to De Grey, 22 August 1843, B.L., Peel papers, Add. MS. 40478, f. 160. These words were deleted in the draft.

classes. This was still true in 1846, when the 'repeal of the Corn Laws' in fact still retained part of the sliding scale:

> He hoped the result of the measure would be so much of increased consumption that there would not necessarily be any reduction of the prices of agricultural produce which would materially interfere with the agricultural interests. He hoped that the measure, by occasioning an increased demand for produce and for labour, would benefit the great body of the people, without any prejudice to the interests of agriculture.[73]

Peel carefully considered whether a fall in prices would cause a fall in wages in both agricultural and commercial sectors and came to the conclusion that:

> the wages of the agricultural labourer did not vary in a direct ratio with the price of corn. He was speaking then of agricultural labourers only, and he thought he had proved his assertion to be founded in fact. But in speaking of the manufacturing and not of the agricultural labourer, he (Sir R. Peel) said he thought he could show that at many times and in many cases the wages of the manufacturing labourer had varied in an inverse ratio to the price of corn.[74]

Peel's support for free trade ideas therefore developed over a period. He put it into practice only when economic problems beckoned (such as the budget deficit in 1842 and the potato harvest failure in 1845) and when he was sure it would serve his purpose of improving the condition of the working classes. He adopted allegiance to full free trade mainly from June 1846, when, facing resignation, he pondered in Cabinet the best strategy with which to fight a general election and decided it would be 'Free Trade and the destruction of Protection'.[75] Yet his intention was still to introduce it gradually, in contrast to the Whigs who were offering full free trade immediately.

Export policy was widely discussed at the time of the famine in Ireland, usually around closing the ports in Ireland with the intention that food should remain in Ireland and prices be kept down. Peel dismissed these calls, emphasising that 'the removal of impediments to import is the only effectual remedy' to scarcity of food supplies.[76] However, since most export duties or 'bounties' had been dispensed with in 1814, powers were taken in the Regulation of the Customs Act of 4 August 1845 to be able to prohibit by Proclamation or Order in Council the export of 'provisions or any sort of victual which may be used as food by man'.[77] Such an

---

73 *Hansard*, LXXXIII, 27 January 1846, c. 305.
74 *Hansard*, LXXXVI, 15 May 1846, cc. 631–32.
75 Cabinet memorandum, 21 June 1846, B.L., Peel papers, Add. MS. 40594, ff. 23–37; transcript, ff. 38–55.
76 Peel to Graham, 13 October 1845, B.L., Peel papers, Add. MS. 40451, f. 380.
77 Geo 3 c. 26 (bounty system abolished); 8 & 9 Vic c. 86 (regulation of Customs Act).

order would have referred to the whole United Kingdom though and not just Ireland. It was never given. There is no evidence as to whether policymakers seriously considered a United Kingdom ban on the export of certain grains that could have prevented demand from other countries raising prices. The freedom to export from Ireland would have allowed expensive foodstuffs, such as beef, to be exported from Ireland and cheaper foodstuffs, such as Indian corn, to be imported and purchased by those who previously grew their own potatoes with money earned from the public-works schemes.

Peel, banking policy and the Currency School

Peel's growing support for moving towards free trade conflicted, in terms of economic ideology, with his equally developing commitment to a gold standard involving a statutory limit on banknote issue. In the context of the 1840s, many protectionists supporting restrictions on trade – such as Robert Torrens – also supported legal restrictions on the issue of banknotes, whereas many free traders – such as Thomas Tooke and James Wilson – tended to also take a *laissez-faire* position on banking regulation. Yet Peel's advocacy for Britain's post-Napoleonic War return to the gold standard in the 1820s and his restrictions on banknote issue in the Bank Charter Act of 1844 and Irish Banking Act of 1845 can be squared with his move towards free trade if his general goal was to constrain and stabilise food prices.

Peel, just like the Currency School, came to the conclusion that the gold standard with a limited circulation of notes would cause a fall in the general level of prices.[78] Copleston's pamphlet, his *Letter to ... Peel*, also had a role in the formation of this opinion. Even today the *Letter* seems a far-sighted document encompassing what were to become both Currency School and Banking School arguments. Re-establishing convertibility to gold at a fixed rate was seen as essential to stabilising food prices to assist the poor, but the Banking School concern that currency should fluctuate with commerce was handled by allowing new discoveries of gold to increase the currency 'in proportion as mankind multiply and commerce is extended'.[79] The Currency School's theory that an increased circulation of currency raised prises is explained and restrictions on banknote circulation are recommended, but mentioned too is the Banking School's theory of investment flows of bullion, in terms of trading in bills with different rates of interest. 'These transactions are in reality conducted on a grand scale: a numerous class of intermediate agents make it

78   *The Economist*, 7 September 1844, p. 1178.
79   Copleston, *A letter to the Right Hon. Robert Peel*, p. 13.

the sole business of their lives to watch the relative value of bills, which is for ever fluctuating, and to derive profit from the exchange'.[80]

Peel ignored the effect of investment flows but picked up on how note restriction could control prices. Sensibly, he wanted to see evidence that the theory worked. Between the 1820s and the 1840s, he gathered plenty of evidence for the theory. After his term as chairman of the currency commission, he recommended the restoration of the gold standard in three stages between February 1820 and May 1823, ending a period of suspension enacted by the government of William Pitt the Younger (1759–1806) in 1797. The government decided to adopt Peel's proposals in general and as a result of this return to the gold standard, prices fell sharply, causing distress as small note circulation was reduced by seven-eighths between 1819 and 1822. Peel had to defend himself against being made responsible for this situation, and this makes it difficult to see that he had accepted that restricting note circulation would keep down prices. In a debate on 13 February 1826, Peel was attacked on all sides by those accusing him of having caused a slump in prices with his legislation. This viewpoint came from William Huskisson's theory that 'we have Banknotes as a substitute for gold, and that it is by an abundant supply of them that prices at home are raised and improved'.[81] It followed that by removing banknotes from circulation, prices would fall. Peel fought back against the attacks by claiming that changes in prices caused the issued number of banknotes to change, in effect the reverse of Huskisson's theory: '… not only would the increase of notes follow the increase of prices, but that they would decrease with the same rapidity, when prices fell; so that the tendency always existed in the system, to aggravate the evils of the country'.[82]

In 1844 Peel was following the same line, stating that an increase in note issue is accompanied by an increase in price levels. Referring to the conduct of the Bank of England, he said '… there is abundant evidence that the principle of unlimited competition, that the increase of issue with the increase of prices, that the unwillingness or inability to regulate the issue of paper by a close observance of the state of the exchange, is fraught with danger'.[83] The 'state of the exchange' referred to bullion flows in and out of the country and the banks' reserves. His belief in the principle that a limited gold standard based note circulation would cause a fall in prices is also clear from his other explanations. He gave this away when answering the question – often still asked today – why he only controlled notes and not other forms of money with

---

80   Idem., prices and circulation, p. 20; limit circulation, p. 89; trading in bills, p. 43.
81   W. Huskisson, *The Question concerning the Depreciation of our Currency stated and examined* (London: J. Murray, 1810), p. 42.
82   *Hansard*, XIV, 13 February 1826, c. 289.
83   *Hansard*, LXXIV, 20 May 1844, c. 1342.

the Bank Charter Act.[84] Apart from considerations of moderation, this was because he believed it was mainly notes (promissory notes) that had an effect on the prices of commodities, his main target: 'There is a material distinction, in my opinion, between the character of a promissory note payable to bearer on demand, and other forms of paper credit, and between the effects which they respectively produce upon the prices of commodities and upon the exchanges'.[85]

The position was made even clearer in the House of Lords by Ripon. He argued against the suggestion that Peel's Act of 1819, returning convertibility, was responsible for recent price increases (rather than the immediate decreases it was originally believed to have caused) and distress amongst the working classes. Ripon was very clear that he believed that with 'increased issues came increased prices ... whilst a depreciating currency produced evils to every class, except debtors, the evil resulting to the labouring class would be greater than that affecting all others'.[86] Limiting banknote issue, by inference, was beneficial to labourers: 'Every attempt, therefore, to produce dissatisfaction against the present Bill, by connecting it with the Act of 1819, and falsely attributing to the latter consequences injurious to the labouring classes, was founded upon a gross misrepresentation', Ripon said, 'or at least a misconception of all the principles which regulated either currency or wages'.[87]

Peel's views on this matter were influenced by the theories of Samuel Jones-Loyd (Lord Overstone from 1850), the intellectual leader of the Currency School. Peel was present when Overstone gave evidence to the 1840 Committee on Banks of Issue. Overstone, who is said to have 'undoubtedly influenced' Peel, was closely questioned on prices.[88] He stated, after some pressure, that if the 1819 Act on a gold standard had been properly constituted 'considerable fluctuations in prices ... would have been avoided'.[89] Peel's pronouncements in Parliament very much reflect Overstone's Currency School line, both being unwilling to predict exact price movements but showing an underlying belief that a gold standard steadied the value of money and brought stability to prices. To reinforce this effect, he believed that paper currency should be limited according to 'the exchanges'. This meant that, as gold bullion tended to flow out of the country, the amount of paper currency in circulation should be

84   Henry Thornton, banker and economist, had suggested bills could stand in the place of notes in H. Thornton, *An Enquiry into the nature and effects of the paper credit of Great Britain* [1802], ed. F. A. v. Hayek (New York: Kelley, 1965), pp. 91–92.
85   *Hansard*, LXXIV, 6 May 1844, c. 733.
86   *Hansard*, LXXVI, 12 July 1844, cc. 714–15.
87   Ibid.
88   M. Reed, 'Loyd, Samuel Jones, Baron Overstone (1796–1883)', *Oxford Dictionary of National Biography* (Oxford: OUP, 2004), online edition., Jan 2008, online at <http://www.oxforddnb.com/view/article/17115> [accessed 26 December 2013].
89   *Report from Select Committee on banks of issue; with the minutes of evidence, appendix, and index*, PP 1840 (602) IV.1, para. 2935, p. 258.

reduced. He quoted a private banker who complained that at the current time 'there is no more regard to the exchanges than the snow upon the mountains'.[90] Alongside his own attempts to gather evidence, he was impressed by the clarity of Overstone's justification of Currency School ideas over six days in 1840 to the Select Committee of the House of Commons on banks of issue.[91]

He was backed up in the adoption of Overstone's theories by an influential Whig, Charles Wood, who had been chairman of a Parliamentary committee on banking and currency in 1840 on which Peel also served.[92] Their views in favour of the ideas of the Currency School became 'very nearly concurrent'.[93] Wood criticised those who opposed Peel and went 'by the specious name of "free-trade in banking"'.[94] In modern literature, this group has been labelled the Banking School, but there was no formal group and the opinions of those who opposed Peel varied widely. Those who had spoken at the 1840–41 Enquiry into Banks of Issue included James Gilbart, manager of the London and Westminster Bank, and Thomas Tooke, an economist, who believed the quantity of notes should be allowed to vary according to commercial needs in order to keep commerce going.[95] Wood argued back, 'now this was precisely the doctrine held by the Bank of England during the suspension of cash payments [the period of non-convertibility between 1797 and 1821] … it was then maintained that so long as their paper was issued on good mercantile security, in compliance with the demands of commerce, it was impossible that there could be an over-issue, or a depreciation of the standard'.[96] That policy, he asserted, was what caused the great inflation of prices at the time and certainly resulted in depreciation of the currency. So Peel, backed by Wood, was prioritising stability of prices over the possibility that the Banking School were right and commercial damage might result from the control of money circulation.

This was to become a bone of contention when the financial crises of 1847 erupted. Those who opposed Peel and Wood then went well beyond Banking School ideas in their criticism and included those that thought that in some respects the 1844 Banking Act had not been rigorous enough. The varieties of unconventional or heterodox economic opinion that surfaced then included the Third Earl Grey, who proposed a whole alternative currency system, similar to a

---

90 *Hansard*, LXXIV, 20 May 1844, c. 1340.
91 *Report from the Select Committee on banks of issue*, PP 1840 (602) IV.1, pp. 211–95.
92 He was also chancellor of the exchequer from July 1846; R. J. Moore, *Sir Charles Wood's Indian Policy 1853–66* (Manchester: MUP, 1966), p. 5.
93 Peel to Wood, 9 May 1844, B.L., Peel papers, Add. MS. 40544, f. 117, cited in Moore, *Sir Charles Wood's Indian Policy 1853–66*, p. 5.
94 *Hansard*, LXXIV, 20 May 1844, cc. 1352–53.
95 Ibid.
96 *Hansard*, LXXIV, 20 May 1844, cc. 1353–54; *Report of Select Committee on banks of issue*, PP 1840 (602) IV.1, pp. 337–72 (Tooke), 231–95 (Overstone); *Second report of Select Committee on banks of issue*, PP 1841 Session 1 (410) V.5, pp. 79–417 (Gilbart).

modern 'currency board' system, which was side-lined in the United Kingdom in 1847 but then was implemented in Mauritius.[97]

A currency board generally refers to a currency system run by appointed Commissioners who issue notes and hold bullion backing. They do not participate in any commercial banking activity and therefore cannot influence interest rates by changing a bank rate. In addition the bullion has to be owned by the Commissioners, it cannot be bullion held on behalf of depositors, which makes the system less vulnerable to bullion flows, but more expensive to start up. Currency boards are seen today as having arisen from Currency School theory because the possibility of a currency administered by National Commissioners was suggested by Ricardo in a pamphlet published after his death.[98] In Ricardo's proposed plan, however, the Commissioners remained as bankers to the government and public bodies. One of Ricardo's drafts stated clearly: 'The commiss. should act as the Banker of the public, in the same way that the Bk. of England now does'.[99] The plan is fairly sketchy, and the published pamphlet was taken from a mixture of notes. Its stated aims were to free more money for commercial deposits and garner to the government the profits available from issuing intrinsically valueless paper money for metallic currency. The complete separation of the currency from banking activities was a step further, added by the Third Earl Grey in a proposal published in 1842. The aim of his scheme (discussed in more detail in Chapter 5) was to provide stability of interest rates. Later, after the financial panics of 1847, he hoped that it would succeed where the restrictions and reorganisations of the 1844 Bank Charter Act, as it turned out, had not. As such, and because Grey's plans directly inspired the arrangement set up in Mauritius, it is the true forerunner of currency boards, whereas Ricardo's was but a first step. Currency boards did not arise from solely the ideas of one School, because Grey's proposal incorporated concepts borrowed from both the Banking and Currency Schools.

Peel included an element of this separation into his Bank Charter Act of 1844 in that the Bank of England was divided into two departments: Banking and Issue. Peel's intention was to separate the commercial lending activities of the Bank from the business of issuing currency. It is not entirely clear what the benefit of this was intended to be, except for a general downward pressure

---

97   See Anon. (Earl Grey), *Thoughts on the Currency* (London: Ridgeway, 1842). This publication is misattributed in some library catalogues. Only Grey's views in correspondence, date of publication and publisher match with it.

98   D. Ricardo, *Plan for the Establishment of a National Bank* (London: John Murray, 1824); J. K. Horsefield, 'The Origins of the Bank Charter Act 1844', *Economica* NS 11:43 (1944), 180–89, at p. 184.

99   D. Ricardo, *Plan for the Establishment of a National Bank*, in D. Ricardo, *The Works and Correspondence of David Ricardo: Pamphlets and Papers 1815–23*, ed. P. Sraffa, M. H. Dobbs (Indianapolis: Liberty Fund, 2005), pp. 289–90, see note 4.

on interest rates, and therefore costs and prices, by discouraging collusion between the two activities. If that had been the case, the Bank Rate set by the Banking Department would not have been influenced by the flows of bullion that affected the amount of notes issued by the Issue Department. But as the Bank of England remained, at the end of the day, a single institution, this did not turn out to be the case. The Bank Rate was sometimes changed to meet the needs of the Issue Department. So the Bank of England ended up a very different type of organisation from a currency board.

The Bank Charter Act was meant to help put these ideas of price stability into practice by legally restricting the banknote issue. The legislation is frequently described only in an English context, but it was drafted to apply to the whole of the United Kingdom. This was a surprise, at the time, to the Repeal Association in Ireland, which complained that the value of notes issued and which banks could do so was restricted in Ireland by the Bank Charter Act of 1844.[100] The fixed limit above which notes had to be backed by gold was calculated on averages from the previous year. Goulburn noted in May 1845 that this had caused an excessive demand for bullion on the Bank of England from Irish banks.[101] The Irish Banking Act of 1845 therefore allowed non-issuing Irish banks to use Bank of England notes, as well as consolidating the existing legislation for Ireland and protecting the position of the Bank of Ireland. Notes worth 25 shillings and 30 shillings were abandoned in favour of using silver as money.

During the discussions on the 1845 Banking (Ireland) Bill, Peel defended the government against the charge that a restriction on notes would damage prosperity in Ireland, saying, 'I feel in my own mind that I am proposing a measure most intimately connected with the growing prosperity of Ireland'.[102] This was followed by an indication of his aim for stability:

> ... he could not conceive how any Government could be supposed to have any motive in imposing a restriction upon the currency of Ireland, unless with a view of securing the welfare of the country. He had had long experience of the effects of an uncontrolled circulation in Ireland. He remembered the years 1819, 1820, and 1825, and the disasters which overtook numberless individuals, who in vain struggled against the misfortunes in which they were involved. So far from treating the Members from Ireland, or the interests of Ireland, with contempt or neglect, he had the strongest impression they

100 *Report of the National Repeal Association on the provisions of the Bill recently introduced into the House of Commons to regulate the Issue of Banknotes in Ireland*, 2 June 1845, B.L., Peel papers, Add. MS. 40568, ff. 195–98.
101 'Memorandum on Irish and Scottish Banking' by Henry Goulburn, 11 May 1845, B.L., Peel papers, Add. MS. 40445, ff. 98–103.
102 *Hansard*, LXXXI, 9 June 1845, c. 248.

were consulting the interests of Ireland, by putting some check to the undue increase of the paper circulation of the country.[103]

The problems in the years Peel quoted were connected with the separate Irish currency which moved away in value from the British pound, causing widespread banking failure in 1825, at which time the Irish currency was assimilated into that of Britain. Peel believed the Banking Acts which tied all notes in the United Kingdom firmly to the value of gold would solve this problem. They were also intended to solve the problem of bullion 'drains', or the movement of excessive amounts of bullion out of the country to pay for foreign goods such as corn.[104] Hilton has described in detail Peel's and Ripon's investigation of data to try to find a link between wheat imports and bullion reserve depletion.[105] The worry, at first, was that the Corn-Law sliding scale caused sudden bursts of wheat imports, and consequent exports of bullion to pay for it, as the tariff changed. It was soon realised, even by the supporters of free trade, that the same problem might apply on the lowering of tariffs under free trade.[106] Peel relied on the theory that restricting the note issue according to bullion reserves would create a self-balancing system in which low bullion reserves caused a low number of notes, increased the value of money, decreased prices which would attract foreign purchasers and return bullion. Conversely, high reserves increased prices which encouraged importation of foreign goods and an outflow of bullion. All this was built on Peel's conviction that 'Bullionist' theory was correct in proposing that gold was a reasonable standard for value. In spite of prices being part of this balancing system, the provisions of the Banking Acts were designed to exert a downward pressure on prices by restricting notes rather than having a free-for-all expansion. But prices would not always decrease (because of other factors), which explains Peel's reticence to predict how prices would move.

Peel did not wish for a deflating economy, despite his desire to keep prices in check. He hoped for moderate increases in sales by farmers, to counterbalance any loss from low prices, and expanding employment as a result of increased volumes of trade. In 1846, when arguing for repeal, Peel had said to agriculturalists that, 'we must take some measures, therefore, to increase the produce of your farm'.[107] This attitude is not quite the same as the modern expectations of rapidly increasing wealth from free trade, but sufficient increases were hoped for to help the labouring population and compensate farmers.

---

103   Idem., cc. 263–64.
104   In the terminology of the time this was known as 'the exchanges turning against us'. Peel did not take investment flows into account.
105   Hilton, 'Peel: A Reappraisal', pp. 602–03.
106   C. Villiers, *Hansard*, LXXV, 25 June 1844, c. 1391.
107   *Hansard*, LXXXIII, 16 February 1846, cc. 1031–32.

Robert Dusty, Esq.—Gemmen—(loud cheers)—should I have the
honnor to be elected, yer representator in the kommon House o' Parleyment, (deafening cheers) for the Dust-hills, (repeated cheering)
depend on it I will do my utmost endeavours to throw *dust* in the eyes
of yer enemies—(vehement cheering). I'll wote for cheap Bread
—(enthusiastic cheering). In fact, I'll propose that yer shall have
Bread for nothin!—(tremendous cheering)—I'll wote for Sugar to be
given away—(reiterated cheering). In short, that it shall be brought
home to yer, that yer shall have only the trouble of popping it into yer
Tea—(thundering cheers). And, as to cheap vood, vy I'll undertake
to say that, if yer send me to Parleyment, yer shall have, in no time,
broom-sticks and shovel-handles laying about in all directions, hollow-
ing out to yer—" Come and take me !"—(vociferous cheering).

Figure 2.2. A candidate for Parliament. *Cleave's Penny Gazette of Variety
and Amusement*, 10 July 1841. Peel is depicted as a clown dustman 'Dusty'
because of his claim to represent the wishes of the working man, by promising
cheap food and goods. The cartoon is a satire of Peel's Tamworth election
speech of 28 June 1841.

Figure 2.3. Peel's cheap bread shop. *Punch*, 24 January 1846, p. 46. The cartoon links Robert Peel, 'R.Peel' of the Corn Laws and cheap bread.

Peel's gradualism

The interpretation of Peel's general economic policy as one of a carefully controlled manipulation of price levels downward was very much how it was seen at the time. As well as the cartoons in the comic papers making this point (see Figures 2.2 and 2.3), a popular book from 1850 assembled quotations from Peel's published speeches to show a consistent theme of concern about lowering food prices.[108] Contrary to common perception among historians, both Peel's trade and banking policies did not take extreme positions. The 'repeal' of the Corn Laws and also the restrictions in the Banking Acts were only partial in nature, and this shows how Peel was trying to introduce legislation which was intended to only have moderate effects – in effect a gradualist approach. Back in 1819, gradualism had been a major theme of Copleston's *Second Letter* to Peel and may have inspired this approach.[109] Privately, Sir James Graham (then home secretary) explained to John Wilson Croker, in 1845, the overall aim of a gradualist approach to lowering food prices and how it seemed to have succeeded so far: '... we have laboured hard and not in vain to restore the prosperity of the country, and to give a measure of security to the Aristocracy by improving the condition and diminishing the discontent of the great Mass of the People'.[110] Moreover, he claimed success when he said, 'We have affected this without inflicting any real injury on the Landed Proprietors'.[111]

The idea was to moderate and stabilise food prices without harming the agricultural sector. Peel made 'repeal of the Corn Laws' a half measure in order to achieve this effect. Peel only abolished the bottom part of the sliding scale of duties with his changes of 1842. Even in Peel's 1846 legislation, it can be seen from Chart 2.1 that duty still rose as prices dropped below a certain level. That was to ensure that food prices would drop far enough to help Ireland while not destroying the livelihoods of farmers. Indeed, as Paul Sharp has described, repeal of more of the sliding scale was provided for in Peel's original legislation but had to wait until 1849. And even then, a duty of one shilling per quarter would be retained from that date. As Sharp goes on to note, this registration duty was not abolished until 1869, only at which point a truly free trade in grain commenced.[112]

---

108   A. Hall, *The Opinions of Sir Robert Peel* (London: Arthur Hall, 1850), pp. 164, 166, 183, 185, 187, 188, 488–89.
109   E. Copleston, *A Second Letter to the Right Hon. Robert Peel* (Oxford: Murray, 1819), pp. 9–10, 31.
110   Graham to Croker, 22 March 1845, B.L., Graham papers, Add. MS. 79618, f. 59.
111   Ibid.
112   P. Sharp, '1846 and All That', *Agricultural History Review*, 58:1 (2010), 76–94, at p. 79.

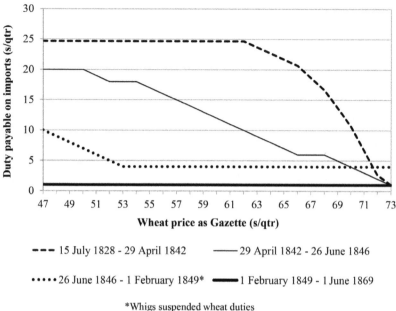

Chart 2.1. Duty payable per quarter of imported wheat according to price, 1828 to 1869. *Sources*: 9 Geo. IV. c. 60; 5 & 6 Vict. c. 14; 9 & 10 Vict. c. 22; *Concept from*: P. Sharp, '1846 and All That: The Rise and Fall of British Wheat Protection in the Nineteenth Century', *University of Copenhagen Department of Economics Discussion Papers*, 06-14 (2006), p. 7.

His phased approach to introducing low tariffs, even in 1846, caused him to be attacked from both sides of the debate. As well as the protectionist members of his own party on one side, who opposed repeal of any sort, he was also attacked by the Whigs for not bringing in free trade in one step. If this happened, Peel believed the agricultural districts, including Ireland, would suffer, and it was better that free trade was introduced slowly by a Conservative government than all at once by a Whig government, who, he worried, were more guided by liberal '*laissez faire, et laissez passer*' dogma than well thought out economic aims.[113] Hilton has indicated that the *laissez-faire* attitudes Peel might have had were generally 'social' in nature.[114] As far as economic policy is concerned, his gradual implementation of free trade confirms such an ideology was not the mainspring of Peel's economic aims. Peel had explicitly stated in 1845 that he 'was not prepared to apply to

113   Russell explains the rise of '*laissez-faire*': *Hansard*, CIV, 2 April 1849, c. 215.
114   Hilton, 'The Ripening of Robert Peel', p. 82.

the rural population of this country those principles of political economy which many hon. Gentlemen were disposed to do'.[115] In contrast, Russell had written an open letter to his constituents in the City of London (known as the Edinburgh letter) on 22 November 1845, declaring 'observation and experience have convinced me that we ought to abstain from all interference with the supply of food' and urging the government to unite to put an end to 'a system which has been proved to be the blight of commerce, the bane of agriculture'.[116] On failing to form a government in January 1846, Russell confirmed he 'would have formed his Ministry on the basis of a complete free trade in corn, to be established at once, without gradation or delay'.[117] In the Corn Laws debate in March 1846, Villiers, the champion of free trade in the House at that time and brother of Lord Clarendon who was to become viceroy of Ireland in 1847, declared:

> The House has very wisely resolved to take into consideration the protective system with a view to its ultimate abolition. The Ministerial measure recognises the policy of perfect freedom in the supply of the necessaries of life to the people of this country; but it has postponed the full application of that principle until the 1st of February, 1849. In my opinion that delay is not called for. It is my conscientious belief that the full advantage of the Ministerial scheme may be extended to this country at once, without danger or inconvenience to any class of the community.[118]

In response, Peel said he would ignore all other points except 'the question whether it be desirable that the repeal of the corn duties should be immediate, or whether they should continue, as Her Majesty's Government propose, for a period of three years', showing how important the issue was for him.[119] He explained that the legislation was dual purpose, helping Ireland and changing permanently the import duties. Although the immediate reduction was not complete, Ireland was catered for because there were immediate complete reductions of duty on Indian corn and rice, foodstuffs used in workhouses to replace the potato.[120] The three-year delay before a further reduction was, he said, to avoid 'a panic greatly depressing the price of wheat' and 'meet the wishes ... of the agricultural interest'.[121] Similarly, he explained the nature of his plans in such a way to Prince Albert, who noted that he was not repealing

115 *Hansard*, LXXXI, 2 July 1845, cc. 1426–27.
116 *Morning Chronicle*, 26 November, p. 5; also, *The Times*, 27 November 1845, p. 5.
117 *Hansard*, LXXXIII, 22 January 1846, c. 107.
118 *Hansard*, LXXXIV, 2 March 1846, c. 422.
119 Idem., c. 450.
120 Idem., c. 451.
121 Idem., c. 455.

the Corn Laws 'in favour of one class and as a triumph over another, but to the benefit of the nation, farmers as well as manufacturers'.[122]

Later on, the Russell government passed the Corn Importation Act in January 1847, which suspended the duties on corn completely from then until 1 September 1847, later extended to 1 March 1848. Peel, in 1849, blamed any 'evil effects from the repeal of the Corn Law before 1st February 1849' on this suspension which interfered with his policy of gradualism.[123] Before that, in February 1848, Peel had opposed an increased income tax which would have been accompanied by immediate full open trade, abandoning his gradual approach.[124] This move, although it indicates again the priority which Peel placed on phasing in slowly full free trade, seemingly contradicts Peel's realisation at the time that Ireland needed the relief funds which would have been supplied by an increased income tax. However, private correspondence with Wood shows that Peel had been trying to get Wood to propose a deficit budget which would have enabled a higher income tax to have been set with little risk of immediate total free trade. Any extra receipts from increased income tax would have been needed to make up the deficit rather than compensate for decreased tariffs. Wood refused, so Peel and the Peelites voted against a proposal to increase the income tax.[125]

Similarly, the Bank Charter Act of 1844 was also only a half measure from the point of view of the theorists behind the Currency School. The 1844 legislation only required that notes issued over a fixed limit had to be backed by bullion and not any other form of credit. Banknote issue under this limit was to be backed by government securities, and therefore not all notes had to be backed by gold under this piece of legislation. The Bankers (Ireland) Act 1845 of 21 July 1845 laid down that Ireland's fixed issue limit was the average issued in the year up to 1 May 1845. Below that level, it did not require any security. Only notes issued above this limit had to be backed by bullion. A full gold standard, however, would require all banknotes to be backed 1:1 with gold. There was, and still is, great confusion as to why the Banking Acts did not follow a full gold standard and why they had exceptions built in.[126] Frank Fetter and Charles Goodhart have thrown some light on this question by rethinking Peel's discussions with his Cabinet in the planning stage of the 1844 Banking Act about whether or not to reorganise the Bank of England. If they did change it, would it be better to set up a scheme like a currency board with a separate institution running the currency, or adopt a compromise solution

122   Prince Albert memorandum 25 December 1845, Royal archives, microfilm 95709/5; Benson, *Letters of Queen Victoria*, vol. 2, pp. 65–66.
123   *Hansard*, CVI, 6 July 1849, c. 1433.
124   Wood to Peel, 26 February(?) 1848 partial letter, B.L., Graham papers, Add. MS. 79713, f. 34.
125   Ibid.
126   T. Tooke, *Bank Charter Act of 1844, its principles and operation* (London: Longman &c, 1856), pp. 21–22.

by creating different departments within the Bank of England? The fact that the compromise solution was chosen confirms that there was an element of gradualism or 'half-measure' in Peel's proposals.[127] The construction of the 1844 Act does make sense if the aim of Peel's policy was to use the price depressing effect of a gold standard, but only in a moderate way. As Walter Bagehot later concluded about the legislation, 'Sir R. Peel's Act is a sort of compromise which is suited to the English people ... it undoubtedly suits no strict theory; it certainly has great marks of incompleteness'.[128]

Peel's economic policies and Ireland

As has been shown, Peel's consistent aim was to improve the welfare of the labouring population across the United Kingdom by means of low and stable food prices. Such an aim was not necessarily based on an attachment to *laissez-faire* or liberal ideas but was intended to ensure the survival of the upper classes while forcing them to contribute to improving the lot of the working classes. Manufacturers and landowners were expected to gain from a release of tension between classes and from increased commercial activity, although the concept of economic growth had not quite arrived yet. The change to free trade was to be managed gradually to avoid harming the agricultural sector and to placate landowners, whose counterparts in Europe were almost as equally quarrelsome as the labourers.[129] It was the failure of this message to get through or be accepted that gave Peel his political difficulties. Yet, he was so concerned about gradual implementation that he sacrificed his political party in order to have control of the way the legislation was enacted. Informed by the ideas of Ricardian economics and the Currency School, Peel believed that his policies of free trade and a firmly controlled currency would lower and bring stability to food prices. In addition, the transfer from indirect to direct taxes would get the country out of economic difficulties and enable a balanced budget to stabilise or reduce the national debt. In these ways, Peel's policies were aimed at satisfying all the conflicting urban and rural interests characterised in the cartoon depicted in Figure 2.1.[130]

---

127 F. W. Fetter, *Development of British Monetary Orthodoxy 1797–1875* (Fairfield, NJ: Kelley, 1978), pp. 183, 192, Ch. 6; C. Goodhart, 'Monetary Regimes: Then and Now', in S. Dow et al. (eds.), *Money, Method and Contemporary Post-Keynesian Economics* (London: Edward Elgar, 2018), 1–11, pp. 3–5.

128 W. Bagehot, *The Works and Life of Walter Bagehot*, ed. R. Barrington, vol. 3 (London: Longmans, 1915), p. 321 [p. 241 in Altenmünster: Jazzybee Verlag, 2015 edition].

129 R. Bidelux, I. Jeffries, *A History of Eastern Europe: Crisis and Change* (London: Routledge, 1998), p. 295.

130 *The Penny Satirist*, 3 June 1843, p. 1.

The strength of this conclusion lies in the way it accounts for many puzzling features of Peel's development of policy. The aim of low prices explains why on some occasions he spoke for free trade and at other times against it. His attitude depended on his changing understanding of the effect of free trade. His concern for the agricultural sector and Ireland is shown by his method of staged or partial introductions of legislation. This approach was intended to help the agriculturalists in his party, but as Stewart explains, they could not be persuaded this was the case.[131] The way in which he pursued his approach, nevertheless, shows integrity and the statesmanship he claimed. It also explains why he was so anxious to implement the policy in stages himself in early 1846, when the Whigs were equally willing to do so, but immediately and in one step. When the price-lowering effect of the Banking Acts perceived at the time is taken into account, Peel's policies seem more coherent. Other intended effects of his policies, including the control of bullion drains and the amendments made to tax legislation in order to run a balanced budget and reduce the national debt, were aimed at producing stability and prosperity in the country, which he hoped would benefit all classes.

In his speech at the opening of Parliament in January 1846, Peel justified his period in office by claiming that he had 'used it for the benefit of the public interest and national good'. He stated that in deciding upon his policy he had to 'consult the public interest'.[132] He repeated the same theme in his *Memoirs*, placing 'public interests' above 'party attachments'.[133] Such an attitude was appropriate for a Protestant Arminian who should wish to 'do more good', as Lady de Grey, one of his political confidantes, put it.[134] It is difficult to reconcile this attitude, for which there is much evidence in his correspondence with Graham, with a historical assessment of Peel which suggests that he used the Irish famine as an 'excuse' for passing legislation to repeal the Corn Laws.[135] That would essentially have involved an extended untruth for which there is little evidence.

An analysis of the Peel papers reveals no striking revelations about his reasoning other than the continuity of the theme of food prices and supply. The sources support Cormac Ó Gráda's approach in taking Peel's explanations at face value.[136] The original letters in the Peel papers, Peel's original manuscript of his *Memoirs*, and the edited published version all agree and have

131   Stewart, *The Politics of Protection*, pp. 37–38.
132   *Hansard*, LXXXIII, 22 January 1846, c. 93.
133   Peel, *Memoirs*, vols. 2/3, p. 182.
134   Henrietta, Lady (Countess) de Grey, to Lady Hardwicke, 28 September 1833, PRONI, Caledon Papers, D2433/D/5/200.
135   For reference to the 'excuse' opinion, see Gaunt, *Sir Robert Peel*, p. 122; N. R. Dunn, 'The Castle, the Custom House and the Cabinet: Administration and Policy in Famine Ireland, 1845–49', University of Oxford, unpublished DPhil dissertation (2007), p. 7.
136   C. Ó Gráda, *The Great Irish Famine* (Cambridge: CUP, 1997), pp. 43–44.

not been altered significantly. The correspondence is summarised to reduce the room it takes up and leaves out some inconsequential items, such as the first letter reporting potato blight in the Isle of Wight (unremarkable on its own) and some of the confusion, including Graham's undecided reporting in four negative and three positive letters on the potato crop.[137] None of the letters omitted has anything of substance to add to Peel's argument except perhaps that the totality of it is more of a convincing imperative for Peel's actions than the published sections suggest.[138] The only significant omission of note is Lord Lincoln's name from a letter criticising Peel's mode of bringing in his legislation, possibly to avoid political embarrassment.[139] There is therefore no reason to view the aim of Peel's repeal of the Corn Laws at that time as anything other than what he describes.

Peel's actions were intended to ensure supplies of food remained available for Ireland by keeping prices down. Peel considered the alternative would hinder relief for Ireland politically and practically. Spending public money buying foodstuffs for the Irish poor – while using tariffs to artificially inflate those prices for the benefit of rich landlords – was not a coherent or sustainable stance to take politically. He asked: 'can we go into the Liverpool market and raise the price of oats by Government purchases, leaving the Corn Law in full operation at the time?' He also foresaw the prospect of 'additional difficulty if the prices of food should range very high, and if we resolve to maintain during the period of pressure the existing Corn Law'.[140]

Even if Peel genuinely hoped that his economic-policy reforms would help Ireland, whether they did is another question. The economic theories upon which Peel's plans were based had not been thoroughly tested before being put into practice and were to have unexpected outcomes. The particular features of the implementation of Peel's Bank Charter Act that could make financial crises worse were highlighted in two letters to the editor of *The Globe* from 'Per Contra', which were republished in *The Economist* in 1847. Firstly, the bullion banking reserve was wholly held in the Issue Department of the Bank of England, with only a small amount of specie as a float in the Banking Department.[141] Depositors to the Banking Department who could withdraw gold at will relied on the same bullion as that which was backing the issued

---

137 Graham to Sewell, 12 August 1845, Home Office papers, PRO HO/43/70, f. 14; Graham to Peel, 18, 19, 28, 30 September 1845; 6, 8, 13 October 1845, B.L., Peel papers, Add. MS. 40451.

138 This view is shared by Dunn, 'The Castle, the Custom House and the Cabinet: Administration and Policy in Famine Ireland, 1845–49', p. 10.

139 Peel, *Memoirs*, vols. 2/3, p. 164; Copy of letter Lincoln to Peel, B.L., Peel papers, Add. MS. 40604, f. 156.

140 Peel, *Memoirs*, vols. 2/3, pp. 193–94.

141 *The Economist*, 13 February 1847, p. 176.

notes in the Issue Department. The 'reserve' in the Banking Department was one of notes, not bullion.[142] Bullion drains were more likely in this situation as gold could be called on both by note holders and depositors. Bullion drains were counteracted by restricting credit or raising interest rates. Both damaged commerce and made the effect identified by the Mundell-Fleming model in the 1960s – a loss of control of interest rates where there is a fixed-exchange rate and free capital mobility – more likely. If another country had high interest rates and attracted bullion away in an external drain, the United Kingdom would be forced to raise its interest rates to prevent or curtail a bullion drain. Secondly, the notes in circulation against which the need for bullion reserve was calculated included the note reserve in the Banking Department. The Bank could therefore cancel out the effect of a reducing bullion reserve on the note circulation by reducing its note reserve – a move that counteracted the self-balancing effect of the price-specie flow mechanism, the principle that the Currency School had originally used to justify the 1844 legislation.[143] Unsurprisingly, these circumstances caused great confusion and made some note holders and depositors nervous, although subsequently they faded from public attention. The lack of confidence in the new regulatory system made investors more likely to cause an internal drain by exchanging their notes for gold or withdrawing their deposits. The increased risk of a financial crisis meant that credit could be short just as a loan needed to be raised for government spending on relief. As the subsequent chapters go on to explain, this is exactly what happened in 1847.

Those problems were not all. Economists now recognise that Peel's aim of falling prices, though microeconomically beneficial for an economy, can act as a drag on macroeconomic growth by increasing real debt and by raising real interest rates.[144] And Peel had no conception of the long timeframes required for some of his policies to work, or for changes in prices to reach a new equilibrium. Wood only pointed out to Peel, as late as 1849, the year before his death, Adam Smith's warning that events which change prices could take 20 years for their effect to work through.[145] Also, the period at the end of 1846 in which the French bought up wheat from any source available because autumn storms had damaged their supplies was characterised by high international wheat prices and not the low American prices that Peel had wanted the effect of free trade to be.

142   Ibid.
143   Idem., 10 April 1847, pp. 414–15.
144   These have been noted to be among the effects of returning to Peel's combination of economic policies between 1925–31 after the First World War; see S. N. Solomou, *Themes in Macroeconomic History: The UK Economy 1919–39* (Cambridge: CUP, 1996), pp. 34–35, 44–47, 94–95, 100.
145   Wood to Peel, 26 September 1849, B.L., Graham papers, Add. MS. 79713, f. 36.

Figure 2.4. The Political Rider, or Peel's Rapid Act of Horsemanship. *Punch*, 28 February 1846. Peel is shown trying to ride two horses, with one foot on 'Protection' and the other one on 'Free Trade'.

Furthermore, Peel was unaware of the extent of his lack of economic knowledge. Recent research has shown that Peel's tariff reductions on agricultural imports in the 1842 budget caused Ireland's rural economy to slump, raising popular support for Daniel O'Connell's Repeal movement sharply between the autumns of 1842 and 1843.[146] Instead, he took an economic rebound from the middle of 1843 as a sign that his budget of 1842 had worked promptly.[147] In short, Peel's economic policies overall were a great leap into

146   C. Read, 'The Repeal Year in Ireland: An Economic Reassessment', *Historical Journal*, 58:1 (2015), 111–35.
147   *Hansard*, LXXIII, 23 February 1844, c. 253.

the dark, and the government lacked the information and economic theory to recognise whether they were working or not. Tragically for Ireland, they were a leap into a 'golden cage' from which the subsequent Whig government struggled to escape.

3

Famine relief before the crises of 1847

I think nothing can have been more marked than the disposition of this House to introduce and to adopt every measure which could, by possibility, mitigate the evils of scarcity, and of disease consequent upon that scarcity, in Ireland; and even those who dissented from the course taken upon many other points by Her Majesty's Government have manifested a most earnest, most eager, desire, to co-operate with us in this great object. Now, I do not think, as has been said, that the evil is of a temporary nature. On the contrary, I think you will find that it has much of a character of permanency, and that, at any rate, it will continue much beyond the present year.

> Sir Robert Peel (Prime Minister), Debate on Fever and Famine, Ireland, 13 March 1846.[1]

The whole credit of the Treasury and means of the country are ready to be used ... to avert famine and to maintain the people of Ireland.

> Lord John Russell (Prime Minister), Debate on Distress in Ireland, 17 August 1846.[2]

'No man died of famine'.[3] Or so the *Freeman's Journal*, the main nationalist newspaper in Dublin, claimed about the first year of the famine in an article published in April 1847. Historians often compare the success of Sir Robert Peel's relief policies in avoiding excess mortality in his final year in government in 1845–46 favourably with the record of Lord John Russell's ministry after 1846.[4] In Russell's period in office, the number of deaths accelerated, and excess mortality remained persistent even after potato yields began to recover from 1847 onwards. As far as the available data for workhouses goes, the number of deaths peaked as late as the winter of 1848–49.[5]

---

1 *Hansard*, LXXXVI, 13 March 1846, cc. 989–90.
2 *Hansard*, LXXXVIII, 17 August 1846, cc. 778–79.
3 *Freeman's Journal*, 5 April 1847, p. 2.
4 Excess mortality is usually defined by demographers and economists as the increase of deaths over the normal level of mortality.
5 C. Ó Gráda, T. W. Guinnane, 'The Workhouses and Irish Famine Mortality', in T. Dyson, C. Ó Gráda (eds.), *Famine Demography* (Oxford: OUP, 2002), 44–64, at p. 44.

Figure 3.1. The Irish Cinderella. As the famine worsened, *Punch* changed from caricaturing Daniel O'Connell and his campaign to split the Union, to criticising England and Scotland for 'keeping' Ireland in poverty. The sympathetic imagery of Ireland as a pretty, young girl with a traditional Irish harp is used. *Punch*, 25 April 1846, p. 181.

In the 1970s researchers found the question as to why Peel's more generous approach to relief was discontinued in 1847 – just at the point that mass mortality surged – 'one of the most surprising aspects of the Whig programme for Ireland'.[6] Since then the explanation for the change that has become favoured among scholars is that adherence to ideology in the form of *laissez-faire* ideas held sway over Russell's incoming government. As Cormac Ó Gráda summarised the state of academic opinion in 1999, the main cause of inadequate relief efforts after 1846 was 'doctrinaire neglect'.[7] He starkly contrasted 'Peel's determined action' with 'the harsh policies of Russell and Wood'.[8] More recently he concluded 'The constraint on [more assistance] happening was ideological, not budgetary', referring particularly to the Russell government.[9] Likewise, Peter Gray, a leading scholar of the impact of ideology on politicians during the famine, emphasised the influence of 'Christian providentialism' and 'commitment to *laissez-faire*' on the formation of relief policy after Russell came to power.[10]

Even so, the records in the archives far from convincingly support the idea that *laissez-faire* ideology alone was responsible for the U-turn in relief policy. This chapter and the next draw on the papers of political leaders, the banking community and other contemporary financial information to argue, instead, that the financial panics of 1847 were the trigger for the change in policy. Peel's macroeconomic policies of the 1840s – supported and continued by Sir Charles Wood as Russell's chancellor of the exchequer – left the Whigs unable to borrow to finance relief efforts in Ireland without panicking financial markets. The problem can be called 'ideology', but the battle was one more fought over monetary policy than a straight choice between *laissez-faire* and intervention on the ground in Ireland. The scaling back of public assistance programmes that resulted from the financial panics of 1847 – and which increased mortality at the height of the Irish famine – was the unintended result of Peel and Wood's economic policies, particularly the Bank Charter Act of 1844. The Whig government's Parliamentary weakness – that meant it was beholden to the commitment of Peel and his followers to that Act – and the strong influence of

6   R. J. Montague, 'Relief and Reconstruction in Ireland 1845–49', University of Oxford, unpublished DPhil thesis (1977), p. 142.
7   C. Ó Gráda, *Black '47 and Beyond: The Great Irish Famine in History, Economy and Memory* (Chichester: Princeton University Press, 1999), p. 10.
8   C. Ó Gráda, *The Great Irish Famine* (Cambridge: CUP, 1995), pp. 43, 45.
9   C. Ó Gráda, 'The Next World and the New World: Relief, Migration, and the Great Irish Famine', *Journal of Economic History*, 79:2 (2019), 319–55, at p. 348.
10   P. Gray, *Famine, Land and Politics: British Government and Irish Society 1843–1850* (Dublin: Irish Academic Press, 1999), pp. 95, 124; idem., 'Potatoes and Providence: British Government Responses to the Great Famine', *Bullán*, 1:1 (1994), 75–90, at pp. 76–8; idem., 'National Humiliation and the Great Hunger: Fast and Famine in 1847', *Irish Historical Studies*, 32:126 (2000), 193–216, at pp. 215–16.

the theories of the Currency School over some senior members of the Cabinet meant that alternative economic policies that could have continued the generous provision of Treasury funds for the relief effort were not implemented.

A conundrum

The focus of historical debate about the Irish famine, rightly, has been on why the initial and relatively successful relief efforts were withdrawn by the British government. In both the popular and academic literature on the subject, British policymakers have received much criticism for their sudden curtailment of relief funding to Ireland from central government in 1847 at the peak of food shortages. Many Irish nationalists argue that this change in policy amounted to purposeful cruelty, and even genocide. However, historians of British politics have found this difficult to reconcile with the intention of policymakers and civil servants, as expressed in their correspondence, that their policies were helping and not hurting the Irish. Even so, they have been unable to find a convincing explanation as to why such a change in policy was undertaken.[11]

   This void was filled with the problematic theory that ideologues advocating a *laissez-faire* ('let it be') policy came to power with the change of government. Blaming the rising influence of *laissez-faire* ideas on this change in personnel has had a long history. Some of the first attacks on the Russell government for its attachment to them came from British politician and leader of the Protectionists in the House of Commons, Lord George Bentinck, in 1847. Seeking to find an easy way to unite his followers after their split from Peel's Conservative Party, he accused the government of purchasing 'free trade with the lives of the Irish people, leaving the people to take care of themselves when Providence has swept the food from the face of the earth'.[12] William Smith O'Brien, a Conservative turned Irish nationalist, echoed these attacks.[13] But the idea has particularly taken off since the 1960s when R. D. C. Black and Cecil Woodham-Smith separately claimed that Peel's measures – the provision of cheap food and employment of the poor on public works – were dismantled by the subsequent Whig government under the ideological influences of *laissez-faire* economic ideas and religious providentialism.[14] 'Adherence to *laissez-faire*

---

11   R. Haines, *Charles Trevelyan and the Great Irish Famine* (Dublin: Four Courts Press, 2004), pp. 542–44.

12   *Hansard*, XCI, 29 March 1847, c. 597; frequently quoted from J. O'Rourke, *The History of the Great Irish Famine of 1847* (London: Duffy and Co., 1875), Chapter X, last footnote, p. 333.

13   *Hansard*, XC, 19 February 1847, c. 283.

14   R. D. C. Black, *Economic Thought and the Irish Question 1817–1870* (Cambridge: CUP, 1960), pp. 175–76, 244–45; C. Woodham-Smith, *The Great Hunger: Ireland, 1845–49* (London: Hamish Hamilton, 1962), pp. 375–83, 408–10.

was carried to such a length that in the midst of one of the major famines of history', Woodham-Smith thundered, 'the government was perpetually nervous of being too good to Ireland and of corrupting the Irish people by kindness, and so stifling the virtues of self-reliance and industry'.[15]

Civil servants as well as politicians have come under suspicion for promoting the use of *laissez-faire* policies during the famine. Since the 1960s, historians have focused on one official in particular: the assistant secretary to the Treasury, Charles Trevelyan, who implemented both the Peel and the Russell government's Irish famine policies. Trevelyan's supposed support and role in implementing *laissez-faire*, and his Christian providentialism, were brought to popular consciousness by Jenifer Hart and Woodham-Smith, who alleged that 'Ireland was ... abandoned to Trevelyan's operation-of-natural-causes system' and '*laissez-faire*'.[16] Their ideas have been widely popularised by works influential on public opinion including by Simon Schama, Robert Kee and Tim Pat Coogan.[17] Ó Gráda has cast the net wider:

> Avoiding deaths was not the prime Whig preoccupation: relief would shift the distribution of food 'from the more meritorious to the less', because 'if left to the natural law of distribution, those who deserved more would obtain it'. Thus in the Commons Russell refused to commit himself to saving lives as the prime objective, and some Whig ideologues such as Nassau Senior and *The Economist*'s Thomas Wilson [sic] ('it is no man's business to provide for another') countenanced large-scale mortality with equanimity ... but historical wrath has been reserved for permanent Treasury Under-Secretary Charles Trevelyan.[18]

However, the literature is beginning to move away from this interpretation. As Ó Gráda has pointed out, Austin Bourke, writing in the 1970s, noted that 'with Russell in command ... Trevelyan's humanitarian instincts could find no voice'.[19] Other historians have gone further still in Trevelyan's defence. In a lengthy book published in 2004, Robin Haines has attacked the impression given by the works by Hart and Woodham-Smith, inspired

15   C. Woodham-Smith, *The Great Hunger: Ireland 1845–49* (London: Penguin Books, 1991), p. 411.
16   J. Hart, 'Sir Charles Trevelyan at the Treasury', *English Historical Review*, 75:294 (1960), 92–110; Woodham-Smith, *The Great Hunger* (1962), pp. 58, 375, 406. Quotation from Woodham-Smith.
17   For instance, see R. Kee, *Ireland: A History* (London: Abacus, 1982), pp. 82–87; S. Schama, *A History of Britain vol. 3: The Fate of Empire 1776–2000* (London: BBC Worldwide, 2002), p. 295; T. P. Coogan, *The Famine Plot* (London: Palgrave Macmillan, 2012), p. 60.
18   Ó Gráda, *The Great Irish Famine*, pp. 44–45. Note: 'Thomas Wilson' is intended as a reference to James Wilson.
19   Idem., p. 45.

by tradition, that Trevelyan was a villain: 'on the evidence of a few selected passages their authors have convinced themselves and others that Trevelyan *was* the fiend he was held to be'.[20] Detailed archival work by Haines instead found Trevelyan to be 'a complex, opinionated man working against the odds, to assist a country to which he was attached by ties of affection, sympathy, and ancestry'.[21] Nevertheless, Trevelyan wrote in an arrogant fashion and the folk-myths about him are strongly held; it would be a brave historian who stood up against them.[22] Yet, Gray, who has used emotive words of disapproval to describe Trevelyan, also rightly said in his book, *Famine, Land and Politics*, which includes an extensive review of some of Trevelyan's correspondence, that 'he was at all times subordinate'.[23] Elsewhere, he has also concluded that Wood, 'as chancellor of the exchequer and Trevelyan's direct superior was the central figure'.[24] Thus, it is necessary to look beyond Trevelyan for the full story of who influenced the British government's policies towards Ireland during the famine.

The influence of some other ideologues has also been exaggerated. For instance, although James Wilson, editor of *The Economist*, believed strongly in *laissez-faire* and free trade for the greater public benefit and thought the Treasury's relief efforts in Ireland would have disastrous financial consequences, his influence on government in the famine period concerning Ireland was limited.[25] Generally he aligned himself with the Banking School, which opposed the Bank Charter Act of 1844, views that were out of favour among several senior members of the government. His advice on the dangers of interference was sharply rebutted by his friend Clarendon as lord-lieutenant of Ireland as 'not at all practicable for a Government having to answer to the humanity and generosity of England for the mortality of Ireland'.[26] In fact Wilson had foreseen, at the end of 1845, that difficulties with trade deficits and the money markets would bring attempts to fund relief from Treasury funds to disaster.[27] The threat to Britain's financial system from the two pressures of the Bank Charter Act and the government's fiscal expansion is what motivated much of his opposition to the government's Irish policies. When Wilson joined the government in 1848, he was appointed as one of the Secretaries of the

---

20   Haines, *Charles Trevelyan and the Great Irish Famine*, p. xii.

21   Idem., editorial.

22   N. R. Dunn, 'The Castle, the Custom House and the Cabinet', University of Oxford, unpublished DPhil dissertation (2009) notes Graham complaining of Trevelyan's 'phraseology', but '<u>not content</u>' (Goulburn to Lincoln, 15 April 1846), p. 125 (original underline).

23   Gray, *Famine, Land and Politics*, p. 231.

24   Idem., 'Potatoes and Providence', p. 83.

25   *The Economist*, 29 November 1845; idem., 21 March 1846.

26   Clarendon to Wilson, 8 March 1847, quoted in E. I. Barrington, *The Servant of All: Pages from the family, social, and political life of my father James Wilson: Twenty Years of mid-Victorian life*, vol. 1 (London: Longmans, 1927), pp. 109–10.

27   *The Economist*, 6 December 1845, p. 1222.

Board of Control, a department that supervised the East India Company's control of British India. It was a position which was often used to side-line away from British domestic policy those with economic views that were considered non-standard.[28]

Neither was the wider British press united in favour of a *laissez-faire* approach towards famine relief. As Michael de Nie has argued in one survey of British newspapers during the famine, 'the press supported the idea of relief for the deserving poor'.[29] The most influential of British newspapers, in fact, initially opposed *laissez-faire* approaches to relief policy. In 1845 *The Times*, the newspaper most associated with the British establishment, argued initially against *laissez-faire*, stating that 'we should at least administer all the natural and commercial relief in our power' in combatting the famine.[30] The editor of *The Times*, John Walters, was enraged when Lord Radnor called on the government to refuse relief to the destitute Irish poor and viciously criticised the aristocrat for this.[31] In 1847 *Punch* satirised the *laissez-faire* views held by opponents of the Russell government's reforms to the Poor Law – naming Radnor and two other Irish landlords explicitly – thereby presenting the government's changes as interventionist by implication (see Figure 3.2).[32] Although several newspapers, including *The Economist* and *The Times*, hardened their attitude towards Treasury spending after 1847, this change occurred under the influence of insights from the Banking School, which saw the financial panics of that year as the consequence of trying to issue government loans for Irish relief while the provisions of the Bank Charter Act remained in force.[33]

Nor is there much evidence that academics thrust *laissez-faire* views upon the Russell government. Nassau Senior did act as a government advisor on the English Poor Law in the 1830s. However, in the 1840s, there is little surviving correspondence between him and Peel or Wood, and in his lectures he disagreed with the government's reliance on an English-style Poor Law for Ireland as part of the 1847 relief reforms.[34] His opposition to government policy clearly suggests that his influence was minimal. Neither did his ideas hold much appeal for the banking community. In the words of one senior Whig banker: 'Mr Senior's

28   The Earl of Ripon (formerly Viscount Goderich), brother of the Second Earl de Grey, was treated in a similar manner in the 1840s.

29   M. de Nie, 'The Famine, Irish Identity, and the British Press', *Irish Studies Review*, 6:1 (1998), 27–35, at p. 30.

30   Leader article, *The Times*, 22 November 1845, p. 4.

31   R. K. Hutch, *The Radical Lord Radnor: The Public Life of Viscount Folkestone, Third Earl of Radnor (1779–1869)* (Minneapolis: University of Minnesota Press, 1977), pp. 162–63.

32   *Punch*, 29 May 1847, p. 217.

33   See, in particular, *The Economist*'s coverage of Ireland and the Irish loan crisis between February and May 1847.

34   N. W. Senior, *Four Introductory Lectures on Political Economy* (London: Longman, 1852), pp. 29–30.

PROTEST AGAINST THE IRISH POOR BILL

WE have seen a document thus headed in the columns of some of our contemporaries, but not believing in the correctness of their report, we have been at some pains to procure the following, which may be relied upon for its authenticity: -

DISSENTIENT.

1. Because the law, giving to the destitute a claim for relief, encourages a notion that it is the duty of somebody to provide for them; and extravagant hopes will inevitably lead to extravagance.

2. Because the Irish people are constitutionally given to starvation, and an interference with national habits cannot be desirable.

3. Because the tendency of the Bill is to increase the distress of the landlords while attempting to relieve the distress of the whole people.

4. Because the Bill, having been framed under an urgent necessity, was framed in a hurry; and as nothing in a hurry is done well, nothing ought to be done when an urgent necessity demands it.

5. Because it will ruin the independence of the poor in Ireland, by giving them something to depend upon.

RADNOR.   MONTEAGLE OF BRANDON.   FITZWILLIAM.

Figure 3.2. Protest against the Irish Poor Bill. In May 1847, after the Irish loan crisis, *Punch* published a fictional letter satirising opponents of the government's Poor Law legislation for their *laissez-faire* views, including two Irish landlords, Lord Monteagle and Lord Fitzwilliam. Note the presentation of the Russell government's policies as interventionist and its critics as *laissez-faire*. *Punch* remained deeply critical of those advocating *laissez-faire* policies in Ireland throughout 1847. *Punch*, 29 May 1847, p. 217 (transcribed).

excellent lectures on political economy, at Oxford, hold in sovereign contempt the practical man'.[35] His main intervention was to supply Lord Monteagle with support during the Anglo-Irish noble's opposition to the introduction of the Irish Poor Law reforms, a move which was interpreted by government ministers to be for Monteagle's own selfish financial interests.[36]

35   A. Baring, *Financial and Commercial Crisis Considered* (London: John Murray, 1847), p. 27.
36   Gray, *Famine, Land and Politics*, p. 235; N. W. Senior, 'Proposals for Extending the Irish Poor Law', *Edinburgh Review*, 84:October (1846), 267–314; Wood to Grey, 19 October 1846, D.U.L., Earl Grey papers, GRE/B122/3/14; Haines, *Charles Trevelyan and the Great Irish Famine*, p. 404.

Meanwhile, Brian Walker's recent research on the change of government has pointed out that, 'the outcome of the 1847 [United Kingdom] general election had no significant effect on the political balance at Westminster and did not cause the government to take a different approach to Ireland'.[37] Although the two Conservative groupings lost a few seats to the Whigs, Russell's government still did not have a majority in the House of Commons, and required Peelite or Repealer votes to get its legislation passed. The change of government had no real political effect on policy for Ireland other than reaffirming the Whig government's reliance on the Peelites and Repealers in Parliament.

A closer examination of the events of 1847 suggests that the change in government in 1846 and the influence of *laissez-faire* ideas do not give a complete explanation for the decisions made. First, rather than the stark contrast presented in much of the literature, Russell and Wood carried on Peel's core economic policies.[38] Second, analysis using the macroeconomic-policy trilemma, a modern concept, suggests why financial forces arose in 1847 that seriously affected the government's ability to raise loans to finance its plans for relief in Ireland. Third, a detailed and chronological examination of policy-makers' papers, contemporary commentary, and economic data shows a clear link between the financial panics of 1847 and a change in policy.

Initially, the new Whig government followed and expanded upon Peel's relief policies, spending upon which surged, albeit in response to increased need as a result of the much greater harvest failure that Ireland suffered in the autumn of 1846.[39] A month after Russell took office in the summer of 1846, he promised to the House of Commons that 'the whole credit of the Treasury and means of the country are ready to be used ... to avert famine and to maintain the people of Ireland' – a statement that both reaffirmed his government's commitment to Peel's generous policies and that unintentionally portended the government's fiscal difficulties in 1847.[40] These policies were largely successful in delaying the onset of mass excess mortality caused by the famine until 1847. Even then, Wood's budget of February 1847 foresaw a further expansion of government relief efforts for the starving Irish, 'assistance which I am confident will not be withheld from them' because of the strength of the public accounts.[41] The decision to cut back spending did not come immediately when the Russell government came to power in July 1846. Initial plans were made to transfer some costs to Irish ratepayers from August 1846 as the government's income

---

37   B. M. Walker, 'Politicians, Elections and Catastrophe: The General Election of 1847', *Irish Political Studies*, 22:1 (2007), 1–34, at pp. 29, 31.

38   A notable exception is Haines, *Charles Trevelyan and the Great Irish Famine*, pp. 542–43.

39   See Chart 4.6; *Correspondence...*, PP 1846 (735) XXXVII.41; *Public income and expenditure ...*, PP 1851 (62) XXXI.159; *Public income and expenditure ...*, PP 1861 (402) XXXIV.139.

40   *Hansard*, LXXXVIII, 17 August 1846, cc. 778–79.

41   *Hansard*, XC, 22 February 1847, c. 317.

deteriorated, as the harvest failure in autumn 1846 worsened, and as problems with the Treasury's public-works system developed. Yet this was initially intended to be accompanied by an expansion in Treasury advances for Relief Committees and Poor Law Unions. The real change came only in May 1847 after financial markets panicked about the scale of public borrowing announced to fund relief efforts.

Some commentators and historians have suggested already that economic conditions were an important influence on the change in policy, but these hunches have not been fully developed. John Mitchel, at the time, blamed policy on the 'gold mongering bullionist' interest.[42] Charles Parker and Norman Gash, both Peel biographers, mentioned that Peel was consulted by Wood about economic policy and Ireland, but omitted any detail of Wood's intended policies.[43] Robin Moore was more explicit, noting that 'neither Black nor Woodham-Smith have given prominence to the restraints that the Whig government' faced in this period, both of whom 'attributed rather too many of the weaknesses of Whig policy to the doctrine of *laissez-faire*'.[44] However, he did not expand much further on this point. Anna Gambles thought Britain imposed 'bullionist policies' on 1840s Ireland, but did not explore their outcome during the famine.[45] Haines has argued that Trevelyan's role has been overstated, but mentions the alternative influence of economic circumstances only in passing.[46] Douglas Kanter has briefly linked the decision to cancel further loans to pay for famine relief to 'the financial panic that unfolded in the summer and autumn' of 1847, but has not fully explored the historiographical implications of this idea.[47] Even Coogan, the most eloquent author in recent times of a nationalist polemic about the famine, mentions it, but merely gives it a curt aside.[48]

In the 1990s Ó Gráda, looking at macroeconomic data and lack of budget deficits, dismissed the possibility of 'a serious fiscal crisis in 1847'.[49] Likewise,

42   *United Irishman*, 2 February 1848, p. 2.
43   C. S. Parker, *Sir Robert Peel from his private papers* (London: John Murray, 1891–99), pp. 480–81; N. Gash, *Sir Robert Peel: The Life of Sir Robert Peel after 1830* (London: Longman, 1972), pp. 622–23.
44   R. J. Moore, *Sir Charles Wood's Indian Policy 1853–66* (Manchester: MUP, 1966), pp. 7–10, 244–45, quotation pp. 8–9, n. 8.
45   A. Gambles, *Protection and Politics: Conservative Economic Discourse, 1815–32* (London/Woodbridge: the Boydell Press in association with the Royal Historical Society, 1999), p. 132; 'bullionist policies' here refers to Currency School bullionist policies.
46   Haines, *Charles Trevelyan and the Great Irish Famine*, pp. 2–6, 72, 75, 555–58.
47   D. Kanter, 'The Politics of Irish Taxation, 1842–53', *English Historical Review*, 127:528 (2012), 1121–55, at p. 1131.
48   Coogan, *The Famine Plot*, p. 143.
49   Ó Gráda, *Black '47 and Beyond*, p. 79; but Ó Gráda has since recognised that the crisis of 1847 may have been significant in E. Vanhaute, R. F. J. Paping, C. Ó Gráda, 'The

Gray identified the 'City panic' of April 1847 and 'financial crisis' of October 1847 and noted that they affected the raising of the Irish loan, but he did not investigate further, presuming that the issue was insignificant.[50] He, Ó Gráda, and wider historical opinion relied on Neville Ward-Perkins, a minor Oxford economist, who claimed in 1950 that 'the financial crisis [of 1847] was exaggerated by the interested parties'.[51] Ward-Perkins is now known as a gold-standard enthusiast who jumped to this conclusion incorrectly as the result of mixing up two columns of data in Bank of England statistics.[52] Using the data correctly, an analysis of the 1847 crises conducted in 1984 by Rudi Dornbusch and Jacob Frenkel demonstrated that they were of a serious nature and entailed 'commercial distress and financial panic, the extremity of which was remarkable'.[53] Mac (H. M.) Boot, in a book published the same year, pointed out that the severity of the first crisis of 1847 was exacerbated by the need to issue debt by the British government and by rising interest rates in America, which attracted bullion flows to the country from Britain. Both these factors put pressure on the Bank of England's reserve ratio (note reserve to total liabilities) and helped to trigger the crisis of April 1847.[54] The next chapter looks at these important triggers in combination with the Irish loan in more detail. These influences have been ignored hitherto by most historians in favour of a focus on railway investment in Great Britain and the Bank of England's interest-rate policy.[55]

European Subsistence Crisis of 1845–1850: A Comparative Perspective', in C. Ó Gráda, R. F. J. Paping, E. Vanhaute (eds.), *When the Potato Failed. Causes and Effects of the 'Last' European Subsistence Crisis, 1845–50* (Turnhout: Brepols, 2007), 15–40, at p. 16.

50   Gray, *Famine, Land and Politics*, pp. 288–89; idem., *The Irish Famine* (New York: Abrams, 1995), p. 48.

51   Ó Gráda, *Black '47 and Beyond*, p. 79; C. N. Ward-Perkins, 'The Commercial Crisis 1847', *Oxford Economic Papers*, 2:1 (1950), 75–94, at p. 89; C. N. Ward-Perkins 'Review', *Economica*, 16:64 (1949), 384–87, at p. 386.

52   Ward-Perkins, 'The Commercial Crisis', p. 94; see R. C. O. Matthew's assessment of Ward-Perkins' approach as not very intellectual, quoted in J. S. Lyons, L.P. Cain, S. H. Williamson (eds.), *Reflections on the Cliometrics Revolution* (Abingdon: Routledge, 2008), p. 157.

53   R. Dornbusch, J. A. Frenkel, 'The Gold Standard and the Bank of England in the Crisis of 1847', in M. D. Bordo, A. J. Schwartz (eds.), *A Retrospective on the Classical Gold Standard 1821–1931* (Chicago: University of Chicago Press, 1984), 233–76; for a contemporary view of their serious nature, see Anon., *The Bank Charter Act in the Crisis of 1847* (London: Richardson Bros., 1854), p. 234.

54   H. M. Boot, *The Commercial Crisis of 1847* (Hull: Hull University Press, 1984), pp. 49–52.

55   The work of E. V. Morgan, and later C. N. Ward-Perkins, particularly pushed historians in these other directions; see E. V. Morgan, 'Railway Investment, Bank of England Policy and Interest Rates, 1844–48', *Economic History*, 4:15 (1940), 329–40.

This and the next chapters show that it is impossible to understand the motivation behind the abandonment of Treasury funding for relief without an understanding of the seriousness of the financial panics. In the case of April 1847, *laissez-faire* or providentialist ideologies can show no changes similar in timing to the relief cuts like those of financial circumstances in the loan market, which correlate exactly – to the week – with announcements of relief-policy changes. This chapter will outline the initial strategy of the Peel government to deal with the harvest failure in Ireland and will expose the continuity between the macroeconomic and relief policies of the Peel and Russell governments. The next chapter will explain how curtailment of central government spending on relief in Ireland exactly followed the Irish loan crisis of spring 1847, rather than occurring at the time of the change of government, and the consequences that followed from this for Ireland.

Peel's successful relief policies in 1845 and 1846

In the words of Gray, 'the reaction of Peel's government to the 1845 potato failure has generally been praised by historians for its promptness and efficiency'.[56] Ó Gráda, in particular, has assessed the fact that few people perished in the 1845–46 harvest season as a 'remarkable achievement', due to the 'efficacy of relief' and 'partly due to the country's ability to handle such a shortfall'.[57] Such interpretations reflect what the press was saying at the time. For instance, in April 1847, the *Freeman's Journal*, a Dublin newspaper sympathetic towards Irish nationalism, could only see Peel's policies as a successful model for the growing harvest failure.[58] What was needed to combat the bigger harvest failure of 1846, the newspaper argued, was an expansion of the same policy deployed in the autumn of 1845. 'Widen the circle of destitution in 1845, and it could be effectually encountered by the proper extension of the same policy'.[59]

Such accounts tend to emphasise Peel's activism in making sure relief was available, while criticising him for mixing up the issue of Irish relief with that of the political crisis surrounding the repeal of the Corn Laws in London.[60] However, the policies that delivered the relief that delayed mass mortality were not particularly innovative. They were simply the ones traditionally used by British officials in Ireland during previous periods of famine.

When it became clear in the autumn of 1845 that the potato harvest had failed, the Peel government swung into action with traditional relief policies

56   Gray, *Famine, Land and Politics*, p. 96.
57   Ó Gráda, *The Great Irish Famine*, pp. 33–34.
58   *Freeman's Journal*, 5 April 1847, p. 24.
59   Ibid.
60   See, for instance, Woodham-Smith, *The Great Hunger* (1991), p. 50.

that had worked well in previous crises. Although the impact of the blight was widely reported in the press from late summer, the government in London first officially heard of the seriousness of the failed harvest in October 1845, in a letter from Lord Heytesbury, the lord-lieutenant.[61] Appeals for extra expenditure from Dublin Castle were a common occurrence. So Peel wanted to be sure of the seriousness of this crisis before taking action. He set up the Scientific Commission, under the auspices of his friend, Dr Lyon Playfair, to investigate the cause and extent of the potato blight, and to recommend measures to combat it.[62] This Commission quickly concluded that there would definitely be a serious shortfall of potatoes fit to eat. That prompted Peel and his government to put into motion a series of policy actions intended to deal with the harvest crisis. The remainder of the efforts of the Scientific Commission – at least in terms of actually combatting the disease – came to nothing. This was unfortunate because the correct chemicals for dealing with the blight – lime, salt and copper sulphate – were published in a letter from Charles Morren on 12 September 1845 in the *Freeman's Journal*.[63] Sadly, it appears that they were never put to the test in Ireland in any significant way.

Peel's government sought to combat the crisis using a mixture of demand-side and supply-side policies. He had consistently shown interest in famine alleviation in Ireland since early in his career. Peel, as chief secretary of Ireland during the famine of 1817 and home secretary during that of 1822, had favoured public-works schemes, working with local Relief Committees and some importation of food by government. This had created a new policy template that was deployed in response to famines in the 1820s and 1830s.[64] With the potato-harvest failure of 1845, the same policies came out of the draw again. On the demand-side, measures to provide paid employment and free food (to the infirm) as relief were adopted. A series of supply-side policies was also implemented, to ensure that there was a steady supply of imported food that the poor were able to buy with their money. Most famous, and controversial, of those on the supply side was his decision to 'repeal' the Corn Laws in 1846.

The policies Peel instigated himself, and took the most interest in, were those aimed at 'increasing the supply of food'.[65] As a matter of priority, Peel resolved

61   Gray, *Famine, Land and Politics*, p. 99.
62   Idem., p. 101; *Copy of the report of Dr Playfair and of Mr Lindley on the present state of the Irish potato crop, and on the prospect of approaching scarcity, dated 15th November 1845*, PP 1846 (28) XXXVII.33.
63   *Freeman's Journal*, 12 September 1845, p. 4; see also C. Morren, *Instructiones populaires sur les moyens de combattre et de'truire la maladie actuelle des pommes de terre* (Paris: Oret, 1845). English abstract in *Journal of Agriculture*, July 1846, pp. 349–53.
64   I would like to thank Liam Kennedy for pointing out this observation to me.
65   R. Peel, *Memoirs by the Right Honourable Sir Robert Peel*, ed. Earl Stanhope, E. Cardwell, vols. 2/3 (London: John Murray, 1857), p. 166.

a territorial dispute with the United States, gifting them 286,000 square miles of the Oregon territory. This precaution was so that a potential war did not disrupt Britain and Ireland's access to cheap food supplies from the North American prairies.[66] These efforts were bolstered by dropping tariffs on Indian corn on an emergency basis ahead of the main legislation that would amend the Corn Laws, in order to encourage importation of the foodstuff as a replacement for the potato.

In his *Memoirs*, Peel claimed that his famine policies were calculated to 'mitigate the evil consequences of a sudden and extensive defalcation in the ordinary supply of food'.[67] This comment suggests that he saw the famine as principally caused by a lack of food availability and explains why he saw reducing tariffs to increase imports as an important step that the government had to take to ameliorate famine hunger.[68] Yet for this to be successful, the poor needed to earn money to buy the imported food. Policies to provide employment were implemented, but Peel left their direction mainly to the Irish government. By not banning exports, landlords and farmers were not impoverished by losing lucrative export markets for their better quality produce. However, in return, they were expected, particularly by the following Russell government, to contribute to and co-operate with the government's programmes to employ unemployed labourers.

Peel has been open to the accusation made by his contemporary John Croker and by several historians since that he used the failure of the potato crop simply as an excuse for repealing the Corn Laws, which they claimed he wanted to do anyway.[69] They often quote his statement to the House of Commons in January 1846 that 'if there be any part of the United Kingdom which is to suffer by the withdrawal of protection, I have always felt that part of the United Kingdom is Ireland', as evidence that he believed that repeal would not help Ireland.[70] Yet this statement, in fact, only refers to the Irish landowning class whom Peel generally did not like, not the Irish economy as a whole, nor the Irish labourers most affected by the blight whom he was most anxious to help. Peel actually used the phrase in the context of a speech about giving Ireland preferential

---

66   F. Merk, 'The British Corn Crisis of 1845–46 and the Oregon Treaty', *Agricultural History*, 8 (1934), 95–123, at pp. 95–100, 121–22; Peel to Hardinge, 16 December 1845, 4 July 1846, B.L. Hardinge papers, Indian Office Records, Neg 11692/17-/32.
67   Peel, *Memoirs*, vols. 2/3, p. 107.
68   Ibid.
69   J. R. Thursfield, *Peel* (London: Macmillan, 1891), pp. 226–27; Thursfield defended Peel against Croker's accusation, Croker to Hardinge, 24 April 1846, in L. J. Jennings (ed.), *J. W. Croker: Correspondence and Diaries*, vol. 3 (London: Murray, 1884): 'the deception of endeavouring to attribute it to the potato failure in Ireland'. Croker was an Irish friend of Peel up to 1845 when he disagreed with him over the repeal of the Corn Laws.
70   *Hansard*, LXXXIII, 27 January 1846, c. 273, cited in B. Hilton, 'Peel: A Reappraisal', *Historical Journal*, 22:3 (1979), 585–614, at pp. 598–99.

treatment in respect of the costs of the legal system. Those costs were payable by wealthy landowners, and this quotation refers to the suffering of landowners rather than the labourer, but Peel privately disapproved of Irish landowners, who he thought were arrogant in believing themselves to be 'a superior and privileged class'.[71] Evidence in a letter from William Gladstone to his father suggests that Peel was in earnest about the issue arising from the food shortage in Ireland. 'It was during the alarm of a potato famine in the autumn of that year [1845] that the movement in the Government about the Corn Laws began', Gladstone explained in response to the suggestion that he had 'made Peel a free trader'.[72] Gladstone denied having had any influence on Peel's trade policies after he left office as President of the Board of Trade in February 1845.

As the previous chapter has shown, Peel's policies were those he thought would benefit the labouring classes over the priorities of landowners in a Ricardian sense. Rather than arguing that protection would hurt the Irish, earlier in the year and long before the arrival of the blight, Peel in fact argued that removing protection would be good for the Irish labourer. He challenged a Mr Shaw who spoke of their poverty: 'will you say that the maintenance of protection is for the benefit of the Irish agricultural labourer, if protection has brought him to this [poverty]?'[73] The key to the improvement of the working classes in general, Peel went on, was plentiful supplies of food, 'You may talk of improving the habits of the working classes, introducing education amongst them, purifying their dwellings, improving their cottages; but believe me the first step towards improvement of their social condition is an abundance of food'.[74]

However, Peel did not believe that free trade alone would bring this about. He also authorised demand-side policies to enable the poor to afford the food supplied but took less direct interest in these. This did not result from a lack of concern. It was simply because these policies were those traditionally used by the Irish executive housed in Dublin Castle in years of crop failure. In contrast to the repeal of the Corn Laws, they were relatively uncontroversial. Peel requested these from Dublin Castle, and initially let the civil servants organise them through the Relief Commission, an organisation set up under the control of Edward Lucas, who had previously been undersecretary, or the head of the civil service, in Ireland.[75] Peel focused on trickier questions concerning the

71   Draft Peel to De Grey, 22 August 1843, B.L., Peel papers, Add. MS. 40478, f. 160; deleted in the draft.
72   W. E. Gladstone to J. Gladstone, 30 June 1849, Gladstone's Library, Glynne-Gladstone papers, MS 229, ff. 132–35. I am indebted to Professor Douglas Kanter for being pointed in the direction of this letter and for a transcription.
73   *Hansard*, LXXXV, 27 March 1846, c. 227.
74   Idem., c. 239.
75   C. R. Dodd, *The Peerage, Baronetage, and Knightage, of Great Britain and Ireland* (London: Whittaker & Co., 1846), p. 253.

raising of revenue to fund these policies and the political difficulties between classes which the abandonment of the Corn Laws was intended to ease.

In November 1845, soon after the Scientific Commission reported the seriousness of the crisis, Peel requested from Edward Pennefather, undersecretary to the lord-lieutenant, a list of policies implemented during previous famines. He replied with a list based, he said, on the returns printed for the House of Commons in 1842.[76] They were mainly the same policies used by the Second Earl de Grey, Peel's lord-lieutenant of Ireland between 1841 and 1844, to combat a downturn caused by Peel's tariff reductions in 1842.[77] These policies were themselves based on what British officials had done in Ireland during previous periods of harvest failure and distress.[78] In general these policies were interventionist and aimed at boosting food entitlements. The items were:

1. Reducing the price of provisions (potatoes and oatmeal) by purchasing cargoes in cheap markets and conveying them to the districts in which the scarcity prevails.
2. Providing employment on public works particularly roads and in some instances piers or harbours for fishing boats.
3. In cases of extreme necessity giving food to those who from infirmity could not earn the means of purchasing it and in some instances giving money to the sick, infirm, and most necessitous.
4. Providing medical attendances ... .
5. Aiding by contributions in money the local efforts for those objects or generally for the relief of the poor.[79]

Peel extended these policies in line with his concentration on food supply. In particular the provision of a supply of Indian corn bought on government account, stored in local depots and distributed at just below market price to 'stabilise market prices' in areas where prices were rising.[80] This was intended to bolster the food supply without flooding potato markets to the point where farmers were unable to make a profit selling what remained of their crop. Most of the other policies used by Peel were driven through by Lucas, who was now chairman of the Relief Commission.

---

76 *Return of Grants or Loans of Public Money in Aid of Distressed in Great Britain,* *1825–42,* PP 1842 (577) XXVI.441.
77 See C. Read, 'Peel, De Grey and Irish policy 1841–44', *History,* 99:334 (2014), 1–18, at pp. 14–16.
78 *Return of Grants ...,* PP 1842 (577) XXVI.441.
79 R. Pennefather, 'Memorandum of the course pursued by Government in seasons of scarcity and distress in Ireland', 4 November 1845, B.L., Graham papers, Add. MS. 79730, ff. 98–104 (original underline).
80 For instance, see Relief Commission papers, Dublin: National Archives of Ireland, RLFC/3/1/1092; RLFC/3/1/1315; RLFC/3/1/1559; RLFC/2/Z4996.

Peel's policies substantially worked, remarkably so in the light of serious infighting at the Relief Commission. Importantly, public-works schemes were set up to provide employment to help unemployed labourers buy food. Most of the infighting was mainly about how relief should be given to the poor rather than about whether it should be given at all. Lucas wanted to follow De Grey's scheme in providing cash relief, funded on the basis of Poor Law Union areas.[81] The alternative scheme proposed was concentrating on public works organised on barony or townland areas.[82] There were many times the number of townland areas as Poor Law Unions, but the government in London thought the smaller townlands provided a stronger link between ratepayers and those implementing relief efforts. However, this often meant there was a slowness to act for fear of incurring expense, and some areas had few wealthy residents to pay the rates. The Poor Law Unions were more impartial, but also remote, yet already had a structure for checking on how relief was administered. Providing relief with money was simple, but providing employment or free food (i.e. in kind) appealed to government on the basis that it would probably attract less abuse of the system. The question was which method was the best to provide and control the relief in a way that minimised the risk of abuse or corruption.

Whereas Lucas supported outdoor relief and the distribution of aid in cash, Edward Twisleton, a Poor Law Commissioner, firmly opposed this course. Henry Goulburn, as Peel's chancellor of the exchequer, was also against the payment of money, and his Memorandum on Measures relating to the potato failure in Ireland, written soon after the problem was noted, stated it was 'expedient to make payment for labour as far as practicable in kind'.[83] This influence was imposed locally through Twisleton, whom Goulburn had appointed to the Commission expecting him to impose strict limitations on relief spending: 'I rely with great confidence on your prudence, moderation and firmness'.[84] Twisleton subsequently agreed with Graham, the home secretary, over the argument within the government over outdoor relief:

> I entirely agree with your views as to the inexpediency of distributing any outdoor relief through the agency of the Boards of Guardians in Ireland. A difficulty undoubtedly exists as to the best way of making localities where relief is given feel an interest in checking imposition. But I do not think the difficulty should be solved by any interference with the existing Poor Law.[85]

---

81   See Read, 'Peel, De Grey and Irish policy 1841–44', pp. 15–16.
82   Twisleton to Graham, 4 February 1846, B.L., Graham papers, Add. MS. 79730, ff. 159–64.
83   Memorandum, [undated], B.L., Graham papers, Add. MS. 79730, ff. 106–07.
84   Graham to Twisleton, 2 December 1845, B.L., Graham papers, Add. MS. 79730, f. 108.
85   Twisleton to Graham, 21 December 1845, B.L., Graham papers, Add. MS. 79730, ff. 134–35.

By February 1846, however, Twisleton was admitting privately that 'it is better to levy money on the Poor Law valuation system than on the Townland valuation system', but he continued to dismiss the Poor Law system and support the Townland system, 'Thou' I entirely agree as to the superiority of the former system to the latter ...'.[86] The reason was the possibility of Parliamentary delay and that new legislation was not required for the Townland system:

> It seems to me desirable to take the 1st and 2nd Victoria c. 21 (a copy of which I herewith transmit) as the basis of any alteration in the law which may be required to meet the present emergency ... the Act even now is sufficient to meet all cases where Public Works can be undertaken in any locality provided that the board of works has sufficient Funds at its disposal and provided that the locality applies for aid in the prescribed form ...[87]

Lucas was unconvinced and resigned, so the Commission was re-formed in February 1846 with Randolph Routh, a former commissary-general working for the Treasury, at its head. De Grey had thought him short of local knowledge and that began to show.[88] Almost immediately the Commission fell apart with Twisleton accusing Routh of illegal interference with the Poor Law when Routh, having little other assistance, issued orders to its officers to help with relief (as Lucas had previously realised would be necessary).[89] To resolve the situation, an attempt was made by George Scrope, a political economist, to persuade the House of Commons to issue 'an Instruction to the Committee, that they have power to make provision therein that the Guardians of the several Poor Law Unions in Ireland be required to relieve with food all such destitute persons within their Unions as may be in danger of perishing from want, or from disease the consequence of want'.[90] This proposal aroused much anger, not from government officials, but from Irish nationalist MPs fearing higher poor-rates, including John O'Connell, son of Daniel O'Connell, who claimed that 'its effects would be disastrous in Ireland'.[91] As a result, Scrope was forced to withdraw the amendment.[92]

In March 1846 Heytesbury was already explaining to Peel the reasons for delays, blaming the procedures run by Trevelyan at the Treasury for the type of demand-side relief implemented. 'The Proprietors ...', he wrote, complained

---

86   Twisleton to Graham, 4 February 1846, B.L., Graham papers, Add. MS. 79730, ff. 159–64.
87   Ibid.; see Russell to Bessborough, 25 September 1846, N.A., Russell papers, PRO 30/22/5C, ff. 312–17.
88   'Earl de Grey's Irish Diary', 1843 vol. 2, B.L.A.R.S., L31/114/17–21, p. 17.
89   Routh to Trevelyan, 9 February 1846, N.A., War Office papers, WO/63/132.
90   *Hansard*, LXXXIV, 18 March 1846, c. 1167.
91   Idem., c. 1213.
92   Idem., c. 1214.

of being called upon for private subscriptions, 'after their compliance with the provisions of the Act 1 Vict c 21 – by which one moiety of the expense exercised is charged upon them', for the official works. They further complained that the Board of Works, under instructions from the Treasury, made these private subscriptions a '*sine qua non*' and was withholding all advances for the employment of the people till they were obtained. 'This may be right in principle, but the delay that it occasions may have serious consequences', Heytesbury claimed, 'this rigid adherence to the rules laid down by the Treasury, will at once explain how little has been done in the way of relief by public works notwithstanding the pressing applications made from so many quarters under the sanction of the commissioners'.[93]

However, in fact the archival evidence in the Relief Commission papers, as described above, clearly suggests that it was disarray among the officers of the Commission that was responsible for delays.

The relationship between the Peel and Russell governments

After the Russell government took over in 1846, Peel's traditional demand-side policies were not only continued, they were also expanded. The Russell government, in its first year in office, spent over four times more on famine relief than the Peel government did the year before despite the concerns of Peel and Goulburn in August 1846 about 'the permanent maintenance of the poor of Ireland out of the national purse' and making temporary relief a permanent institution.[94] Historians have emphasised the contrasting policies of the two governments, whereas in fact they both shared a core set of economic policies.[95] This should not entirely be a surprise when Parliamentary arithmetic is taken into account. Russell's Whig government did not hold a majority in Parliament between 1846 and 1852 and relied on groupings such as Peel and his remaining followers from the Conservative Party to get its policies passed into law.[96]

Historians' focus on Russell as responsible for famine policy after 1846 has obscured the more important influence of Wood and Peel. Wood controlled Irish policy because of Russell's lack of economic understanding and the need for the chancellor to find the financial resources necessary for the relief efforts. Peel had a longstanding influence over Wood as the government relied on the

---

93 Heytesbury to Peel, 16 March 1845, B.L., Peel papers, Add. MS. 40479, ff. 557–60.
94 Goulburn to Peel, 13 August 1846, B.L., Peel papers, Add. MS. 40445, ff. 365–66; Peel to Goulburn 14 August 1846, Surrey Record Office, Goulburn papers, 304, box 42; Gray, *Famine, Land and Politics*, p. 230.
95 For instance, see Ó Gráda, *The Great Irish Famine*, pp. 43, 45.
96 See P. Scherer, *Lord John Russell: A Biography* (Selinsgrove: Susquehanna University Press, 1999), pp. 177–78.

Parliamentary group he led to stay in power. Together, they both generally agreed that economic policy should be used to promote stability and reduce food prices and that this could be achieved with the gold standard, the Bank Charter Acts and lower tariffs.[97] Peel's government had set a precedent that the budget should be balanced at all times. Wood also attempted to follow this as far as possible, a policy which relied on low interest rates to reduce debt servicing costs. In the 1830s, Wood had witnessed the Whigs' in-built electoral advantage in Parliament after the Reform Act of 1832 be annihilated by 1841 as a result of Peel's accusations of Whig financial mismanagement.[98] The out-of-control spending and rising budget deficits of the Melbourne government suggested to Wood that the Conservative leader had a point. To stay in power, Wood thought the Whigs would need to broadly follow Peelite policies, including a balanced budget, to avoid a repeat of the electoral disaster of 1841. So Peel's policies became a shared agenda, which set the background for their co-operation over both financial policy and Ireland. The Lords of the Treasury were happy to implement the policies that followed from this meeting of minds, and as the archives show, Trevelyan was directed accordingly.[99]

The second prime minister during the famine, Russell, must take some of the blame for poorly constructed policy, despite the dominance of Wood. He was at the time known by contemporaries, as well as by historians more recently, as a politically weak and financially inept leader. Neither are good qualities in a prime minister, and this was particularly so during the Irish famine, when the economic and political environment faced by his government was so inclement. As Paul Scherer has rightly noted, Russell 'could carry neither his cabinet nor the British members of Parliament with him'.[100] He failed to form a government in December 1845 because of arguments among the Whigs, after which even Queen Victoria thought Russell could never 'be Prime Minister, for he has not a shadow of authority' over his own party.[101] Moreover, he was widely held to 'think of economics as a necessary evil', and Sir John Young (the Peelites' whip) reported Wood's belief that 'Lord John Russell knows nothing of trade or finance'.[102] Gray has judged that 'it is unlikely that his grasp of the subject was ever much more than superficial'.[103] Russell often had to ask Wood for

97 Moore, *Sir Charles Wood's Indian Policy 1853–66*, pp. 5–6.
98 R. Stewart, *Party and Politics, 1830–1852* (New York: Macmillan, 1989), p. 60.
99 See, for example, N.A., Treasury papers, T64/370B/1 cover note 9 September 1848 with Wood's instructions to Trevelyan, copied by the latter in Trevelyan to Twisleton, 14 September 1848, N.A., Treasury papers, T64/370B/1; Trevelyan follows Wood's instructions.
100 Scherer, *Lord John Russell: A Biography*, p. 176.
101 Queen Victoria to Prince Leopold, 23 December 1845, Royal archives, 92/36; Scherer, *Lord John Russell: A Biography*, p. 148.
102 Scherer, *Lord John Russell: A Biography*, p. 151; Young to Peel, 16 January 1847, B.L., Peel papers, Add. MS. 40598, ff. 38–42.
103 P. Gray, *Famine, Land and Politics*, pp. 238–39.

help in understanding his own government's economic policies and to make decisions. Russell was prepared to admit to Bessborough, over a matter as small as security issues in Dungarvan, 'I felt I could not act alone in it. I wrote to Charles Wood ...'.[104] Unable to understand railway policy, he once wrote to Wood, 'I wish you would send over here some person qualified to explain the Railway propositions'.[105] Wood told Russell he was 'a little alarmed at [his] finance' and worried by his lack of understanding of economic issues.[106] Wood started to remove the full detail of the financial problems facing the government from his correspondence.[107] Wood also used the Cabinet and the Royal Family to out-manoeuvre Russell over economic and financial issues.[108]

This dependent relationship increased the powers over economic and expenditure matters of Wood and the other Treasury Lords, who have been hitherto somewhat overlooked in accounts of the famine. These included Denis O'Conor Don and Richard Bellew, who were both Irish Catholics with some influence over Irish policy.[109] O'Conor was replaced by Bellew in July 1847. Bellew was more sympathetic to the new policy and may have been chosen because of that. O'Conor was a strong supporter of public works, whereas Bellew was of the opinion that Irish relief should be self-financing and saw the Poor Law system as the best way of organising it. Even before he was appointed, he advocated from the backbenches 'making the property of Ireland responsible for the poverty of Ireland' by shifting the cost of Irish relief onto the Poor Law so that Ireland 'would no longer be in the position of a burden upon the Imperial State'.[110] Another overlooked figure of importance is John Parker, Whig secretary to the Treasury, who directed Trevelyan (officially his 'assistant') in policy and its application. Trevelyan demurred from discussing some matters when Parker and Wood were away.[111] Parker's correspondence shows Trevelyan was under a huge amount of pressure from him, as well as others, to exercise 'economy' in Irish relief expenditure over the summer of 1847, when centralised relief was ended and the Poor Law relief system was introduced.[112]

Nevertheless, the greatest influence over policy came from Wood, with the support of Peel. The chancellor of the exchequer and leader of the opposition's

---

104   Russell to Bessborough, 4 October 1846, N.A., Russell papers, PRO 30/22/5D, ff. 62–63.
105   Russell to Wood, 21 December 1846, N.A., PRO 30/22/5F, Russell papers, ff. 240–41; Russell to Bessborough, 4 October 1846, N.A., Russell papers, PRO 30/22/5D, ff. 62–63.
106   Wood to Russell, 26 August 1847, N.A., Russell papers, PRO 30/22/6E, ff. 218–21.
107   Wood to Russell, 3 September 1847, N.A., Russell papers, PRO 30/22/6F, ff. 28–29.
108   Scherer, *Lord John Russell: A Biography*, p. 183; Prince Albert to Earl Grey, 23 November 1847, D.U.L., Earl Grey papers, GRE/B75/3A/11/1.
109   *Hansard*, LXXXVII, 6 July 1846, c. 1063.
110   *Hansard*, LXXXIX, 25 January 1847, cc. 457–58.
111   Trevelyan to Creed, 30 December 1846, O.B.L., Trevelyan letter books, vol. 10, p. 279.
112   Parker to Wood, 10 August 1847, C.U.L., Hickleton Papers, MS MF A4.52 reel 1490.

close co-operation over policy is understandable as the Russell government never held a majority in Parliament. As the two Conservative groupings together continued to hold more seats than the Whigs after 1846, Russell and Wood were forced to approach the Peelites and co-operate in passing their initial legislation for Ireland, coming to rely on them for votes and advice over the next few years.[113] Peel returned to his approach of 'opposition in government' that he had pioneered in the 1830s, offering the government his support on some measures in exchange for influence on the formulation of public policy.[114] Communication between Peel and Wood and the Whigs – initially through Goulburn, Graham and Young, and then directly – began as early as August 1846. By 1847 Wood was writing to Peel describing the 'serious satisfaction' which his 'approbation' of the government's proposals gave him.[115] Their relationship became so close, Gash has said that 'Peel was almost an unofficial member of Russell's cabinet' between 1846 and 1850.[116] Peter Mandler has noted that the influence of the Peelites over the government was so great by 1847 that Russell was forced to appoint Clarendon – the Peelites' preferred choice – as lord-lieutenant of Ireland after Bessborough died in May 1847, over the prime minister's initial preference to appoint his own brother, the Duke of Bedford, to the position.[117]

Peel's policies and the Russell government

Wood and Peel together supported three important macroeconomic policies in the 1840s. They were an interventionist mixture of restriction and openness, not philosophically consistent, which was intended to boost the economy by the reduction and stabilisation of food prices, an overall aim Peel had promised in his Tamworth election speech of 1841.[118] First, both Wood and Peel agreed that the value of the British currency should be firmly fixed to a gold standard, with the pound freely convertible by the Bank of England and a limited banknote

113   Scherer, *Lord John Russell: A Biography*, pp. 147–48.
114   E. J. Evans, *Sir Robert Peel: Statesmanship, Power and Party* (London: Routledge, 1991), p. 39.
115   Wood to Peel, 4 December 1847, B.L., Graham papers, Add. MS. 79713, ff. 22–23.
116   N. Gash, 'Peel and the Party System 1830–50', *Transactions of the Royal Historical Society*, 5th series:1 (1951), 47–69, at p. 66.
117   P. Mandler, *Aristocratic Government in the Age of Reform: Whig and Liberal 1830–52* (Oxford: OUP, 1990), p. 251, citing L. Strachey, R. Fulford (eds.), *The Greville Memoirs, 1814–1860*, vol. 5 (London: Macmillan, 1938), p. 445 (3 May 1847), and Greville to Normanby, 30 April 1847, 7 May 1847, Mulgrave MSS, O/490–1.
118   R. Peel, *Tamworth Election: speech of Sir Robert Peel, June 28, 1841* (London: John Ollivier, 1841), p. 12.

supply, based on a multiple of gold reserves after a fiduciary allowance.[119] This currency arrangement was implemented under the Bank Charter Act of 1844. Wood was chairman and Peel a member of the Parliamentary committee which had in 1840 proposed such legislation, with the assumption it would stabilise and lower prices.[120] The resulting legislation followed the theories of the Currency School, which were based on the principle that the excessive issue of banknotes caused price inflation and that their circulation should be restricted by making the Bank of England hold a proportion of the equivalent of the notes issued in gold, to maintain convertibility and the value of the pound.[121] The Irish Banking Act of 1845 extended this requirement to Ireland, but with very manageable limitations. When these pieces of legislation came under attack in 1847, Peel redrafted Wood's Treasury letter for him in defence of the policy.[122] The second point of agreement was on free trade, or more accurately, lower tariffs. That policy encouraged the flow of capital abroad partly as payment but also to earn high rates of short-term interest as bills of exchange that were used as credit for exporting goods, repaid when they were sold.[123] Free capital flows had been allowed with the establishment of convertibility according to Peel's recommendations in 1819–21, but free trade gave additional impetus for flows to actually occur. Gash and Haines have described how Peel worked closely with Wood in fending off protectionist attacks after 1846 and repealing the Navigation Acts in 1849.[124] Wood passed Peel the necessary information and Peel made the speeches to further this agenda in Parliament.[125] Lastly, control of interest rates and a balanced budget was necessary to keep the cost of servicing the national debt, which stood at nearly 140% of GDP in 1845, affordable.[126]

Given Peel and Wood's close agreement and co-operation on economic matters, it therefore should not come as a surprise that when the Whigs, led by Russell, took over government from 30 June 1846, they initially continued the

119   Peel to Wood, 9 May 1844, B.L., Peel papers, Add. MS. 40544, f. 117, cited in Moore, *Sir Charles Wood's Indian Policy 1853–66*, p. 5.

120   *Report from Select Committee on Banks of Issue; with the minutes of evidence, appendix, and index*, PP 1840 (602) IV.1, prices, pp. 258–60, Peel's questioning of Overstone (leader of Currency School), p. 251.

121   Currency School: as based on the writings of Ricardo in *Plan for the Establishment of a National Bank* (London: John Murray, 1824); appendix to *The high price of Bullion* (London: John Murray, 1811), pp. 101–28l; and *Proposals for an Economical and Secure Currency* (London: John Murray, 1816); D. P. O'Brien, *Foundations of Monetary Economics*, vol. 4: *The Currency School* (London: Routledge, 1994).

122   Gash, *Robert Peel: The Life of Sir Robert Peel after 1830*, pp. 628–29.

123   Moore, *Sir Charles Wood's Indian Policy 1853–66*, pp. 5–6.

124   Gash, *Robert Peel: The Life of Sir Robert Peel after 1830*, pp. 634–35; Haines, *Charles Trevelyan and the Great Irish Famine*, p. 213.

125   For example, Wood to Peel, 19 June 1849, B.L., Peel papers, Add. MS. 40601, f. 281.

126   B. R. Mitchell, *British Historical Statistics* (Cambridge: CUP, 1988), pp. 575–93.

majority of Peel's financial and local relief policies. Casual assertions, like those by Norbert Götz, Georgina Brewis and Steffen Werther recently that 'the new Whig government was unwilling to interfere with the almost complete failure of the potato crop', are substantial misinterpretations of the Russell government's policies in its first year in office.[127] After an initial uncertainty in which relief efforts were suspended on 7 August 1846 by a Treasury minute to ensure there were enough available workers to collect the harvest in, within weeks the government reverted to Peel's policies when the almost complete failure of the potato crop became clear. Under another Treasury minute dated 31 August 1846, the public works were restarted, as was Peel's policy of providing Indian corn at near market rates via food depots.[128] Wood told Bessborough that to change policy would be 'too dangerous' at that time.[129] Russell praised Peel's famine measures in the House of Commons and proposed to continue Peel's programme of works.[130] Wood did announce the purchase of corn would be discontinued because private merchants could now take over, leading the *Freeman's Journal* to complain bitterly of a 'no importations' policy.[131] However, this was simply window-dressing for Whig supporters in commerce: in reality, as Wood admitted in January 1847, the government had continued to discreetly import food in late 1846 in spite of his previous statements to the contrary.[132] Secret imports of Indian corn were arranged by Barings Bank on behalf of the government until Trevelyan changed over to Eric Ericksen, another broker, on 28 August 1846, the main motive being to save money on broker fees to spend more on corn rather than any underlying ideological change. The operation then continued until July 1848.[133] Although deliveries were made to the Commissary General, the supplies were for relief, not just military use.[134]

When it became clear that the potato blight had destroyed at least 80% of the 1846 crop and was going to make the famine crisis worse, the new government felt that they should put the relief effort on a permanent legal footing. However, worries over the effectiveness and cost of Peel's policies

127 N. Götz, G. Brewis, S. Werther, *Humanitarianism in the Modern World: The Moral Economy of Famine Relief* (Cambridge: CUP, 2020), p. 149.
128 C. E. Trevelyan, *The Irish Crisis* (London: Longman, 1848), p. 51.
129 Wood to Bessborough, 16 September 1846, C.U.L., Hickleton Papers, MS MF A4.99, reel 1509.
130 *Hansard*, LXXXVIII, 17 August 1846, c. 770.
131 Idem., 27 July 1846, cc. 29–32.
132 *Hansard*, LXXXIX, 21 January 1847, cc. 224–32.
133 Generally, documents are contained in ING Baring Archives, HC3.16 and HC3.75, Trevelyan papers, Ericksen files, in N.A., Treasury papers, T64/365A/1–3; Trevelyan to Barings, 8 July 1846, 27 August 1846, ING Baring Archives, HC3.75.
134 See the numerous correspondence confirming the situation in *Correspondence relating to the measures adopted for the relief of distress in Ireland from July 1846 to January 1847 (Commissariat Series)*, PP 1847 (761) LI.1.

soon emerged in government circles, thanks to the surging number of people employed on public works and the fiscal burden of doing so. In the week ending 3 October 1846 the total number of people employed was 20,135, but by the week ending 5 December 1846 it had increased to 321,066. Expenditure in the week ending 19 December 1846 was running at £158,890 16s 4d per week, which if sustained for an entire year would have cost over £8m.[135]

Yet, even as the numbers employed accelerated, it became clear that the large-scale public-works scheme was not achieving its aim of helping those most at risk. Those who had pawned their clothes to buy food, for example in Skibbereen, were unable to work in the cold weather.[136] There were continual arguments over the level of wages and the introduction of piecework to combat idleness. Relief officers were subject to threats and attacks, often by men with blackened faces in women's clothes.[137] Women and child workers and those such as fishermen unused to 'spade labour' were disadvantaged.[138] Groups without relatives able to perform manual work, including the infirm, the disabled, orphans and widows with young children, went uncatered for. Earnings in silver coin were difficult to spend, and the demand for silver put pressure on the Bank of Ireland.[139] Small holders were attracted away from their crops, threatening future food supplies, and a 20% reduction to the scheme was made early in 1847 to encourage labourers to return to agriculture to ensure the next season's crops were sown.[140]

Wood wrote to Russell on 7 October noting that there were complaints that some of the expenditure was being misused by proprietors: 'The scheme in principle is good, but it requires the very greatest care to guard it from abuse in the execution ...'.[141] The problem was that 'the Irish proprietors perverted the scheme into a mode of executing public works where they were not needed for the relief of distress. They are now perverting it into a mode of improving their own estates'.[142] Distrust was encouraged by letters of complaint to the British press that Irish landlords were exempt from the income tax that their equivalents on the island of Great Britain had to pay.[143]

Another growing worry was the fiscal hole these policies were opening in the government's accounts. Wood, quick to foresee problems, wrote to

---

135 Idem., pp. 116, 376, 412.
136 Parker to Larcom, 21 December 1846, idem., p. 431.
137 For example, idem., pp. 176, 187, 189, 190, 309.
138 *Commissioners of Public Works (Ireland), Reports on Measures for Relief of Distress, March–June 1847*, PP 1847 (838) XVII.589, p. 5.
139 *Correspondence relating to the measures*, PP 1847 (761) LI.1, pp. 154, 134, 263; F. G. Hall, *History of the Bank of Ireland* (Dublin, Hodges, Figgis & Co., 1949), pp. 218–19.
140 *Commissioners of Public Works*, PP 1847 (838) XVII.589, p. 4.
141 Wood to Russell, 7 October 1846, N.A., Russell papers, PRO 30/22/5D, ff. 105–10.
142 Ibid.
143 For example, letter from 'Euclid', *Morning Chronicle*, 26 October 1846, p. 5.

Russell, in October 1846, that although 'what we are doing now is easy enough, advancing money out of a full exchequer' – as Peel had been able to do during his government – the fiscal situation was rapidly deteriorating, and they could not continue such policies for much longer.[144] It was clear the government was facing two economic problems: a budget deficit and a trade deficit. The summer of 1846 had marked the end of the early-1840s boom and the start of a sharp downturn in the business cycle. The failure of the potato and wheat crops across Europe had pushed up the cost of Britain's food imports, but the price of its manufactured exports had not increased. The simultaneous failure of the cotton crop in the United States and fall in demand from Europe for textile imports reduced Britain's trade balance and ability to pay for food imports. Falling tax revenues were exacerbated by the revenue lost from Peel's repeal of the Corn Laws earlier that year. All these factors made the level of expenditure the Peel government had committed to before 1846 unsustainable, as there was no longer a budget surplus to fund them. Wood sought to persuade Russell that they needed to 'retrace their steps' on Irish relief, quoting Peel, who had admitted 'the danger of the course [of famine relief policy] he had adopted' in 1845–46; if the Whigs persisted in it, with declining tax revenues, the consequences could be 'most serious'.[145]

This greatly disturbed Russell. Shortly afterwards, Russell's election agent reported to F. Baring that Russell was 'rather apprehensive of being brought into financial difficulties' in Ireland 'by Labouchere's and L. B.'s [Lord Bessborough's] compassion for the Irish'.[146] After a cabinet in early November 1846, the Third Earl Grey noted in his diary 'the Irish govt. insisted on going beyond what was sanctioned' in providing relief.[147] He had been contacted by Wood for support in curbing expenditure in the Cabinet meeting because 'John [Russell] was disposed to yield to them', but he did not attend the meeting.[148] Afterwards, Russell accused Bessborough of undertaking relief efforts with such enthusiasm that it appeared he was trying to court popularity in Ireland by means of them.[149] Bessborough complained in reply that he was 'bothered to death' by agriculturalists and landlords trying to get him to 'employ their able-bodied labourers at the expense of the Counties'.[150] Clarendon, then the

144   Wood to Russell, 14 October 1846, N.A., Russell papers, PRO 30/22/5D, ff. 191–94.
145   Ibid.
146   Le Marchant to Baring, 18 October 1846, C.U.L., Hickleton papers, MS MF A4.54 reel 1490.
147   Earl Grey diary, 6 November 1846, D.U.L., Earl Grey papers, GRE/V/C3/13, p. 34.
148   Ibid.
149   Russell to Bessborough, 13 November 1846, N.A., Russell papers, PRO 30/22/5E, ff. 88–89.
150   Bessborough to Russell, 14 November 1846, N.A., Russell papers, PRO 30/22/5E, ff. 106–08.

President of the Board of Trade, wrote to Wood saying he should make public 'the check upon expenditure' in case the level of relief spending should damage financial confidence in the Treasury.[151] The Cabinet in mid-December refused to sanction the Board of Works employing people without the agreement of the Irish Government in an attempt to curb expenditure.[152] Spending was not just under pressure in Ireland: public works in the colonies were reduced, and two regiments were to be withdrawn from Canada to save money.[153]

On the ground in Ireland, the beginning of 1847 saw the worst effects of the famine since its start. The reduced potato harvest from 1846 ran out in the majority of areas from the beginning of January 1847, and prices at their peak rose to between three and five times those in January to March 1846.[154] Wheat and Indian corn prices continued their rise from November 1846 through into 1847.[155] As Ó Gráda has described, all the horrors of widespread famine, including death and disease, began to show themselves from January, starting with the worst areas such as Skibbereen.[156] The number employed on public works did not stop increasing and was to reach a high of 734,792 in the week ending 6 March 1847, despite some early efforts to substitute outdoor relief for public works.[157] In other words, nearly one in ten Irish residents were employed on public works; including their dependents, up to half the Irish population may have received some sort of support from the scheme.[158] Never before had the British government directly employed such a large share of the Irish population.

It was during the first weeks of 1847 that Wood, with the assistance of the Third Earl Grey, developed a revised policy for Ireland to maximise the efficiency and effectiveness of relief funds in view of the looming fiscal crisis in Britain and general dissatisfaction with the effectiveness of public works as a relief measure. Wood's policy was communicated to Peel via Sir John Young, in January 1847, as an attempt to establish political co-operation,

151 Clarendon to Wood, 25 November 1846, C.U.L., Hickleton Papers, MS MF A4.57, reel 1495.
152 Earl Grey diary, 16 December, D.U.L., Earl Grey papers, GRE/V/C3/13, p. 34.
153 Idem., 17 December 1846, p. 62.
154 Market reports in *Belfast Commercial Chronicle, Champion or Sligo News, Colerain Chronicle, The Constitution, Drogheda Argus and Leinster Journal, Dublin Gazette, Enniskillen Chronicle and Erne Packet, Fermanagh Mail, Freeman's Journal, Galway Vindicator and Connaught Advertiser, Kerry Evening Post, Kilkenny Journal, Limerick Reporter, Londonderry Sentinel, Londonderry Standard, Mayo Constitution, Meath Herald, Nenagh Guardian, Newry Commercial Telegraph, Telegraph or Connaught Ranger, Tipperary Constitution, Tipperary Free Press, Tralee Chronicle, Tyrawly Herald, Waterford Mail, Western Star.*
155 Ibid.
156 Ó Gráda, *Black '47 and Beyond*, pp. 39, 40, 52–56, 58.
157 *Commissioners of Public Works*, PP 1847 (838) XVII.589, p. 3.
158 Haines, *Charles Trevelyan and the Great Irish Famine*, p. 271.

ten days before Russell was due to state his plan for Ireland in the House of Commons. He proposed to continue advancing Treasury funds for drainage projects, the reclamation of waste lands, the development of fisheries and subsidising emigration.[159] The critical change was 'cessation of all employment on public works and substitution of gratuitous relief in the form of food by Relief Committees, to be nominated by the Lord-Lieutenant with the cost to be borne partly by the public, partly by the electoral District'.[160] This meant that instead of Treasury funds being spent directly on its own public-works scheme, they would henceforth be mainly used as grants and loans for enabling relief efforts by local-government bodies, with some of the costs reclaimed at a later date. The underlying idea was to ensure that the available funding was used in a way which would relieve as many people as possible, rather than to defer to a *laissez-faire* philosophy. It was intended that for every pound raised locally, a further two would be advanced by the Treasury, one of which had to be paid back; the relief effort would be one-third from local taxes, one-third repayable loan and one-third grant. It was realised that, in reality, 'not ... much of the money to be advanced will ever be recovered'.[161]

The plan aimed to resolve the many criticisms of public works and help Unions 'to effectively relieve their poor'. The adoption of outdoor relief proposed in Grey's plan offered direct assistance to the infirm, widows and orphans, who were not catered for by the public works, and was to be extended to every destitute person.[162] Trevelyan consulted with his relief officers immediately and concluded that it was 'sufficiently comprehensive to embrace the destitute of every class'.[163] The arrangement was intended 'to be the foundation of a permanent measure on the same principle'.[164] It was believed that local management of relief and public works, as well as the realisation among ratepayers that they would eventually have to pay some of the Treasury advances

159   Young to Peel, 16 January 1847, B.L., Peel papers, Add. MS. 40598, ff. 38–42; John Young (Lord Lisgar) had been one of Peel's Parliamentary Secretaries to the Treasury (i.e., whips).
160   Ibid.; Third Earl Grey, Paper on Relief for Ireland (which contains the policy adopted), 13 January 1847, D.U.L., Earl Grey papers, GRE/B155/19, pp. 8–11.
161   Third Earl Grey, Paper on Relief for Ireland (which contains the policy adopted), 13 January 1847, D.U.L., Earl Grey papers, GRE/B155/19, pp. 15–16; Grey noted that 'the system ... of employment seems practically to have failed': idem., p. 1; Grey's policy paper accorded with the adopted government policy: Grey's diary entry 2 February 1847, Diary 31 July 1846 to 2 December 1847, D.U.L., Grey papers, GRE/ V/C3/13, pp. 72–73; for Wood's related speech see: *Hansard*, LXXXIX, 1 February 1847, cc. 675–90.
162   Third Earl Grey, Paper on Relief for Ireland, 13 January 1847, D.U.L., Earl Grey papers, GRE/B155/19, pp. 8–9; Haines, *Charles Trevelyan and the Great Irish Famine*, p. 275.
163   Trevelyan to Jones, Routh, 14 January 1847, O.B.L., Trevelyan letter books, vol. 11, pp. 125–30, cited in Haines, *Charles Trevelyan and the Great Irish Famine*, p. 275.
164   Ibid.

back, would provide better oversight than Treasury officials could that the
money was being spent wisely on the ground. Charging Irish landlords for some
of the costs was intended to increase the amount of money available for relief, as
well as forestall criticism that Irish landlords, who did not pay the income tax,
were being subsidised by British taxpayers. The government clearly intended
the new scheme to be an expansion of Peel's policies, but in a way which was
more fiscally and politically sustainable than they had been.

On 25 January 1847 Russell cleared the way in the House of Commons for
Wood's budget in February, that would finance these measures, by explicitly
stating that he did not blame the ordinary Irish for the crisis: 'I do not think,
therefore, that either the fertility of the land or the strength and industry of
the inhabitants are at fault'.[165] Government funding for relief efforts would
continue, but through local Relief Committees and the Poor Law system, rather
than by means of public works organised by the Treasury.

> I must always recollect that those sums [for relief] are not to be granted by
> Government or Parliament without the most serious consideration; that these
> are sums derived from payments by the people of this country; from the taxes
> which they pay on their soap, their sugar, their tea, their coffee. It is that which
> forms the surplus by which we are able to come to the assistance of Ireland …
> The fact is, that the system of task-work is no longer beneficial employment
> to many; their bodily strength is gone, and their spirits depressed, they have
> not power to exert themselves sufficiently to earn the ordinary day's wages;
> this necessary outlay will be stigmatized as a wasteful expenditure, and the
> works will be left incomplete … Relief Associations will be empowered to
> receive subscriptions, levy rates, and receive donations from the Government;
> that by means of these they should purchase food, and establish soup kitchens
> in the different districts; … [so that] labouring men should be allowed to work
> on their own plots of ground.[166]

Russell hoped that the government's revised policy would help the Irish poor
by maximising the amount spent on them – much of the money spent on public
works had ended up paying surveyors' fees and the like. The new policy was also
intended to reduce the crippling physical toll on famished labourers working
on the public-works programmes. Even so, the cost to the Treasury of the new
policy in meeting Ireland's continuing needs for relief remained enormous, as
Wood himself admitted. The important point to note, though, was that this set
of reforms, as set out before the financial crises of 1847, was part of an attempt
to raise and put the necessary money to use. In his February 1847 budget Wood
revealed his intention to take out an Irish loan worth £8m – much more than
the £5m the Treasury had hitherto spent on Irish relief since the appearance

165   *Hansard*, LXXXIX, 25 January 1847, c. 452.
166   Idem., cc. 426–79.

of the blight in 1845 – to pay for the advances, and privately had plans to raise another loan for Ireland worth £5m–£6m later in the 1847/48 financial year.[167] As the next chapter explains in detail, this was the crucial announcement that triggered a financial panic in the spring of 1847 and which caused the course of Irish relief policy to change dramatically, removing Treasury support from the new arrangements.

167   *Hansard*, XC, 22 February 1847, c. 329.

4

Famine relief during and after the crises

It has pleased Providence to afflict not only this country, but the greater part of the rest of Europe, with scarcity and dearth, which have pressed with peculiar severity on that part of the United Kingdom which, from its poverty, is least able to bear it. Thousands of suffering and famishing people, chiefly in Ireland, claim from us sympathy and assistance, which I am confident will not be withheld from them. If I were only to refer to the past and the present state of the finances of the country, I should certainly say, that there never was a time when the finances of the country were so well able to bear the demands which are now about to be made upon them.

> Sir Charles Wood (chancellor of the exchequer),
> debate on the February 1847 Budget.[1]

I have no money & therefore I cannot give it. The Revenue is at last as we have been expecting, falling off very much. According to the last account ending August 7th, the revenue from April 5 to August 7 is £850,000 less than last year – the expenditure £2,000,000 more. You may guess from these figures in what state my Exchequer is. The unused balance of the loan carries me over the October quarter and a paltry plight I shall then be in. Therefore, assistance to Ireland means only a further loan and in the present state of the money market and depression in all our manufacturing towns, this is out of the question. Ireland must keep herself somehow or other. This, at least, is certain: the public funds of this country will not. I plead guilty to being very hard hearted.

> Wood to Lord Clarendon (lord-lieutenant of Ireland), 15 August 1847.[2]

When last year we were much pressed to adopt measures for emigration, I objected to any such attempt on the ground that no measures of this kind could be adopted which would not involve a considerable outlay of capital in the first instance ... at that time it cannot be forgotten there was an obvious deficiency of disposable capital in the country and that it would have been

---

1   *Hansard*, XC, 22 February 1847, c. 317.
2   Wood to Clarendon, 15 August 1847, C.U.L., Hickleton papers, MS MF A4.186, reel 1523.

Figure 4.1. Little Jack Horner. Lord John Russell is shown as overconfident that the £8m Irish loan will be a success. *Punch*, 3 July 1847, p. 271.

impossible for the Government to have gone into the market to borrow money
for any such purpose as that now adverted to without still further aggravating
this deficiency, and increasing the severe pressure then bearing upon the trade
of the country.

> Third Earl Grey (war and colonial secretary),
> memorandum to Cabinet, 14 April 1848.[3]

Sir James Graham (Sir Robert Peel's home secretary) had predicted in April
1846 that if the famine continued beyond the end of the year, then given the
Irish landowners' continuing exemption from income tax, 'charging the Land
of Ireland with the maintenance of the Poor of Ireland will become inevitable'.[4]
When that situation became reality in early 1847, Lord John Russell and Charles
Wood attempted to avoid charging the land of Ireland upfront with the entire
cost of relief, either through local rates or the income-tax system, by raising
Treasury loans from the London money markets to fund grants and repayable
advances for Irish relief efforts (Figure 4.1).

At this point, they almost certainly did not realise that this was as risky a
strategy as it turned out to be thanks to Peel's banking reforms and macroeconomic policy. Many in the City of London were already nervous of loans raised
that increased expenditure outside of Great Britain. The loan to fund compensation for slave owners in the 1830s, many believed, had caused bullion drains.
Henry Burgess, editor of the influential *Circular to Bankers*, had criticised
the British government for taking out 'the West-Indies' loan of £15m (to
compensate slave owners affected by the abolition of slavery in Britain's directly
held colonies in October 1833) as it had drained the Bank's resources because
much of the money was invested abroad by its recipients.[5] The government
also stood accused of encouraging the Bank of England to make foreign investments including 'the transmission of British capital to the United States', a
habit that carried on into the 1840s.[6] The 1837 crisis had arisen apparently,
as predicted by Burgess, as a 'manifestation of [American] pecuniary power'.[7]

There was controversy about whether Peel's Bank Charter Act of 1844 made
Britain still more vulnerable to such drains because the legislation forced the
Bank of England to contract credit whenever there were bullion outflows. As
introduced in Chapter 1, the Currency School thought that external drains
were connected with trade, but the bullion would return because of David
Hume's price-specie flow mechanism. The Banking School agreed that this

3   Third Earl Grey, memorandum to Cabinet, 14 April 1848, D.U.L., Earl Grey papers,
GRE/B144/20.
4   Graham to Heytesbury, 25 April 1846, B.L., Graham papers, Add. MS. 79611, 21.
5   *Circular to Bankers*, 3 February 1837, p. 236.
6   Idem., 3 February 1837, p. 234.
7   Idem., 1 January 1836, p. 188.

might happen with trade but countered that external investment flows could cause bullion to leave permanently unless interest rates were raised. After the 1850s, the Currency School came to agree that raising interest rates would attract bullion as well, but on the basis of the 'price' of capital.[8] Internal bullion drains, where the gold remained within the country, could occur when specie or bullion was needed for transactions, or where the bullion was taken out of the financial system and hoarded, particularly when investors anticipated a banking crisis or the suspension of the gold standard.

All these various bullion drains took place during 1847, but the examples with the most serious consequences that this chapter will emphasise are the drains in April and October.[9] The internal April drain was caused by the first Irish loan of £8m, announced in February 1847, and the actions the government subsequently took to restore financial confidence in London hampered the government's efforts to fund the relief effort in Ireland upfront. The external drain to America in October caused interest rates to rise significantly, led to considerable panic, and ensured that no further loans were attempted. Although the Irish loan was not the only cause of the crises of 1847, it was far bigger than the proverbial straw that broke the camel's back. David Morier Evans, a financial journalist working for *The Times*, wrote up the 1847 crisis in terms of the background influences of a strong demand for funding for the construction of railways and the need for the large importations of food. However, significantly, he recorded the general opinion that the market was coping with these demands 'until it was ascertained … the necessities of Ireland through the failure of the potato crop would have to be satisfied by the national treasury' and 'the negotiation of a loan [seemed] a matter of extreme probability'.[10]

---

8   D. P. O'Brien, *The Correspondence of Lord Overstone* (Cambridge: CUP, 1971), vol. 2, p. 626. Lord Overstone, in 1856, wrote a paper on the Bank Charter Act of 1844 for George Cornewall Lewis, the chancellor, claiming that, despite wars, there was enough bullion to 'effectually suppress … all alarm and anxiety', but writing in private to Gladstone, in 1855, he had been alarmed at the bullion flows: 'our Gold is all going to the Mediterranean, and our Silver to India and China – if nothing remains – What then?' In a January 1857 draft letter to *The Times* (as Mercator), he wrote 'When all the civilised world is competing for capital no country can retain its due proportion which will not consent to pay the necessary price in the form of a high rate of interest. When peculiar causes create a general and severe demand for the precious metals, the country which will not consent to bear her proportionate share of the pressure, must consent to yield to other countries in which there is more firmness and more regard to principle, those precious metals, and to abandon that metallic standard which she has neither the virtue nor the resolution to maintain': O'Brien, *The Correspondence of Lord Overstone*, vol. 2, pp. 667–74, 626; Lord Overstone, *Tracts and Other Publications on Metallic and Paper Currency* [1857], ed. J. R. McCulloch (London: published privately by Lord Overstone, 1857), pp. 355–57.
9   See Wood's classification of crises, Wood to F. Baring, 3 November 1847, C.U.L., Hickleton papers, MS MF 54, reel 1490.
10   D. M. Evans, *The commercial crisis 1847–48: being facts and figures* (London: Letts, 1849), p. 55.

This chapter will explain the relationship between these bullion drains, the financial crises they caused, and the catastrophic impact they had on the government's new relief policies for Ireland. The chapter starts by exploring why Peel's banking and wider economic reforms had made Britain's financial system more susceptible to bullion drains and crises. It will then go on to show how the government's new plans for Ireland were derailed by the first Irish loan crisis, and how the commercial crisis in the autumn of 1847 dissuaded the government from attempting any more loans. Further, it will be shown that other means of providing funding for relief, such as limiting the convertibility of notes to reduce outflows of bullion and the consequent limiting of credit facilities, or the raising of income tax, were not possible because the Russell government lacked the Parliamentary strength to get the necessary legislation through Parliament. The resulting drop in spending by the Treasury on Irish relief after 1847 caused high rates of excess mortality to persist in Ireland for many more years than was inevitable.[11]

Peel's economic-policy reforms and the crises of 1847

Peel and Wood did not realise two important points about the economic-policy reforms of the 1840s. First, the Bank Charter Act they did so much to construct and defend produced a very unstable gold standard vulnerable to bullion drains that needed to be restrained with interest-rate rises. As the Bank of England was a profit-making institution, the legislation gave it an incentive to keep its interest rates as low as possible in order to gain market share in the discount market, as well as an incentive to hold its reserves in interest-paying assets rather than in gold.[12] The result of this – its relatively low level of bullion reserves – meant that sterling was especially vulnerable to international bullion flows and external interest-rate shocks.[13] In addition, the rules about the bullion that backed its banknotes allowed bullion deposited by clients of the commercial arm to be counted against notes in the Issue Department, as well as bullion owned by the Bank. If this had not been the case, only note-holders could have withdrawn bullion. As it was, bullion could be withdrawn by depositors at will, forcing a decrease in note circulation, yet the published tables in the *London Gazette* disguised the situation. As Bonamy Price, an economist, pointed out in 1876 (at which time the arrangement was still news to most of the public):

---

11   See Chart 4.6; *Correspondence...*, PP 1846 (735) XXXVII.41; *Public income and expenditure ...*, PP 1851 (62) XXXI.159; *Public income and expenditure ...*, PP 1861 (402) XXXIV.139.
12   B. Bernanke, H. James, 'The Gold Standard, Deflation and Financial Crisis', in R. G. Hubbard (ed.), *Financial Markets and Financial Crises* (Chicago: University of Chicago Press, 1991), 33–68, at p. 38.
13   Ibid.; the Bank of England only managed to find a way to manage this low level of reserves successfully later in the nineteenth century with the help of Banking School policies.

it is a great misfortune that the framers of the Act of 1844 should have made the exceedingly unintelligent blunder of mixing up together in the weekly reports of the bullion at the Bank, two absolutely dissimilar and distinct things – the gold stored away by one office to face the banknotes, and the gold belonging to the Bank of England as a banker.[14]

The Bank Charter Act of 1844 also had many contemporary critics. The legislation particularly came under attack from the Banking School. Typical of their views were those of Thomas Birkbeck, who represented the Country Bankers at the Enquiry into Commercial Distress, where he stated that 'the Act of 1844 … has no effect on monetary pressure, it destroys confidence at a time of pressure coming on … and there is a want of confidence some time after'.[15] In the year the Act was passed, Thomas Tooke, one of the main theorists of the Banking School, described 'regulating the country circulation by the foreign exchanges', in other words limiting the circulation according to the bullion in the reserve, as being utterly impracticable.[16] At the 1840 Enquiry into Banks of Issue Tooke had given an irritable outburst that he doubted that the quantity of circulation 'operate[d] upon prices at all' according to the views of the 'partisans of the currency theory'.[17]

John Fullarton, a Scottish surgeon and banker, attempted to mitigate this disagreement by pointing out that a direct relationship between quantity of money and commodity prices only operated in a closed system. In an open system, with a high level of international trade and cross-border investment flows, as Britain had in the 1840s, other factors would come into play. He took 'the case of a nation having no commercial intercourse with its neighbours' and a circulation 'which preserves a high rate of exchangeable value merely by the limitation of its amount' and compared it with a highly open economy in terms of trade and capital flows.[18] He concluded that the quantity of circulation effect on prices would be easy to see in the former but not in the latter, because to 'add permanently to the note circulation of the country' in the open economy, it would be necessary to spread the effect 'throughout the world'. However, 'the prices of all commodities, estimated in banknotes, would after a time, infallibly rise'.[19] Tooke later explained international bullion movements, in addition to trade payments, as investment flows resulting from interest-rate

---

14   B. Price, *Currency and Banking* (New York: Appleton, 1876), p. 66. The situation probably confused Neville Ward-Perkins.

15   *First Report from the Secret Committee of the House of Commons on Commercial Distress*, PP 1847–48 (395) VIII Pt.I.1, p. 479.

16   T. Tooke, *An Inquiry into the currency principle* (London: Longmans, 1844), p. 43.

17   *Select Committee on Banks of Issue*, PP 1840 (602) IV.1, p. 298; J. Fullarton, *On the Regulation of Currencies* (London: John Murray, 1844), p. 58.

18   Fullarton, *On the Regulation of Currencies*, pp. 60–62.

19   Idem., p. 58.

differentials between countries: 'securities of the country where high rates of interest prevail, fall, in effect, into the category of its exports, and the remittances received for payment of these exports tend to equalise the supply of capital'.[20] This suggested that when interest rates equalised, investment flows would suddenly stop and a financial crisis might occur as credit came under pressure in the country that had been previously the subject of investment. In turn losses might occur in the investor country.

The reaction of Peel and Wood was to deny any link between the Bank Charter Act of 1844 and the crises of 1847. Wood strongly supported the Currency School.[21] After the first crisis of 1847 he declared to the House of Commons that, 'the present state of the money market is owing, not to the operation of that [1844 Bank Charter] Act, but to a neglect of the sound principles on which that Act was framed', blaming excessive note issue by country banks.[22] Wood believed that the principles of the Currency School had not been sufficiently included in the Bank Charter Act of 1844 and this was the problem behind the bullion drains. In May 1847 he told Francis Baring, the previous Whig chancellor of the exchequer and a member of the Baring banking family, that he would have preferred 'a national issue', in other words just a single one, without any country and Irish and Scottish banknotes still in circulation, so that the question of bullion drains 'would not have arisen for the notes out would have corresponded with the bullion in'.[23]

The second point which Peel and Wood could not have realised was that, according to the modern economic theory of the macroeconomic-policy trilemma, their three policies of free capital flows, a gold standard, and low interest rates would prove impossible to maintain while financing Irish relief with a loan. In the 1960s Robert Mundell and Marcus Fleming showed that it was only possible for governments to follow at one time two of the three following policy objectives when central bank reserves are low: fixed-exchange rates, free capital and trade flows, and an independent monetary policy, which would include control of interest rates (Figure 4.2).[24] Peel and Wood did not know this, and so as it turned out, when a series of structural shocks hit the British and Irish economies in 1846–47, the attempt to pursue all three policies at once resulted in a loss of control of interest rates and an adverse impact on credit.

20   T. Tooke, *History of Prices*, vol. 5 (London: Longman, 1857), pt. II, p. 314.
21   Wood to Russell, 14 April 1847, N.A., Russell papers, PRO 30/22/6C, ff. 80–86.
22   *Hansard*, XCII, 30 April 1847, c. 213.
23   Wood to F. Baring, 12 May 1847, C.U.L., Hickleton papers, MS MF A4.54, reel 1490 (original underline).
24   R. A. Mundell, *International Economics* (New York: Macmillan, 1968); J. M. Fleming, 'Domestic Financial Policies under Fixed and under Floating Exchange Rates', *IMF Staff Papers*, 9 (1962), 369–79.

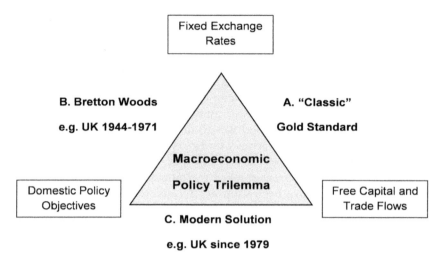

Figure 4.2. Diagram of the 'trilemma'. Solutions A, B and C control only their two adjacent economic-policy objectives.

The trilemma has a theoretical basis in Mundell's model, which considers the extreme policies of perfect capital mobility and fixed-exchange rates. Fleming took into account that in reality adherence to these conditions was partial, but the implications were similar. The model is a short-term one and assumes that reaching equilibrium between countries mainly takes place quickly through interest rates rather than prices. If local interest rates move away from the world rate – for instance by alteration of the central bank's base rate – unrestricted arbitrage by capital holders under the gold standard will drain the central bank of its reserves until it can no longer honour the pre-existing parity. As Maurice Obstfeld, Jay Shambaugh and Alan Taylor have shown with data from 1870 to the present, for 16 countries, this trade-off can be seen clearly in practice for a period of at least 130 years.[25]

Some monetarist economists are reluctant to accept the model and inappropriately apply modern concepts, such as real interest rates, to the gold standard of the nineteenth century. However, nominal interest rates were then the generally accepted measure, as inflation was so low. As Milton Friedman, the intellectual father of monetarism explained: 'In the major Western countries, the link to gold and the resultant long-term predictability of the price level meant that, until some time after the Second World War, interest rates behaved as if prices were expected to be stable and both inflation and deflation were unanticipated'.[26] In addition, investors causing capital flows look at the comparative returns of countries from a single country. Therefore, comparative prices are not an issue because value is judged in one country only.

Some confirmation of the trilemma effect in 1847 can be shown in the context of trade with the United States by comparing British and American interest rates. It is an assumption of the Mundell-Fleming theory that interest-rate parity is in effect and is able to move interest rates together.[27] In other words, that, with sufficient capital transfer between countries, the returns on investment in both countries will equalise over time. When the exchange rate is fixed this means interest rates will equalise apart from any anticipation of rate changes and transaction costs. If a gold standard is strong enough, no exchange-rate changes will be anticipated and interest rates will become virtually the same in both countries. Before 1847 there was not sufficient arbitrage for the short-term interest rates to move together, except briefly after the tariff reductions in 1846. Rates were influenced more by domestic money markets. From the beginning of 1847 the trilemma policies were implemented in a severe manner. The Whigs' Corn Importation Act of 26 January 1847 suspended all duties on corn completely from then until 1 September 1847, later extended to 1 March 1848, increasing bullion flows.[28] Trade was effectively restricted to payment with specie by the Bank Charter Act of 1844 in Britain and Independent Treasury Act of August 1846 in America (intended to provide financial stability as Mexican war loans were raised). Moreover, during the first three quarters of 1847 the dollar–pound exchange rate remained stable for most of the period, varying significantly from its official parity of 1:4.8665 only very rarely.[29]

Chart 4.1 shows that interest-rate equalisation can be seen between May and October 1847. Free and significant flows in capital, together with a gold standard, meant nominal interest rates came together by arbitrage against British attempts to control them, a powerful trilemma effect. British gold had flowed to France initially and America by the discounting of American bills in Britain.[30] Now the movement of capital to the United States suddenly faltered

26   M. Friedman, 'Quantity Theory of Money', in *The New Palgrave Dictionary of Economics*, 6 (London: Palgrave Macmillan, 2008), 793–815.

27   For further explanation, see the Nobel Prize Press Release on Robert Mundell, 13 October 1999 where the phenomenon is referred to as a special case. It reoccurs in 1855–58, alongside the next banking crisis, and in 1866. See Royal Swedish Academy of Sciences, 'Press Release: The Bank of Sweden Prize in Economic Sciences in Memory of Alfred Nobel, 1999, to Professor Robert A. Mundell', 13 October 1999, online at <http://www.nobelprize.org/nobel_prizes/economic-sciences/laureates/1999/press.html> [accessed 4 April 2016].

28   & 11 Vict. c.1.

29   L. H. Officer, *Between the Dollar-Sterling Gold Points: Exchange Rates, Parity and Market Behaviour* (Cambridge: CUP, 1996), p. 88.

30   *First Report from the Secret Committee of the House of Commons on Commercial Distress*, PP 1847–48 (395) VIII Pt. I.1, p.74.

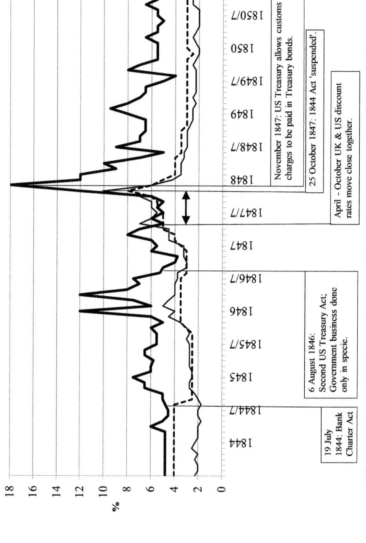

Chart 4.1. United Kingdom and United States monthly discount rates (%). The period of equalised rates is shown by the horizontal double headed arrow and coincides with the temporary reduction of the corn tariff to nil by the Corn Importation Act 1847 and trade being paid for principally in specie. *Sources:* United Kingdom: *Report from the Select Committee on bank acts*, PP 1857 (220) (220–1) X, pt. I, pt. II.1, pp. 463–64; *Burdett's Official Intelligence* (1894), p. 1771. United States: *New York Daily Tribune*, 'Commercial and Money Matters' column, author's dataset.

Within the chart:

19 July 1844: Bank Charter Act

6 August 1846: Second US Treasury Act; Government business done only in specie.

November 1847: US Treasury allows customs charges to be paid in Treasury bonds.

25 October 1847: 1844 Act 'suspended'.

April – October UK & US discount rates move close together.

Discount rate: —— UK free market   - - - UK official Bank Rate   —— US free market

due to the reversal of investment flows causing a sudden, but temporary drop in the $/£ exchange rate. The *Mississippi Free Trader* reported a local flash crash of the dollar against gold of up to 50% and that the banks would only accept payment in specie.[31] The practical reason why rates came together was an attempt to prevent net outflows of bullion. Britain had to raise its rates to prevent bullion outflows to America, or at least that was how the Banking School saw it. The Currency School also criticised the Bank for not raising its minimum discount rate quickly enough.[32]

The trilemma helps to explain the convergence of British and American interest rates during the two crises of 1847. The Bank of England was forced to raise interest rates significantly in May and October 1847 alongside worries about falling bullion reserves before each crisis. After October British rates fell when Russell and Wood wrote a letter to the Bank of England allowing the temporary suspension of the Bank Charter Act, but confirming that the government continued support for the gold standard.[33] The relaxation of the gold standard in the United States and the decision to accept payment of taxes using Treasury bonds again allowed the countries' interest rates to move apart as means of exchange other than bullion came back into use.[34]

The Irish loan and the first financial panic of 1847

Of the 'two major crises' of April and October that Rudi Dornbusch and Jacob Frenkel identified, the October one was most serious. Nevertheless, the April one was still a serious banking shock and commercial crisis.[35] By following events closely, it can be shown that the government initiated the April crisis as a result of the announcement of the Irish loan, which provoked a bullion drain. The two crises of spring and autumn convinced policymakers that further financial panics would be sparked by the continued provision of Irish relief from Treasury funds using loans. Worse still, the circumstances in April suggested that the Irish loan could not be expended quickly without causing a worse financial panic. The background to these events was a fiscal squeeze caused

31   *Mississippi Free Trader*, 22 June 1847, p. 2; general measures of Anglo-American exchange rates based on bills show sharp fluctuations in this period: L. E. Davis, J. R. T. Hughes, 'A Dollar-Sterling Exchange, 1803–1895', *Economic History Review*, 13:1 (1960), 52–78, at pp. 73, 79.

32   For example, Wood: *Hansard*, XCV, 30 November 1847, c. 383.

33   Russell and Wood to Morris and Prescott, 25 October 1847, in Evans, *The commercial crisis*, p. 87.

34   'Commercial and Money Matters', *New York Daily Tribune*, 13 November 1847, p. 3.

35   R. Dornbusch, J. A. Frenkel, 'The Gold Standard and the Bank of England in the Crisis of 1847', in M. D. Bordo, A. J. Schwartz (eds.), *A Retrospective on the Classical Gold Standard 1821–1931* (Chicago: University of Chicago Press, 1984), 233–76, at p. 236.

by a downturn in the business cycle, an adverse balance of payments due to large grain imports and a shortage of credit due to demands made by largely uncontrolled railway investment.

In the 1847 budget Wood decided to raise large loans to fund the government's new policy for Irish relief for two reasons. First, a downturn in Britain meant there was no longer a budget surplus to fund Irish expenditure, in the same way as Peel had financed his relief policies in the last year of his government. Second, there did not appear to be enough support in Parliament from the Whigs' Parliamentary allies – particularly the Peelites – for raising the income tax to pay for it instead of raising loans. This could have been done by increasing the rate charged on incomes in Great Britain and/or abolishing Ireland's exemption from the income tax. Without support from the Repealers or Irish Whig backbenchers – who furiously opposed any move that could have led to the Irish exemption being abolished – in theory the government could have got its way with Peelite support. However, that was not forthcoming. At the start of 1847 Peel rejected Wood and Edward Ellice's suggestion of funding Irish relief with an increased income tax in the budget of February that year, recommending that the government should raise loans instead and wait until the tax came up for renewal in 1848. As Russell later noted in May 1847, after the Irish loan crisis of March and April had triggered a financial panic, Peel's 'advice ... to raise a loan has turned out unfortunately'.[36] Douglas Kanter has explained that the Whig government (and the Peelites as well) thought that imposing an income tax on Ireland would cause a resurgence of Repeal enthusiasm. In addition, the rest of the United Kingdom would resist an increased income tax to pay for Irish relief because they saw Ireland's exemption as unfair.[37] The Parliamentary situation caused Wood to advise Russell against raising the income tax as late as August 1847, saying 'people won't stand for more than 5 per cent income tax', never mind the required 6 per cent.[38]

Therefore, under Peel's advice, Wood went ahead with loans instead.[39] Wood made public in clear terms his fears for the future due to the downturn in the business cycle in his budget speech of 22 February 1847: 'I should only be holding out delusive hopes if I were to say that we are entitled to expect a continuance of the present financial prosperity'.[40] Nonetheless, he also stated at the start of the budget that the government would make provision for the 'thousands of suffering and famishing people, chiefly in Ireland, claim from

36 Russell to Wood, 5 May 1847, C.U.L., Hickleton papers, MS MF A4.56, reel 1495.
37 D. Kanter, 'The Politics of Irish Taxation, 1842–53', *English Historical Review*, 127:528 (2012), 1121–55, at p. 1123.
38 Wood to Russell, 23 August 1847, N.A., Russell papers, PRO 30/22/6 E, ff. 199–202; Wood to Russell, 25 August 1847, N.A., Russell papers, PRO 30/22/6 E, ff. 211–14.
39 Russell to Wood, 5 May 1847, C.U.L., Hickleton papers, MS MF A4.56, reel 1495.
40 *Hansard*, XC, 22 February 1847, c. 318.

us sympathy and assistance, which I am confident will not be withheld from them'.[41] To fund the government's new relief policy, Wood intended to raise two government loans, together worth up to £14m, to fund advances for Ireland up to that value during the 1847–48 financial year. The first of these, worth £8m, was announced at the end of Wood's budget speech and became known as 'the Irish loan'.[42]

The loan was to be paid out in eight equal instalments between 9 April and 15 October 1847, which implied a significant amount of money coming onto the food market quite quickly.[43] Tenders were to be submitted by 1 March, and a large group of wealthy capitalists were invited to a meeting with Wood. In the event, the tenders of Baring Bros. and Co. and N. M. Rothschild and Sons were accepted as they were the only ones suitable. Their offers were at the level of 89.5% of 3% consols stock, whereas Irish stock had originally been offered.[44] The loan had to be issued in 3% consols at that discount to par (at an increased interest rate) stoking fears of a credit squeeze.[45]

While the initial relief reforms had been motivated by the need to maximise the impact of finite Treasury funds as the number of those requiring assistance soared, the sharp cut in funding at the beginning of May 1847 was the direct result of the financial panic caused by the raising of this loan. The April crisis of 1847 was characterised by falling consol prices and a drain of a quarter of the Bank of England's bullion reserves in six weeks; while deposits rose and note reserves fell, long- and short-term interest rates increased and credit became scarce. The Bank issued notes from its reserves, partially defeating the provisions of the 1844 Act, and raised the Bank Rate. The outcome was extensive commercial failure and a threat to the Bank and the Treasury, the fear of which crippled future funding for relief.

The announcement of the loan in the last week of February immediately sparked off a financial panic. 3% consols, a type of bond used as an indicator of long-term interest rates, and of which half the government's debts were composed, rose to a yield of almost 3.5% in April 1847 (Chart 4.2). This movement was significant because long-term rates are normally very stable. Senior members of the government quickly became aware of problems in the London money markets. The Third Earl Grey recorded in his diary that he visited Wood at home on 7 March 1847, less than one week after the loan was contracted, 'where I found the two Rothschilds very anxious something will be done after an increased demand for capital and fall in government

---

41 Idem., c. 317.
42 Idem. cc. 331–37; for details see *Bell's Life in London*, 28 February 1847, p. 8; also known as 'the Government loan'.
43 *The Era*, 28 February 1847, p.11.
44 *Yorkshire Advertiser*, 4 March 1847.
45 *Hansard*, XC, 1 March 1847, cc. 612–16, 614.

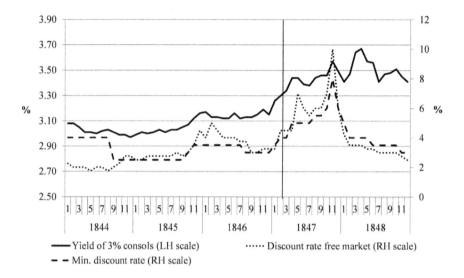

——Yield of 3% consols (LH scale)   ······ Discount rate free market (RH scale)

– – Min. discount rate (RH scale)

Chart 4.2. Bank of England's Bank Rate, free-market discount rate and yield of British government 3% consols from 1844 to 1848, monthly. Vertical line denotes issue of Irish loan. *Sources:* J. G. Hubbard, *A letter to Sir Charles Wood on the monetary pressure and commercial distress of 1847* (London: Longman, 1848), p. 51; *Burdett's Official Intelligence* (1894), p. 1771; *Report from the Select Committee on bank acts*, PP 1857 (220) (220–1) X, pt. I, pt. II.1, pp. 463–64.

securities'; 'Wood showed me letters from Ireland more frightful than ever'.[46] Acutely aware of the potential situation, the Rothschilds had set up the British Association for the Relief of the Extreme Distress in the Remote Parishes of Ireland and Scotland at the start of 1847 to help fund relief efforts through charitable donations.[47] F. Baring wrote to Wood on 20 March 1847 warning him not to crash the market with further loans and discussing non-standard ways of obtaining money.[48] He quoted Trevelyan's suggestion that any further loan should be named as being for government expenditure more generally and not particularly called 'Irish'. However, Baring demanded that 'you will of course make the cause of the issue clear and Irish' for the sake of accountability to investors and to Parliament.[49] Although the loans had been contracted on 1 March, the monies still had to be raised from the market, and this extended over the period of credit shortage in April 1847 and panic in October 1847.

46   Earl Grey diary, 7 March 1847, D.U.L., Earl Grey papers, GRE/V/C3/13, pp. 86–88.

47   N. Ferguson, *The House of Rothschild, vol. 1: Money's Prophets, 1798–1848* (Harmondsworth: Penguin, 1999), p. 443.

48   F. Baring to Wood, 20 March 1847, C.U.L., Hickleton papers, MS MF A4.54, reel 1490.

49   Ibid.

The records in the Baring Archive show that, before the contracting of the loan at the beginning of March, Baring Bros. and Co. had raised promises of the money from investors adequately (in a process that in modern terms is called 'book running'). Over a hundred offers were refused and some applicants only received a third of their offered allocation. However, as the April difficulties developed, deposits had to be paid and the list of those actually paying shows considerable changes from the offers accepted only weeks ago.[50] Interest rates had become raised and credit tight, and Wood had decided the deposits could not be paid by discounting stock. Wood wrote to Russell on 14 April 1847 with an indication Barings were have difficulties collecting the funds, 'certainly they have reason to reject the terms of the loan, and they not unnaturally complain of anything and everything'.[51]. The records of subscriptions suggest that groups of investors such as the staff of the Bank of England bought into the loan on a virtually charitable basis to help raise the necessary money.[52] Furthermore, it was at this time that tight money-markets meant that there was a shortfall of £2.5m in a sale of Treasury bills, a form of government debt issued on a regular basis to pay for the interest on the national debt, forcing the Bank of England to step in and provide £2m of funds instead.[53] This increased pressure further on the Bank of England's reserve ratio (note reserve to total liabilities). It was unusual for the government to fail to raise the money it required each quarter through this method, and this circumstance would have sparked worries at the Treasury and with Wood that the government was unable to finance itself.

Wood realised by 11 April 1847 some of the impact of the Irish loan upon financial and political confidence, writing to Russell to inform him that, 'it is evident that bad money times are coming upon us and a second loan to be spent upon Irish paupers will not be so easily raised … we shall not meet with unanimous support in borrowing another 5 or 6 millions even with an Irish income tax'.[54] At this stage he was therefore considering an additional loan to finance the entire sum (of up to £14m a year) required for relief efforts. Even so, he was also worried about the economic situation and about growing resentment in Great Britain that Ireland was having huge sums spent on it while its upper classes were excused from paying income tax. The full extent of the financial panic was made clear to Wood a few days later by a letter from F.

---

50 Irish loan, unsuccessful and successful applications, ING Baring Archives, HC3.75A.1, 2; List of allocations and deposit payments, ING Baring Archives, 3.75A.7.
51 Wood to Russell, 14 April 1847, N.A., Russell papers, PRO 30/22/6C, ff. 80–86.
52 Letters of application from staff of the Bank of England, with lists of allocations, ING Baring Archives, HC3.75A.6.
53 Boot, *The Commercial Crisis of 1847*, p. 50; it should be noted that this sale of bills was a regular event and not part of the Irish loan; *Return of Number and Amount of Exchequer Bills issued, June 1847–48*, PP 1847–48 (454) XXXIX.153, p. 5.
54 Wood to Russell, 11 April 1847, N.A., Russell papers, PRO 30/22/6C, ff. 65–70.

Baring on 'the loan and the conduct of the Bank', detailing the steps taken to reduce circulation, by raising interest rates using direct and indirect methods, in line with the sudden outflow of bullion caused by panic over the loan.[55]

John Horsley Palmer (pseudonym the 'Vindicator'), a former governor of the Bank of England, wrote to *The Times* on 29 April 1847, pointing out how advances on loans for Irish relief could induce financial panics by suddenly producing a drop in the Bank of England's bullion reserve because of the weekly tables published in the *London Gazette* as required by the 1844 Act.[56]

> I will suppose a case. The chancellor of the exchequer has calls on him for money to carry on the works there, or may have to pay for corn to feed the people, has not a farthing on his account, and comes to the Bank and asks an advance to the amount of the next instalment of the loan, or upon any other receipt he may expect in a few days – say to the amount of £2,000,000 … If this should happen the day before the publication of the account what a panic may be raised by interested parties?[57]

As he pointed out, the possibility of a panic depended on how quickly any such advance was repaid and the nature of future demands. This letter was written shortly after a recovery in the bullion reserves which coincided with an indication that changes to proposed Irish Poor Law legislation would slow down the use of loan payments, the implication of his letter being that this was a good thing for the credit situation. An article in *The Economist* published on 8 May 1847, but presumably written some time before, explained further why the London banking community thought that the Irish loan would damage confidence in the currency:

> During the next five months the whole of the eight million loan for Ireland will be abstracted from the capital of the country, and being chiefly if not wholly, destined for the purpose of provisions will in reality be sent out of the country to meet out foreign payments. The money it is true goes to Ireland first where it is expended on provisions … [but eventually] is transmitted to the United States to pay the balance of trade caused by the imports of food.[58]

The article reflected the widespread view in the City of London that, if the loan were expended within six months as many originally believed the Poor Relief Act intended, the gold standard would become impossible to maintain,

55   Wood to Russell, 14 April 1847, N.A., Russell papers, PRO 30/22/6C, ff. 80–86; Wood describes Barings' letter.
56   *The Times*, 29 April 1847, p. 6; for the identity of the 'Vindicator' see *The Spectator*, 1 May 1847, p. 11.
57   *The Times*, 29 April 1847, p. 6.
58   J. Wilson, *Capital, currency and banking* (London: The Economist, 1847), p. 206.

causing a run on the Bank of England, as holders of banknotes and sterling-denominated securities tried to convert them to gold before the bank's reserves were exhausted. What the banking community thought would happen usually came to pass as investors traded in a way that sought to anticipate future changes, thereby accelerating them. The feared drain did indeed begin to occur in March and April 1847. The situation made the City very sensitive to signs of how the money might be spent.

Dornbusch and Frenkel's analysis can be used to confirm that there was a link between the April panic and announcements on how the money was to be spent (Charts 4.3, 4.4 and 4.5). It can be seen from Chart 4.3 that the contracting and announcement of the Irish loan on 1 March 1847, followed two weeks later by the first reading of the Poor Relief (Ireland) Bill 1847, which dealt with how the money would be spent, corresponds to a dip in bullion reserves at the Bank of England in March and a crisis depicted by a low note-reserves to deposits ratio. However, the third reading and passing of the Bill then corresponds with a complete reversal of this trend to the exact week of its announcement in the papers.[59] The reason for this was that the revised Bill at the third reading transferred the expense of relief off the government account altogether, and the indications were that a large amount of money would not be expended on food suddenly.

At the commencement of the Bill's progress, it was generally assumed about half of the expense was to be funded by Treasury grants and the rest would be provided as a Treasury loan (as with the Poor Relief [Ireland] Act that February), according in general terms with Grey's original policy proposal.[60] The Bill also proposed Grey's outdoor relief of the able-bodied but destitute poor, potentially a costly and uncapped expenditure commitment. However, during the third reading of the Bill on 16 April 1847, it became clear that the entire loan used in Ireland was to be repaid by ratepayers, and that the money would only be released slowly, as the Poor Law Commissioners could control whether outdoor relief was given.[61] Wood emphasised the point about limiting the rate and total amount of expenditure on 30 April 1847 in the House of Commons: 'I never said, that the whole of that loan would be devoted to the relief works, ... I do not understand how anybody can fancy that I intend to issue additional Exchequer-bills, or to raise an additional loan for Irish purposes'.[62]

59   The line on the graph appears to rise before this because it connects the low data point before the bill was passed with the next, higher data point after the bill was passed.
60   Poor Relief (Ireland) Act 1847 (10 & 11 Vict c.7); Third Earl Grey, paper on Relief for Ireland, 13 January 1847, D.U.L., Earl Grey papers, GRE/B155/19.
61   *Hansard*, XCI, 16 April 1847, cc. 915–17; idem. c. 879.
62   *Hansard*, XCII, 30 April 1847, cc. 215–16.

The link between how quickly the Irish Loan was likely to be spent and financial confidence (or lack of it) was a very serious blow to the Russell government's plans for relief in Ireland. It meant that, not only would it be difficult to raise a further loan, but for the purposes required, the £8m loan taken out was virtually useless because it could not be expended quickly. Suddenly all the plans about reducing Treasury funding on relief and costs in general that had been slowly put together over the previous period of declining finances were implemented. Massive relief cuts, the largest proportion at one time during the famine, were made between 1–8 May 1847, when 40% of employment on the public works was cut, and in due course was replaced with soup kitchens and then the Poor Law, as contemporary maps show (see Figures 4.3 and 4.4). The May cuts of 40% were sudden and were intended to immediately save money; in contrast to the previous cut of 20% which was made slowly (from 20 March to the end of April) and was primarily intended to free up agricultural labourers to plant the next season's crops. The cuts were both mitigated by the temporary provision of soup kitchens, which was regarded as a more direct and efficient way of providing relief than the much-criticised public-works system.[63] Moreover, it was at this time that the Treasury contribution to support the replacement outdoor-relief system through grants and loans, as originally proposed, evaporated with little comment, leaving historians ever since bemused as to why.

Despite being considered since January 1847, the poor-relief legislation had been delayed by landlord protests, but now, according to Gray, it was implemented 'as rapidly as possible'.[64] The Poor Relief (Ireland) Act 1847 c. 31, of 8 June 1847, and Poor Relief (Ireland) (No. 2) Act 1847 c. 90, of 22 July, transferred relief costs to the Poor Law system and separated them from those of England, in order to placate the London financial markets, for whom the level of uncertainty about the total cost of public relief efforts was so threatening.[65] As the Acts were passed, Wood confirmed that 'he was not aware that any part of any rate had been actually collected in repayment of the sums advanced for relief in Ireland; but he was informed that some rates had been struck; and he believed that several were in progress of collection'.[66] In making the link

---

63   Treasury Minute, 11 March 1847, *Report of Commissioners of Public Works (Ireland)*, PP 1847 (834) XVII, pp. 4–6; Earl Grey noted in his Journal 'relief works had failed because the Irish of all ranks had thwarted [them] in every way': 2 February 1847, D.U.L., Earl Grey papers, GRE V/C3/13.

64   P. Gray, *Famine, Land and Politics: British Government and Irish Society 1843–50* (Dublin: Irish Academic Press, 1999), p. 283.

65   Landed Property Improvement (Ireland) Act 1847 (10 & 11 Vict c.32); Poor Relief (Ireland) Act 1847 (10 & 11 Vict c.31); Poor Relief (Ireland) (No. 2) Act 1847 (10 & 11 Vict c.90).

66   *Hansard*, XCIV, 8 July 1847, c. 73.

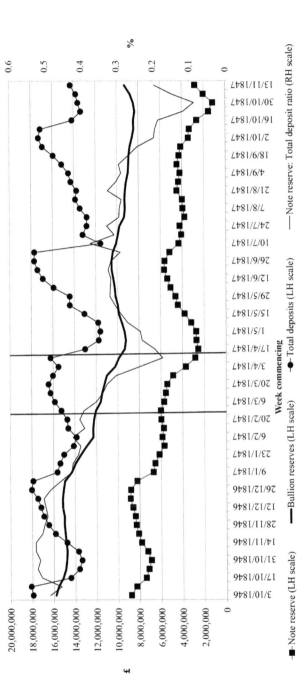

Chart 4.3. Bank of England note reserve, bullion reserve, total deposits and note reserve: total deposit ratio 3/10/1846 to 13/11/1847, weekly. Vertical lines represent 1/3/1847 and 17/4/1847, the announcement of the loan and newspaper report of the third reading of the Poor Relief (Ireland) Bill 1847. The first data indicating recovery is on 17/4/1847. *Sources:* Dornbusch, 'The Gold Standard', pp. 261–62; *Second Report from the Secret Committee of the House of Commons on Commercial Distress*, PP 1847–48 (584) VIII.505, Pt. I, appendix 6, pp. 16–21.

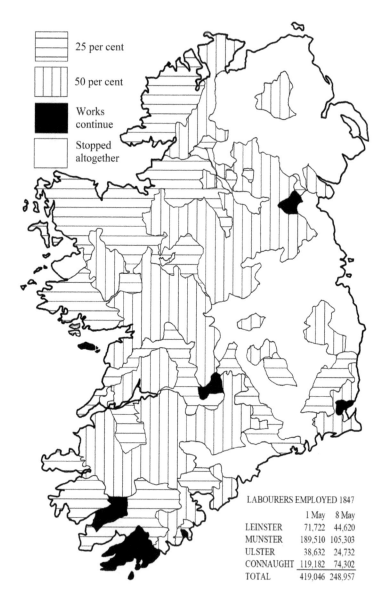

	25 per cent
	50 per cent
	Works continue
	Stopped altogether

LABOURERS EMPLOYED 1847		
	1 May	8 May
LEINSTER	71,722	44,620
MUNSTER	189,510	105,303
ULSTER	38,632	24,732
CONNAUGHT	119,182	74,302
TOTAL	419,046	248,957

Figure 4.3. Map based on a contemporary map showing the cuts in relief made 1–8 May 1847, after the Irish loan crisis in April. (N.A., Treasury: Trevelyan papers, T64/ 370 C/3). To the right are the details of the changes in employment made 1–8 May 1847.

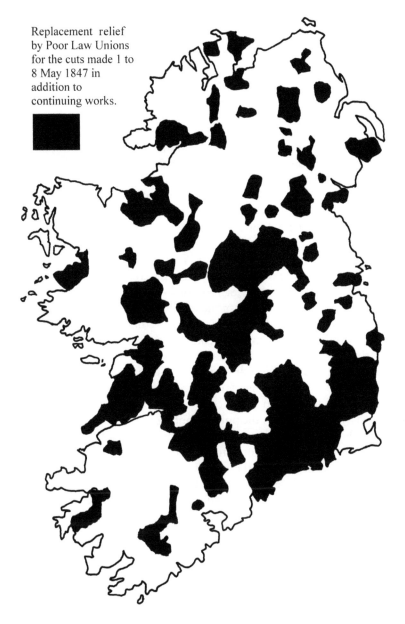

Replacement relief
by Poor Law Unions
for the cuts made 1 to
8 May 1847 in
addition to
continuing works.

Figure 4.4. Map based on contemporary map showing the replacement relief by Poor Law Unions for the cuts made 1–8 May 1847, after the Irish loan crisis, as at January 1848. (Treasury: N.A., Treasury: Trevelyan papers, T64/ 370 C/3).

between events, it is important to be aware that proposed legislation mentioned by previous historians from August 1846 onwards actually had little monetary effect on Ireland until the first financial panic of 1847 associated with the Irish loan forced politicians to act.[67] Immediately after Wood's speech Russell wrote to Clarendon to tell him, 'it is impossible to extend the [Irish loan] again – nor is it desirable – yet how are the people to be fed?'[68] *Laissez-faire* or providentialist ideologies can show no changes similar in timing to those of financial circumstances, which correlate exactly to the week with relief-policy changes.

The timing of the discussion of Irish legislation and the bullion drain crisis coincide so exactly, it is surprising that economic historians have not uncovered this before. The reason is that Neville Ward-Perkins in 1950 discredited the idea of an internal drain such as would be caused by an Irish loan panic by confusing the 'note reserve' column in the Bank of England data with private 'bullion reserves'. In fact, he correlates the reduction in the size of bullion and note reserves, not private bullion reserves.[69] Ward-Perkins tended to sympathise with the Currency School's viewpoint, but Palmer, who had preferred the Banking School view, recognised the April bullion drains as mostly internal in the Commons' Secret Committees on the Commercial Crisis.[70] Wood, whose views aligned with the Currency School, realised in May 1847 that the drain was internally influenced. In correspondence with Francis Baring he discussed bullion flows and note withdrawal and concluded that importations of bullion were being withdrawn to convert to coin to use instead of notes which had gone 'firstly to the public'.[71] This letter shows that at this time Wood had accepted that the April bullion drain was an internal drain of bullion caused by its withdrawal by its commercial owners and conversion of some of it to coin which could be used in commerce.[72] There was a shortage of notes as well, caused by demand from the public wanting to use them instead of credit. However, although this explanation is convincing, his attitude is not one of great understanding, wishing for simpler times and a purely metallic currency that 'does not oscillate (that is the word I believe) so readily'.[73] More recently, Dornbusch and Frenkel used the Bank of England figures correctly and showed that they point to significant serious internal drains not only in April but in

---

67   Gray, *Famine, Land and Politics*, p. 229.

68   Russell to Clarendon, 9 July 1847, O.B.L., Clarendon papers, Ms. Clar. dep., Irish box 43.

69   C. N. Ward-Perkins, 'The Commercial Crisis 1847', *Oxford Economic Papers*, 2:1 (1950), 75–94, at p. 94; see R. C. O. Matthew's assessment of Ward-Perkins' approach as not very intellectual, quoted in J. S. Lyons, L.P. Cain, S. H. Williamson (eds.), *Reflections on the Cliometrics Revolution* (Abingdon: Routledge, 2008), p. 157.

70   *First Report from the Secret Committee of the House of Commons on Commercial Distress*, PP 1847–48 (395) VIII Pt.I.1, p. 156.

71   Wood to F. Baring, 12 May 1847, C.U.L., Hickleton papers, MS MF A4.54, reel 1490.

72   Ibid.

73   Ibid.

October 1847 as well.[74] Dornbusch and Frenkel have shown that the note reserve:total deposit ratio is a good indicator of crisis. If there was a low ratio, an unstable equilibrium could make the Bank fail when a refund of deposits and the redemption of a large amount of notes in the hands of the public was demanded at a time of low bullion reserves.[75] The enquiries of the Lords' and Commons' Secret Committees on the Commercial Crisis, by contrast, mainly concluded that the initial April crisis was caused by an external drain of bullion payments to the United States for imports of high-priced wheat.[76] This conclusion served to defend the reputation of the Bank Charter Act.

However, wheat prices cannot have been the entire story because the wheat price-fluctuations do not correspond well with the bullion drain crisis in April. After a rise in 1846, they were steady, a surge in price occurring only after the worst period of the drain (Chart 4.4). Moreover, the lowest point of the ratio graph recovers too quickly for the drain to be external and for the gold to be physically re-imported into the country. In the case of an external drain the recovery from crisis is gradual as trade has to take place and bullion be moved between countries. In an internal drain, recovery can be instant as domestic holders of gold exchange their bullion back again for banknotes.

Another background issue was the railway mania, as described in recent research by Gareth Campbell.[77] A large number of new railway companies set up since 1845 had sold shares in exchange for small deposits. Afterwards, substantial additional sums were 'called' throughout 1847. While this absorbed much spare money-market liquidity and certainly created a situation vulnerable to a credit panic, weekly domestic railway-share calls by date payable show no unique features that correlate specifically with the start and end of the April panic (Chart 4.4). The research of Mac (H. M.) Boot has also shown that factors other than railways calls were substantially responsible for the crises of 1847.[78]

Further analysis shows that the sharp worsening of the crisis caused by the loan is a separate issue from a background trend caused by grain imports leading to a trade deficit and credit shortages or calls on railway shares soaking up available liquid funds. If the variations of the note reserve:deposit ratio

74 Dornbusch, Frenkel, 'The Gold Standard', p. 236.
75 See idem., p. 247 for a full explanation; also C. Goodhart, 'Monetary Regimes: Then and Now', in S. Dow et al. (eds.), *Money, Method and Contemporary Post-Keynesian Economics* (London: Edward Elgar, 2018), 1–11, at p. 6 gives further historiography for the use of 'the unused notes to liabilities' ratio.
76 *Report from the Secret Committee of the House of Lords on Commercial Distress*, PP 1847–48 (565 & 565-II) VIII Pt. III.1, 537, pp. iii–v; *First Report from the Secret Committee of the House of Commons on Commercial Distress*, PP 1847–48 (395) VIII Pt.I.1, p. iv.
77 G. Campbell, 'Government Policy during the British Railway Mania and the 1847 Commercial Crisis', in. N. Dimsdale, A. Hotson (eds.), *British Financial Crises since 1825* (Oxford: OUP, 2014), 59–68.
78 Boot, *The Commercial Crisis of 1847*, pp. 14–24, 81.

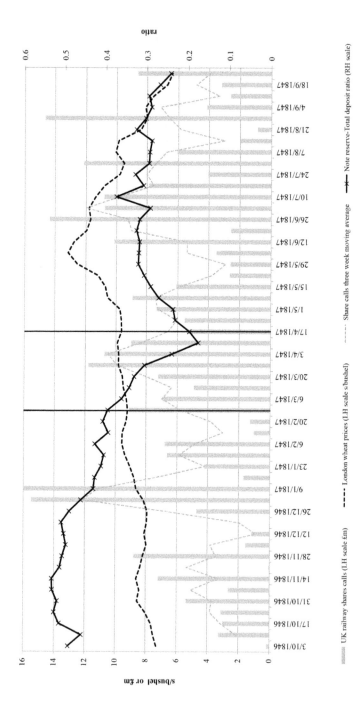

Chart 4.4. London wheat price (s/bushel), railway-share calls by date payable and note reserve: total deposit ratio 3/10/1846 to 25/9/1847, weekly. The vertical lines are as Chart 4.3. See G. Campbell, 'Two Bubbles and a Crisis: Britain in the 1840s', *Cliometric Society ASSA Session* (2011), p. 5, concerning calls. *Sources: London Gazette*, London, Middx. prices, dataset supplied courtesy of Corn Returns Online; D. M. Evans, *The Commercial Crisis, 1847–48: being facts and figures* (London: Letts, Son and Steer, 1849), p. 125; *Herapath's Journal and Railway Magazine; The Economist*; as Chart 4.3.

and bullion reserves from their annual trends (estimated using ordinary least squares) over the entire 1846–47 harvest year are graphed (Chart 4.5), the enhanced results show the start and end of the panic again correlate exactly with the announcement of the loan and the change in relief policies.

The overall explanations of the crises produced by the Parliamentary enquiries into the financial crises of 1847 conceal the underlying variety of opinions of the witnesses from the commercial and banking worlds, a considerable proportion of whom refer to an explicit link between the government's Irish policies, the Bank Charter Act of 1844 and financial panic. They also indicate attitudes that explain the reaction of the financial community to the loan and to proposed Irish legislation. Alexander Wylie, who represented business in Liverpool, which was particularly badly hit by commercial distress, blamed price rises in food on 'the Irish loan, or a great part of it, being thrown upon the market'.[79] Charles Turner, representing Liverpool merchants, was asked what he believed caused the commercial distress in Liverpool. 'The fundamental cause I believe to be the famine'; increased imports of food, bills of exchange limited by limited credit, had to be paid for in bullion, he explained. 'How do you consider the Government loan [Irish loan] aided in increasing the pressure?' he was asked. He answered that the loan was 'a very proper course for the Government to pursue; but it is clear that if Government had not issued that loan, the same importation of food would not have taken place'.[80] He did not blame the 1844 Act, however, mainly the loan. George Muntz, an industrialist and MP from Birmingham, believed the Bank made a mistake in not 'increasing the [Bank] rate in the months of October and November 1846' ... 'I have always supposed that they were influenced by a wish to assist the government in making the [Irish] loan'.[81] In contrast to Turner, he thought that the difficulties were made worse by the 1844 Act. Joshua Bates, a partner in Barings Bank (Baring Bros. and Co.), thought the April panic was due to a great need for deficiency bills.[82] These bills were to tide the government over because of cash-flow problems paying interest on existing debt, a problem that swallowed the unspent remainder of the Irish loan at the end of the year.[83] He

79 *Report from the Secret Committee of the House of Lords on Commercial Distress*, PP 1847–48 (565 & 565-II) VIII Pt. III.1, 537, q. 2144, p. 246.

80 *First Report from the Secret Committee of the House of Commons on Commercial Distress*, PP 1847–48 (395) VIII Pt. I.1, p.50.

81 Idem., p. 101.

82 Idem., p. 183.

83 *The Economist* counselled against allowing this to happen again as it did in 1847: 'it would be objectionable for the chancellor of the exchequer to rely upon again running in debt to the Bank every quarter, to the amount of *three or four* millions on deficiency bills in order to enable him to pay the dividends' ... 'But for the residue of the Irish loan, the dividends in October could not have been paid without a considerable advance from the Bank, which the Bank could not have made': *The Economist*, 15 January 1848, p. 57.

thought the process of publicising the Bank of England tables according to the 1844 Act facilitated the alarm. He would have preferred it if contractors for the Irish loan had been allowed to pay up on discount, in other words in exchange for stock, rather than the stock having to be sold and the loan funded with cash. This was initially refused by Wood as chancellor 'saying "that he only wanted the loan as instalments fell due"'.[84] As has been described, Parliament, and the public, had been assured that the expenditure of the loan would only take place gradually, which was presumably the reason for this restriction, and the fact that the whole of the loan was not expended on Irish relief in the end. Speaking in June 1848 in answer to the question of whether the effects of the crises were over yet, Bates replied, 'I should think not; things are not yet settled'.[85]

James Morris and Henry Prescott, Governor and Deputy Governor of the Bank of England, confirmed that a planned rise in interest rates was deferred to ease the rate at which the Irish loan was raised. They were of the opinion it should have been raised earlier. It was queried whether this had been fair to those bidding for the loan because afterwards the rates went up.[86] They believed the cause of the April pressure was the famine and consequent importation of food. The result was 'an almost total prostration of credit'.[87] Generally, they supported the 1844 Act on the basis it maintained convertibility, although at the cost of commercial pain, but even this could have been less than it might have been without the Act. Samuel Gurney, a Banking-School inclined London bill-broker, believed 'had there been no such Act ... the Alarm that rose in April 1847 would not have occurred'.[88] The shortage of food would have been better managed in that case and 'have gone off imperceptibly and lightly'.[89] Tooke attributed 'exclusively to the 1844 Act' the financial problems of April 1847.[90] William Brown, a Liverpool trader and member of Parliament for South Lancashire, put the 1847 crises down to the Bank of England, 'carrying on business without a sufficient available capital'.[91]

In a similar way to *The Economist*, *The Bankers' Magazine* also argued that the potato blight and the Irish loan weakened Britain's monetary system, in particular pointing out that the loan competed with commercial and

84   *First Report from the Secret Committee of the House of Commons on Commercial Distress*, PP 1847–48 (395) VIII Pt. I.1, p. 183; Wood did allow discounting eventually: Evans, *The commercial crisis*, pp. 56, 65; *The Times*, 18 October 1847, p.2.
85   *First Report from the Secret Committee of the House of Commons on Commercial Distress*, PP 1847–48 (395) VIII Pt.I. 1, p. 184.
86   Idem., p. 230.
87   Idem., p. 205.
88   Idem., p. 126.
89   Ibid.
90   Idem., p. 411.
91   *Report from the Secret Committee of the House of Lords on Commercial Distress*, PP 1847–48 (565 & 565-II) VIII Pt. III.1, 537, p. 253.

manufacturing interests for the same capital.[92] In the immediate aftermath of the crisis, Alexander Baring, whose son was a close relative and friend respectively of Wood and Peel, published a pamphlet in which he said that it was 'doubtful' the Irish loan would be paid back and it had damaged the public finances and shaken confidence in the Bank of England: 'it imposes upon us this year the scandal of a large loan in time of profound peace'.[93] These financial problems in London soon became known to those administrating relief on the ground in Ireland. Later, Twisleton said that when administrating relief efforts, he had 'to prevent the Irish Unions from making demands upon the national funds at a time when such demands ... might be seriously injurious to the Empire'.[94]

At the time of the Irish loan, the 'minimal terms that the government was willing to accept from the bidders were apparently decided in the morning of the day for the bidding'.[95] Trevelyan was generally too lowly an official to be involved in such matters, which were managed by the Lords of the Treasury themselves, and so does not comment a great deal on them. Even so, the sudden change in the tone of his letter books shows the dismay of Wood at the outcome of the tenders on 1 March 1847. Beforehand Trevelyan is optimistic, referring to children being fed in schools and saying, 'I think we shall be able to dispense with the new Relief Act', on 27 February 1847. (This ended up being delayed and the British Association, in fact, only started feeding children in schools from October 1847, thanks to Count Strzelecki.)[96] However, afterwards, on 2 March 1847, he writes in intimidating terms to a specific Board that: 'Sir Charles Wood requests' it close its public works, unable to 'describe in too strong terms the degree in which the public credit and safety are considered to be involved'.[97]

As a result of the crisis, the government discouraged any further discussion which might have led to renewed panic. In the House of Commons, Wood cut off debate in Parliament, forcing Major Samuel Blackall to sit down and withdraw his motion when, after a debate on the commercial panic, he

92   The Bankers' Magazine, February 1847, p. 261; The Bankers' Magazine, August 1847, p. 390.
93   A. Baring, Financial and Commercial Crisis Considered (London: John Murray, 1847), pp. 25–26.
94   Twisleton to Trevelyan, 3 February 1848, N.A., Russell papers, PRO 30/22/7A, ff. 271–73.
95   A. Odlyzko, 'Supplementary Material for Economically Irrational Pricing of 19th Century British Government Bonds', March 2015, online at <http://www.dtc.umn.edu/~odlyzko> [accessed 22 February 2020], p. 95.
96   British Relief Association, Report of the British Relief Association for the Relief of Extreme Distress in Ireland and Scotland (London: Richard Clay, 1849), p. 35.
97   Trevelyan to Burgoyne, 27 February 1847, compared with Trevelyan to Jones, 2 March 1847, O.B.L., Trevelyan letter books, vol. 12, pp. 242–44, 257–58.

suggested the Irish loan might have to be increased.[98] Politicians also wanted to avoid talking about the crisis to avoid criticism of the Bank Charter Act. Peel's correspondence with Edward Cardwell, who had been his financial secretary to the Treasury and was later the co-editor of his *Memoirs*, shows how discussion of the Bank Charter Act of 1844 was repressed after Peel was informed how unpopular it was.[99] While Cardwell was seeking election in 1847 for the constituency of Liverpool, talking with commercial interests in that city he noted 'the strange prejudice they have taken up against the Bill of 1844'.[100] The 'prejudice' was a complaint that the Act had caused an unstable commercial environment of widely fluctuating interest rates.[101] When the Bank of England bullion reserves were filling, rates were too low for them; when the reserve was emptying, the rate was too high. Cardwell informed Peel, after the April 1847 financial crisis, that he had been 'told the Country Bankers could at any moment have gone to the Bank of England and brought it to a dead lock'.[102] When Peel wrote his address to electors in Tamworth for the 1847 general election, he concentrated on the religious question of fair treatment of Catholics and on the commercial question of free trade, sidestepping the issue of the 1844 Act.[103] Cardwell used the same themes in Peel's *Memoirs*, in which the 1844 Act received only a brief mention, thus helping to remove the relationship between Peel, the Bank Charter Act and the financial crises of 1847 from the historical spotlight.[104]

Outside of Parliament, the aim of Trevelyan's original *The Irish Crisis* article in the *Edinburgh Review*, as opposed to the later book, was to calm any fear that more Irish loans might have to be issued by claiming that the Irish problem had been 'solved' and all was for the best according to the theories of political economy.[105] Trevelyan even ensured that incoming letters on monetary policy and Ireland with a different viewpoint were destroyed.[106] This discretion inhibited historians from linking the loan and the April crisis and generally discouraged

98   *Hansard*, XCV, 30 November 1847, cc. 477–78, cc. 374–477.
99   For biographical details see A. B. Erickson, 'Edward T. Cardwell: Peelite', *Transactions of the American Philosophical Society*, ns 49 pt. 2 (1959), 1–107, at pp. 8–11.
100   Cardwell to Peel, 20 May 1847, B.L., Peel papers, Add. MS. 40598, ff. 260–65.
101   Ibid.
102   Idem., f. 263.
103   'Election Address to the Electors of the Borough of Tamworth', 15 July 1847, B.L., Peel papers, Add. MS. 40599, ff. 263–43.
104   The only indirect mention of the Bank Charter Act in Peel's published memoirs is Peel, *Memoirs*, vols. 2/3, pp. 300–01.
105   C. E. Trevelyan, 'The Irish Crisis', *Edinburgh Review*, 87:175 (January 1848), 229–320.
106   For instance, see Trevelyan to Wood, 26 July 1847, C.U.L., Hickleton papers, MS MF A4.59, reel 1498.

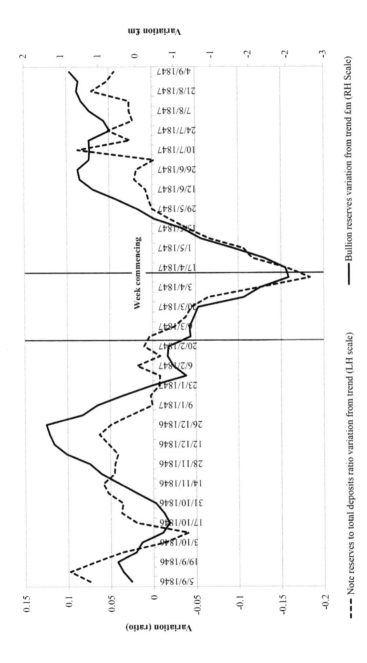

Chart 4.5. Bank of England note reserve: total deposits ratio and bullion reserve, variation from annual trend 5/9/1846 to 4/9/1847, weekly. The vertical lines are as Chart 4.3. The variation from trend is calculated by determining the straight-line trend for the data using ordinary least squares and deducting the trend figure for each week from the actual figure for that week. The result represents variation from the trend line as if it was horizontal and thus identifies any effect which is not part of the trend. *Sources:* Calculated from same sources as Chart 4.3.

--- Note reserves to total deposits ratio variation from trend (LH scale)   —— Bullion reserves variation from trend £m (RH Scale)

discussion of relief funding from early 1848 onwards.[107] However, in private, Trevelyan regularly refers to the effect of the crisis in his outgoing letters from April onwards. To Routh he wrote 'the state of the money market would prevent us getting another loan … and it is therefore particularly incumbent upon us to husband what we have and make it go as far as possible'.[108] This admission links directly Trevelyan's perceived parsimony in Ireland with the financial crisis. To others he wrote in similar terms, complaining 'our difficulties are aggravated by the money market' and of 'the excessive prices of food and the difficulty in which our monied interest, our trade and above all our <u>manufacturers</u> are involved'.[109] High food prices were no longer a useful inducement for merchants to boost imports, as in October to November 1846, but had become a threat to Britain's financial system as its trade deficit increased.

Interest rates were to continue to rise throughout the second crisis in the autumn of 1847.[110] Free-market short-term interest rates, which affected about a tenth of government debt, reached 7% in May. Haines has pointed to the way in which historians have dismissed budget and financial problems as an important governing influence of the Russell government's famine policy on the basis that the expenditure was a small proportion of Britain's GDP or military spending.[111] Nevertheless, these interpretations ignore an obvious point. In the 1845–46 financial year, servicing the national debt took up 56.25% of government expenditure, high even by today's standards.[112] While much British government debt was financed with consols, which are perpetual and recallable only by the issuer, the high consol rates from the last century had been reduced by payment and reissue in times of low rates, to cut the rate of interest on the debt. This became impossible and the spectre of a rate spiral where interest on loans is repaid with loans at an increasingly high rate damaged confidence in British government debt, which did not build its reputation for stability until after William Gladstone's period as chancellor.[113] Bankers claimed that the markets considered it 'doubtful' the loan would be paid back, envisaging many

107   For the strange silence on the famine see N. O'Ciosain, 'Was there "Silence" about the Famine?' *Irish Studies Review*, 4:13 (1995–96), 7–10, at p. 7.
108   Trevelyan to Routh, 13 April 1847, O.B.L., Trevelyan letter books, vol. 12, pp. 36–38.
109   Trevelyan to Gayle, 13 May 1847, O.B.L., Trevelyan letter books, vol. 14, pp. 270–71; Trevelyan to Campbell, 10 May 1847, Trevelyan to Burgoyne, 11 May 1847, O.B.L., Trevelyan letter books, vol. 14, pp. 247–53 (original underline).
110   Dornbusch, Frenkel, 'The Gold Standard', p. 271.
111   R. Haines, *Charles Trevelyan and the Great Irish Famine* (Dublin: Four Courts Press, 2004), p. 75.
112   *Public income and expenditure. Return of the net income and expenditure of the United Kingdom, for the several years ending 5th April 1842, 1843, 1844, 1845, 1846, 1847, 1848, 1849 and 1850, respectively*, PP 1851 (62) XXXI.159.
113   See discussion of 'Gladstonian finance' in D. Needham, 'Covid-19 and the UK National Debt in Historical Context', History & Policy paper, 22 April 2020, online at <http://www.

years of increasing rates.[114] New debt was difficult to issue in this environment. In fact, it took until 1 February 2015 for the Irish loan to be repaid by the redemption of 4% consols.[115] Throughout 1847, a proportion of Treasury bills, government debt sold to pay interest on existing debt, remained unsold and the government had to borrow funds owned by the Bank of England, putting in jeopardy the country's whole financial system. Charles Manners, Marquess of Granby, volubly if not lucidly, blamed this on the Bank Charter Act of 1844 and free trade.[116]

The more pressing problem which panicked markets in both crises, more than the fear of a debt-interest spiral, was the worry about what the Irish loan meant for the balance of payments. The problem was not mainly the scale of public borrowing itself; neither crisis in 1847 was a sovereign-debt crisis in modern terminology. The problem was that the markets feared that the money that had been raised at home was to be spent suddenly abroad on food imports for Ireland, in other words that government borrowing and spending was about to trigger a sterling crisis and to crash the Bank of England. The announcement of the loan caused a deeply damaging run on the currency system, including the Bank of England, through which the government financed itself. Bullion was demanded as an external drain for investment and to pay for foreign imports of food and as an internal drain because credit was short and it was feared notes would become inconvertible into gold. The crisis and the principles behind it were understood by the public at the time, as is shown by the *Punch* cartoon on the front cover of this book. Published a month after the first crisis of 1847, Peel is depicted standing in front of the Bank of England's gold reserves, paralysing John Bull into thinking he is bankrupt with the Bank Charter Act.[117] The reference is to an opera, Robert the Devil – about a knight who discovers that he is the son of the devil – playing at Her Majesty's Theatre in Haymarket, London, at the time.[118] The implication was obvious.

---

historyandpolicy.org/policy-papers/papers/covid-19-and-the-uk-national-debt-in-historical-context> [accessed 29 April 2020].

114   Baring, *Financial and Commercial Crisis Considered*, p. 25.

115   J. Kollewe, S. Farrell, 'UK Bonds that Financed First World War to Be Redeemed 100 Years Later: Treasury's Redemption Scheme Stretches All the Way back to Napoleonic and Crimean Wars and Irish Potato Famine', *The Guardian*, 31 October 2014, online at <http://www.theguardian.com/business/2014/oct/31/uk-first-world-war-bonds-redeemed> [accessed 5 November 2014].

116   *Hansard*, XCII, 14 May 1847, cc. 856–64.

117   'Robert the [Devil] paralysing John Bull with his Mystic Branch', *Punch*, 29 May 1847, p. 221.

118   Her Majesty's Theatre, *Roberto il Diavolo: Robert the Devil an Opera in Four Acts* (London: Her Majesty's Theatre, May 1847).

The second financial panic of 1847

Fear that another bullion crisis was on the way meant that the decisions made in 1847 to restrict further advances to Ireland to pay for relief were never reversed. After the first crisis of 1847 Wood became increasingly nervous about further loans. 'In order to lend or give to Ireland we must <u>borrow</u>', Wood told Russell in August 1847. 'It may be necessary to do this ... but it will be well to avoid borrowing again if we can'.[119] He put this in clearer terms to the lord-lieutenant of Ireland on 15 August 1847 to manage expectations. Wood took five pages of economic detail to spell out to Clarendon that he had 'no money & therefore I cannot give it ... therefore assistance to Ireland means only a further loan and in the present state of the money market and depression in all our manufacturing towns, this is out of the question' (see full quotation at the start of this chapter).[120] Historians have tended to downplay or ignore the importance of that reasoning, in spite of all the economic data that shows a close relationship between the announcement of the Irish loan that February and the financial panic that followed.[121]

More emphasis has been placed on Wood's providential kicker at the end of the letter, which curtly ends with a reference to Ellice, a senior Whig backbencher, saying 'all our difficulties arise from our impious attempt to thwart the dispensation which was sent to cut the Gordian knot in Ireland'.[122] This comment is flimsy evidence for supporting the idea that Wood was primarily influenced by a providentalist agenda. Scherer notes that 'many thought [Ellice] to have great influence on Russell' and Wood was probably cynically using his comment to intimidate Clarendon. Wood did not agree with Ellice's views; the chancellor thought it was he who was responsible for the failure of the Whigs' economic policies when the party was previously in government before 1841.[123] The treatment of Clarendon's response by historians demonstrates a wider problem with the current literature on the Irish famine: government policy during the crisis is not placed in its full financial context. The Irish viceroy replied, 'Ireland cannot be left on its own resources which are manifestly

---

119   Wood to Russell, 26 August 1847, N.A., Russell papers, PRO 30/22/6E, ff. 218–21 (original underline).
120   Wood to Clarendon, 15 August 1847, C.U.L., Hickleton papers, MS MF A4.186, reel 1523.
121   Dornbusch, Frenkel, 'The Gold Standard'; C. Read, 'Laissez-faire, the Irish Famine and British Financial Crisis', *Economic History Review*, 69:2 (2015), 411–34, at pp. 419–27.
122   Wood to Clarendon, 15 August 1847, C.U.L., Hickleton papers, MS MF A4.186, reel 1523; Gray, *Famine, Land and Politics* (reference given as A4.185.2), pp. 292–93.
123   P. Scherer, *Lord John Russell: A Biography* (Selinsgrove: Susquehanna University Press, 1999), p. 171.

inadequate', as quoted by Joel Mokyr, who left out the next phrase, 'whatever may be the state of trade and credit', the real difficulty at the time.[124]

Although some confidence in the markets was restored after it was announced the entire loan would be paid back from local-government funds and expended slowly, investors remained shaken and consol yields did not return to their previous levels before a second crisis developed, started by another gold drain to America that July.[125] By the autumn, falling corn prices, railway securities and confidence in the Bank of England led to many banks and businesses in London failing, culminating in the 'Week of Terror' in October.

This crisis was partly triggered by soaring interest rates in America, caused by a war between the United States and Mexico over territory. Texas had been annexed in 1845, and President James Polk, who had been elected on a platform of territorial expansion, persuaded Congress to declare war on Mexico on 13 May 1846. Mexico City was captured by the United States in September 1847 and negotiations over a peace treaty began. The direct cost of the war to the United States has been estimated at around $70m, and about $38m was raised in Treasury notes. Interest rates soared from August 1847. The Treasury notes issued to raise the capital were at a rate of up to 6% and it was expected that the price of them would increase when the Mexicans had been defeated. Investors piled in, lured by the prospect of making a sizable capital gain. This added to the flow of bullion from the United Kingdom. As an indication of the volume of flow, the net importation of coin and bullion into the United States for 1847 amounted to $22.2m compared with a net exportation of $0.127m in 1846.[126] This was from all countries, but Britain at the centre of the world's financial system would have provided a significant proportion. When the United Kingdom started to collect better information about the destination of bullion after the 1847 crises, it was discovered that bullion flows did move in the ways described above, just as the Banking School's theories predicted.[127]

In his book on the 1847 crises, Evans listed over 500 firms which failed between August 1847 and December 1848.[128] In Ireland the commercial community that had benefitted from sales of food at very high prices in 1845 and 1846 were suddenly in a difficult financial position. They had bought stocks of grain at high prices, which they could now only sell at a loss, so they needed to raise credit and hope prices would rise again. All Irish banks found themselves under pressure to provide coin, which was already scarce due to the increased amount

124 Clarendon to Russell, 25 October 1847, N.A., Russell papers, PRO 30/22/6F, ff. 209–20; J. Mokyr, *Why Ireland Starved: A Quantitative and Analytical History of the Irish Economy, 1800–1850* (London: George Allen & Unwin, 1983), p. 292.
125 Evans, *The commercial crisis*, p. 65.
126 *The Merchants' Magazine and Commercial Review*, April 1848, p. 427.
127 *Gold and Silver bullion*, PP 1854 (516) XXXIX.439, pp. 2–3.
128 Idem., Appendix, pp. lxxxviv–ci.

needed for small payments for day work on the public-works schemes. The Bank of Ireland had made an arrangement with the other Irish banks to provide coin in times of shortage and had to import £0.2m in coin from Great Britain in order to keep to their commitments.[129]

The second crisis left Wood too nervous to attempt to issue further loans. It threatened the Bank of England's ability to honour the gold standard as laid out in the Bank Charter Act, and brought real fear to the government, such that in October Clarendon hung back from disturbing Russell about Irish affairs: 'For the last few days I have abstained from writing to you as I knew how you must be worried by the state of things in the City'.[130] Worse still, as the result of a combination of factors, including the repeal of the Corn Laws, depressed export volumes and an implosion in railway construction, tax revenue fell while expenditure on Ireland continued to increase. The estimated surplus of £332,000 Wood had predicted for the 1847/48 financial year in the February 1847 budget transformed into an actual deficit of £3,092,285 for that year – and that outturn was only achieved after severe mid-year spending cuts.[131] On 1 September 1847 Wood wrote to Russell warning of impending fiscal and financial crisis if relief spending in Ireland were not reduced:

> I hope that you are not too sanguine and that I am not too gloomy in my views of the prospects of the country, but I confess that I cannot participate in your bright expectations – I am at present disposed to wish not speaking of financial prospects at all, they are anything but bright ... if a high rate of interest prevails for some time ... my present impression therefore is that far from devising further on other modes of spending money in Ireland, I shall be glad of every shilling which can be saved in our present expenditure there, in order to enable the Exchequer to meet the demands which we are pledged in that country or elsewhere for advances to individuals or to pay the sums required to be spent for the ordinary services.[132]

Wood calculated that the Irish loan would be entirely expended by the end of December, and that revenue and expenditure after that time needed to balance in order to avoid defaulting on payments to creditors.[133] Just as the second commercial panic began, Irish MPs were told that finance precluded further

129   F. G. Hall, *History of the Bank of Ireland* (Dublin: Hodges, Figgis & Co., 1949), pp. 218–19.
130   Clarendon to Russell, 18 October 1847, N.A., Russell papers, PRO 30/22/6F, ff. 186–92.
131   S. H. Northcote, *Twenty years of financial policy* (London: Saunders, Otley and Co., 1862), p. 381.
132   Wood to Russell, 1 September 1847, N.A., Russell papers, PRO 30/22/6F, ff. 5–14.
133   Wood even developed contingency plans to raise tariffs that the government had only just lowered, in order to generate more revenue; see A. Howe, *Free Trade and Liberal England 1846–1946* (Oxford: OUP, 1997), pp. 45–46.

wide-scale Irish assistance. John O'Connell sent a circular letter to all provincial Irish newspapers saying 'We are told *there is no money in the Treasury!* Yes, that has been repeated to us over and over again within the last few weeks. THERE IS NO MONEY – THERE IS NO MONEY TO KEEP THE PEOPLE ALIVE!!!' O'Connell took this seriously, warning that local organisation was necessary to combat starvation.[134]

At the beginning of October Wood was reporting to Russell daily on the cash balance in the exchequer account.[135] It was feared that the government could cause another collapse in financial confidence by needing to borrow from the markets, as it did in March 1847, if it tried to raise any more loans. The price of exchequer bills had fallen to 20% below face value, raising substantially the interest rate that the government had to pay to borrow.[136] It was at this point, Trevelyan briefly broke ranks with the government and wrote to *The Times* asking the public for charity.[137] As the crisis worsened, Trevelyan wrote to Clarendon confirming that the government really meant business over the Poor Law and that a reliance on charity was the best hope. 'It is the intention of the government ... to insist upon the Poor Law being carried out to the utmost possible extent', he insisted, and 'in the present state of the public finances nothing can be more plain and reasonable [sic] than our right to require that all private funds applicable to the purpose should be expended ... before the public purse is opened'.[138] The move minimised expenditure based on loaned funds by replacing it with charitable donations that normally came from cash-in-hand.

Through October further bullion drains took place. The Bank of England was worried that it did not have sufficient bullion to maintain convertibility and it gave up trying to hold down interest rates. The Bank dumped £0.2m of 3% consols on 22 October that it had been previously buying to hold down long-term rates, after a fall in consol prices of over 400 basis points in a week and a related rise in yield (long-term interest rates) that did not abate until well into 1848 (Chart 4.2), affecting the cost of government borrowing.[139] On 25 October 1847, in a Treasury letter to the markets, Russell and Wood (with Peel's approval) announced the government's intention to maintain 'the vital principle of preserving the convertibility of the Banknote', by briefly suspending the

---

134 J. O'Connell, letter, *Athlone Sentinel*, 1 October 1847, p. 3.
135 Wood to Russell, 7 October 1847, N.A., Russell papers, PRO 30/22/6F, ff. 162–65.
136 Idem., ff. 144–45.
137 *The Times*, 12 October 1847, p. 5.
138 Trevelyan to Clarendon, 16 October 1847, O.B.L., Clarendon papers, Ms. Clar. dep. Irish box 60.
139 Dornbusch, Frenkel, 'The Gold Standard', p. 271; *Second Report from the Secret Committee of the House of Commons on Commercial Distress*, PP 1847–48 (584) VIII.505, appendix 34, p. 262; *The Economist*, 'Bankers' Price Current', 9 October 1847, p. 1173, 16 October 1847, p. 1202, 23 October 1847, p. 1229; in this context 400 basis points amounts to 4 percentage points of the face value.

requirements of Peel's legislation, a move repeated to restore confidence in 1857 and 1866.[140] To boost the Bank of England's gold reserves to a level where it could maintain the gold standard and the original requirements of the Bank Charter Act, the government told the Bank to raise official short-term interest rates from 3.5% at the start of the year to 8% – a record high since the Bank's foundation in 1694. This policy was believed by the Banking School to cause bullion to flow into the country and by the Currency School, at the time, as following the market interest rate as part of a self-balancing flow of bullion and adjustment of prices. The British government also planned to balance its books in subsequent years to avoid the need for any more borrowing, out of fear that it could trigger another financial panic.[141] Around half the Irish loan was spent on other expenditure because the government had not spent it on relief and was unable to refinance a total of about £4m of deficiency bills from April 1847 to April 1848 due to the second crisis.[142]

Unable to borrow from the markets and failing repeatedly to gather enough cross-party support in Parliament to raise income-tax rates in 1848, the government made the decision to reduce spending on Irish relief programmes and end most of its financial support for them by 1848.[143] Trevelyan had to write to Richard Pennefather in July 1848 passing on instructions 'for preparing for the entire cessation of this expenditure at the earliest practicable period'.[144]

The sharp reduction in expenditure from the time of the 1847 crises can clearly be seen in the British national accounts (Chart 4.6). Loans advanced to Poor Law Unions amounted to £4,080,000 in the financial year 1846–47 and £2,139,000 in 1847–48, but were completely ended by March 1848.[145] Treasury grants from central government funds for Irish relief also sharply fell after 1847, from £682,000 in 1846–47 and £975,000 in 1847–48 to just £389,920 in 1848–49.[146] After 1849 central government fiscal assistance for Irish relief was virtually non-existent. The reductions coincide with an increase in famine-related mortality, workhouse data suggest the peak of which occurred in the

140   Evans, *The commercial crisis*, p. 87.
141   Northcote, *Twenty years of financial policy*, pp. 381–82.
142   *The Economist*, 15 January 1848, p. 57; *Return of Number and Amount of Exchequer Bills issued, June 1847–48*, PP 1847–48 (454) XXXIX.153, p. 5.
143   Scherer, *Lord John Russell*, pp. 183–84; Howe, *Free Trade and Liberal England 1846–1946*, p. 46; Wood to Russell, 25 August 1847, N.A., Russell papers, PRO 30/22/6E, ff. 211–14.
144   Trevelyan to Pennefather, 3 July 1848, N.L.I., RLFC3/1/4068; earlier instructions in Treasury minute, 29 June 1847, C.U.L., Hickleton papers, MS MF A4.59, reel 1498.
145   *Public income and expenditure. Return of the total income of each year from 1829 to 1860–61 inclusive, as estimated in the budget, and of the actual income received ...*, 1861 PP (402) XXXIV.139.
146   *Public income and expenditure. Return of the net income and expenditure of the United Kingdom, for the several years ending 5th April 1842, 1843, 1844, 1845, 1846, 1847, 1848, 1849 and 1850, respectively*, PP 1851 (62) XXXI.159.

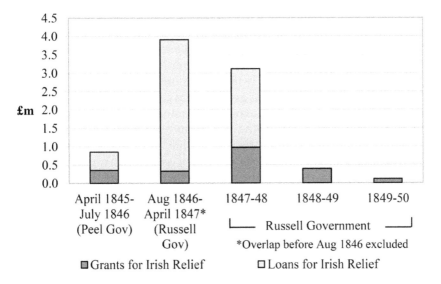

Chart 4.6. Expenditure on relief by Treasury loans and grants, by government, 1845 to 1850. *Sources: Correspondence...*, PP 1846 (735) XXXVII.41; *Public income and expenditure...*, PP 1851 (62) XXXI.159; *Public income and expenditure...*, PP 1861 (402) XXXIV.139.

winter of 1848–49.[147] As Haines has shown, Trevelyan made it clear in the book version of *The Irish Crisis* that 'crisis' referred to the fiscal crisis at the Treasury, not the harvest failure or famine itself.[148] The 'crisis' had ended, not with the end of crop failure and excess mortality in Ireland, but once Treasury funding for relief had ceased in 1848, leaving local government in charge.[149]

The British Association ran many of the soup kitchens and food depots in Ireland up to the middle of 1848 to provide relief after the early shut down of Treasury advances due to the crises that had 'paralysed' credit and the British financial system. However, the Association, now under the chairmanship of Lord Overstone, the main protagonist of Currency School ideas, voluntarily chose to close itself down, even though both the Treasury and the Irish Poor Law Unions were still desperately short on funds for relief and it had the opportunity to raise more donations.[150] Sir Randolph Routh, superintending

---

147 C. Ó Gráda, 'The Workhouses and Irish Famine Mortality', in T. Dyson, C. Ó Gráda (eds.), *Famine Demography* (Oxford: OUP, 2002), 44–64, at p. 44.
148 Haines, *Charles Trevelyan and the Great Irish Famine*, p. 406.
149 Ibid.
150 W. Stanley, Secretary Poor Law Commission, to Strzelecki, 20 December 1847, in *Papers relating to proceedings for the relief of distress and state of the unions and workhouses in Ireland*, fifth series 1848, Poor Law Commission Office, Dublin, p. 5.

the relief in Ireland, thought the Association had rushed and wasted its relief, as Overstone was well aware, but in vain Routh hoped that more would be available in 'the real time of trial' to come.[151] James Donnelly Jr. has put the phasing out of voluntary relief down to 'donor fatigue', but Count Strzelecki, who was closer to events in 1849, blamed it on the tendency to consider 'the distress which now exists in Ireland as an ordinary case' in the way Overstone considered financial crises as an unavoidable natural 'storm or tempest', an idea that came to be associated with the Currency School.[152]

A nervous Wood sent Peel information in July 1849 that suggested their macroeconomic plans were failing, as part of communications with him over free trade matters and legislation such as the Navigation Laws.[153] Large quantities of foreign wheat were being imported, and Poor Law reports showed that there was intense distress in the agricultural districts.[154] Wood pointed out wheat imports for the entire United Kingdom in the 1848–49 period were over three times those of 1846–47, which were believed to have triggered the bullion crisis, and the Poor Law reports 'disclose[d] a good deal of distress in the agricultural districts from want of employment'. Wood realised that the social benefits of their policies would be less than expected; 'small, unskilled farmers will have the fate of hand loom weavers: and though the people at large will be most materially benefited, I am afraid that there must be a good deal of class suffering'.[155] This realisation that the lower classes would suffer appears to have been news for both parties, and against their original intentions. However, potential bullion outflows prevented the government from reversing its decisions in 1847 because of Wood's fears that more Irish relief expenditure – or even discussions of it – might trigger yet another financial crisis.

Alternative policies to finance relief efforts

The Cabinet did attempt to find alternative economic policies that would allow the government to either continue borrowing to fund relief efforts, or to finance them without borrowing. The first to be considered was a plan by Grey for

151   Routh to Trevelyan, 7 September 1847, copy sent by Trevelyan to Overstone; O'Brien, *The Correspondence of Lord Overstone*, vol. 1, pp. 392–94.
152   J. S. Donnelly Jr., *The Great Irish Potato Famine* (Stroud: Sutton, 2002), p. 127; *Select Committee of House of Lords to inquire into Operation of Irish Poor Law, Fourth Report, Minutes of Evidence*, PP 1849 (365) XVI.543, p. 862; S. J. Loyd (Lord Overstone), *Remarks on the Management of the Circulation* (London: P. Richardson, 1840), p. 104.
153   Various letters Wood to Peel, May 1849, B.L., Peel papers, Add. MS. 40601, ff. 277, 281, 284, 288, 290.
154   Wood to Peel, July 1849, B.L., Peel papers, Add. MS. 40602, ff. 1–4.
155   Idem., ff. 11–14.

a currency which incorporated ideas of the Banking School in addition to the basic principles of the Currency School and the Bank Charter Act of 1844.[156] The problems of the Bank of England counting depositors' bullion 'twice' – both as deposits and as backing for notes – would be solved by having a Commission that owned all the bullion. His suggestion, which was the model for currency boards (an alternative to central banks), would have avoided, he believed, the need to raise interest rates and limit credit during crises. In that way, he hoped, it would have avoided the problem of government loans for Irish famine relief panicking markets.

The Third Earl Grey had published the basis of the plan in a pamphlet, *Thoughts on the Currency* in 1842.[157] It formed the model for the currency board which was set up in Mauritius after it suffered problems in 1847. Enquiries into the impact of the Bank Charter Act of 1844 on the crises of 1847 were held in response to Grey's pressure on the matter, but they had little effect.[158] The Lords Report suggested that amendments to the Act were necessary, but the Commons Reports concluded that they were not. The records of a series of votes on various motions are very instructive as to the views of the committee, but they also show that they were almost evenly split between Currency and Banking views.[159] Wood and Peel supported the Currency School line consistently, and this won through in the end. The views of those with a Banking School tendency varied from individual to individual and perhaps it was this inconsistency which allowed the ideas of the 1844 Act to emerge victorious.

The enormity of the conflict of ideas here should not be underestimated. The kernel of the argument was as to whether currency should be restricted in a financial crisis or whether it should be allowed to increase in quantity as commercial need demanded. According to Louise Davidson this is a basic argument about the nature of money and can be traced back to Aristotle.[160] It has evolved into the present-day conflict between Monetarists and Keynesians about fiscal policy and public investment. Monetarists often want credit restraint in a crisis; in contrast Keynesians tend to want more public investment.

156   Russell to Grey, 15 October 1847, D.U.L., Earl Grey papers, GRE/B122/3/91.

157   Anon. (Earl Grey), *Thoughts on the Currency* (London: Ridgeway, 1842); Wood to Grey, 10 January 1843, D.U.L., Earl Grey papers, GRE/B105/3/55; Pennington to 'author of "Thoughts on the Currency"', D.U.L., Earl Grey papers, 9 January 1843, GRE/B105/3/56.

158   *Reports from the Secret Committee of the House of Commons on Commercial Distress*, PP 1847–48 (395) VIII.1, VIII.379; *Second Report from the Secret Committee of the House of Commons on Commercial Distress*, PP 1847–48 (584) VIII.505; *Report from the Secret Committee of the House of Lords on Commercial Distress*, PP 1847–48 (565, 565-II).

159   *First Report from the Secret Committee of the House of Commons on Commercial Distress*, PP 1847–48 (395) VIII.1, pp. xii–xxii.

160   L. Davidson, 'Can Money be Neutral Even in the Long Run? Chartalism vs. Monetarism', in L. Davidson (ed.), *Uncertainty, International Money, Employment and Theory* (London: Palgrave Macmillan, 1999), 196–210, at pp. 196–97.

The argument has developed into a political one between the right and left extremes of political views, each eager to obliterate the viewpoint of the other.

Grey's ideas, as he expressed them in *Thoughts on the Currency* in 1842, contained a mixture of both. He retained the idea of limiting the circulation of notes according to the amount backing them as specie and stock, in line with the ideas of the moderate Currency School theorists.[161] However, in line with the ideas of the Banking School, he also incorporated the idea that the amount of specie should be grown by means of the interest earned on stocks and a method of limiting capital flows to lessen the possibility of 'hot' money flows making crises worse (by only making currency notes exchangeable for specie for amounts larger than 100 ounces of gold).[162] So Currency School and Banking School ideas were combined. In 1847 the change required to the United Kingdom's currency to implement Grey's ideas would have been significant, and the Russell government simply did not have the confidence or Parliamentary strength to alter Peel's banking legislation. In addition, the resolve on the part of Peel and Wood to defend the 1844 Bank Charter Act should not be underestimated. Currency School theory was in reality the ideology where adherence to it worsened the Irish famine.

The other alternative policy considered by the government was to fund relief spending in Ireland by increasing the income tax. Wood had hoped that an increase in income tax could either raise more money for relief efforts in Ireland directly or enable the government to borrow from the markets again by showing that Parliament was willing to raise taxes to cover the extra interest payments, just as had happened during the Napoleonic Wars.[163] However, by 1848, it had become difficult politically to get the income tax for Great Britain renewed, let alone increased. Much fuss has been made by historians about radical Whig backbenchers galvanising opposition to tax rises during the commercial downturn of 1847–48, yet in fact many were more than happy to see Ireland's income-tax exemption disappear to help fund Irish relief efforts.[164] The archives

161   Anon. (Earl Grey), *Thoughts on the Currency*, pp. 51–64.

162   Idem., pp. 47–48, 59.

163   Attempted policy summarised in: Wood to Russell, 31 March 1848, N.A., Russell papers, PRO 30/22/7B/64, ff. 186–89; ff. 190–91 typescript; for the history of debt finance during the Napoleonic War, see M. D. Bordo, E. White, 'A Tale of Two Currencies: British and French Finance during the Napoleonic Wars', *Journal of Economic History*, 51:2 (1991), 303–16, at pp. 310–12.

164   For instance, Gray states that: 'The UK general election of summer 1847 returned a turbulent group of around eighty *laissez-faire* radical MPs, led by Richard Cobden, who held the Parliamentary balance of power and demanded fiscal retrenchment': P. Gray, 'The Great Famine, 1845–1850', in T. Bartlett, J. Kelly (eds.), *The Cambridge History of Ireland* (Cambridge: CUP, 2018), 639–65, at p. 655; D. Kanter, in contrast, shows that Irish MPs were the greatest block on government action, with the increase in the number of Irish Repeal MPs in the 1847 election also a problem: 'Wood's plan failed because ministers were

suggest that a lack of support from Irish MPs, as well as the other parties that the minority Whig government needed to get its legislation passed, proved more troublesome for the government.[165] Kanter has described the series of events which resulted in Wood's first budget, proposed for 1848, being abandoned. It would have supported spending in Ireland by increasing the income tax from 7d to 12d in the pound in Great Britain and by partial abolition of the Irish exemption, but it failed because of a lack of support from Irish MPs, and this constrained relief expenditure.[166]

The failure to increase the income tax was the tragic consequence of a partisan squabble over Ireland's income-tax exemption in 1847–48.[167] Peel, when he reintroduced the income tax in Great Britain in 1842 at a rate of 7d, had excluded Ireland from paying it in exchange for some tax increases on spirits and stamps.[168] The Repealers (Irish supporters of Repeal of the Act of Union) opposed any increase of the tax in Great Britain out of the fear that it would eventually lead to its introduction in Ireland, where it had always been regarded as an obnoxious impost and was electorally unpopular. The Repeal Association had won 36 seats in the 1847 general election, 16 more than in 1841, making the Parliamentary arithmetic more difficult still for an income tax increase.[169] Irish MPs – Repealers, Conservatives and Whigs – appear to have all opposed the increase; when Wood consulted Clarendon about his proposals in February 1848, the Irish viceroy replied stating, 'that there will be a violent opposition to the Income Tax, modify it as you will, & resistance in every shape & from every class to its payment – it will exasperate every holder of place, smash every squireen, & certainly give an impetus to the expiring cry of Repeal'.[170]

However, what was seen by Irish landowners and their representatives of all parties in Parliament as defending their legitimate financial interests was easily seen by British MPs and the British press as rank hypocrisy. Ireland had been exempted from Britain's original income tax introduced during the Napoleonic Wars, as well as its re-introduction in Peel's budget of 1842. The greatest beneficiaries of this were clearly Ireland's landowners, as Schedule A (the tax on rental income from land and other real estate) was the most lucrative

---

unwilling to impose the income tax in the absence of Irish consent'; Kanter, 'The Politics of Irish Taxation', p. 1132; see p. 1131 for the point about the support among Radical MPs for abolishing Ireland's income-tax exemption.

165   Kanter, 'The Politics of Irish Taxation', pp. 1131–32.
166   Ibid.
167   Idem., pp. 1130–34.
168   *Hansard*, LXI, 11 March 1842, cc. 444–48.
169   Kanter, 'The Politics of Irish Taxation', p. 1132.
170   Ibid., citing Clarendon to Wood, 9 February 1848, Borthwick Institute for Archives, Hickleton papers, A4.57.

part of the system in Great Britain.[171] Their opposition towards the abolition of their exemption fuelled the growing hostility towards Irish landowners in Parliament and in the press from then onwards, particularly as Peel's public-works system came to be seen as a bailout for the Irish rich, a group already massively favoured by the tax arrangements.

In reaction to protest from Irish MPs in Parliament, the Cabinet then decided to 'defer' the abolition of the Irish exemption in the budget, but press ahead with a temporary increase for Great Britain.[172] When Russell presented that proposal to Parliament in another budget statement on 18 February 1848, the frosty reception it received from MPs of all parties showed that Parliament would not approve even a temporary income-tax increase in Great Britain if the Irish exemption was continued.[173] Even so, the key Parliamentary group was, once again, the Peelites. At the end of February 1848, Peel signalled his opposition to a higher rate of income tax in private correspondence in an attempt to try and extract concessions from the government on trade policy.[174] Although the Peelites supported the income tax's renewal in Great Britain in 1848, they did not favour any rise in the rate levied as a result of their worries about whether the extra revenues would be diverted from Irish relief to end Peel's policy of gradualism by bringing in free trade too quickly (see Chapter 2).[175] So on 28 February 1848, approximately two days after Peel's letter made it clear that the government did not have enough votes in Parliament for its revised proposal, Wood was forced to abandon it too, in favour of renewing the income tax at its original level.[176] The chancellor conceded 'that, under ordinary circumstances, Ireland ought to pay the tax', but 'it would be ... unwise and inexpedient to impose that tax upon Ireland at the present moment'.[177]

The failure to raise the income tax contributed towards the almost complete cessation of advances for Irish relief from the end of March 1848, as the government's deficit on ordinary expenditure had to be met via spending reserves which would have otherwise been available for making further advances for relief in Ireland.[178] Wood justified further funding restraint to Clarendon in

---

171   R. Peel, *Financial Statement of Sir R. Peel in the House of Commons, March 11, 1842* (London: William Edward Painter, 1842), pp. 16–17.
172   Kanter, 'The Politics of Irish Taxation', p. 1132.
173   *Hansard*, XCVI, 18 February 1847, cc. 900–81; Kanter, 'The Politics of Irish Taxation', p. 1134.
174   Wood to Peel, 26 February(?) 1848, B.L., Graham papers, Add. MS. 79713, f. 34.
175   Wood to Russell, 25 August 1847, N.A., Russell papers, PRO 30/22/6E, ff. 211–14; *Hansard*, XCVII, 3 March 1848, cc. 162–231; idem., 13 March 1848, c. 534; Wood to Peel, 26 February(?) 1848, B.L., Graham papers, Add. MS. 79713, f. 34.
176   *Hansard*, XCVI, 28 February 1848, c. 1410.
177   *Hansard*, XCVII, 17 March 1848, c. 743.
178   *Hansard*, XCVI, 28 February 1848, cc. 1414–15; *Public income and expenditure ...*, PP 1851 (62) XXXI.159; *Public income and expenditure ...*, PP 1861 (402) XXXIV.139.

Dublin by blaming Parliamentary arithmetic for the debacle: 'I do not think you have a notion on how strong the feeling is [in Parliament] … against further expenditure for a country that does not pay the income tax'.[179] In short, once again, the weakness of the Russell government in Parliament prevented alternative funds being raised to maintain advances to Ireland for relief.

More policies blocked

Even after the financial panics of 1847 and the humiliating failure to raise the income tax in 1848, Russell had not given up on finding ways to help Ireland. As the decade wore on there were further attempts to produce policies which would assist Ireland. These were provoked in 1848 by a fear of revolution. Grey, in particular, attempted to produce policies that bridged the gap between the Irish middle classes who wished to emigrate and the colonies, particularly Canada, who were fearful of receiving them. This put him into conflict with Russell who believed that policies could be implemented by raising taxes. Grey recognised that his brother-in-law, Wood the chancellor of the exchequer, was traumatised by the financial events of 1846–47 and the failed budgets of early 1848. Wood was unable to contemplate either taking on more public loans or raising taxes, and Grey, who understood more than most about the insecurity of the financial position of Britain, looked to source funding from elsewhere. The resultant conflict and Russell's weak political leadership meant that very little in the way of policy actually came to fruition.

Aside from its effects on relief funding for the famine in Ireland, the 1847 financial crisis had caused commercial pain and thrown many working people out of employment in Great Britain. There was general discontent about the economic situation, and politicians feared that the revolutions on the Continent early in 1848 would revive the Irish Repeal lobby and the Chartists in Britain. On 30 March 1848 Russell wrote a letter to members of his Cabinet proposing a number of policy ideas to help the Irish poor for their comment. It proposed in summary:

1. that ejectments of tenants be more rigorously controlled.
2. that further loans be made to landlords for improvements.
3. that an additional £1m borrowed by the issue of exchequer bills be provided for drainage and other useful works in Ireland.
4. that the Habeas Corpus Act be suspended for one year.
5. that £1.4m, levied by a land tax, be used to support Catholic priests.[180]

179   Wood to Clarendon, 3 April 1848, C.U.L., Hickleton papers, MS MF A4.57, reel 1495.
180   Russell to members of Cabinet, 30 March 1848; this letter only exists by the transcription in Sir S. Walpole, *Life of Lord John Russell*, vol. 2 (London: Longmans, 1889),

Wood replied, agreeing that ejectments should be carried out more fairly towards the tenants, not believing that suspending Habeas Corpus was a good idea, and agreeing to further loans for landlords. However, he leapt to reject other expenditure. He believed that the Commons would not agree to pay the interest on loans for more drainage works and that a land tax would fail.[181] Russell pushed the matter further and Wood exploded, in a passage worth quoting in full:

> Look at our financial state, a probable deficiency of £150,000 – heavy demands for advances, for reserves purposes, New Zealand, Immigration, Tobago distress, drainage and – borrowing is becoming too possible, and that without the means of paying interest without just taxation. The manufacturing districts in great distress, operatives not on wages largely and no prospects of reviving trade; on the contrary in many districts every chance of its becoming worse: and, during the process which is sure to aggravate the suffering and discontent of the lower orders and the constant necessity for conciliating the better classes. They are complaining bitterly of taxation. It is essential to retain their support. In order to do so we have been obliged to abandon the additional income tax – and now you propose to conciliate them by an advance – for whom? The Irish landlords, who don't pay the income tax, to which they have just been exempted. Depend upon it, we cannot in these days, afford to set the populous districts, high and low, against us. We have had one pretty severe lesson this session [this is a reference to Wood's failure to get an increased income tax through Parliament in 1847–48] and we cannot afford to try any more experiments of the same kind. It is our bounden duty to prevent starvation, it is not our bounden duty to secure a dozen Irish candidates who ask us for money ... If money matters of 1846 and 1847 do not carry conviction, no future years will ... But I really cannot conceive what Liverpool, Manchester and Glasgow will say to income tax, no navigation laws and further advances for Ireland [if they] are to be heaped upon their devoted heads – I am sure that coals of fire will be heaped upon ours.[182]

Tellingly, Lord Palmerston, the foreign secretary, said the proposals two and three 'would be useful', but with an important qualifier – they should only be pursued 'if financially easy'.[183] Grey agreed in principle with all the proposals except for suspending Habeas Corpus. With the proposal to fund Catholic clergy he entirely approved but thought that the Catholic hierarchy and the Pope should approve the idea (whose approval was not forthcoming in the end). This

pp. 64–65, but the original replies are in the National Archives, Kew.
181   Wood to Russell, 31 March 1848, N.A., Russell papers, PRO 30/22/7B, ff. 186–89, typescript ff. 190–91.
182   Wood to Russell, 9 April 1848, N.A., Russell papers, PRO 30/22/7B, ff. 249–52.
183   Palmerston to Russell, 31 March 1848, N.A., Russell papers, PRO 30/22/7B, ff. 181–82, typescript ff. 183–84.

response matched his support for a pluralist religious society in Mauritius, but he did not think 'to add to the burdens upon Irish land' to pay for it was 'practicable' though.[184] Trevelyan's advice on how to respond to criticism by Repealers suggested more funding should be available when charitable donations ran out:

> All the measures that have been recently adopted and that are now in progress for the good of Ireland should be recapitulated – the great expenditure and the immense efforts, public and private made for the relief of the distress – the large amount of Loan which has been remitted – the further amount which <u>may be</u> remitted when time shall be afforded to make a satisfactory adjustment of Taxation between the two countries – the million and a half Loan for the Improvement of Private Estates and affording employment to the people – the large Drainage Loans and the further Loans for similar purposes which will be made as our financial condition may allow (This may be called blackmail, but it will be a cheap way of encouraging the Irish gentry and we can hold out these expectations <u>now</u> without loss of character) – the Bill for Encumbered Estates – the Bill for the reorganisation of the medical charities – the Bill for the reorganisation of the local financial Grand Jury system – and further assistance from the Consolidated Fund in aid of the most distressed Districts under the Poor Law, when the fund of the British Association is exhausted. This may be safely promised.[185]

Emigration assisted by public funds was also discussed at this time and, more generally, since the Whigs came to power in the summer of 1846. The problem with this policy option was, yet again, the government's lack of funding for such a scheme on any large scale. The proposals put forward were hampered by financial concerns from the start. Stephen Spring Rice, a son of the Irish Whig peer Lord Monteagle, came up with a plan for a large, government-funded emigration scheme from Ireland. Copies of the plans were distributed to ministers in October 1846. 'I cannot say I think there is much in it' was the comment of the Third Earl Grey, the colonial secretary in charge of emigration matters.[186] Wood thought 'he [Monteagle] has only one object in mind, namely the relief of the Irish landlords from the pressure of their tenantry they have, to their cost, permitted or even encouraged on their estates'.[187] Nevertheless, Grey worked out the details of a scheme based on village settlements in Canada, but when it came to costings, the scheme fell apart. Grey reported to Russell that, 'the cost of settling immigrants in villages would be so enormous (the

184   Grey to Russell, 30 March 1848, N.A., Russell papers, PRO 30/22/7B, ff. 178–79, typescript f. 180.
185   Trevelyan memorandum on Chartists and Ireland, 4 April 1848, N.A., Russell papers, PRO 30/22/7B, ff. 217–22 (original underline).
186   Grey to Russell, 16 October 1846, N.A. PRO 30/22/5D, ff. 216–17.
187   Wood to Grey 19 October 1846, GRE/B122/3/14.

estimate I have had given to me is £48,000 for settling 500 families) that it would be practically impossible to attempt it'.[188] Lord Monteagle obtained approval for an Enquiry, but by this time the financial problems of 1847 had begun and Grey warned, 'they could not be ignorant of the present state of the money market'.[189] The Enquiry took evidence to explore other means of funding but came to no firm conclusions in July 1847, and was still to report in June 1848.[190] It was during this period Grey told Clarendon that Monteagle's emigration plan was 'entirely impracticable' and a loan to fund it was not possible because of its impact on British money markets:

> The financial considerations are by no means the only ones which stand in the way of adopting it and yet these by themselves ought to be conclusive. In the present state of the country, grievously as we are suffering from the want of capital immediately available, when we know that the state's coming into the money market to borrow five million for such as this would necessarily have the effect of withdrawing that large sum from the resources of the country applicable to railroads and the various industrial enterprises, stopped in many cases from the deficiency of those resources, and when we further consider that this must aggravate all the evils under which we are suffering, throw more labourers out of employment and render more intense the vicious competition for money now going on, it certainly appears to me that it would be perfectly unjustifiable to the people of this country to expose them to these consequences for the sake of the Irish for whom they have already made such sacrifices.[191]

The other problem the Whigs faced with assisted emigration was the rising realisation that the colonies were resistant to receiving Irish immigrants, who were increasingly viewed as troublesome by their local elites. In general, Irish protest had been peaceful, as encouraged by Daniel O'Connell and his supporters. The attitude in many colonies towards Irish immigrants at the start of the famine was broadly sympathetic. However, in July 1846, Thomas Meagher gave his 'sword speech' and started Young Ireland's split with the O'Connellites over the use of physical force to achieve Irish nationalism's goals. The decisive moment that swayed politicians against more Irish emigration to the colonies was Young Ireland's attempted 'cabbage patch' revolution in rural County Tipperary in 1848. Grey at the Colonial Office was heavily swayed by

188   Grey to Russell, 29 January 1847, N.A. PRO 30/22/6A, ff. 217–18; see Black, *Economic Thought and the Irish Wuestion 1917–1870*, p. 228.
189   *Hansard*, XCIII, 4 June 1847, c. 116.
190   *Report of the Select Committee of the House of Lords on Colonisation from Ireland*, PP 1847 (737 737-II) VI.1, 563; *Report of the Select Committee of the House of Lords on Colonisation from Ireland*, PP 1847–48 (415) XVII.1.
191   Grey to Clarendon, 4 December 1847, D.U.L., Earl Grey papers, GRE/B81/3/17.

Edward Gibbon Wakefield, a member of the legislative council of Canada, who by 1849 had become indignant about being asked to take more immigrants from Ireland, 'In Canada the Orange and Milesian [traditionally the first Christian inhabitants of Ireland] factions have been effectually transplanted and wage a perpetual war ... producing terror and disgust for other people', he thundered.[192] The growing protests from the colonies can clearly be seen in Grey's letters about Ireland. 'But even if we had the money it would be difficult to do anything', the colonial secretary protested to Clarendon as Irish viceroy in 1849, 'The Colonies are already angry beyond measure at the manner in which Irish Emigrants have been sent out and I must say not without good reason ... Canada cannot absorb more than a limited number at a time'.[193]

Grey, nevertheless, was not initially discouraged by the problems at the Treasury. In the aftermath of the crises of 1847, Grey initially believed that funding could be found from other sources than the Treasury for Irish emigration to Canada as a form of famine relief. He knew that Canada wanted to build a railway line from Halifax to Quebec, but needed finance and workers; 'The way in which I think we might do this, and to which to my surprise even Wood, with all his hatred of expense and of new taxes, seemed inclined to agree, is to borrow £5m for the purpose (it would be wanted in about three years), charging the interest upon a duty to be imposed on colonial timber, and looking to the sale of land on the line for a sinking fund'.[194] Part of the funding would pay for workers to emigrate to Canada to build the line. This arrangement removed Wood's objection that the House of Commons would not pay interest on loans for Ireland through an increased income tax, while attempting to keep Canadian officials on board by helping with one of their priority projects.

However, Russell persisted into 1848 with his proposal to raise money through domestic taxation. He suggested that money for emigration schemes in Ireland as well as the rest of the United Kingdom could be funded with 'a tax on property rated to the relief of the poor to the amount of 6d in the pound [2.5%] in Ireland, and of 3d in the pound in England and Scotland.[195] Grey was less keen on this proposal, replying that 'I am opposed to the proposal for borrowing money on the security of the rates'. For England and Scotland, he did not believe large-scale emigration was necessary; why 'are we to pay additional poor rates to remove able-bodied labourers from the country?' As to Ireland, he pointed out, on reflection, that in 1847 those who arrived in Canada 'were almost exclusively labourers of the lowest and most destitute

---

192 E. G. Wakefield, *View of the art of colonisation* (London: J. Parker, 1849), pp. 186–87.
193 Grey to Clarendon, 4 December 1847, D.U.L., Earl Grey papers, GRE/B81/3/17.
194 Walpole, *Life of Lord John Russell*, vol. 2, p. 79; see also D.U.L., Earl Grey papers, GRE/B109/7B/2-6.
195 Russell, emigration plan, 1848(?), N.A., Russell papers, PRO 30/22/5G, ff. 215–17.

class'. After that most who arrived were 'tolerably well off'. The likelihood was that public money would end up being utilised by those who could already afford their journey, using the passage to Canada as part of a subsidised journey to the United States.[196] James Wilson wrote to Grey backing him up by saying that further taxes on Ireland would be counterproductive, by disincentivising investment in Ireland and leading to 'the improbability of continuing even good land in cultivation ... unless some kind of limit is placed on the rates to which land shall be exposed'.[197] Others had similar reservations about raising taxes on land further. Archbishop Whately of Dublin, for instance, noted that already the 'law, as far as respected the mode of administering relief, and the circumstances under which it was given, operated as a penalty upon industry, and an impediment to the cultivation of the land'.[198]

In February 1849, with the public finances improving, Wood encouraged Russell to 'chip up Somerville as to his scheme for financing emigration', for the coming Select Committee on the Poor Law. At that Committee, enabling the emigration of paupers was considered 'on pecuniary grounds' with a plan to: '... cut the Gordian knot of Irish pauperism, because I believe it is universally admitted, that if the funds were forthcoming by which the surplus population of Ireland could be safely and successfully placed within the reach of the almost unlimited demand for Colonial labour, the carrying out of such an arrangement would meet with universal sanction'.[199] In the event, the Poor Relief (Ireland) Act of 1 August 1849 allowed Poor Law Unions to borrow from the Exchequer Bill Loan Commissioners, but only 2,592 people and children were assisted.[200] Once again, restraints on borrowing by the Treasury, which still feared another bullion drain, limited what could be done to help Ireland with grants and advances from the Treasury. As Russell sadly admitted to Clarendon, 'Now without borrowing and lending we could have no great plan for Ireland – and much as I wished it, I have got to see that it is impracticable'.[201]

The 'mare's nest' of financing famine relief

The argument that the Russell government's economic policy during the famine was driven mainly by the application of *laissez-faire* principles alone is therefore unconvincing. The political papers of Peel, Russell and Wood

196 Grey to Cabinet, 18 December 1848, D.U.L., Earl Grey papers, GRE/B144/12.
197 Wilson to Grey, 16 February 1849, D.U.L., Earl Grey papers, GRE/B132/11/15–16.
198 *Hansard*, CV, 11 May 1849, c. 277.
199 *Select Committee on Irish Poor Laws*, PP 1849 (194) XV.347, paragraph 4751.
200 G. Moran, *Sending out Ireland's Poor* (Dublin: Four Court's Press, 2004), pp. 89, 136.
201 Russell to Clarendon, 24 February 1849, O.B.L., Clarendon papers, Ms. Clar. dep. c. 126, also cited in Mandler, *Aristocratic Government in the Age of Reform*, p. 252.

show that a concern for financial issues did more to shape their relief policies towards Ireland than a providential attitude of *laissez-faire* towards the Irish poor. Indeed, Wood claimed 'everything in Ireland resolves itself into a money question'.[202]

Whether Wood saw economic forces he did not understand as the hand of God is possible, but the words historians use to justify this view of him can also be interpreted as his use of another's philosophy as a refuge from or disguise for the reality of the government's failure to finance the relief effort.[203] Trevelyan's *The Irish Crisis*, a book often held up by historians as evidence that he advocated a *laissez-faire* approach to famine relief, performed a similar function.[204] It appeared first as an article in the *Edinburgh Review* and the overall focus was an attempt to justify the policies of putting the whole relief effort on the Irish Poor Law and trying to force landlords to employ the poor according to the laws of political economy, without disclosing that these solutions were a necessity for reasons of financial failure of the government's previous policies.[205] Privately, Trevelyan was collecting evidence to suggest that the policy was not producing enough employment to end the crisis. The answers he received to a survey sent out asking Poor Law officials whether enough employment could be generated to replace relief efforts were strongly in the negative.[206] This important information about the context of his published book – that it was spinning government policy in an optimistic way rather than really stating the situation – has been hidden from historians until now because the answers to the survey had been mis-catalogued by the National Archives in Kew under 'non-Irish famine subjects'. The financial panic caused by the Irish Loan was not mentioned until the book version.[207] This was because, to avoid another panic, Trevelyan was not initially, in his *Edinburgh Review* article, allowed to explicitly state that the crises of 1847 were the reason why the costs of Peel's relief policies could no longer, let alone indefinitely, be met from the Treasury. In 1848, when the book was published, Trevelyan described the loan as causing 'serious injury' to Britain.[208] The aim, he stated clearly, was now to prevent a recurrence of financial crisis by assuring the public that the famine problem had been resolved.

202   Wood to Clarendon, 25 September 1847, C.U.L., Hickleton papers, MS MF A4.57, reel 1495.
203   For instance, see Gray, *Famine, Land and Politics*, p. 292 and Wood to Clarendon, 15 August 1847, C.U.L., Hickleton papers, MS MF A4.186, reel 1523.
204   Trevelyan, *The Irish Crisis* (London: Longman, 1848).
205   Idem., 'The Irish Crisis'.
206   *Poor Law Inspectors: entry book of their replies to a Treasury Circular on Unemployment*, January 1848, N.A., Treasury papers, T 64/400.
207   Trevelyan, *The Irish Crisis*, p. 194.
208   Ibid.

Trevelyan was not the only figure to use *laissez-faire* ideas to justify the government's line in public, while being motivated by a different agenda in private. In 1853 the Third Earl Grey published a book about his time as colonial secretary entitled *The Colonial Policy of Lord John Russell's Administration*, which also gave *laissez-faire*-sounding reasons for the lack of government-funded assisted-emigration schemes from Ireland during the famine.[209] But the justification he gave in private correspondence is different, particularly in a memorandum circulated to the Cabinet dated 14 April 1848. In it he unequivocally blames the financial panics of 1847: 'there was an obvious deficiency of disposable capital in the country and that it would have been impossible for the Government to have gone into the market to borrow money for any such purpose as that now adverted to without still further aggravating this deficiency'.[210]

The idea that the Russell government was ideologically more parsimonious in providing famine relief than Peel's should be put to rest. The descriptive statistics showing that this notion is false are stark. The Russell government, in its first year in office, spent over four times more on famine relief than the Peel government did during the first year of the crisis. In its second year, it had initially been prepared to spend up to £14m, according to the correspondence relating to the budget of 1847. This proposed level of spending on famine relief, it seems, was unprecedented anywhere in the British Isles up to this point. The spirited public and private defence of the government's interventionist policies by Russell, Wood and Clarendon in 1846–47, even when the contrary position may have been a politically easier position to take, suggests the influence of *laissez-faire* ideology does not fully explain the government's actions when it cut funding for Irish famine relief efforts in 1847.[211]

Instead, it was economic crisis and financial panic in Britain that helped to push the Russell government away from their initial plans to offer Ireland generous grants and loans to fund the relief effort. Wood's commitment to a set of macroeconomic policies laid out by Peel before 1846 left him with limited options when financial crisis hit Britain in 1847. Rather than *laissez-faire* ideology it was the Currency School's ideology of applying a gold standard with limited resources of bullion, which induced a squeeze on credit as interest rates increased abroad, that prevented loans being available to fund relief efforts. The reason that the crises were short lived is that they were policy induced and resolved by policy changes such as holding back on future loans and the brief suspension of the Bank Charter Act. But this does not mean they were not

---

209   Earl Grey, *The Colonial Policy of Lord John Russell's Administration* (London: Richard Bentley, 1853).
210   Earl Grey memorandum to Cabinet, 14 April 1848, D.U.L., Earl Grey papers, GRE/B144/20.
211   *Hansard*, LXXXIX, 25 January 1847, cc. 426–79.

serious. The downturn in the British business cycle, a trade deficit, a collapse in tax revenues, rising interest rates in America and the need to borrow to fund Irish relief, all contributed towards the panics over falling gold reserves in 1847.

Wood and Peel believed that they needed to maintain the gold standard, the Bank Charter Acts and free trade as the only way of saving the entire British economy from collapsing while ensuring food prices remained low in Ireland.[212] However, to do this, they had to cut famine relief spending, which was placed off the Treasury's main balance sheet and under the control of local government. To Trevelyan, this change also removed some responsibility from central to local government: 'we must not be chargeable with neglect ... the Relief Committees may leave the people to starve ... we cannot force them if they will do so'.[213] When the financial panic subsided, Treasury expenditure was still limited. Wood was fearful of the effects of loans, and Whig Parliamentary weakness meant that they were unable to raise income tax in Parliament to provide the additional funding to provide more assistance in Ireland without resorting to borrowing.

Thus, it should be the unintended consequences of Peel's and Wood's economic policies, their adherence to the principles of the Bank Charter Act, as promoted by Overstone, and the weakness of the Russell government in Parliament which bear the responsibility for the change in relief policy in 1847 and the persistence of excess mortality after this period. Peel and Wood were firmly convinced that the policies they had adopted in 1847 would help the Irish poor only at the cost of Ireland's wealthy. Advances for relief were curtailed because contemporary politicians did not fully understand the economic forces at work. Wood confided to Russell during the Irish loan crisis that from what he could gather of some of the Bank's actions, 'I am puzzled by the whole story – and I suggest there is a mare's nest at the bottom of it'.[214]

Contemporaries certainly saw the government's reaction to the events of 1847 as confused and unsatisfactory. A caricature published in *Punch* magazine in September 1848 illustrates the common opinion at the time that Wood's limited expertise on economic matters had resulted in the Russell government becoming incapable of effective action to raise the necessary funds to combat the famine after the financial panics of 1847 (Figure 4.5).[215] The result was the destruction of Ireland. Pointing to a map on the wall of Ireland in pieces, *Punch* presents his sarcastic 'prizes' 'to Master Charles Wood, for the pursuit of financial knowledge under difficulties'.[216] Also given

212   Wood to F. Baring, 12 May 1847, C.U.L., Hickleton papers, MS MF A4.54, reel 1490.
213   Trevelyan to Routh, 14 December 1846, O.B.L., Trevelyan letter books, vol. 10, pp. 115–17.
214   Wood to Russell, 14 April 1847, N.A., Russell papers, PRO 30/22/6C, ff. 80–86.
215   *Punch*, 9 September 1848.
216   Ibid.

Figure 4.5. Punch's prizes for the session. *Punch*, 9 September 1848, p. 116.

'to Master John Russell, the head boy of the establishment, [is] the First Prize, for *General Inefficiency*; and an extra prize ... for an essay, illustrated with practical examples, "On the Art of doing the Least Possible Work in the Greatest Possible Time"'.[217]

The fiscal disaster of 1847 – and the consequences it had for Ireland – were not easily forgotten by Victorian politicians. Wood, as secretary of state for India in the 1860s, cut back Trevelyan's public-works schemes there so that a proposed loan for the Indian government could be cancelled, out of the fear that the events of 1847 could repeat.[218] At home, it also contributed to a paradigm shift over fiscal policy. So traumatic were the problems associated with raising the Irish loan in 1847 that it inspired the parsimony of Gladstonian finance in subsequent decades. When Gladstone became chancellor of the exchequer in December 1852, at the very end of the famine, he vowed to ensure the Treasury would never again have to go 'begging to the Bank'.[219] The Treasury needed to be, Gladstone wrote, 'provided with an instrument sufficiently powerful to make him independent of the Bank and the City power when he has occasion for sums in seven figures' – a reference to the difficulties that Wood faced with

217   Ibid.
218   Read, 'Laissez-faire, the Irish Famine and British Financial Crisis', pp. 427–28.
219   J. Tomlinson, *Problems of British Economic Policy, 1870–1945* (Abingdon: Routledge, 2006), p. 46.

deficiency bills when he tried to borrow £8m for Ireland in 1847.[220] Gladstone decided to build fiscal capacity by paying down debt and he borrowed directly from the public by setting up the Post Office Savings Bank in order to ensure that the problems of 1847 would never again beset a chancellor.[221] Therefore it is clear that Gladstone had not forgotten the financial problems of 1847, even if some historians writing recently have.

220 Undated fragment quoted in J. Morley, *The Life of William Ewart Gladstone* (Cambridge: CUP, 2011), p. 651.
221 Tomlinson, *Problems of British Economic Policy, 1870–1945*, pp. 46–47.

5

The intentions and consequences of redistributive relief policy

If you had gone through the Irish Famine as I did, you would I think agree with me. In vain I strove to make them do something for themselves, I reconstituted the supply of money – but I begged, prayed, and urged and tried to force them by every means in my power to help in at least managing the relief, not a bit of it. It was entirely thrown on the Govt. officers ... We could not let the people starve – but we had to find the means of administering food to hundreds of thousands, unassisted by any Irish residents, high or low.

> Halifax (Sir Charles Wood in retirement) to William
> Gladstone (as prime minister), 16 December 1870.[1]

The effect of the law was to reduce the middling and struggling classes to abject poverty. Their cattle and stock were distrained for rates to support pauperism, and then they became paupers themselves. He knew, himself, the case of a gentleman who had a large estate lying waste and profitless. The tenants [themselves also] all emigrated to America with the rent, and everything they could scrape together, and the owner of the land could not even let the land as pasture for cattle, lest the stock should be seized for payment of poor-rates. Such was the position of this gentleman, who was now dependent upon private charity for support. He believed that the working of the present law, as far as it respected the mode of administering relief, and the circumstances under which it was given, operated as a penalty upon industry, and an impediment to the cultivation of the land.

> Richard Whately, Archbishop of Dublin, 11 May 1849.[2]

As the previous chapter has shown, the year 1847 was a turbulent one for London's money markets. In Ireland it is one that has become infamous as the worst point of the famine. 'Black '47' is not only referred to by historians but in popular discourse too.[3] A recent film about the famine, *Black '47*, has

---

1 Halifax (Wood) to Gladstone, 16 December 1870, B.L., Gladstone papers, Add. MS. 44185, ff. 103–05.
2 *Hansard*, CV, 11 May 1849, c. 277.
3 C. Ó Gráda, *Black '47 and Beyond: The Great Irish Famine in History, Economy and Memory* (Princeton: Princeton University Press, 1999).

immortalised the suffering on the ground in Ireland that year.[4] Yet like all historical myths, the reality is more complex. As Peter Gray has recently noted in the *Cambridge History of Ireland*, there were some economic signs in 1847 that 'provided the illusion that the Famine emergency was now over'.[5] Food prices halved between February and August, while imports of Indian corn that summer surged.[6] That autumn saw potato yields per-acre-planted recover to pre-famine levels (although the total area under cultivation had dropped because of a shortage of seed potatoes).[7] However, in spite of an improving agricultural backdrop, excess mortality remained persistent. Research by Cormac Ó Gráda suggests that deaths in workhouses did not peak until the winter of 1848–49.[8] Even at that late stage of the famine, well past the worst period of harvest failure, travellers still frequently reported finding dead corpses at the roadside between settlements on the west coast of Ireland.[9] The persistence of excess mortality, the failure of potato yields to fully recover and continued emigration and economic stress into the 1850s has made it difficult for historians to date the end of the famine, with 1849, 1850, 1852 and 1853 used by different scholars.

Given the gradual recovery of the agricultural sector from 1847, the intensification of suffering in Ireland may have had less to do with total calorie availability and more to do with other issues, such as 'entitlements', the financial ability to buy food, and nutritional diseases.[10] 'Entitlements' is the term that development economists use to refer to the ability of individuals to access food either by producing it, by purchasing it in an accessible marketplace or by being given access to it through social welfare. The organisation of relief policy in Ireland after 1847 has, rightly, received a bad press from historians for failing to provide to the Irish poor the level of 'entitlements' required to avoid excess mortality or loss of population after 1847. So why were these policies introduced, in spite of the mounting evidence of their ineffectiveness? Moreover, what, in terms of policy design, should be blamed for their failure to meet the scale of the crisis?

---

4   'Black '47: Brain-Twitching Great Irish Famine Revenge Thriller', *The Irish Times*, 5 September 2018.
5   P. Gray, 'The Great Famine, 1845–1850', in T. Bartlett & J. Kelly (eds.), *The Cambridge History of Ireland* (Cambridge: CUP, 2018), 639–65, at p. 655.
6   Idem., p. 654.
7   P. M. A. Bourke, 'The Extent of the Potato Crop in Ireland at the Time of the Famine', *JSSISI*, 10:3 (1959/60), 1–35, at pp. 11–12.
8   C. Ó Gráda, T. W. Guinnane, 'The Workhouses and Irish Famine Mortality', in T. Dyson, C. Ó Gráda (eds.), *Famine Demography* (Oxford: OUP, 2002), 44–64, at p. 44.
9   C. Ó Gráda, *The Great Irish Famine* (Cambridge: CUP, 1995), p. 39.
10   Many other scholars of the famine reach this same conclusion, including Gray, 'The Great Famine, 1845–50', 654; C. Ó Gráda, *Ireland before and after the Famine: Explorations in Economic History, 1800–1925* (Manchester: MUP, 1993), pp. 106–10; idem., *Black '47 and Beyond*, pp. 122–25.

THE CAUSES OF EMIGRATION IN IRELAND.

Figure 5.1. The causes of emigration in Ireland. *The Lady's Newspaper*, 13 January 1849, p. 15. The papers are marked 'County Cess', 'Poor Rate', 'Charge' and 'Rack Rents and Arrears'.

This chapter examines the policy of forcing the landlords to either employ the poor or to pay for their relief on the rates, instigated by Sir Charles Wood as chancellor of the exchequer while a lack of funds held back other plans. It was an attempt at the redistribution of 'entitlements' from the Irish rich to the Irish poor. However, the intention behind this policy was frustrated by poor design and implementation; it failed to avoid further excess mortality or loss of population after 1847. This chapter explains what went wrong, and why.

The policy of extreme redistribution

The policies of the British government from 1842 onwards generally had a growing element of redistribution in them. Sir Robert Peel had attempted transfers of wealth from the rich towards the labouring classes by the lowering of tariffs on grain in 1842 and 1846.[11] The intended transfer was from the landowners to those who had to purchase their food in the form of bread.[12] After Lord John Russell's government came to power in 1846, Wood targeted the better-off in Ireland. He wanted them to employ as labourers those who currently lived a subsistence lifestyle. This policy entailed a transfer from farmers to the poorest in society. By charging local taxes to fund the relief required for those not employed he hoped to encourage those being taxed to offer employment instead of being forced to pay extra in rates to maintain them via the Poor Law.[13] In Wood's own words, 'employ the people at wages or you will have to keep them by rates'.[14]

At the start of his period as the chancellor of the exchequer, Wood regarded local taxation as a fall-back solution if the poor could not be employed through public or private funding.[15] Wood had intended that generous advances would be available from the Treasury to initially finance relief spending. However, this source of funds dried up after the financial panic caused by the announcement of the first Irish loan to pay for the advances in 1847. As the government soon found it could not borrow from the London money markets to finance Irish relief efforts, employment by landlords and local taxation to redistribute wealth became the main planks of Wood's policies. The result of this series of events was that the Poor Law amendment legislation in 1847 increased the immediate fiscal pressure on taxpayers in Ireland beyond what was originally intended,

11   C. Read, 'The Political Economy of Sir Robert Peel', in J. Hoppit, A. B. Leonard and D. J. Needham (eds.), *Money and Markets: Essays in Honour of Martin Daunton* (Woodbridge: Boydell Press, 2019), 71–89, at pp. 77–78.

12   Idem., pp. 74–83.

13   Wood to Bessborough, N.A., Russell papers, PRO 30/22/5 F, f. 248.

14   Ibid.

15   Young to Peel, 16 January 1847, B.L., Peel papers, Add. MS. 40598, ff. 38–42.

with local taxes collected rising as a share of Ireland's GDP from around 2% in 1845 to approximately 5% in 1847.[16] The system began to break down as some Poor Law Unions went bankrupt or failed to act. To remedy the situation, the Rate-in-aid legislation transferred wealth from better off to poorer parts of Ireland. The Encumbered Estates Act was also envisaged as encouraging a transfer of wealth, one from landlords to their populations.

Wood's policies in Ireland were far from *laissez-faire*. Together they amounted to an interventionist attempt at redistribution, and redistribution on a dramatic scale within Ireland. Wood did hope that falling land prices in Ireland would trigger an inflow of capital investment from English investors, without intervention, according to the theories of political economy.[17] However, Wood was also intent on using the machinery of state to ensure that landlords and wealthy farmers in Ireland, whom he believed had made themselves rich from the misery and toil of their tenants when harvests were good, should bail out those who had made them wealthy now that times were bad.[18] This is a coercive vision of interference in the economy that did not match contemporary definitions of *laissez-faire*. The overall thrust of the government's legislation was to redistribute entitlements – to use the modern phraseology deployed by Amartya Sen – from the rural rich to their poor labourers, one way or another through voluntary initiative or state coercion.[19]

Even so, just like the U-turn over the financing of relief policy in 1847, existing interpretations substantially blame ideology as the root cause of the government's failure. Charles Trevelyan, as the official in charge of implementing policy, also receives much of the blame for the inadequacy of relief efforts throughout the rest of the famine. 'The decision, taken in the summer of 1847, to throw the burden of relief on the Irish Poor Law and the Irish taxpayer was the most cynical move of all', Ó Gráda argued in the 1990s.[20] 'This callous act, born of ideology and frustration, prolonged the crisis'.[21] More recent research echoes a similar conclusion, although acknowledging fiscal limitations. To Gray, the evidence suggests that 'ideological fixations with free trade, eliminating moral hazard and enforcing self-help on Ireland' should be held responsible for the failure to provide enough 'food aid and employment to

16   For tax data sources see note to Chart 5.3; Irish GDP data taken from K. H. O'Rourke, 'Monetary Data and Proxy GDP Estimates: Ireland 1840–1921', *Irish Economic and Social History*, 25:1 (1998), 22–51, at p. 48.

17   This has already been noted, for instance, in R. D. C. Black, *Economic Thought and the Irish Question 1817–1870* (Cambridge: CUP, 1960), p. 39.

18   Grey to Russell, 16 October 1846, N.A., Russell papers, PRO 30/22/5D, ff. 216–17; Wood to Grey, 19 October 1846, GRE/B122/3/14.

19   A. Sen, *Poverty and Famines: An Essay on Entitlements and Deprivation* (Oxford: OUP, 1981), p. 177.

20   Ó Gráda, *The Great Irish Famine*, p. 39.

21   Ibid.

the starving masses'.[22] He attributes 'a providentialist theodicy and a moralist obsession with self-help, liberal political economy', but also 'the ascendancy of British middle-class pressures for budgetary restraint' as responsible for the failure of the Russell government's policies.[23]

Various scholars have also blamed land policies supposedly aimed at modernising and transforming the Irish countryside for the persistence of excess mortality. Historians generally view that 'policy' as having amplified the effect of the famine in order to create larger and more profitable farms that benefitted landowners at the expense of the poor.[24] At worst, this is described as purposeful from the start. Over the past decade, some academics have increasingly argued that the outcomes of the relief effort 'were largely determined by the structures of colonial subordination and economic exploitation established over centuries'.[25] 'Relief strategies became increasingly bio-political in nature and intent', as David Nally, a historical geographer, put it, aimed at removing an excess population no longer required.[26] In his view, the British response to the Famine was driven by imperial and colonial prejudice towards the Irish; the chief imperative was the maintenance of British economic interests in Ireland rather than saving lives.[27] William Smyth, in the same volume, has further argued that relief policy during the famine continued a pattern of British domination over Ireland that played out over the *longue durée*.[28]

Although these interpretations do well in terms of explaining some of the context, they do not present a full picture of the specific intentions behind how relief policy was supposed to work once Poor Law Unions assumed the burden from the summer of 1847. Neither do they pinpoint precisely why the policies implemented fell so short of the continuing expectations of their creators. The archival evidence clearly shows that British officials wanted to save lives, but found themselves in an impossible position, trapped between a money market fearful of government loans and bullion drains, on the one hand, and unhelpful Parliamentary arithmetic on the other. In 1846 Wood promised Lord John

22   P. Gray, 'Polemic without Plausibility', *The Irish Times*, 19 January 2013.
23   Gray, 'The Great Famine, 1845–1850', 645–46.
24   G. O'Brien, *The Economic History of Ireland from the Union to the Famine* (London: Longman, 1921), p. 197; P. Gray, *Famine, Land and Politics: British Government and Irish Society 1843–1850* (Dublin: Irish Academic Press, 1999), p. 327.
25   Gray, 'The Great Famine, 1845–1850', p. 640.
26   D. P. Nally, *Human Encumbrances: Political Violence and the Great Irish Famine* (Notre Dame: University of Notre Dame Press, 2011), p. 163.
27   D. P. Nally, 'The Colonial Dimensions of the Great Irish Famine' in J. Crowley, W. J. Smyth, M. Murphy (eds.), *Atlas of the Great Famine, 1845–52* (Cork: Cork University Press, 2012), 64–74.
28   W. J. Smyth, 'The Longue Durée – Imperial Britain and Colonial Ireland', in J. Crowley et al. (eds.), *Atlas of the Great Irish Famine, 1845–52* (Cork: Cork University Press, 2012), 46–63.

Russell 'government interference to an extraordinary degree', even as economic conditions deteriorated.[29] Russell took Lord Bessborough, his first Irish viceroy, to task on reports of a single death caused by the non-payment of wages on a public-works scheme.[30] His successor as lord-lieutenant, Clarendon, insisted when the financial crisis of October 1847 was at its worst that 'we cannot let the public die of starvation'.[31] In 1848 Trevelyan became emotional in mid-letter to Clarendon as funds ran out.[32] Even in the winter of 1848–49, during one of the worst periods for mortality, Clarendon admitted that the only two alternatives were the exhaustion of 'the Treasury or death – the first we cannot afford and the second we dare not permit'.[33]

Wood claimed to his prime minister that 'so much was never done for any country by another in the history of the world'.[34] Later, in retirement, he wrote of the Irish famine to a later prime minister in 1870, 'We could not let the people starve', but complained that the government could not get sufficient co-operation locally for his policies to work.[35] The importance of localism for the Whigs of this period in both Great Britain and Ireland is a factor that has often been forgotten by historians.[36] As Robin Moore pointed out after a detailed survey of Wood's correspondence, principles of local control were important here: 'neither Black nor Woodham-Smith has given prominence to the restraints that the Whig government's attachment to the traditional principle of local self-government imposed upon government action during the famine'.[37] Moore cites Wood's correspondence as evidence that this principle weighed heavily on him: 'from Wood's letters on Irish policy, and from his expression of his views upon local government in England at that time ... it seems certain that the influence of the principle must have been considerable'.[38]

That opens a pertinent historical question. If the wish to save lives was there, why did so many people die after 1847? The traditional commentaries do not

29 Wood to Russell, 16 October 1846, N.A., Russell papers, PRO 30/22/5D, ff. 214–15.
30 Russell to Bessborough, 21 October 1846, N.A., Russell papers, PRO 30/22/5D, ff. 268–69.
31 Clarendon to Russell, 25 October 1847, N.A., Russell papers, PRO 30/22/6F, ff. 209–20.
32 Trevelyan to Clarendon, 24 April 1848, O.B.L., Clarendon papers, Ms. Clar. dep. Irish box. 60. See p. XYZ.
33 Clarendon to Grey, 13 January 1849, D.U.L., Earl Grey papers, GRE/B81/2/91.
34 Wood to Russell, 9 April 1848, N.A., Russell Papers, PRO 30/22/7B/87, ff. 249–52.
35 Halifax (Wood) to Gladstone, 16 December 1870, B.L., Gladstone papers, Add. MS. 44185, ff. 103–05.
36 However, it will be emphasised in a forthcoming book: L. Darwen, B. Gurrin, L. Kennedy, D. MacRaild, The Death Census of Black '47: Eyewitness Accounts of Ireland's Great Famine (London: Anthem Press, forthcoming).
37 R. J. Moore, Sir Charles Wood's Indian Policy, 1853–66 (Manchester: MUP, 1966), pp. 8–9, n. 8.
38 Ibid.

fully unravel this question. Wood's policy, in his own words, was to 'recon-stitute ... the supply of money' through Treasury advances and local taxation, and then force the landlords 'to help in at least managing the relief', either by providing employment or through the Poor Law.[39]

In hindsight, this approach clearly failed to raise the funds needed to replace the Treasury's earlier relief efforts. Neither did it produce the employment required to feed the rural population. Structural changes to Irish agriculture wrought by the potato blight meant that the extra employment Wood envisaged did not materialise. Employment in agriculture could only be increased if tillage was maintained at or increased from pre-famine levels. However, three parallel developments encouraged farmers to shift from tillage to pasture, reducing the available employment in agriculture. First, the blight reduced average potato yields by almost half, reducing the returns on using land for this form of tillage.[40] Second, the land required to sustain each labourer from arable crops rose, thanks in part to falling potato yields, but also to the rising price of Indian corn and oatmeal, which would need to be purchased with money wages as a substitute for potatoes. Third, the repeal of the Corn Laws subjected Irish farmers to lower grain prices, a trend which was especially evident in 1849–51.[41] It may have taken policymakers some time to realise that average potato yields had fallen permanently. However, by 1847, it was already clear to other commentators that the potato was no longer a reliable subsistence crop.[42]

The situation over employment had become clear relatively early on, when Trevelyan sent a circular to the Poor Law Officers in Ireland on 19 January 1848 asking whether 'all the unemployed able-bodied persons' could be 'profitably and permanently employed by the Landed Proprietors and Farmers'. The exercise was a test of whether Wood's policy of encouraging employment was going to work as the chancellor originally intended. There are about 120 pages of replies from Ireland; almost all of them are in the negative.[43] The mounting pile of evidence that government policy would fail was gathered together shortly before Trevelyan showed emotion in his letter of 24 April 1848, claiming

39 Halifax (Wood) to Gladstone, 16 December 1870, B.L., Gladstone papers, Add. MS. 44185, ff. 103–05.
40 *Returns of Agricultural Produce in Ireland, 1848*, PP 1849 (1116) XLIX.1, p. v: 1847 potato yield 57 tons per acre, 1848 30 tons per acre.
41 L. Kennedy, P. M. Solar, *Irish Agriculture: A Price History from the Mid-Eighteenth Century to the Eve of the First World War* (Dublin: Royal Irish Academy, 2007), p. 194 (table A.18).
42 *The Economist*, 19 June 1847, p. 693.
43 *Poor Law Inspectors: entry book of their replies to a Treasury Circular on Unemployment*, T 64/400. p. 11. This document was found in a cupboard at the Treasury and transferred to the Public Record Office in February 1932 and since then until time of writing has been mis-catalogued under 'non-Irish subjects' and therefore widely ignored in histories of Ireland.

Ireland was 'in our hearts'.[44] In reaction, Wood heaped further pressure on Poor Law Unions to raise their rates further either to cover the shortfall or to encourage sufficient employment to be created, culminating in the Rate-in-aid legislation of 1849. At the same time, the government began its search for any *ad hoc* policy, within the severe political and economic constraints that the government faced after the financial panics of 1847, to provide relief in Ireland without doing so from central funds. It was from this search that a smorgasbord of cheap-to-implement policies, such as the Encumbered Estates Act of 1849 and the Rate-in-aid, appeared.

The failure of the hoped-for employment to materialise and the fallback policy of keeping the poor on the rates resulted in local taxes collected in Ireland doubling from around £1.5m a year in 1845 (approximately 2% of GDP) to about £3m in 1848 (approximately 5% of GDP).[45] This was an eye-watering sum in the context of annual Poor Law spending in Great Britain. In that country, one which boasted wealthier taxpayers than Ireland, annual Poor Law spending fell from around 2% of its GDP in 1830 to just 0.7% in 1880.[46] Worse still, in Ireland, this tax burden was disproportionally heaped on the areas most affected and impoverished by harvest failure. As a result, tax rates in some areas reached crippling levels. By 1849 the rates in at least 62 Poor Law Unions reached over 10 shillings in the pound (50%).[47] Rates in Ballinrobe Union reached 34 shillings 3¼ d in the pound – in other words a tax on a theoretical rental income of over 170%.[48] This, moreover, was not charged upon actual rental income, but an assessment of rental yields conducted before the famine had slashed them. In short, these policies represented unprecedented levels of taxation and intervention in the Irish economy.[49]

Thus, the important question that should be asked is why did the intervention that took place in Ireland prove so ineffective, rather than whether *laissez-faire* held sway. Large sums had been expended by the Treasury earlier during the famine and, later on, by local taxpayers, and yet the deaths Clarendon, as lord-lieutenant, 'dare[d] not permit' still took place.[50] The rest of this chapter

44   Trevelyan to Clarendon, 24 April 1848, O.B.L., Clarendon papers, Ms. Clar. dep. Irish box. 60.
45   For tax data sources see note to Chart 5.3; Irish GDP data taken from O'Rourke, 'Monetary Data and Proxy GDP Estimates: Ireland 1840–1921', p. 48.
46   See P. H. Lindert, 'Poor Relief before the Welfare State: Britain versus the Continent, 1780–1880', *European Review of Economic History*, 2:2 (1998), 101–40, at pp. 113–14 for data about poor-relief expenditure in England, Wales and Scotland in the nineteenth century.
47   *Treasury minutes June 1850 prescribing arrangements for repayment of advances to Poor Law unions in Ireland – Report of Poor Law Commissioners in Ireland, December 1851*, PP 1852 (19) XLVII.113, pp. 13–15.
48   Idem., p. 13.
49   The situation was gradually corrected following Griffith's valuation 1847–64.
50   Clarendon to Grey, 13 January 1849, D.U.L., Earl Grey papers, GRE/B81/2/91.

examines Wood's redistributive policies on the ground in Ireland and uncovers why they did not work as he intended. It is shown that Wood hoped for the employment of former smallholders, whose livelihoods had been wiped out by the potato blight, by larger farmers. Clearance and emigration were not his primary aims. The initial implementation of redistributive policies of the Russell government by placing the burden of relief efforts on the Poor Law is shown to be flawed by local taxes in some areas rising to levels which made them impossible to collect. The mistake was corrected by the Rate-in-aid Act of 1849 to support underfunded unions but not before much suffering had been caused. The Encumbered Estates Acts of 1848 and 1849 removed bankrupt landlords who could not pay taxes and unblocked the transfer of land ownership. However, the legislation also incentivised capital flight, the opposite of what the leading backers of the legislation intended. The consequence was that the impact of the famine was made worse by rising levels of capital flight and emigration among the better-off to escape high taxation at a time when Ireland desperately needed more investment. It is these features that particularly characterise the failure of Wood's redistributive policies.

The 'Twisleton effect' and policy after 1847

Rather than acknowledging Wood's actual focus on finding employment for the Irish poor, many historians argue that the government's post-1847 policies, including the use of the Irish Poor Law, the Rate-in-aid and the Encumbered Estates Acts, grew from a faith in liberal political economy to modernise the Irish economy.[51] While Cecil Woodham-Smith was prepared to excuse the government on the basis of its 'short-sightedness and ignorance', others refer to the viewpoint of government attempting to 'complete the work begun by the Famine'.[52] Nally has more recently taken this viewpoint further to argue that these policies were designed to take advantage of the crisis to implement 'social and economic engineering' by modernising Irish society.[53] Yet if modernisation through raising efficiency and productivity were the goal of the government, it was a complete failure. As Ó Gráda has pointed out, it was not the landlord's incomes which grew fastest in the post-famine period; neither was there any great increase in efficiency as measured by total factor productivity.[54] The analysis here suggests that, in fact, Wood's aim was the

---

51   Gray, *Famine, Land and Politics*, pp. 225, 325; C. Woodham-Smith, *The Great Hunger: Ireland, 1845–49* (London: Hamish Hamilton, 1962), pp. 54, 410.
52   Woodham-Smith, *The Great Hunger*, pp. 409–10; Gray, *Famine, Land and Politics*, p. 327.
53   Nally, *Human Encumbrances: Political Violence and the Great Irish Famine*, p. 160.
54   Ó Gráda, *Ireland before and after the Famine*, p. 80.

employment of labourers, and it was the redistribution of entitlements that was the priority well into 1849, rather than efficiency or landlords' profits. Any social engineering was intended to support these immediate aims.

Yet again, an over-focus on Trevelyan – ever the red herring – has distracted historians from Wood's policies of redistribution and full employment. Most notably, Trevelyan's letter of 14 September 1848 to the Poor Law Commission has been used as evidence of plans to emphasise the effects of the famine, in which he said:

> I do not know how farms are to be consolidated if small farmers do not emigrate, and by acting for the purpose of keeping them at home we should be defeating our own object. We must not complain of what we really want to obtain. If small farmers go and their landlords are reduced to sell portions of their estates to persons who will invest Capital, we shall at last arrive at something like a satisfactory settlement of the country.[55]

However, some authors have (misleadingly) assumed that these are Trevelyan's wishes and do not put the quotation in its correct context, that of him passing on instructions from his political masters. In fact, here Trevelyan is paraphrasing Wood's instructions, which contained more distinction between classes, in an answer to Poor Law Commissioner Edward Twisleton (through Trevelyan) over the question of what the optimal revenue-raising rate of local taxation is, in view of the low collection rates in some Unions. On 21 August 1848 Trevelyan wrote to Russell concerned that 'there will be another scarcity of food and prices will seriously advance' and that an addition 'to the actual stock of food' was necessary to help 'the lower order of people'.[56] That meant Unions had to be sufficiently financed, he concluded. Shortly afterwards, on 2 September 1848, the Poor Law Commission complained to Trevelyan that they were being asked to raise a tax of more than 3/- in the pound in order to pay past debts and raise funding for this new challenge. He passed their letter to Wood with a note recommending that although the high rate should be maintained, payment could be deferred. Wood replied to Trevelyan, writing on 9 September 1848 that 'for the purposes of maintaining their own poor, a vigorous collection of rates must now be made'. The Commissioners' made the point that some farmers might be driven abroad, which was answered by Wood:

> I never know how farms were to be consolidated unless small farmers will emigrate, and if we are to act for the purpose of helping them at home, we

---

55   C. Kinealy, *A Death-Dealing Famine: The Great Hunger in Ireland* (London: Pluto Press, 1997), p. 148; see also idem. 'Peel, Rotten Potatoes and Providence', in A. Marrison (ed.), *Free Trade and its Reception 1815–1960: Freedom and Trade: vol. 1* (London: Routledge, 1998), 50–62, at p. 61.

56   Trevelyan to Russell, 21 August 1848, N.A., Russell papers, PRO 30/22/7C, ff. 369–76.

are defeating our own object. Nobody can suppose that the population will be hired unless some emigrate. If small farmers go and their landlords are induced to sell portions of their estates to persons who will invest capital it will do good, but it seems to me absurd to complain of that we really want to attain, a clearance of small farmers.[57]

By comparing this with Trevelyan's reply above it can be seen that Wood was in control, his primary concern in the letter being the hiring of labourers as a form of relief and the achievement of full employment: 'Nobody can suppose that the population will be hired unless some emigrate'.[58] Trevelyan merely toned down the blunt reply, which, as a consequence, lost some of its meaning.

Twisleton, on behalf of the Commissioners, defended a rate of no more than 3/- by anticipating by a century Arthur Laffer's observation that high tax rates can reduce the amount collected: 'I have not the slightest doubt that more money will really be collected throughout Ireland from a 3/- Rate than would have been collected from a 5/- Rate with the general opposition against it'.[59] However, Wood insisted on having his way. He felt undermined by the issue of Circular no. 6, which stated, 'the Commissioners *will not insist on a higher rate than 3 shillings in the pound*', and wrote to Trevelyan, 'I wish you would <u>privately</u> ask Twisleton whether this is their doing or the act of Lord Clarendon and Lord John'; in fact it was both.[60] By November, Redington was writing to Somerville: 'The 5/- Rate which with an armed force we are endeavouring to collect … will if paid do little beyond paying off the old debts'.[61]

Twisleton initially stated, 'it is very desirable that the <u>small</u> Tenants should emigrate'. But as its effects became clear, Clarendon wrote twice to Russell, once on behalf of Twisleton, heavily criticising Wood's policy of high taxes and acceptance of the possibility that it would lead to small farmers leaving their land and, if they were to escape the workhouse, leaving the country.[62] He reported that Twisleton was calling it 'a policy of extermination', a phrase which Woodham-Smith quoted, and which has been extensively re-quoted by

57 Cover note, 9 September 1848, N.A., Treasury papers, T64/370B/1.
58 Ibid.
59 Twisleton to Trevelyan, 17 September 1848, N.A., Treasury papers, T64/366A.
60 Circular no. 6, N.A., Treasury papers, T64/366A (original italics); Wood to Trevelyan, 19 September 1848, N.A., Treasury papers, T64/370B/1 (original underline); P. Scherer, *Lord John Russell: A Biography* (Selinsgrove: Susquehanna University Press, 1999), p. 174; Wood to Russell, 6 September 1848, N.A., Russell papers, PRO 30/22/7D, f. 4.
61 Reddington to Somerville, 8 November 1848, O.B.S., Clarendon papers, Ms. Clar. dep. Irish vol. 3.
62 Twisleton to Trevelyan, 17 September 1848, N.A., Treasury papers, T64/366A (original underline).

others, without any explanation of its contemporary meaning.[63] Since the
Second World War the word's meaning in most dictionaries has been limited
to 'total extirpation' or 'utter destruction' and, referring to the Holocaust
in particular, 'mass murder'.[64] However, the *Oxford English Dictionary* also
quotes the word's original, though (since the Second World War) obsolete,
meaning of 'expulsion from the bounds or limits of a country, state, or
community' from the Latin *ex* (out of) and *terminus* (boundary), referring to
eviction.[65] Twisleton and Clarendon were both within the Irish Government,
and would have used the local Irish version of this meaning, as explained by
Lord Eliot, chief secretary to Ireland, in 1842: 'an exterminator – that was
to say ... a person who ejected many of his poorer tenants for the purpose
of gratifying a political feeling'.[66] The legal background was explained in
Parliament in 1856: 'the system was ... checked in England when the law of
settlement was adopted. In the reign of Charles II, if a landlord cleared off
his tenantry, the law of settlement obliged him to maintain them at his own
expense; and from that time to the present there had been in England no such
system of extermination as that which now existed in Ireland'.[67] There are
numerous references elsewhere in *Hansard* to this usage and in the contemporary press, including an article in *The Spectator* explaining the situation
in Ireland.[68] Nevertheless, the disapproval in the word is always heightened
by its implication of associated deaths, as the alternative meaning of 'utter
destruction' was also used occasionally in the 1840s. However, what Wood
really intended was for the employment of the Irish poor by their former
landlords, not their 'utter destruction' or 'mass murder'.[69]

63   Kinealy, *A Death-Dealing Famine*, pp. 138, 145; Clarendon to Russell, 12 March 1849,
28 (not 26 as commonly quoted) April 1849, O.B.L., Clarendon papers, Ms. Clar. dep. Irish
vol. 4. 'I saw Twisleton yesterday – he is determined upon resigning, but as to the moment of
leaving his office I have no doubt he will consult your convenience. He thinks the destitution
here quite horrible, and the indifference of the House of Commons to it so manifest that he
is an unfit agent of a policy that must be one of extermination'.
64   'extermination, n.', *OED Online*, OUP, March 2020, online at <www.oed.com/view/
Entry/66984> [accessed 11 April 2020].
65   Ibid.
66   *Hansard*, LXV, 18 July 1842, c. 266.
67   *Hansard*, CXLI, 29 April 1856, c. 1712.
68   For example, *Hansard*, CII, 1 February 1849, c. 144; CII, 19 February 1849, c. 883; XCV,
23 November 1847, c. 5; LXIX, 30 May 1843, c. 1119; *The Spectator*, 20 November 1847.
Ó Gráda in *Ireland before and after the Famine*, p. 138, is more specific in using the word
'extirpation' to mean mass killing.
69   Wood to Bessborough, N.A., Russell papers, PRO 30/22/5 F, f. 248; 'extermination, n.',
OED Online, OUP, March 2020, online at <www.oed.com/view/Entry/66984> [accessed
11 April 2020].

The Rate-in-aid and the Encumbered Estates Acts

The Rate-in-aid and the Encumbered Estates Acts were originally part of a set of ideas by Peel to help Ireland after the financial panics of 1847, born out of a shortage of Treasury funds. They replaced a list of expensive plans that Peel had proposed and Wood had rejected on the grounds there was no money, involving investing in fisheries and agriculture, funding priests from the Crown Estate, running a model estate, or public-works schemes building roads and bridges.[70] However, funds still needed to be found in order to help bankrupt Unions in the south and west of Ireland, even if central-government money was unavailable owing to the crises of 1847 and the government's weakness in Parliament. Therefore, the Rate-in-aid legislation (Rate-in-aid of Distressed Unions Act 1849 c. 24) was brought in to solve the kind of problem which Clarendon described to Wood in cases where Poor Law Unions went bankrupt: 'I found that the Ballina Union was said to be insolvent and ... for 24 hours the inmates were starving'.[71]

Russell threatened to abolish Ireland's income-tax exemption to intimidate Irish MPs into voting for Rate-in-aid, which then came into effect on 24 May 1849 temporarily until 31 December 1850.[72] The Act gave the Poor Law Commissioners control over the raising of funding of relief in failing Unions. If the entire sums collected proved to be insufficient to defray the expenditure of relief in those Unions, the Commissioners would be permitted to obtain the necessary funds by the levy of a rate on all other Unions in Ireland. This created an off-Treasury-balance-sheet source of income to support Unions in distress without having to spend central-government money. A one-off advance of £50,000 from the Treasury to provide immediate help with distressed Unions in the west of Ireland was voted for at the same time.

Russell felt he had to justify applying the legislation to the north of Ireland: 'I cannot believe that the loyalty of Ulster is of that nature that it will be impaired by the imposition of a tax of this kind for the relief of persons who are destitute and suffering the extremity of hunger'.[73] This was indeed to become an issue, as James Grant has described, because many felt it was unfair to charge those areas in the north that had run their Poor Law and relief arrangements comparatively

---

70   Cover note Trevelyan to Wood, 9 September 1848, N.A., Treasury papers, T64/370B/1. Suggested policies in copy of memo by Peel given to Clarendon 2 April 1849, B.L., Peel papers, Add. MS. 40601, ff. 90–100; *Hansard*, CIII, 2 March 1849, cc. 99–156.

71   Clarendon to Wood, 12 July 1847, C.U.L., Hickleton papers, MS MF A4.57, reel 1495.

72   *Memorandum on financial proposal for relief of distress in Ireland 1849*, unsigned, N.A., Russell papers, PRO 30/22/7, ff. 103–09: a proposal to introduce income tax into Ireland; it was used to make Irish MPs aware of the alternative to voting for the Rate-in-aid legislation.

73   *Hansard*, CIII, 2 March 1849, c. 111.

well.[74] Twisleton resigned for this explicit reason.[75] Such rebellion inflamed the resentment towards local taxation and exacerbated sectarian tensions, particularly in Ulster.[76]

In contrast, the idea of an Encumbered Estates Act was well received in Ireland. When Trevelyan had sent a Circular to all the temporary Irish Poor Law Officers on 19 January 1848 asking whether 'all the unemployed able-bodied persons' could be 'profitably and permanently employed by the Landed Proprietors and Farmers', most of the 120 replies referred to the waste and idleness of much land and blamed the proprietors being 'heavily incumbered'.[77] Wood, referring to the initial Encumbered Estates (Ireland) Act 1848 c. 48, claimed 'I have never heard anybody recede from the opinion that this was one of the most essential measures for the real and permanent improvement of the country'.[78] The lord chancellor in seeking approval of the bill in the House of Lords emphasised the advantages to owners: 'if the owners of those estates were enabled to convert them into money, the balance, or residue, coming to such owners would often be of considerable amount, and would, if prudently invested, yield handsome incomes'.[79]

However, very few properties were sold, mainly because of the problems left in the bill, even though it had been significantly altered in its progress through Parliament. A memorial from representatives of existing lenders on estates in Ireland objected that landlords could sell their estates without reference to existing lenders and without making arrangements to pay them and complained about the 17 amendments of the bill.[80] The second attempt, the 1849 Bill (that became the Encumbered Estates [Ireland] Act 1849), was the result of co-operation between Peel and Wood. Peel suggested a process to sort out the legal problems that had been holding up sales.[81]

The actual records of policymakers' discussions during the genesis of the legislation paint a different picture about their intentions from some recent

74   J. Grant, 'The Great Famine and the Poor Law in Ulster: The Rate-in-aid Issue of 1849', *Irish Historical Studies*, 27:105 (1990), 30–47.
75   *Fifth Report from the Select Committee on Poor Laws (Ireland)*, PP 1849 (170) XV.325, evidence of Edward Twisleton, pp. 1–3.
76   H. Verdone, 'Sectarianism in Belfast during Ireland's Great Famine, c.1847–50', University of Cambridge, unpublished MPhil thesis (2021).
77   *Poor Law Inspectors: entry book of their replies to a Treasury Circular on Unemployment*, N.A., Treasury papers, T 64/400, p. 11. Note: as of January 2020 this was mis-catalogued under 'non-Irish subjects'.
78   Wood to Russell, 20 May 1848, N.A., Russell papers, PRO 30/22/7C, ff. 69–72.
79   *Hansard*, XCVI, 24 February 1848, cc. 1249–50.
80   Memorial, May 1848, B.L., Peel papers, Add. MS. 40600, f. 346.
81   P. G. Lane, 'The Management of Estates by Financial Corporations in Ireland after the Famine', *Studia Hibernica*, 14 (1974), 67–89, pp. 69–70.

scholarship that sees Ireland during the famine as a 'laboratory of modernity'.[82] The archives align more with Ó Gráda's version of what followed.[83] The Encumbered Estates Acts attempted to replace what were felt to be the unsatisfactory and financially insolvent landlords in Ireland with what most hoped would be responsible persons acting in the best traditions of moral economy and *noblesse oblige*, or at least persons who had a co-operative relationship with the occupiers of land. Russell had great regard for the model 'relation of landlord and tenant – which binds men together by the ties of protection ... and of regard [for each other]'.[84] He hoped that it would create a better social compact between landlords and tenants in Ireland as well as assist in redistribution through employment and the Poor Law. Wood, too, was enthusiastic over Peel's idea of an Encumbered Estates Act. 'I have been thinking over your sketch of a plan for Irish matters. I go any length you like as to facilitating the transfer of estates and I hope that we shall be able to do something in spite of the lawyers'.[85] Wood thought this would encourage English capital to flow into Ireland without requiring subsidy from central-government funds.[86]

The Encumbered Estates (Ireland) Act 1848 c. 48 was the first attempt to pass legislation to free up the sales process for estates with mortgages that had become too large to be serviced from their revenues. Sometimes the mortgage absorbed all the income from the estate in interest charges, and sometimes the loan exceeded the value of the estate. Both Peel and Russell saw the Act as 'a measure which may lay the foundation for a sounder state of society in Ireland'.[87] They hoped that more solvent proprietors would do a better job in financially supporting the Poor Law, just as landlords had in the eighteenth-century age of moral economy in Great Britain.[88] 'I trust that the encumbered estates which may be sold may come into the possession of landlords who may be sensible of the policy of attending to the improvement of the estate, and the

82   R. Hartigan, 'Review: *Human Encumbrances: Political Violence and the Great Irish Famine*', *Irish Geography*, 45:3 (2012), 292–94.
83   Ó Gráda, *Black '47 and Beyond*, pp. 127–28.
84   *Hansard*, LXXX, 2 June 1845, c. 1238.
85   Wood to Peel, 6 April 1849, B.L., Peel papers, Add. MS. 40601, ff. 139–44.
86   Ibid.
87   *Hansard*, CI, 30 August 1848, c. 711.
88   For the development of the concept of 'moral economy' in British economic and social history see W. W. Rostow, *British Economy in the Nineteenth Century* (Oxford: OUP, 1948), pp. 122–25; E. J. Hobsbawm, *Labouring Men: Studies in the History of Labour* (London: Weidenfeld and Nicolson, 1964); T. S. Ashton, *Economic Fluctuations in England, 1700–1800* (Oxford: OUP, 1959) (this economic historian endowed a prize awarded by the Economic History Society won in 2017 by a much earlier version of Chapter 4 of this book); E. P. Thompson, 'The Moral Economy of the English Crowd in the Eighteenth Century', *Past & Present*, 50:1 (1971), 76–136, at pp. 76–79.

wants of the population'.[89] Wood encouraged this view, calling the legislation
'... one of the most essential measures for the real and permanent improvement
of the country', but from an early stage had seen it as the natural follow on
from his attack on the Irish nobility and gentry by means of the Poor Law.[90]

> I showed to Sir W Somerville the copy of my letter to Labouchere which
> went furthest in the necessity of breaking up estates and selling portions of
> the landlords' property &c. and he said he entirely agreed in it. I am sure
> that we must look forward in Irish matters, and pay regard not only to the
> temporary, but the ultimate tendency of our measures.[91]

The legislation was therefore intended to transfer entitlements from large
landowners to smaller ones (not *vice versa*) and assist in redistribution of wealth
as a product of their benevolence, particularly after estate sales. Much the same
mistake has been made over the Gregory clause in the Poor Relief (Ireland) Act
1847 (10 & 11 Vict c.31), which Christine Kinealy blames at length, correctly,
for the ejections.[92] However, the notion that the legislation was intentionally
'callous' – supported by a quotation from *Hansard* that Sir William Gregory,
a Peelite MP for Dublin, 'did not see of what use such small farmers could
be' – has been convincingly and overwhelmingly demonstrated to be incorrect
by Brian Walker.[93] Gregory himself was noted by contemporaries as a good
landlord and tried to avoid evictions on his own estates in Ireland.[94] His father
was a particularly vigorous Relief Committee chairman in Kinvar, who died in
April 1847 from an epidemic disease spread by the famine in the area.[95] Walker
has shown Gregory produced two amendments to the Poor Law Amendment
Act of 1847, both of which were passed. The first was that any tenant rated at a
net value not exceeding £5 should receive assistance, if in need, to emigrate from
the Guardians of the Union; and that the landlord should commute outstanding
rent and assist the tenant and his family to emigrate. The fiscal burden of this
was counterbalanced by Gregory's second amendment which stated that a test
be applied to ensure that no undeserving person should get relief. He proposed
that if a tenant held more than a quarter-acre of land, he should not be entitled
to assistance. The passage of the amendment in the third reading of the bill on

---

89 *Hansard*, CI, 30 August 1848, c. 711.
90 Wood to Russell, 20 May 1848, N.A., Russell papers, PRO 30/22/7C, ff. 69–72.
91 Wood to Russell, 28 September 1847, N.A., Russell papers, PRO 30/22/6F, ff. 126–29,
at f. 129.
92 C. Kinealy, *This Great Calamity: The Irish Famine, 1842–52* (Dublin: Gill and
Macmillan, 1994), pp. 218–26.
93 Kinealy, *A Death-Dealing Famine*, p. 123; *Hansard*, XCI, 29 March 1847, c. 595.
94 B. M. Walker, 'Villain, Victim or Prophet? William Gregory and the Great Famine',
Irish Historical Studies, 38:152 (2013), 579–99, at p. 580.
95 Idem., p. 581.

16 April 1847 may well have helped calm the financial markets over the burden of Irish spending at the end of the first financial panic of 1847.[96]

Walker has rightly suggested that the *Hansard* record is a misquotation and a more correct version exists in *The Times*: 'As for the clause destroying the small farmers, of what value could their farming be if this would affect them', meaning if their farming was no longer viable they would have access to public assistance.[97] Perhaps this slightly dismissive attitude to questioning shows why unintended consequences were often not avoided in policymaking during the famine, as the political weakness of the government meant it had to accept all sorts of unwanted backbench amendments to get its legislation passed. Later, Russell blamed 'the obscurity and confusion of our laws' on 'political interests and opinions' which meant that 'every man brings his patch and wants it inserted in the act – the Govt – as the Mover, anxious to carry his bill and to conciliate, agrees to patch …'.[98] John Reynolds, a Repealer who succeed Gregory as MP for Dublin, commented the next year in Parliament that the legislation, 'appeared to have been prepared for the particular benefit of the landlords', and that its outcome 'furnished them with a powerful weapon for dispossessing the poorer sort of tenantry'.[99]

Thus Gregory's intentions, which were potentially empathetic with the Irish poor, were turned to bad by the actions of some landlords. Even suggestions of legislation had the same effect. Proposals to give tenants rights in respect of the value of improvements to their land if they moved away also caused landlords to evict their tenants. Sir William Somerville in introducing the Landlord and Tenant Bill of 1848 did not intend this result and yet his promise that 'it will provide compensation for the improvements made by the tenants during their holding, if they are dispossessed previous to the expiration of a certain period', flagged up an unintentional warning to landlords to remove their tenants before legislation was passed.[100]

The policymakers' reaction to the failure of their policies to relieve the poorer classes was to blame the lack of co-operation given by local administration and infighting within them, rather than the design of their own initiatives. The arguments between factions may have been made worse because of Peel's previous policies of favouring Catholics for public appointments in Ireland before 1846 had already exacerbated sectarian tensions across rural Ireland.[101] The reaction

96   See Poor Relief (Ireland) Act 1847 (10 & 11 Vict c. 31); *Hansard*, XCI, 16 April 1847, cc. 875–928.
97   *The Times*, 30 March 1847, p. 2.
98   Russell to Clarendon, 18 September 1849, O.B.L., Clarendon papers, Ms. Clar. dep. Irish box. 26.
99   *Hansard*, XCVII, 9 March 1848, cc. 338–61, c. 355.
100   *Hansard*, XCVI, 15 February 1848, cc. 673–700, c. 673.
101   See C. Read, 'Peel, De Grey and Irish Policy 1841–44', *History*, 99:334 (2014), 1–18 for some of the background relating to this issue in the early 1840s.

by policymakers to the chaos would eventually contribute to initiatives affecting the entire United Kingdom to professionalise the civil service and provide a paid replacement for voluntary administrators from the nobility and gentry.

The Relief Commission archives show that its bureaucrats from the start of the famine were unnecessarily burdened by having to referee fights between Protestant and Catholic clergy over the control of local Relief Committees.[102] The problem was noted at the highest levels. In 1849 Trevelyan told Russell that sectarian divisions over allocation of jobs between Catholics and Protestants were damaging the 'local machinery' of relief, and suggesting that the answer would be a shift towards appointment on the sole basis of merit.[103] Russell admitted that both 'the Popish and Protestant mind is disturbed by our calm impartiality'.[104] However, as 'impartiality' inevitably involved favouring one side or another, he was confirming the Second Earl de Grey's earlier warnings before the famine that attempts to interfere, except on the basis of merit, would please no-one.[105]

The inability or unwillingness of the local gentry to organise or take part in famine relief programmes became clear to those in Dublin Castle and London. The necessity of extracting rates from Ireland to pay for Irish poverty and the lack of co-operation from voluntary Poor Law Guardians led to demands for the appointment of stipendiary Guardians from Twisleton in 1848. He explained that as 'it seems essential for the common good of all to throw the Irish on their own resources ... the best means for extracting money from unwilling ratepayers is to appoint paid Guardians'.[106] Similar attitudes were also shared by policymakers in London. Wood was quite sure that 'the starvation has arisen from the misconduct of the Irish officials and Guardians'.[107] In due course Trevelyan, based on his experience in Ireland, suggested to Russell, at the prime minister's instigation, that the most able persons should be recruited for paid public service in the Treasury in general: 'think what Anderson, Bromley, Hoffey, Elliot, Murdoch, Pressley who were selected on the ground of superior qualification are doing for the public ... as compared with [those] ... appointed merely from motives of patronage'.[108]

102   For instance, see Dublin, National Archives of Ireland, Relief Commission papers, RLFC 3/1/1067.
103   Trevelyan to Russell, 19 August 1849, N.A., Russell papers, PRO 30/22/8A, ff. 76–78.
104   Russell to Clarendon, 16 September 1849, O.B.L., Clarendon papers, Ms. Clar. dep. Irish box. 26.
105   Read, 'Peel, De Grey and Irish policy 1841–44', pp. 8–16.
106   Twisleton to Trevelyan, 3 February 1848, N.A., Russell papers, PRO 30/22/7A, ff. 271–73.
107   Wood to Russell, 9 April 1848, N.A., Russell papers, PRO 30/22/7B, ff. 249–54.
108   Trevelyan to Russell, 19 August 1849, N.A., Russell papers, PRO 30/22/8A, ff. 76–78.

This letter in which Trevelyan made the argument for professionalism in the civil service basically marks the start of the system for which he is known in the history of Whitehall.[109] On becoming the chancellor of the exchequer in 1852, Gladstone commissioned Stafford Northcote and Trevelyan to write the *Report on the Organisation of the Permanent Civil Service*, which recommended recruitment and promotion on the basis of merit only.[110] Recruits were to have a good general education and would be placed in a hierarchical staffing structure. Although the report does not mention Ireland directly, it praises the appointment and promotions system in the Army Commissariat – the part of the civil service responsible for the central government's relief efforts in Ireland.[111] More tellingly, even as late as 1870, the, by then, retired Wood petitioned Gladstone in favour of professionalisation, citing the behaviour and inefficiency of the Irish gentry as voluntary administrators during the famine as the reason to do so.[112]

The impact of redistributive taxation

Wood's policies for employment, the Rate-in-aid and the Encumbered Estates Acts were all intended to redistribute entitlements from rich to poor in the absence of further Treasury advances from London. It was not a policy of *laissez-faire*, but rather of state intervention and reorganisation within Irish society by local government. This policy fell woefully short of raising enough funds to fully relieve the continuing famine. This should be no surprise: Russell, Wood and Grey initially intended that Ireland's Poor Law Unions would be backed up by an extensive system of Treasury grants and loans – providing up to two-thirds of the upfront cost – which never fully materialised because of the financial panics of 1847. Historians have extensively written about the consequence of the failure of this revised policy on the Irish poor. However, they have not yet answered the question of why a policy of fiscal redistribution within the Irish economy failed so badly, particularly when, at first glance, it appears to anticipate Amartya Sen's framework of thinking about entitlements and famine. The rest of this chapter explores how this policy of intervention failed.

The impact on the poor of the raising of taxation locally, even though they did not pay it, has been well documented. The position of Poor Law Guardians torn between supplying the basic needs of an increasing flood of

109   Ibid.
110   S. Northcote, C. E. Trevelyan, *Report on the Organisation of the Permanent Civil Service* (London: Eyre and Spottiswoode, 1854).
111   Idem., p. 20.
112   Halifax (Wood) to Gladstone, 16 December 1870, B.L., Gladstone papers, Add. MS. 44185, ff. 103–05.

paupers and the political unpopularity of issuing rating demands to those who elected them has been described by Margaret Preston.[113] John O'Connor has collected descriptions of the dirty and diseased conditions which prevailed in workhouses because of this situation.[114] Gerard O'Brien has laid out the evidence of pre-famine maladministration by well-to-do administrators which indicated that a centralised relief structure would be difficult to run in Ireland, a lesson learnt only slowly by the British government.[115] Olwen Purdue has emphasised the consequent effect on future politics.[116] The mistake which the British government made of imposing taxes which went beyond what the wealthy classes were prepared to or could part with will be analysed here using data for tax rates and payment received for Unions in distress. The assumptions which the government made were similar to those made by Sen's analytical framework: that increased taxation on the wealthy would produce increased revenue for redistributing entitlements to food towards the poor. This relationship can be queried by pointing to the effects of the Laffer curve, which suggest that it is possible to raise less money by raising tax rates beyond a certain level. This section of the chapter will demonstrate that this effect occurred during the famine period in Ireland and inhibited the effective funding of the relief effort through the Poor Law in the way that Wood had expected.

In proposing the transfer of entitlements as a remedy for famine, Sen claims to counter Thomas Malthus, who held out that transfer of wealth from rich to poor would mean 'all would have the same quantity of money. All the provisions of the country would be consumed and all the people would starve together'.[117] Sen proposes that the transfer should be increased as long as the income of the poor is insufficient to purchase an adequate ration of food and the income of the poor is less than the rich.[118] The transfer should stop when the income of the poor will buy an adequate ration. There is an obvious flaw in this argument in that the position in which the incomes of rich and poor equalise before the income of the poor buys an adequate ration is the one to which Malthus refers. However, a more appropriate analysis, where there is sufficient food to be shared out, is whether it is actually economically and politically possible to make this transfer happen.

113   M. Preston, 'We Cannot but Regret the Delay: Reflections on the Writings of the North Dublin Union Guardians during the Famine', in D. A. Valone (ed.), *Ireland's Great Hunger*, vol. 2 (Lanham: University Press of America, 2009), pp. 26–27.

114   J. O'Connor, *The Workhouses of Ireland* (Dublin: Anvil Books, 1995), pp. 146–47.

115   G. O'Brien, 'Workhouse Management in Pre-Famine Ireland', *Proceedings of the Royal Irish Academy*, 86C (1986), 113–34, at p. 113.

116   O. Purdue, 'Poverty and Power: The Irish Poor Law in a N. Antrim town 1861–1921', *Irish Historical Studies*, 37:148 (2011), 567–83.

117   T. R. Malthus, *An Investigation of the Cause of the Present High Price of Provisions* (London: Johnson, 1800), pp. 17–18.

118   Sen, *Poverty and Famines*, pp. 177–78.

The period 1848–49, the period just before the Rate-in-aid legislation in which deaths in workhouses were at their highest, can be used to test whether the redistribution policies through the Poor Law system were effective. Local taxes were at their height in this period. It can be said that an increased rate of taxation is effective if it is accompanied by a proportionate increase in tax revenue. Laffer called this the arithmetic effect of higher taxes, but he also points out the economic effect of higher taxes which can lead to diminishing returns. He quoted John Maynard Keynes, one of the most influential economists of the twentieth century, to explain this:

> … taxation may be so high as to defeat its object, and … given sufficient time to gather the fruits, a reduction of taxation will run a better chance than an increase of balancing the budget. For to take the opposite view today is to resemble a manufacturer who, running at a loss, decides to raise his price, and when his declining sales increase the loss, wrapping himself in the rectitude of plain arithmetic, decides that prudence requires him to raise the price still more – and who, when at last his account is balanced with nought on both sides, is still found righteously declaring that it would have been the act of a gambler to reduce the price when you were already making a loss.[119]

The loss of revenue as tax rates become very high can be caused by tax avoidance or a refusal or inability to pay. The curve, as discussed in economic theory, can be represented as shown in the top part of Chart 5.1. The first section of rising revenue approximates to a straight line (shown dotted), the arithmetical effect of rising revenue with rising tax rate. However, as the economic effect of resistance to payment becomes stronger a maximum revenue point is reached and the revenue collected declines. Zsolt Becsi has demonstrated that the second part of the Laffer curve can shift about causing a wide spread of points seen in reality, although the first section tends to shift far less.[120]

A similar pattern can be seen in tax records during the Irish famine that supports Twisleton's observation that a lower tax rate was optimal.[121] The historical data for Chart 5.1 (bottom) have been collected from Parliamentary papers.[122] Figures for total local tax-rate poundage, including Poor Law, cess

---

119   A. Laffer, 'The Laffer Curve: Past, Present and Future', *Backgrounder*, Heritage Foundation, 1 June 2004, p. 2. For recent exploration and verification of the Laffer curve effect in a modern context, see M. Trabant, H. Uhlig, 'How Far Are We from the Slippery Slope? The Laffer Curve Revisited', *NBER Working Paper* no. 15434 (2009 rev. 2011); idem., 'How Do Laffer Curves Differ across Countries?', in A. Alesina, F. Giavazzi (eds.), *Fiscal Policy after the Financial Crisis* (Cambridge, MA: NBER Books, 2013), 11–49.
120   Z. Becsi, 'The Shifty Laffer Curve', *Federal Reserve Bank of Atlanta Economic Review*, Q3 (2000), 53–64.
121   Twisleton to Trevelyan, 17 September 1848, N.A., Treasury papers, T64/366A.
122   *Sources*: see Chart 5.1.

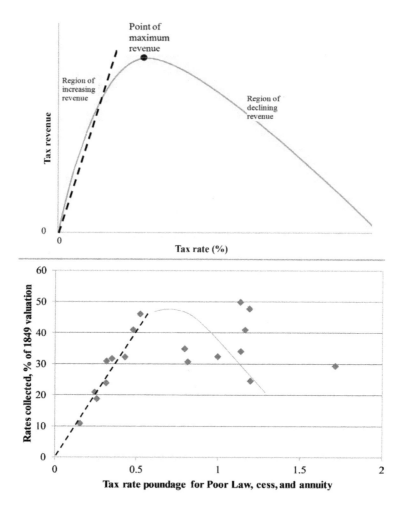

Chart 5.1. Top: theoretical Laffer curve diagram. Bottom: Scatter diagram of rates collected for each Poor Law Union while paid Guardians were in place as a percentage of 1849 valuation against the tax-rate poundage for poor law, cess and annuity in the same year (1 = 100% tax rate). Below: a tax rate of about 50%, revenue rises with tax rate more or less in a straight line, but at rates higher than 50%, revenues begin to decline. *Sources:* Combined poundage for Poor Law, cess and annuity for government loan to Poor Law Unions: *Treasury minutes June 1850 prescribing arrangements for repayment of advances to Poor Law unions in Ireland – Report of Poor Law Commissioners in Ireland, December 1851,* PP 1852 (19) XLVII.113, pp. 13–15. Rates collected and not collected: *Return of Financial state of unions in Ireland at time of appointment of paid Guardians: Reports and Resolutions relating to the management of unions under paid Guardians,* PP 1850 (251) L.109, pp. 4–5. Valuation: *Rate-in-aid (Ireland) An account of all sums levied and issued ...,* PP 1851 (554) XLIX.513.

and annuity charges for government loans is only available for unions with annuities, and the amount of rates collected is only available for the period when unions had paid Guardians. Therefore, the data cover the Unions most in distress, having government-loan annuities and paid Guardians, for the period just before the Rate-in-aid legislation. It can be seen from Chart 5.1 (bottom) that whatever the rate charged, the maximum revenue extracted was about 50% of the valuation in 1849. Even the theoretical poundage producing a maximum income was unlikely to have gone beyond 70%. However, the total rates for local taxation in 1849 went up to a height of 34 shillings 3¼d in the pound (20s) for Ballinrobe Union, the highest in the country, and there were altogether 62 unions in which local taxation was over the 10s in the pound rate.[123]

As Bruce Kinzer has noted, John Stuart Mill predicted in 1846 that if the Poor Law was extended from England to Ireland it would 'in short time … absorb the whole rental of the country', and many others felt the same.[124] In fact, as the total valuation of Ireland in 1849 was £12,908,763, it would have been possible to collect £6.4m in tax (at ten shillings in the pound or 50%), across the whole of Ireland, before revenues would have begun to stagnate. This would have more than covered the annual expenditure of approximately £2.1m on the Poor Law and £1m on other local bodies each year, so the Rate-in-aid would have in theory and in practice helped to raise extra relief funds.[125] Even so, it is questionable whether Ireland could have continued to fund relief policies on the scale required to avoid any excess mortality after 1846 through local taxation alone. Relief spending by the Treasury in early 1847 was reaching £1m a month, and Wood's plans to borrow up to £14m to finance them in 1847 suggests that rates of 100% a year would have been needed across Ireland.[126] Had the taxes to fund Irish-relief efforts been spread to Great Britain, however, it would have become much more affordable. Local opposition within Ireland to workhouse expenditure would have also likely decreased. Therefore, it is clear that the policy of transferring entitlements on a local level from the wealthy to the poor, to a greater extent than actually was the case, would not have worked on its own during the Irish famine as the wealthy would have resisted payment in order to maintain their lifestyles. However, a Rate-in-aid on a United Kingdom basis would have raised the necessary funds without crippling rates of taxation. Yet it is hard to see the politics of this working out. The price for British MPs to have agreed to a United Kingdom-wide Rate-in-aid would have been the

---

123   *Treasury minutes June 1850 prescribing arrangements for repayment of advances to Poor Law unions in Ireland – Report of Poor Law Commissioners in Ireland, December 1851*, PP 1852 (19) XLVII.113, pp. 13–15.

124   *Morning Chronicle*, 7 October 1846, p. 4, quoted in B. L. Kinzer, *England's Disgrace: J. S. Mill and the Irish Question* (Toronto: University and Toronto Press, 2001), p. 68.

125   *Rate-in-aid (Ireland) An account of all sums levied and issued …*, PP 1851 (554) XLIX.513, p. 8.

126   *Hansard*, XC, 22 February 1847, cc. 331–37; Wood to Russell, 11 April 1847, N.A., Russell papers, PRO 30/22/6C, ff. 65–70.

abolition of the Irish income-tax exemption, something that would have been electoral suicide for Irish MPs, who collectively held the balance of power at Westminster from 1847.

However, using the results of the Laffer curve analysis above, the original policy outlined by Wood and Grey at the start of 1847 could have raised money on the sort of scale that Ireland required. At this stage, before the financial crises resulted in the cancellation of the necessary Treasury advances, the plan was that the funding would be one-third from local taxes, one-third from Treasury grants and one-third from repayable Treasury loans (with the intention that most of the loan would never be recovered).[127] With a ratings valuation for Ireland of £12,908,763 in 1849, and the ability to collect 50% of this a year in tax revenue, up to £6.4m could have been gathered from Irish ratepayers a year (just over £1m of which would have been required for other local services). If a further £6.4m in Treasury grants and a further £6.4m in Treasury loans had been issued to match what was raised in Ireland, just over £18m could have been raised for Irish relief a year. In total, that is not far off £20m, the annual amount by which the potato blight and famine had reduced Irish GDP between 1846 and 1847.[128] It should be noted that the c. £13m in Treasury grants and loans in this calculation tallies with the £13m–£14m that Wood was planning to borrow as two Irish loans in the 1847–48 financial year, before the financial crises of 1847 threw the government off course. The original plan would have still been far from a perfect solution: a mechanism for wealthier Poor Law Unions to help stricken ones would have been needed, and nutritional diseases caused by the use of maize as the main relief food would have caused excess mortality however much money officials on the ground had. Yet the important point is the following. The Whig government is often accused of having been unwilling to intervene in Ireland after 1846 and of a lack of generosity. The evidence in the archives and the back-of-an-envelope calculations above, however, suggest that they were planning to fund the relief effort on the full scale required – at least, until the financial crises of 1847 intervened.

Another well-documented adverse effect of higher taxes on the poor was a wave of evictions and the loss of small holdings, leading to a higher proportion

---

127   Third Earl Grey, Paper on Relief for Ireland (which contains the policy adopted), 13 January 1847, D.U.L., Earl Grey papers, GRE/B155/19, pp. 8–11; Grey's diary entry 2 February 1847, Diary 31 July 1846 to 2 December 1847, D.U.L., Earl Grey papers, GRE/ V/ C3/13, pp. 72–73.
128   c.£20m is from calculations of Irish GDP by O'Rourke, 'Monetary Data and Proxy GDP Estimates: Ireland 1840–1921', pp. 47–48 and F. N. G. Andersson, J. Lennard, 'Irish GDP between the Famine and the First World War: Estimates Based on a Dynamic Factor Model', *European Review of Economic History*, 23:1 (2019), 50–71, at p. 70.

of medium- and larger-sized farms.[129] William Vaughan has suggested that there were around 70,000 evictions between 1846 and 1853 but notes that 'eviction accounted for only 27% of those who gave up agricultural holdings between 1847 and 1850'.[130] While starvation may have caused many to move from what would have been the smaller holdings, this leaves the possibility that the lifestyle was no longer viable and the famine caused a release of economic forces pushing towards larger holdings. Parallel with this is the reduction in poor quality 'Class 4' housing between the 1841 and 1851 Censuses (shown in Table 5.1).

Table 5.1. Class of houses in Ireland in the 1841 *Irish Census* and 1851 *Irish Census*.

Class of house	number		percentage	
	1841	1851	1841	1851
First	40,080	50,164	3.02%	4.79%
Second	264,184	318,758	19.88%	30.47%
Third	533,297	541,712	40.13%	51.78%
Fourth	491,278	135,589	36.97%	12.96%
Total	1,328,839	1,046,223	100.00%	100.00%

Source: *Census of Ireland 1851 General Report* (Dublin: HMSO, 1856), p. xxiii.

The actual outcome of legislation on farm size is difficult to assess because of the lack of data, so a longer time period has to be considered. The short-term human effect of clearances and poverty in removing very small holdings is evident from accounts at the time, such as pictures of the ruined village of Tullig published by the *London Illustrated News* in December 1849, and this analysis does not detract from that.[131] However, the assumption that the long-term increase in larger units was a specific characteristic of the famine in Ireland as a result of legislation, as Theodore Hoppen mentions, is disputable.[132] If the rates of change (shown by the gradient of the trend-lines on Chart 5.2) of percentages of holding and farm types in Ireland and England, which are comparable by their position in the spread of size of farm in each country, are placed side by side they look remarkably similar. This suggests that parallel economic forces were at work in both countries, rather than the change being a result of the

129   K. T. Hoppen, *Elections, Politics and Society in Ireland 1832–1885* (Oxford: OUP, 1984), pp. 91, 165; Kinzer, *England's Disgrace: J. S. Mill and the Irish Question*, p. 91.
130   W. E. Vaughan, *Landlords and Tenants in Ireland 1848–1904* (Dublin: Dundalgan Press, 1984), p. 23.
131   *Illustrated London News*, 15 December 1849, p. 393.
132   Hoppen, *Elections, Politics and Society in Ireland*, p. 91.

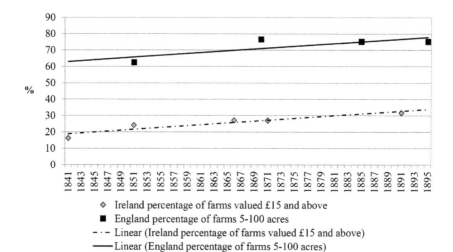

Chart 5.2. A comparison of the rate of increase in the percentage of farms of comparable standard sizes in England and Ireland, 1840s to 1890s. *Sources:* Ireland: K. T. Hoppen, *Elections, Politics and Society in Ireland 1832–1885* (Oxford: OUP, 1984), p. 92; England: D. Grigg, 'Farm Size in England and Wales from Early Victorian Times to the Present', *Agricultural History Review*, 35:2 (1987), 179–89, at p. 185.

Encumbered Estates Act or other legislation connected with the famine, as the Irish data include 1841. Tyler Goodspeed has provided corroboration of this by showing that blight severity (and therefore local tax rates) did not correlate with farm size in the aftermath of the famine.[133] Michael de Nie has described how English attitudes to the loss of small farms and poor housing in Ireland changed from sympathy over evictions in places such as Tullig to the feeling that they were what the *Illustrated London News* called a 'natural process'.[134]

What is not so commonly noted, because of a lack of data for England, is the contemporary demise of small farms in England and the consequent feeling that this process was inevitable. However, references to this assessment of the situation can be found. *The Economist* refers to 'the yeomen, the men who occupied their own small farms' in England nearly ceasing to exist, in

133   T. B. Goodspeed, 'Microcredit and Adjustment to Environmental Shock: Evidence from the Great Famine in Ireland', *Working Paper* (2014) University of Oxford, Table 7; also idem., *Journal of Development Economics*, 121:SI (2016), 258–77.
134   M. de Nie, *The Eternal Paddy: Irish Identity and the British Press, 1798–1882* (Wisconsin: University of Wisconsin Press, 2004), p. 117; *Illustrated London News*, 20 October 1849, p. 257.

the context of discussing the inevitable change from small to large farms.[135] Even so, small farms were still prevalent in counties such as the West Riding of Yorkshire and Cornwall.[136] Nevertheless, the difference between the countries is that Ireland's changes took place within a very short period over the famine; the decrease in numbers of Class 4 houses in the Census shows the suddenness with which the poor vacated the countryside. Yet it is not possible to cite the changing size of farms as an intended or unintended consequence of redistributive legislation with confidence if it might have been a long-term trend across Britain and Ireland.

Kilworth: a case study of the better-off fleeing from redistribution

It is difficult to separate the demographic effects of legislation on the wealthy from that of the poor over the whole of Ireland because most of the detailed records of the Censuses of 1841 and 1851 were destroyed. The surviving grouped data do not answer many questions about the economic processes which occurred during that decade. However, some detail can be glimpsed from considering the unusually detailed 1851 Census records that have survived for Kilworth parish just outside Cork, where the Census enumerator noted where people had recently moved or were about to move.[137]

These are not the only interesting records about Kilworth that have survived. The Robert Bennet Forbes papers contain a list of deaths, including names, in Kilworth due to starvation from 1 January to 17 April 1847.[138] This appears to have been sent with a letter from Stephen Moore, Lord Mountcashel, to a captain R. B. Forbes to encourage him to bring the USS *Jamestown* on a trip together with '800 tons' of grain for Ireland, donated by the Irish Relief Society of Boston. Discounting six deaths that occurred outside the Kilworth parish, the list of deaths amounts to 112, and they coincide with a period when supplies of potatoes in Cork markets suddenly disappeared and when the import of comparatively expensive Indian corn began. It is recorded by *The Nation* in mid-May 1847 that the Kilworth Relief Committee threatened to resign as costs soared, at which time they stated that just over half the population

135   *The Economist*, 25 November 1848, p. 1330.
136   *The Times*, 26 December 1850, p. 6.
137   J. Masterson, *County Cork, Ireland, a Collection of 1851 Census Records* (Baltimore: Genealogical Publishing Co., 2004) and Dublin, National Archives of Ireland, M4685 and 999/643.
138   Robert Bennet Forbes papers, Massachusetts Historical Society, box 1, quoted in E. Garner, *To Die by Inches: The Famine in North-East Cork* (Fermoy: EIGSE Books, 1988), p. 151.

was receiving rations.[139] Other famine-related deaths which are recorded in Kilworth are 32 in a temporary fever hospital in the town between April 1847 and May 1848.[140] The position of the poorest appears to begin to stabilise after this, as the Fermoy workhouse, which covered the area, took the load (though further deaths would have also occurred there); the percentage of population receiving relief in the Fermoy Union dropped from 40.6% in 1848–49 to 19.4% in 1849–50.[141] However, Lord Mountcashel, who despite living a lavish lifestyle, mostly in Canada, was a Guardian of the Poor Law Union, continued to object to increased rates (which reached a maximum of 5s 5d in the pound in 1849) and in 1850 his estate near Kilworth was sold under the 'Encumbered Estates Court'.[142] In 1852 he was implicated in a fraud on emigrants.[143]

After 1847, as Edward Garner has put it, came the 'diaspora of cottier, middle class farmer and small business people'.[144] The detailed 1851 Census records for Kilworth demonstrate this class differentiation, but they also show something hitherto unrecognised: that many of the remaining poor moved into the empty properties in towns, replacing the departing trades-people. Kilworth Parish was composed of 13 townlands and Kilworth town. For Kilworth town, out of 846 names, 88 are noted as in the process of emigrating to America. They all come from families where the head of household had a skilled occupation, such as clerk, schoolmaster, stonemason, millwright, shoemaker, etc., except for two paupers and two labourers. Labourers in the poorer street of Pound Lane were already noted as moving into the better houses left vacant. In the rural townlands, communities had shrunk from 1841 to leave mainly those which were immediately adjacent to and dependent upon local gentry for support. Nearby Monadrishane (also spelt Monedrisane), which must have seen a great growth in poor housing since 1841, had 330 names listed against the 31 actually shown in the summary tables of the Census. This is because the remainder, 299, were noted as moving, mainly to Kilworth town, explaining the disparity between the 846 names noted and the 1,185 given in the tables. By 1861 many of the abandoned plots in Monadrishane were occupied again.

Thus a different picture from the bare Census data shown in Table 5.1 is presented. It is usually assumed that because centres of wealthy housing correlate with the retention of population (e.g. Whitebog retains 21% against

139   *The Nation*, 15 May 1847, p. 5, see also *Kerry Evening Post*, 12 May 1847, p. 2.
140   *Census of Ireland for the year 1851* (Dublin: HMSO, 1856) Tables of Death vol. II, p. 32.
141   Garner, *To Die by Inches: The Famine in North-East Cork*, p. 147.
142   *Freeman's Journal*, 23 August 1847; *Returns from each Poor Law Union in Ireland ... 1845–55 ...*, PP 1857 Session 2 (288) XLII.447; *Nenagh Guardian*, 4 May 1850, p. 3.
143   *Lloyd's Weekly Newspaper*, 26 September 1852; 3 October 1852 (references are to Lord Kilworth, his name until 1822 which he continued to use on occasion).
144   Garner, *To Die by Inches: The Famine in North-East Cork*, p. 71.

Kilworth town keeping 67%) generally it is the poor who either left Ireland or died.[145] However, if the analysis of Kilworth can be used as an indication of what was happening elsewhere, the position was complicated by the poor replacing the better-off who were more able to leave. The tendency was long lived: it is notable that the population of Kilworth town continued to decline rapidly from 1851 to 1861 (see Table 5.2). Commercial directories show a decline in tradesmen from before to after the famine period: from 54 in 1846 to 32 in 1856 and 25 in 1870.[146]

Table 5.2. Population data for the Parish of Kilworth, 1841 to 1861, by townlands and town.

Townlands and Town in Kilworth Parish (using spelling from report)	Population		
	1841	1851	1861
Ballinrush	284	156	112
Ballinvoher	279	135	113
Glansheskin	54	70	52
Graigue	132	119	92
Killally East	119	16	22
Killally West	126	97	46
Kilworth	63	.	47
Knockanohill	120	13	10
Maryville	39	21	21
Monadrishane	43	31	214
Moorepark	25	22	32
Toor	68	52	23
Whitebog	122	26	35
Kilworth Town	1772	1185	621
Total	3246	1943	1440

Source: Census of Ireland for the year 1861, Area, population and number of houses, Ireland, vols. 1/2 (Dublin: HMSO, 1863), p. 62.

145   K. Hourihan, 'The Cities and Towns of Ireland', in Crowley et al. (eds.), *Atlas of the Great Famine, 1845–52*, pp. 228–39, at p. 234; C. Ó Gráda, K. H. O'Rourke, 'Migration as Disaster Relief: Lessons from the Great Irish Famine', *European Review of Economic History*, 1:1 (1997), 3–25, at p. 8.

146   *Slater's Commercial Directory 1846* (Manchester: I. Slater, 1846–70), p. 254; 1856, p. 285; 1870, p. 130.

It is therefore quite possible that elsewhere the poor moved to and within the towns and replaced some of the better-off who had emigrated. Consequently, Wood's social engineering may have happened to a degree, but not in the fashion he had hoped. The poor may have replaced the better-off who had fled, rather than have been employed by them. Further descriptive evidence confirms that many of the poor from the countryside migrated to the areas around Irish towns generally. Bessborough wrote to Russell in March 1847 referring to 'the able-bodied vagrants ... who have been forced into these towns by the clearance of properties and other causes'.[147] This insight may explain what happened to some of those who were evicted.

Census data from County Cork for 1841 and 1851 shows that there was a significant concentration of people into 15 local town areas between these two years.[148] Rural areas with numbers of houses that decreased during the famine tended to be in the surroundings of towns with populations that increased. The number of houses in the countryside fell and the population of these towns and cities rose. Cork city's population rose from 92,038 in 1841 to 102,334 in 1851; while its population relying on independent means or managerial work halved, the number of manual labourers doubled.[149] Even so, there is evidence that the poor replaced the better-off in rural areas too. In 1850 Clarendon sent Russell a note explaining how paupers were taking over small estates:

> A noble Lord not liking the liabilities attached to a small estate gave it to his brother, who finding it impossible to extract from it the Poor rates for which he, as immediate lessor was liable has assigned it to a labourer. I know two other similar small estates ... [one owner] has lately passed through the Insolvency Court, the proprietor of the other is a virtual Pauper.[150]

Clarendon's worry about this was that the owners avoided rates by not culti-vating the soil and would therefore produce neither tax nor employment for the poor. Future research into detailed population changes may help identify to what extent the pattern of population movement around Cork is reflected in the rest of Ireland during this period.

The preliminary conclusion to be drawn is that the poor reached a crisis immediately at the start of 1847, while the wealthy suffered longer lasting problems because of high taxation. This could be used to query traditional attitudes towards the causes of migration. Ó Gráda has already noted the

---

147   Bessborough to Russell, 17 March 1847, N.A., Russell papers, PRO 30/22/6B, f. 243.
148   A.S. Fotheringham, M. Kelly, C. Treacy (2011), NCG Online Atlas Portal, online at <http://ncg.nuim.ie/historical-atlas> [accessed 30 July 2014].
149   W. Smyth, 'The Roles of Cities and Towns during the Great Famine', in Crowley et al. (eds.), *Atlas of the Great Famine, 1845–52*, 240–52, at p. 252.
150   Note by Clarendon, January 1850, N.A., Russell papers, PRO 30/22/8C, ff. 142–45 (original underline).

change in the relationship between regional poverty and emigration over the nineteenth century. Before the Famine, arguably, 'those living in richer areas ... [were] more prone to leave', but between 1891 and 1911 'the lower the wage, and the higher the proportion of poor housing, the higher the proportion of the cohort lost'.[151] The situation in the famine period may have been a mixture, with most emigration in richer areas going to America. As over 95% of Irish emigrants were forced to pay for their emigration without government subsidy, only the wealthier could afford to travel to long-haul destinations such as the United States.[152] Contemporary accounts typically describe emigrants to America as 'comfortable in appearance, young and healthy'.[153] Witnesses at the 1849 Select Committee on Irish Poor Laws included Alfred Power, Twisleton's successor, who gave his impression 'that those who have emigrated have been of the farming [i.e. better-off] class', and George Hamilton, who confirmed 'the better class of farmers are much more anxious to emigrate than they were'.[154] The higher socio-economic status of emigrants to America is confirmed by a recent analysis of savings accounts of emigrants in the United States, which indicates that Irish emigrants in the 1840s and 1850s were disproportionately richer and better educated than the Irish-American population already living in New York City.[155]

Figure 5.2 shows the results of an investigation of the link between emigration and poverty for 1850. The areas of the country have been classified according to the results of a commission enquiring into whether Poor Law Union distribution was adequate and recommending changes between 1848 and 1850. As William Smyth has shown, the distribution of new Unions and boundary changes points up the areas of greatest need.[156] The poorest areas are assumed to be those in which a new Union was established (dark grey), the next most impoverished

151   C. Ó Gráda, *Ireland: A New Economic History 1780–1939* (Oxford: OUP, 1994), pp. 232–33.

152   See O. MacDonagh, 'The Irish Famine Emigration to the United States and the British Colonies during the Famine', in R. D. Edwards, T. D. Williams (eds.), *The Great Famine: Studies in Irish History 1845–52* (Dublin: Browne & Nolan, 1956), 319–90, at p. 335; D. Fitzpatrick, *Irish Emigration 1801–1921* (Dundalk: Dundalgan Press, 1984), pp. 19–20.

153   *Cork Constitution* quoted in *Reynold's Newspaper*, 16 March 1851.

154   *Select Committee on Poor Laws (Ireland), seventh report*, PP 1849 (194) XV.347, paras. 746, 4592.

155   T. Anbinder, 'Moving beyond "Rags to Riches": New York's Irish Famine Immigrants and their Surprising Savings Accounts', *Journal of American History*, 99:3 (2012), 741–70; R. J. Ernst, *Immigrant Life in New York City 1825–63* (New York: Columbia University Press, 1949), pp. 214–18.

156   *Poor Law Unions and Electoral Divisions: reports of the Commissioners for inquiring into the number and boundaries of Poor Law Unions and Electoral Divisions in Ireland*, nos. 1–14, HMSO, 1849–50; Smyth, 'The Roles of Cities and Towns during the Great Famine', p. 252.

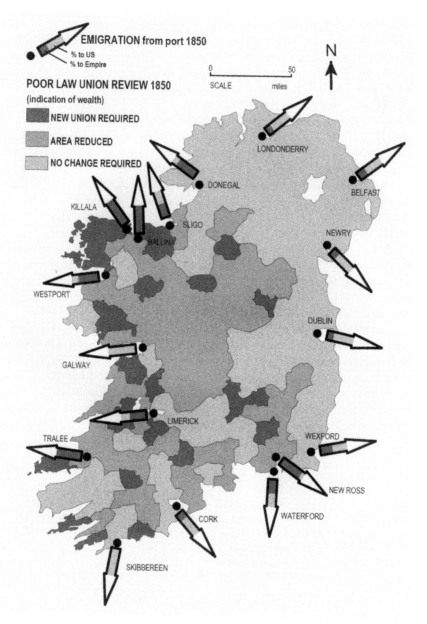

Figure 5.2. For 1850 a comparison of poverty shown by shading on the map (dark is the most impoverished, medium less so and light the least) and the destination of emigration shown as the comparative share of emigration from each port by shading on the arrow (light to the United States of America, dark to destinations in the British Empire outside the United Kingdom).

are those whose area was significantly reduced (mid-grey) and lastly comes the parts of the country where no change was made (light grey). The proportion of emigrants leaving from each port in 1850 and going either to the United States or areas of the British Empire outside the United Kingdom, such as Canada or Newfoundland, was published in a Parliamentary paper, and these have been indicated by shades of grey in the arrows, by proportion along the length.[157] It can be seen by eye that the light grey for destination United States in the arrows correlates with light grey for less poverty or stress in the surrounding areas to the ports. Obviously, this is a considerable approximation and generalisation but underlines a trend for the less impoverished to leave for the United States.

These results clarify the differences in patterns of emigration by the better-off who mostly went to America and the poor who generally migrated to Great Britain or parts of its Empire. The immediate urgency for the poor to escape in early 1847 is clear but the reason for the pattern of emigration by the better-off is still open to question. An answer is suggested by a comparison between local tax rates and emigration levels to America. This exercise identifies a link between the two, caused by the economic stress of local taxation. It suggests a process that underlies the results from the Laffer curve analysis and that was pointed out at the time by the Church of Ireland's Archbishop of Dublin, Whately.[158] As Chart 5.3 shows, the data for Irish emigration to the United States closely follow the overall burden of local taxation in Ireland (comprising Poor Law rates, presentments and county cesses), with about a three-year lag.

The co-movement of local taxation and emigration data suggests that it was not simply the rise of American nativism in the 1850s, as Raymond Cohn has suggested, but the cutting of local taxation which helped curb the flood of the better-off leaving the country.[159] The final reduction in local taxes in this period was due to Gladstone's budget of 1853, which wiped away the entirety of the Poor Law's debts from the famine in Ireland, in return for the long-deferred abolition of the Irish income-tax exemption.[160] The prediction of Wood and Grey at the start of the famine that very little of the Treasury's advances to Ireland would ever be demanded in repayment had come true.

The impact of taxes on the better-off farmers who concentrated on cattle and tillage products was amplified by the falling prices of their products towards the end of the famine. Liam Kennedy and Peter Solar have recorded in their extensive study of Irish agricultural prices that tillage products in the South of Ireland fell from an indexed value of 102.4 in 1845 and 103.1 in 1847 to 92.7 in

157   *Tables of the Revenue, Population, Commerce &c. of the United Kingdom and its Dependencies Part XX 1850*, PP 1852 (1466-I) LII.1, pp. 216–17.
158   *Hansard*, CV, 11 May 1849, cc. 277.
159   R. L. Cohn, 'Nativism and the End of the Mass Migration of the 1840s and 1850s', *Journal of Economic History*, 60:2 (2000), 361–83.
160   *Hansard*, CXXV, 18 April 1853, cc. 1350–427, at cc. 1402–03.

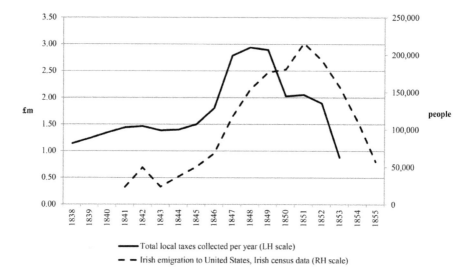

3.50
3.00
2.50
2.00
£m
1.50
1.00
0.50
0.00

250,000
200,000
150,000
people
100,000
50,000
0

1838 1839 1840 1841 1842 1843 1844 1845 1846 1847 1848 1849 1850 1851 1852 1853 1854 1855

——— Total local taxes collected per year (LH scale)
– – Irish emigration to United States, Irish census data (RH scale)

Chart 5.3. A comparison of emigration to the United States of America and local taxation in Ireland (£m), 1837 to 1853. *Sources:* for Presentments: *Presentments (Ireland.) Grand jury presentments. Abstracts of the accounts of presentments made by the grand juries of the several counties, cities and towns in Ireland… in the year 1837*, PP 1837–38 (207) XLVI.377; *Presentments (Ireland.) Grand jury presentments. Abstracts of the accounts of presentments made by the grand juries of the several counties, cities and towns in Ireland… in the year 1838*, PP 1839 (104) XLVII.573; *Presentments (Ireland.) Grand jury presentments. Abstracts of the accounts of presentments made by the grand juries of the several counties, cities and towns in Ireland… in the year 1839*, PP 1840 (41) XLVIII.211; *Presentments (Ireland) Grand jury presentments. Abstracts of the accounts of presentments made by the grand juries of the several counties, cities and towns in Ireland… in the year 1840*, PP 1841 Session 1 (143) XXVII.265; *Presentments Grand jury presentments (Ireland). Abstract of accounts of presentments made by the grand juries of the several counties, cities, and towns in Ireland, in the year 1850…*, PP 1852 (20) XLVII.409; *Presentments Grand jury presentments (Ireland). Abstract of accounts of presentments made by the grand juries of the several counties, cities, and towns in Ireland, in the year 1851…*, PP 1852 (152) XLVII.413; *Presentments Grand jury presentments (Ireland). Abstract of accounts of presentments made by the grand juries of the several counties, cities, and towns in Ireland, in the year 1852 (pursuant to acts 49 Geo. 3, c.84, s. 31, and 4 Geo. 4, c.33, s. 18)*, PP 1852–53 (366) XCIV.573; *Presentments Grand jury presentments (Ireland). Abstract of accounts of presentments made by the grand juries of the several counties, cities, and towns in Ireland, in the year 1853…*, PP 1854 (207) LVIII.367; for Poor Law: *Poor rate. Return of the gross amount of sums levied under the head of poor rate in England and Wales, in each year, from 1830 to 1851, and in Scotland and Ireland, from 1840 to 1851, stated in pounds sterling…*, PP 1852 (319) XLV.51; *County rates, &c. charges. Return for each year of all charges formerly paid out of county rates, but now paid out of the public taxes, from the year 1849 inclusive to the present time…; also, return of the sums paid for poor rates in Ireland, in each of the years since the year 1844 inclusive; &c.*, 1864 (538) L.185; *Report of the Colonial Land and Emigration Commissioners*, PP 1842 (567) XXV.55, pp. 55–102.

1848 and 80.4 in 1849, the years of highest emigration, before rising steadily again.[161] Market forces reduced the yield from farmers' lands just as they were expected to pay peak local taxes based on high valuations. Falling emigration in the 1850s may have resulted from falling local taxation as well as the strong recovery in agricultural prices and incomes that coincided with the outbreak of the Crimean War.[162] Britain's armed forces may have also drawn off many young men who might have otherwise been lured away to better financial opportunities in the United States.

The impact of nutritional ignorance

Even if the financing problems had been eased successfully earlier in the famine, another issue hampered relief efforts – one that may have, in many places, reduced the central government's and local Poor Law Unions' efforts to naught. The food provided as relief often caused nutritional diseases. It is now widely recognised by economists and scientists that nutritional disease and famine are intimately linked.[163] In recent decades the World Food Programme and other United Nations agencies have shifted their focus from simply relieving calorie deficiency towards promoting good nutrition to avoid disease, as well.[164] Yet it was not until 1984 that the first detailed study was published about nutritional diseases and mortality during the Irish famine.[165] This is in stark contrast to the role of epidemic diseases and social dislocation (which aided their spread) in raising mortality during the famine, which has been already widely discussed by historians. This chapter focuses on nutritional diseases, though, as this aspect was an explicit result of policy-design decisions made in London about the main form of food to be offered as part of the relief effort.

Even today, the role of nutritional failures in the famine-relief effort is relatively underexplored. For instance, Leslie Clarkson and Margaret

---

161   Kennedy, Solar, *Irish Agriculture: A Price History from the Mid-Eighteenth Century to the Eve of the First World War*, p.194 (table A.18). The index is 100 for 1840–45.

162   Idem., p.194 (table A.18).

163   E. M. Crawford, 'Dearth, Diet, and Disease in Ireland, 1850: A Case Study of Nutritional Deficiency', *Medical History*, 28:2 (1984), 151–61, at p. 151.

164   J. Hoddinott, personal interview with author, 11 February 2014; see also P. Webb, G. A. Stordalen, S. Singh, R. Wijesinha-Bettoni, P. Shetty, A. Lartey, 'Hunger and Malnutrition in the 21st Century', *British Medical Journal*, 361:k2238 (2018) for a general discussion of the issue.

165   Crawford, 'Dearth, Diet, and Disease in Ireland, 1850', p. 151; there had only been two very general surveys of the subject before this time, W. P. McArthur, 'Medical History of the Famine', in R. D. Edwards, T. D. Williams (eds.), *The Great Famine: Studies in Irish History 1845–52* (Dublin: Brown & Nolan, 1956), 263–315 and Woodham-Smith, *The Great Hunger*, pp. 188–205.

Crawford, relying on official records and Census data, concluded in 2001 that there were few deaths due to scurvy or pellagra during the Irish famine.[166] Yet since then, archaeologists have excavated workhouse graveyards in the famine period and found a different story. When they analysed the bones of 970 people buried in the Kilkenny workhouse graveyard they found that up to 52% of the skeletons exhibited symptoms of scurvy.[167] The authors of that study find that the 'scurvy was very probably misdiagnosed by the workhouse physicians during the famine', noting that the classic symptoms of scurvy were wrongly recorded by Dr Joseph Lalor, one of residing physicians in the Kilkenny workhouse, as 'gastric fever', or typhoid fever.[168] Recent medical research has also strengthened the link between malnutrition (particularly the nutritional diseases pellagra and kwashiorkor) and the sort of immune dysfunction which would have increased susceptibility to contagious diseases during the famine.[169] Clarkson and Crawford suggest, quoting official figures from the Irish Census of 1851, that a quarter of those who died from nutritional diseases died from marasmus, a quarter from Dropsy (mostly kwashiorkor) and just under half from 'starvation', the total of starvation deaths being less than the number killed by contagious diseases during the period.[170] The archaeological and medical evidence increasingly suggests that even this assessment grossly under-states the role of nutritional diseases, caused by imbalanced diets, in directly killing people as well as making them susceptible to contagious infections during the famine.

Many of the nutritional diseases that occurred during the famine can be seen as an unintended consequence of the decision to try and replace the potato with Indian corn during the relief effort. This, alongside oatmeal, became the dominant form of food relief after 1846. Workhouses were permitted to serve Indian corn instead of potatoes (which were in short supply) from 1846 onwards.[171] By 1848 only three out of 140 workhouses in Ireland were

166   L. Clarkson, M. Crawford, *Feast and Famine: Food and Nutrition in Ireland 1500–1920* (Oxford: OUP, 2001), p. 146.

167   J. Geber, E. Murphy, 'Scurvy in the Great Irish Famine', *American Journal of Physical Anthropology*, 148:4 (2012), 512–24.

168   Idem., pp. 521–22; J. Lalor, 'Observations on the Late Epidemic Fever', *Dublin Quarterly Journal of Medical Science*, 5 (1848), 12–30.

169   See, for instance, C. D. Bourke, J. A. Berkley, A. J. Prendergast, 'Immune Dysfunction as a Cause and Consequence of Malnutrition', *Trends in Immunology*, 37:6 (2016), 386–98; P. Katona, J. Katona-Apte, 'The Interaction between Nutrition and Infection', *Clinical Infectious Diseases*, 46:10 (2008), 1582–88.

170   Clarkson, Crawford, *Feast and Famine*, citing *The Census of Ireland for the year 1851*, Part V. Table of deaths, vol. 2, PP 1856 (2087-II), XXX.1.

171   I. Miller, 'The Chemistry of Famine: Nutritional Controversies and the Irish Famine, c.1845–47', *Medical History*, 56:4 (2012), 444–62, at p. 457, citing *Twelfth Annual Report*

reported to be serving neither meal made from Indian corn or oats.[172] The policy of importing Indian corn from abroad was adopted, in part, in order to introduce new supplies to the Irish market from America. It was also thought this would ensure that Irish markets for the more usual grains did not receive direct competition from subsidised imports. This, it was hoped, would avoid the government depressing prices and investment in domestic production of Irish staple crops by more than was necessary. Indian corn was also thought, incorrectly, to be a good nutritional substitute for potatoes. The staple rural diet before the famine, potatoes supplemented by a little milk, is almost a nutritionally complete diet. There is some evidence that, as a consequence, the Irish population was healthier and taller than the English before the famine.[173]

Policymakers thought Indian corn was a good substitute for the potato as a staple food that could provide the same wide variety of nutrients. Peel described Indian corn as 'a better and more generous description of food' when arguing for the reduction of tariffs for its importation.[174] Wood attributed what he saw as the indolence of the Irish peasant to the potato which he regarded as 'unwholesome food', and so saw Indian corn as an improvement.[175] Trevelyan even tried to serve it to his family at home as an experiment and sent cornmeal biscuits to Peel as prime minister to try.[176] The arrival of Indian corn in Ireland was also initially greeted warmly by the Irish press (although its introduction caused riots in some workhouses).[177]

The reputation of maize as a good replacement for the potato in the diet arose from an article dating from 1833 in *Tait's Edinburgh Magazine*, which described healthy communities in the Tyrol living on it alone.[178] However, the authors of the article did not emphasise that the Tyrolean diet was supplemented by large quantities of milk, which overcame the protein deficiency of Indian corn. Faced with surging demand for relief during the famine, milk was judged by Poor Law Guardians to be too expensive to purchase on any large scale for their workhouses. The resulting protein deficiency almost certainly

---

of *Poor Law Commissioners, Reports of Commissioners, Commons,* 1846 (Cmd. 704) XIX.1, 25.

172   Miller, 'The Chemistry of Famine', p. 457.

173   For the latter point see J. Mokyr, C. Ó Gráda, 'Height and Health in the United Kingdom 1815–1860: Evidence from the East India Company Army', *Explorations in Economic History*, 33:2 (1996), 141–68.

174   *Hansard*, LXXXV, 8 April 1846, c. 694.

175   Wood's memorandum to Cabinet, 20 November 1846, O.B.L., Clarendon papers, Clar. dep. Irish box 74.

176   R. Haines, *Charles Trevelyan and the Great Irish Famine* (Dublin: Four Courts Press, 2004), p. 183.

177   Miller, 'The Chemistry of Famine', p. 457.

178   H. D. Inglis, 'Travels in the Tyrol', *Tait's Edinburgh Magazine*, 3:15 (June 1833), 287–98, at p. 293.

caused nutritional diseases such as kwashiorkor and pellagra, as well as scurvy caused by a lack of vitamin C, another micronutrient present in potatoes but not in Indian corn. These nutritional diseases became widespread in workhouses alongside typhoid and cholera.

The exact nature of the link between Indian corn and kwashiorkor has been generally accepted among nutritionists and scientists since the 1950s.[179] The disease particularly affects the young, and the symptoms are discolouration and lesions on the skin, sometimes swelling, and diarrhoea, as well as a loss of interest in surroundings or will to do anything. Those affected sit around with curious 'crouching attitudes', as was noted during the famine itself.[180] Descriptions by witnesses abound of the symptoms of kwashiorkor and pellagra including 'frightful swelling' – hunger oedema – among victims of the famine in early 1847.[181] Woodham-Smith tells the horrific story of men employed on public works whose abdomens had swelled to twice their natural size and the body of a 12-year-old boy whose body had swelled to three times its normal size 'and actually burst the garment he wore'.[182] Other contemporary descriptions speak of children with 'their heads bald and their faces wrinkled like old men and women of seventy or eighty years of age' and others 'too weak to rise, pale and ghastly ... [with] little limbs ... swollen and ripening for the grave', which are all symptoms of kwashiorkor and pellagra.[183]

The question of why harvest failure caused so many deaths in Ireland, but not in France or elsewhere in Europe, perplexed many contemporary Irish commentators. Nutritional disease could explain these observations of excess deaths, as well as the number of reports from Ireland of the resignation of the population in the face of suffering. Many of the newspapers of the time contrasted the placid behaviour of the Irish compared with the French in the face of similar food shortages. The *Cork Examiner*, on 8 March 1847, asked: 'We are told of food being as high priced in France as it is in Ireland' and questioned 'how comes it that the French people do not drop dead on the roads as well as those of Ireland?'[184] An article published in the same newspaper on 29 March 1847 continued the same theme, noting 'that there has been no famine

179   C. D. Williams, 'Kwashiorkor: A Nutritional Disease of Children Associated with a Maize Diet', *Nutrition Reviews*, 31:11 (1973), 350–51, originally: 'Kwashiorkor, a Nutritional Disease Associated with a Maize Diet', *Lancet*, no. 224 (1935), 1151–52.
180   E. Broderick, 'The Famine in Waterford as Reported in Local Newspapers', in D. Cowman, D. Brady (eds.), *The Famine in Waterford, 1845–50* (Dublin: Geography Publications, 1995), 152–213, at pp. 162–63; *Illustrated London News*, 13 February 1847, p. 100.
181   Woodham-Smith, *The Great Hunger*, p. 194; Woodham-Smith refers to this as 'famine dropsy', a non-specific term.
182   Ibid.
183   Clarkson, Crawford, *Feast and Famine*, pp. 144–45.
184   *Cork Examiner*, 8 March 1847.

in France, but only a partial scarcity, and yet [it is] exciting the people to great discontent'.[185] In contrast, 'In Ireland thousands upon thousands of young stalwart men have laid down in their wretched hovels, on the road side, in the streets of populous cities, to die ... and yet they have borne their unexampled distresses with patience, meekness and forbearance'.[186]

It is true that more recent scholarship has challenged Kevin Nowlan's assumption in the 1950s that the famine years were 'conspicuous for their tranquillity rather than their turbulence'.[187] Yet, although James Kelly and others have more recently shown that there was a rise in petty crime and food rioting, the overall impression and point the *Cork Examiner* made remains valid.[188] In France harvest failure and rises in food prices were met by a political revolution that shook the establishment in 1848. In Ireland, however, the only serious revolutionary insurgency that year was a damp squib led by a few middle-class people, beginning and ending in a cabbage patch in County Tipperary.[189] Other sources suggest an inactive population, quiescent in the face of disaster. Contemporary descriptions abound from the time of starving people sitting around in 'crouching attitudes' and with an 'unmeaning staring stare', losing the ability to do anything for themselves.[190] The *Illustrated London News* often published sketches of people in crouching positions in Ireland (see, for instance, Figure 5.3).[191] In Youghal and Dungarvan, the same newspaper described the 'miserable spectacle of haggard looks, crouching attitudes, sunken eyes, and colourless lips and cheeks'.[192]

185   Idem., 29 March 1847.
186   Ibid.
187   K. B. Nowlan, 'The Political Background', in Edwards, Williams (eds.), *The Great Famine: Studies in Irish History 1845–52*, 131–206, at p. 136; challenged by Ó Gráda, *The Great Irish Famine*, p. 36 and E. Delaney, B. Mac Suibhne (eds.), *Ireland's Great Famine and Popular Politics* (New York: Routledge, 2015), p. 3.
188   J. Kelly, *Food Rioting in Ireland in the Eighteenth and Nineteenth Centuries: The 'Moral Economy' and the Irish Crowd* (Dublin: Four Courts Press, 2017); Ó Gráda, *The Great Irish Famine*, p. 36; Delaney, Suibhne (eds.), *Ireland's Great Famine and Popular Politics*, p. 3.
189   For instance, see recent comments in D. Kanter, 'Post-Famine Politics, 1850–1879', in T. Bartlett, J. Kelly (eds.), *The Cambridge History of Ireland* (Cambridge: CUP, 2018), 688–715, at p. 688: 'In Ireland, however, the collapse of the agitation for the repeal of the Act of Union in 1848 was followed by a period of relative quiescence, and a sustained nationalist campaign enjoying broad popular support re-emerged only with the advent of the home rule movement in the 1870s'.
190   Broderick, 'The Famine in Waterford as Reported in Local Newspapers', pp. 162–63; *Illustrated London News*, 13 February 1847, p. 100; Woodham-Smith, *The Great Hunger*, p. 195, citing James Hack Tuke, MS. Notes, February 1847, Borthwick Institute for Archives, Tuke Papers.
191   *Illustrated London News*, 13 February 1847, p. 100.
192   Idem., 7 November 1846, p. 293.

Kwashiorkor is characterised by a loss of will to do anything that would explain the docile nature of the afflicted in Ireland, and it is fatal if left untreated.[193] It is believed to be caused by a lack of proteins and niacin, of which maize (and its variant Indian corn) contains an indigestible form that cannot be absorbed. The disease pellagra, which has similar symptoms, also has the same cause.[194] In the words of Barratt Brenton, 'traditionally, the symptoms were characterised as the four D's: dermatitis, diarrhoea and dementia, with the fourth and final "D" being death'.[195] There is a wealth of knowledge and literature from the southern United States on such health risks because they are maize-growing areas.[196] In 1879–80, medical practitioners in Ireland made this association, reporting on whole families with the symptoms which match the disease and the specific observation that they had not eaten anything but Indian corn for several months.[197] This shows how long lasting the impact of the introduction of Indian corn in Ireland was. It may also explain why stories circulated in London in March 1847, which were quoted in the Greville memoirs, of people dying of 'starvation' in Ireland even though food and money to buy it were available.[198] The young and old would still look like they were starving, even if they had been fed with enough calories in the form of Indian corn. Later, deaths occurred for an extended period past 1847, when the food supply situation began to improve, possibly for the same reason. In 1849 Count Strzelecki returned to give evidence to an Irish Poor Law Enquiry. He was certain, from observation, that the new forms of grain distributed had caused deaths by 'inflammatory diseases of the stomach'.[199] These types of diseases are still a problem in refugee camps and during famines in the developing world in the modern era and so their presence in Ireland during its Great Famine should be no surprise.[200]

193   R. Cook, 'The General Nutritional Problems of Africa', African Affairs, 65:261 (1966), 329–40, at p. 330.
194   B. P. Brenton, 'Pellagra and Nutrition Policy Lessons from the Great Irish Famine to the New South Africa', Nutritional Anthropology, 22:1 (1998), 1–11.
195   Idem., p. 1.
196   K. J. Carpenter, 'The Relationship of Pellagra to Corn and the Low Availability of Niacin in Cereals', in J. Mauron (ed.), 'Nutritional Adequacy, Nutrient Availability and Needs', Experientia Supplementum, 44 (Basel: Birkhäuser, 1983), 197–222; M. K. Crabb, 'An Epidemic of Pride: Pellagra and the Culture of the American South', Anthropologica, 34 (1992), 89–103; K. Clay, E. Schmick, W. Troesken, 'The Rise and Fall of Pellagra in the American South', Journal of Economic History, 79:1 (2019), 32–62.
197   G. Sigerson, Report of the Medical Commission of the Mansion House Committee (Dublin: Browne and Nolan, 1881), p. 166.
198   C. Greville, The Greville Memoirs pt. II, vol. III (London: Longmans, 1885), p. 71.
199   Select Committee of the House of Lords to enquire into the operation of the Irish Poor Law, Fourth Report, minutes of evidence, PP 1849 (365) XVI.543, p. 854.
200   See, for instance, O. Müller, M. Krawinkel., 'Malnutrition and Health in Developing Countries', Canadian Medical Association Journal, 173:3 (2005), 279–86.

Figure 5.3. Figures in Skibbereen crouching in the street even though a coffin is passing. *Illustrated London News*, 13 February 1847, p. 100.

Wood's policies of extreme redistribution failed the poor

In conclusion, the results of attempts by the government to redistribute wealth in Ireland after 1847 without Treasury advances on the scale originally intended can be seen as disastrous and full of unintended consequences. Russell yearned for the days when responsible landlords looked after their populations. However, the employment by the landowners that Wood hoped would occur in the countryside did not materialise. Generally, the poor did not benefit as intended and the wealthy did not pay in wages or relief what policymakers intended them to. It is not surprising that Wood confided to Peel in 1849: 'I fear very much for the interposition of the government. Every day shows this more clearly'.[201] For Wood, his experience in Ireland had shown voluntary organisers of relief were not to be relied upon, and this view contributed to the development of a professional, paid, British civil service by Trevelyan in the 1850s.

201   Wood to Peel, 6 April 1849, B.L., Peel papers, Add. MS. 40601, ff. 139–44.

The
IRISH EMIGRANT'S ADDRESS TO HIS IRISH LANDLORD
On attempting to get him a small loaf in place of his big

I'm now going to a country, where
From Poor-rates I'll be free,
For *Poor* Iriland's going to the dogs
As fast as fast can be;
You know you'd like to *stop me*,
So I'll do it on the *sly*,
With Me I'll take a half year's Rent,
Your Honor—Won't you *cry*?

CHORUS
O your honor, what do you think of that
Upon the yellow Indian-buck your honor
    will get fat?

Now, that the Corn Laws are gone,
Our Grain's so Mighty cheap,
I'll hardly find it worth my while
My Plot of Oats to reap;
So when it's cut and all sold off
Off to Yankee land I'll fly,
But sure I'll leave you all your Land,
Your Honour don't you cry?

O your honour's now reduced to misery
When I am in America, I'm safe from
    perfidy.

I don't believe I ped the rint,
Within the last three years,
And so I owe your honour
Some trifle of arrears;
I mention this because I think,
You'd like to say *good-bye*?
For those arrears—I have them snug,
Your honour, don't you cry.

O Your honour the poorhouse is your dart,
Before, like those by Famine died, your
    honour breaks *your heart.*

Now I'm sure your head is breaking,
For arrears of rent it's true
But, *Kind Friend*, be not mistaken
For you'll never get *a screw*;
Now you sadly do regret it,
As I have it on my thigh,
Dont you wish that you may get it?
And you know the reason why!

O your honour, may jolt your granny still
When I'm in America you may do what
    you will.

Sure your honour though to hold me
Till I'd pay you what was due
And you sent an old bum-baliff,
To the house to watch me too,
For fear I'd stir the corn,
but his efforts they did fail,
For I tied him in the barn,
And that night I took leg bail.

Oh your honours, the Bread Tax must take
    leg!
As the Dublin Coal-porters have won o'er
    Butt and Trasham Gregg!

Now all your sooty mud-wall cabins,
You may hang them on the shelf,
And when you sell on your mansion,
You can live in one yourself,
but with the change of diet I fear,
Your guts they won comply,
When the India-buck you try it,
Oh, your honour dont you cry.

Oh your honour is crying now again,
You remind me of the Fable where the wolf
    had hired a crane.

I hope your honour may have luck
When all the counrry's waste,
And when they give outdoor relief,
May your honor get a taste,
but if they build a Union,
For Landlord's there to fly,
And you get in—why then I think, your
    honour need not cry.

O your honors, the poor beggars you do
    offend
You'll have your own hands out e'ere long
    but you won't get a Friend.

Now when I'm landed in New York, that
    moment I will get,
A gallon of rum and drink your health
With what I'm in your debt
As I dont intend to pay you
I'll tell you the reason why,
Sure you though to seize upon me
Oh, your honour that's no lie.

O your honor will get a ticket for the soup
when we get English Landlords hear, they'll
    put you through the hoop!

Figure 5.4. *The Irish Emigrant's Address to His Irish Landlord On attempting to get him a small loaf in place of his big*, 2 April 1850, N.A., Treasury papers, T64/370C/1 (transcribed). Trevelyan noted the irony of this ballad in that, though protesting on behalf of small farmers, it 'tends to the increase of emigration and the consolidation of the small holdings, by which the landlords will be ultimately benefitted'.

The increase in local taxation after the placing of relief costs on the Poor Law proved a disincentive to the collection of revenue in the areas worst affected by famine. The lack of funding consequently made conditions in the workhouses worse than intended. The introduction of the Rate-in-aid solved this to some extent, but the continued increase in local taxation caused a surge in emigrations of the better-off, together with their human and financial capital. The fiscal burden was only lifted when Gladstone's budget of 1853 wiped out the remaining debt owed by ratepayers.

The conclusion that a high proportion of emigrants to the United States was drawn from the better-off, who were politicised and anxious to improve themselves, provides an explanation for the observation made by David Doyle that: 'the major scholars of Irish migrations to Britain, Australia and Canada have by now demonstrated that, while their Irish populations increased after [the famine], that event neither reshaped nor originated Irish subcultures and communities therein to anything like the degree that was the case of the United States'.[202] That subculture in America has had a tendency to retain a strong animosity to Irish landlords and the United Kingdom, carried with it from the period of the famine. That resentment arose to a great extent from the inability for middle-class economic advancement due to the tax system and from the feeling that they had effectively been exiled from Ireland as a result of it, as the ballad in Figure 5.4 illustrates.

The economic analysis presented above also shows that development economists have missed an important point about redistributive policy during famines. As the Laffer curve analysis suggests, many of the rich in Ireland preferred to hide their wealth, or to emigrate, rather than contribute to redistribution. This experience calls into question the universal applicability that the transfer of entitlements within a society is a generalised solution to all famines. It suggests that, unless the load can be spread over a wide population or geographical area to make the level of contributions manageable, raising the wealth of all classes should be the preferred aim. That redistribution was difficult, despite vigorous attempts by the government to get the system to work to help the destitute poor, shows that many wealthier Irish people resisted assisting their fellow residents. Genuine fiscal 'Union' did not exist within local Poor Law Unions let alone between Great Britain and Ireland during this period. In the face of the resistance of the better-off in Ireland to help their poorer neighbours, and their continued exemption from the income tax, British taxpayers became less and less willing to pay extra to help the situation across the Irish Sea as time passed. Unfortunately, legislation such as the Encumbered Estates Act and the continued fallout from the Bank Charter Act hampered

---

202   D. N. Doyle, 'Cohesion and Diversity in the Irish Diaspora', *Irish Historical Studies*, 39:123 (1999), 411–34, at p. 414.

rather than helped economic recovery in the short term in Ireland.[203] As a result, the consequences of problems of finance and politics that prevented the geographical redistribution of wealth from Great Britain to Ireland after 1847 transformed a misfortune into a catastrophe.

203   Some historians argue that the Encumbered Estates Act helped the Irish economy in the much longer term; the point made here does not attempt to take anything away from this.

6

Ireland and Mauritius: the British Empire's other famine in 1847

With respect to food: nearly the whole of the cultivation of the Island being Sugar – the food consumed by the population (rice) is imported entirely from India, and by the houses engaged in cultivating the Island. Most of these houses having failed, and such a shock having been given to the credit of those which remain that their Bills will not be negotiable as usual for the purchase of Rice. There is a great risk that the island will be left without its necessary supplies. ... the peculiar circumstances of the labouring population ... having no other means whatsoever but the sugar estates, the great proportion of which must be immediately suspended, we feel strongly [there are] – reasons for some interference – which might not be justifiable under ordinary circumstances.

James Wilson to Third Earl Grey, 'The Island of Mauritius', 17 October 1847.[1]

Mauritius is an island in the Indian Ocean over 1,200 miles from the southeast coast of the African continent, and over 6,000 miles away from Ireland. It is, perhaps, best known as the former home of the Dodo (*raphus cucullatus*), a flightless species of giant pigeon that became extinct within a century of the arrival of the first Europeans to reach the island in 1598.[2] Mauritius is also known as a former sugar plantation with a history of slavery and indentured labour.[3] It is natural therefore to approach its history with an expectation that there would be poverty, resentment against its former coloniser, and internal

---

1   J. Wilson, 'The Island of Mauritius', 17 October 1847, D.U.L., Earl Grey papers, GRE/B145/D9, p. 2, paper enclosed in letter Wilson to Grey, 17 October 1847, GRE/B132/11/5.
2   H. E. Strickland, A. G. Melville, *The Dodo and Its Kindred; or the History, Affinities, and Osteology of the Dodo, Solitaire, and Other Extinct Birds of the Islands Mauritius, Rodriguez, and Bourbon* (London: Reeve, Benham and Reeve, 1848), especially p. 40; B. Shapiro, D. Sibthorpe, A. Rambaut, J. Austin, G. M. Wragg, O. R. P. Bininda-Emonds, P. L. M. Lee, A. Cooper, 'Flight of the Dodo', *Science*, 295:5560 (2002), 1683.
3   A. Sheriff, V. Teelock, S. Wahab, S. Peerthum, *Transition from Slavery in Zanzibar and Mauritius* (Dakar: Council for the Development of Social Science Research in Africa, 2016), p. 86.

Figure 6.1. Statue of Queen Victoria outside Government House in Port Louis, Mauritius.

racial and class conflict far worse than that of Ireland. Yet the reality has turned out very differently. The roots of this can be traced to 1847 and the British government's decision to restart Mauritius's economy at the time of the Irish famine. Without that effort, some of the Mauritian population and its economy could well have ended up 'as dead as a Dodo'. This chapter describes how the British government's intervention avoided this outcome and how this should change the way historians think about policy mistakes made in Ireland during its famine.

In terms of civil war and conflict, Mauritian history could not be more different from that of modern Ireland. Aside from a few riots in the 1930s, 1960s and 1990s, it has witnessed no major warfare since the British invaded and took the colony from the French in 1810. Since independence in 1968, it has mostly been a democratic and well-governed country.[4] According to the Institute for Economics and Peace, at the time of writing Mauritius is one of just four countries in the entire world free from both ongoing domestic and international conflict.[5] It is currently one of Africa's few 'high middle income' countries, according to the World Bank's definitions, with a gross domestic

4   R. Saylor, 'Probing the Historical Sources of the Mauritian Miracle: Sugar Exporters and State Building in Colonial Mauritius', *Review of African Political Economy*, 39:133 (2012), 465–78, at p. 466.
5   Institute for Economics & Peace, *Global Peace Index 2019: Measuring Peace in a Complex World* (Sydney: Institute for Economics & Peace, 2019), p. 96.

product per head of population six times its regional average.[6] Travellers and citizens alike have fallen in love with the country: 'Mauritius was made first, and then heaven', a resident told Mark Twain when the American humourist visited the island in 1896, 'and that heaven was copied after Mauritius'.[7]

So rarely does anything dramatic happen in well-governed Mauritius that journalists at *The Economist* nowadays jokingly refer to 'Mauritian monetary policy' as an example of the sort of predictably unexciting good-news story only included in an edition for completeness of coverage.[8] Yet it is exactly this subject that should be regarded of great interest and importance to historians of Ireland's Great Famine. For it was in 1847, during the worst year of the Irish famine, that Mauritius's main crop failed and its banking system imploded, threatening mass starvation amongst the agricultural labourers on the island. However, unlike the situation in Ireland, there was little excess mortality, in spite of the monetary crisis there being more serious than in Ireland. The comparative success of the British relief and reform effort in Mauritius challenges many interpretations championed by anti-revisionist historians about what exactly went wrong in Ireland. It also does much to explain why the two islands have enjoyed very different historical trajectories since.

Mauritius and Ireland had a surprising amount in common in the 1840s. Both were threatened with catastrophic famine at the same time as a financial crisis in 1847. On both islands, the agricultural sector was dominated by a monoculture crop that was decimated by new diseases: potatoes for Ireland (hit by *Phytophtora infestans* from 1845 onwards) and sugar cane for Mauritius (probably infested by gumming disease, *Xanthomonas axonopodis pv. Vasculorum*, and the sugar-cane moth borer from 1847 onwards).[9] Reduced crop yields persisted for some time beyond the appearance of the new afflictions.[10] Both also suffered from severe trading and financial problems. In Ireland banknotes in

---

6   Saylor, 'Probing the Historical Sources of the Mauritian Miracle', p. 466.

7   M. Twain, *The Writings of Mark Twain, vol. 6: Following the equator: a journey around the world*, part 2 (New York: Harper, 1899), p. 316.

8   Author's conversations with *The Economist*'s employees, unattributable.

9   R. Antoine, A. C. Hayward, 'The Gumming-Disease Problem in the Western Indian Ocean Area', *Proceedings of the International Society of Sugar Cane Technologists*, 11:1 (1962), 789–894, at p. 789, citing W. Bojer et al., 'Rapport de la Commission charge par Son Excellence le Gouverneur de faire une enquête sur la maladie de la canne à sucre' (1848); R. W. Rawson, *Rapport fait par le Comité d'Agriculture de la Société Royale des Arts des Sciences de Maurice au Conseil de la Société sur une maladie du cannes*, 9 October 1848, National Archives of Mauritius, HA/66/8; 'Sugar-Cane Disease in Barbados', *Bulletin of Miscellaneous Information (Royal Botanic Gardens, Kew)*, 100/101 (1895), 81–88, at p. 85.

10   For Ireland see K. H. O'Rourke, 'Did the Great Irish Famine Matter?', *Journal of Economic History*, 51:1 (1991), 1–22; for Mauritius see Saylor, 'Probing the Historical Sources of the Mauritian Miracle', pp. 474–75 for a discussion of the initial failure to eliminate the sugar-cane borer.

circulation halved from £7.4m in January 1846 to a trough of £3.8m in August 1849, while in Mauritius banknote circulation fell by nearly 95% between 1845 and 1847, as virtually all the precious metal drained out of the colony to finance food imports.[11] While the Bank of Ireland managed to stay afloat during the Irish famine, in Mauritius one of the two main banks collapsed in 1848, as well as many sugar estates and four of the five British commercial houses that had financed most of the island's sugar production.[12] The similarities do not end there. Weak local government institutions and legal problems with the transfer of real estate hampered effective governance in both. Like Ireland, Mauritius had a substantially Catholic population, large numbers of whom did not speak English. The elites of both places were viewed with distrust by British public opinion and politicians. Both the Anglo-Irish landlords in Ireland, presiding over mass poverty on their estates, and the French plantation class in Mauritius, who used to be slave owners, were seen by most politicians in London as not understanding 'British values' concerning the social responsibility of elites. More surprisingly still, the Trevelyan family played a role in implementing the government's response to the crisis in both places: Charles Trevelyan as a Treasury official for Ireland and his brother-in-law, Charles Zachary Macaulay, as the manager of the new currency commission in Mauritius.

In terms of overall policy structure, the British responses in Ireland and Mauritius were also remarkably similar. The government reconstituted the money supply in both places so that relief efforts could be financed upfront, while the assistance on the ground itself was to be organised by the local elites and partly funded by local taxes. In Ireland this policy meant that the Treasury advanced loans for purchasing Indian corn, for public works, for soup kitchens and then for relief on the Poor Law. In Mauritius this meant advances for the importation of rice to feed the labouring population, as well as for the financing of the next sugar crop.

Yet there were some important differences. The authors of Irish policy, Sir Robert Peel and Sir Charles Wood as chancellor of the exchequer, were devotees of the Currency School, sacrificing all – including the loans necessary to finance the relief efforts in Ireland – to the note-issue restrictions of Lord Overstone's (Samuel Jones-Loyd until 1850) theories and the Bank Charter Act of 1844.[13] In contrast, policy in Mauritius arose from the Third Earl Grey, as colonial

---

11   C. Ó Gráda, *The Great Irish Famine* (Cambridge: CUP, 1995), p. 40, citing *Thom's Directory*, 1847–50; O. Griffiths, J-M. Huron, M. Carter, *Piastres to Polymer* (Mauritius: Bioculture Press, 2018), p. 73, citing *Le Mauricien*, 7 April 1848.

12   *The Times*, 25 October 1847, p. 8, supplement, from *Allgemeine Zeitung*; *Le Cerneen* 13 December 1847; R. B. Allen, 'Maroonage and its Legacy in Mauritius and in the Colonial Plantation World', *Outre-mers: revue d'histoire*, 89:366–67 (2002), 131–52, at p. 148.

13   *Reports from the Secret Committee of the House of Commons on Commercial Distress*, PP 1847–48 (395) VIII.1, VIII.379, p. vi.

secretary, and James Wilson, as his informal advisor and then as secretary to the Board of Control, both of whom tended to heterodox economic views, which in general did not support such restrictions. The two devised urgent policies to fund the purchase of food in Mauritius. Grey's Colonial Office also set up an innovative new currency, which became the first currency board in the world, and which enabled the Mauritian economy to refinance itself.

In terms of outcome, the policy for Mauritius was more successful. The risk of widespread famine and starvation there was averted, whereas in Ireland excess mortality dragged on into the 1850s. The strange part of this situation is that Grey and Wilson are normally seen as more *laissez-faire* than the Currency School, because of their opposition to the rigid regulation by government of banknote issues under the provisions of the Bank Charter Act. Yet their '*laissez-faire*' policies, on the face of it, appear to have been more successful in Mauritius than the interventionist ones of Wood and Peel for Ireland.

The threat of famine in Mauritius in 1847 has been overlooked by scholars because of the prompt response of the British government that autumn and the limited demographic consequences it had for the island. Rather like the other famines in nineteenth-century Ireland where there was little, if any, excess mortality, historians have passed over the subject as a non-event. The concurrent financial crisis has been discussed in greater detail by scholars as the trigger for the decision to set up Mauritius's new currency board, the first in the world, at the end of that decade.[14] It has also been noted how the new currency and banking system encouraged greater investment in the island, a success which encouraged the idea of currency boards to spread to 45 countries by the 1940s. Richard Allen's insightful book about indentured labour in Mauritius, published in 1999, used data from Parliamentary papers about Mauritius to show how the availability of capital there as a result of these reforms enabled many of the population of former indentured labourers to acquire land and become owner-occupier farmers.[15] Much has also been written about the economic and social development of the island into a successful multi-ethnic and multi-religious society, and most scholars acknowledge the economic legacy that modern Mauritius received from the mid-nineteenth century in what appears, at first glance, to have been, until then, simply an exploitative and cruel history of slavery.[16]

14   Griffiths, Huron, Carter, *Piastres to Polymer*, pp. 71–74; M. Lagesse, *150 Années de Jeunesse* (Port Louis: Caravelle, 1988), pp. 35–37; *The Mauritius Commercial Bank, 1838–1963* (Port Louis: Mauritius Commercial Bank, 1964), pp. 9–10.

15   R. B. Allen, *Slaves, Freedmen, and Indentured Labourers in Colonial Mauritius* (Cambridge: CUP, 1999), pp. 105–71.

16   M. Carter, 'The Transition from Slave to Indentured Labour in Mauritius', *Slavery and Abolition*, 14:1 (1993), 114–30; F. Fessha, N. H. T. Nam, 'Is it Time to Let Go, the Best Loser System in Mauritius', *Afrika Focus*, 28:1 (2015), 63–79, at pp. 63–64; Saylor, 'Probing the

The reason why the threat of famine in Mauritius should be of wider interest is that the British response was modelled on Grey's ideas to change the United Kingdom's currency to help Ireland, which were rejected by the British government in late 1847.[17] Grey at the Colonial Office had suggested a set of reforms for the Bank of England, which by reducing capital flows and turning it more into a currency board, it was hoped, would lower interest rates and enable borrowing to fund advances for Irish relief to resume. Wood in the Cabinet, advised by Overstone, and Peel in Parliament successfully killed off Grey's proposals in Britain and defended the principles of the Currency School embodied in the Bank Charter Act.[18] In any case, Ireland was not formally a colony and so not dealt with by the Colonial Office; the Irish famine was a matter for the Treasury and the Home Office. However, as Mauritius came under the Colonial Office's responsibilities when Grey received an appeal for assistance from the island in October 1847, he eagerly seized the opportunity to use it as a laboratory for the ideas and principles he had pushed for in vain, as ways to help Ireland, and forced them past Wood and Overstone.[19]

Mauritius after 1847 therefore offers a comparison that can inform a counterfactual for Ireland. It is often asked whether the British government would have behaved the same way if the famine had struck the island of Great Britain as hard as it did that of Ireland; a question raised as early as April 1847 by the *Dublin University Magazine*.[20] Peter Gray has pointed out, more recently, that it really did hit parts of Scotland and Cornwall as hard as it did Ireland, and so the crisis should really be called the 'Great British Famine of the 1840s'.[21] The problem with the counterfactual of Great Britain losing as great a share of its overall harvest as Ireland did after 1845 is that the much greater imports of food required in that situation may well have triggered the

---

Historical Sources of the Mauritian Miracle', p. 476; J. H. Shaver et al., 'The Boundaries of Trust: Cross-Religious and Cross-Ethnic Field Experiments in Mauritius', *Evolutionary Psychology*, 16:4 (2018), 1–15.

17   See Russell to Grey, 16 October 1847, D.U.L., Earl Grey papers, GRE/B122/3/92.

18   Russell to Grey, 26 November 1847, D.U.L., Earl Grey papers, GRE/B122/3/103; *Reports from the Secret Committee of the House of Commons on Commercial Distress*, PP 1847–48 (395) VIII.1, VIII.379, p. vi; Memorandum by Grey for the Cabinet on the 1844 Act and its amendment, 3 November 1847, D.U.L., Earl Grey papers, GRE B153/35/1.

19   D. P. O'Brien, *The Correspondence of Lord Overstone*, vol. 1 (Cambridge: CUP, 1971), pp. 431–36.

20   I. Butt, 'The Famine in the Land: What Has Been Done, and What Is to Be Done?' *Dublin University Magazine*, 29:172 (1847), 501–40, pp. 514–15.

21   P. Gray, 'The Great Famine, 1845–1850', in T. Bartlett, J. Kelly (eds.), *The Cambridge History of Ireland*, vol. 3 (Cambridge: CUP, 2018), 639–65, at p. 639; see also P. Gray, '"The Great British Famine of 1845–50"? Ireland, the UK and Peripherality in Famine Relief and Philanthropy', in D. Curran, L. Luciuk, A. Newby (eds.), *Famines in European Economic History: The Last Great European Famines Reconsidered* (London: Routledge, 2015), 83–96.

panic that drained the Bank of England's gold reserves much sooner than it did in reality. If supporters of the 1844 Act had still won the battle against reform of this legislation, as they did in 1847–48, the balance of payments would have provided a powerful constraint on government action just the same. However, what if Grey had won the battle of ideas on currency inside the Cabinet in 1847? What actually happened in Mauritius provides a tantalising glimpse of the outcome that could have been possible in Ireland if similar policies had been pursued. It is a comparison from which Grey and Wilson emerge with much greater credibility, by modern standards, than historians usually give them.

The aim of this chapter is to uncover the reasons for the comparative success of the British relief and reform effort in Mauritius and what this can say about why it went so wrong in Ireland. Most scholars seeking colonial comparisons with Ireland have sought to uncover links between Ireland and India.[22] Anti-revisionist scholarship has increasingly emphasised the role that colonial institutions and capitalist modernisation played during the Irish and Indian famines in encouraging the British government to adopt 'faminogenic behaviour' that raised the death toll.[23] In Mauritius, in contrast to Ireland, there is an example of a prompt and effective British response to a potential famine in what was explicitly a colony with semi-feudal institutions. The colony's capitalist and social modernisation, imposed on its elites in return for British assistance with the relief effort, produced improved conditions for indentured labourers as well as laying the institutional foundations for Mauritius's more recent social and economic success. Therefore, the role of colonialist attitudes and capitalist modernisation just by virtue of their existence does not provide a good explanation for why Ireland's relief effort failed so badly compared to that of Mauritius.

The first section of this chapter explores what the colonial secretary thought was the explanation for the failure of the funding of the relief effort in Ireland: the credit restrictions caused by the Bank Charter Act of 1844. Private correspondence and other paperwork show that Grey believed it was the credit restrictions during the financial panics of 1847 which curtailed Irish relief and his plans to subsidise emigration from Ireland. It explains the different

22   C. Bayly, 'Ireland, India and the Empire: 1780–1914', *Transactions of the Royal Historical Society*, series 6, 10 (2000), 377–97; J. Ohlmeyer, 'Eastward Enterprises: Colonial Ireland, Colonial India', *Past and Present*, 240:1 (2018), 83–118.

23   See, for instance, C. Kinealy, 'Was Ireland a Colony?', in T. McDonough (ed.), *Was Ireland a Colony? Economics, Politics and Culture in Nineteenth-Century Ireland* (Dublin: Irish Academic Press, 2005), 48–65; W. J. Smyth, 'The Longue Durée – Imperial Britain and colonial Ireland', 64–74, and D. P. Nally, 'The Colonial Dimensions of the Great Irish Famine', in J. Crowley et al. (eds.), *Atlas of the Great Irish Famine, 1845–52* (Cork: Cork University Press, 2012), 46–63; D. P. Nally, *Human Encumbrances: Political Violence and the Great Irish Famine* (Notre Dame: University of Notre Dame Press, 2011), p. 227.

approaches of the Currency and Banking Schools to providing a paper currency convertible to gold on demand as well as Grey's particular proposals, which contained elements of both and which were side-lined in the United Kingdom. The second section explains how these plans influenced the British response to the crisis in Mauritius, which involved intervention to secure the island's food supplies, to refinance its sugar industry and to develop a new currency system after it suffered a severe financial crisis in 1847 that threatened to lead to famine. The third section explains how greater co-operation between British officials and landowners in Mauritius made the relief effort there more effective than in Ireland. The fourth section compares the available data on how Ireland and Mauritius fared after 1847, as a result of the relief policies. The final section describes how the success of Grey's policies in Mauritius inspired him to campaign for the establishment of currency boards throughout the British Empire and how it came to influence his views on Ireland later in the century.

Thoughts on the currency and Ireland

When the Russell government came into power in June 1846, Grey was appointed the secretary of state for war and the colonies.[24] His department dealt with emigration to the colonies, such as Canada, Australia and a number of smaller territories including Mauritius. Although he suggested policy, he did not deal with Ireland directly, which was under the Home Office and Treasury as part of the United Kingdom, or with India, whose rule by the East India Company was regulated by the Board of Control.

He was youthful and intelligent, the scion of perhaps the most politically influential and well-connected Whig aristocratic dynasties of the period (his father, the Second Earl Grey, as prime minister, has been credited with buying the party a decade in office with the Reform Act of 1832).[25] However, his headstrong personality squandered much of his inherited political capital. Other leading Whigs blamed him for undermining the tail end of the ministry of Lord Melbourne in the 1830s. His subsequent refusal to join a cabinet in which Lord Palmerston was returned to the Foreign Office meant that Russell was unable to form a government when Peel temporarily resigned in December 1845.[26]

24   P. Burroughs, 'Grey, Henry George, Third Earl Grey (1802–1894), politician', *Oxford Dictionary of National Biography* (Oxford: OUP, 2004), online at <https://www.oxforddnb.com/view/10.1093/ref:odnb/9780198614128.001.0001/odnb-9780198614128-e-11540> [accessed 26 February 2020].

25   E. A. Smith, 'Grey, Charles, Second Earl Grey (1764–1845), Prime Minister', *Oxford Dictionary of National Biography* (Oxford: OUP, 2004), online at <https://www.oxforddnb.com/view/10.1093/ref:odnb/9780198614128.001.0001/odnb-9780198614128-e-11526> [accessed 26 February 2020].

26   P. Scherer, *Lord John Russell: A Biography* (Selinsgrove: Susquehanna University Press, 1999), pp. 146–50.

His reputation as a competent Cabinet minister was high because of his performance as secretary at war from April 1835 to September 1839. However, by the end of his second period of office, in the Colonial Office, he had many critics and even enemies because of a seeming lack of action.[27] Despite the problems of persuading colonies to take Irish emigrants who had a reputation for riotousness, the main problem remained how assisted emigration schemes would be financed. The general depression leading up to the 1847 financial crises had already reined in spending. Grey wrote to Charles Buller complaining of his inability to proceed with 'systematic colonisation' because 'there is not a farthing to be had from the Treasury and without some money, very little seems possible'.[28] Grey was subservient to Wood's control of the Treasury because the rest of the Cabinet felt that he had 'been unreasonable' in causing the collapse of Russell's attempts to form a government by opposing Palmerston 'holding the seals of the Foreign department'.[29]

Although Grey gave *laissez-faire* sounding reasons for the lack of emigration projects in his book, *The Colonial Policy of Lord John Russell's Administration* (1853), it was written under Wood's influence, just as Trevelyan's *The Irish Crisis* had been, which also gave similar sounding excuses for the withdrawal of relief funding for Ireland in 1847.[30] They plugged into a public understanding of 'political economy' which made their excuses more acceptable to contemporary opinion. The explanation Grey gave in his private correspondence during the period is different. It is unequivocally the shortage of credit caused by the 1847 financial crises. However, unlike some members of the Cabinet, Grey fought against this restriction. As soon as he thought the second crisis was over, Grey wrote to the Cabinet trying to persuade them to take out a loan to fund military protection for the colonies, which had been cut back along with other expenditure. He reminded them that when they had been pressed to adopt emigration measures in 1847 he had advised against it. This was for reasons of finance because, 'it cannot be forgotten there was an obvious deficiency of disposable capital in the country and that it would have been impossible for the Government to have gone into the market to borrow

---

27 For modern criticism of the Third Earl Grey and Sir Charles Wood for the lack of assisted emigration schemes to the colonies see C. Ó Gráda, 'The Next World and the New World: Relief, Migration, and the Great Irish Famine', *Journal of Economic History*, 79:2 (June 2019), 319–55, at pp. 339, 348.
28 Grey to Buller, 23 February 1847, D.U.L., Earl Grey papers, GRE/B79/11/55.
29 Russell to Grey, 21 December 1845, N.A., Russell papers, PRO 30/22/4E, ff. 257–58; Bessborough to Russell, 23 December 1845, N.A., Russell papers, PRO 30/22/4E, ff. 275–77.
30 Earl Grey, *Colonial Policy of Lord John Russell's Administration*, vol. 1 (London: Bentley, 1853), pp. 239–43; Wood was bullying: 'I prefer the appearance of your book to your own appearance in Parliament': Wood to Grey, 20 October, 2 November 1852, Howick Papers, quoted in J. M. Ward, 'The Colonial Policy of Lord John Russell's Administration', *Australian Historical Studies*, 9:35 (1960), 244–62, at p. 248; see also for Wood's influence on Grey, Wood to Grey correspondence, 7 March 1853, 8–14 March 1853, 3 April 1853, D.U.L., Earl Grey papers, GRE/B105/7/24–32.

money for any such purpose'.[31] Even though it was still too soon to spend
on emigration that year he thought cautious measures 'would help solve the
difficulty of providing suddenly for the defence of our distant populations'.[32]
Thus the 1847 crisis obstructed not only advances to Ireland to pay for relief
efforts, but any government-funded resettling of paupers by emigration or
expansion of imperial defences. Grey blamed Peel's policies for the credit
shortage in 1847 because of the Bank Charter Act of 1844 and so campaigned
against the legislation for most of the rest of his life.[33] He sought other ways
of organising a convertible currency which would avoid the problem of frequent
periods of sharply restricted credit.

Grey had drawn together ideas on how he thought a currency should be
organised prior to the introduction of Peel's Bank Charter Act in a pamphlet
entitled *Thoughts on the Currency* (1842).[34] His proposals firmly marked him
out as producing unusual ideas that combined principles taken from the Banking
School and the Currency School. Both 'Schools' believed that a currency should
have its value based on specie to ensure that its market value remained the
same as a metallic currency. To maintain that value a paper currency had to be
convertible on demand into gold or silver. In order to perform this function,
the issuing banks had to keep enough bullion in reserve to fulfil any demand
that arose. Grey's proposals planned to achieve that aim while avoiding the
Banking School's criticisms of the Currency School's methods of doing so.[35]

The Currency School relied on restricting the amount of money that could
be issued (in the form of banknotes under the 1844 Act) to ensure that bullion
which flowed out of the Bank of England would return.[36] The Banking
School, in contrast, thought that the amount of banknotes should be allowed to
fluctuate with commercial needs; bullion should be attracted into the country
by other means, such as by raising interest rates. The method used by Horsley

31   Grey memo to Cabinet, 14 April 1848, D.U.L., Earl Grey papers, GRE/B144/20.
32   Ibid.
33   See for instance his article on a plan for a government currency in *The Economist*, 27
February 1875, p. 242, and *The Economist*'s comments: 6 March 1875, p. 270.
34   Anon. (Third Earl Grey), *Thoughts on the Currency* (London: Ridgeway, 1842). This
publication is misattributed in some library catalogues. Contemporary correspondence,
Grey's views, date of publication, and publisher match with Grey as the author. The letter
Pennington to 'author of "Thoughts on the Currency"', 9 January 1843, D.U.L., Earl Grey
papers, GRE/B105/3/56, was passed from Wood to Grey as the author: Wood to Grey, 10
January 1843, D.U.L., Earl Grey papers, GRE/B105/3/55.
35   For a discussion of the differences between the Banking School (and its variant, the Free
Banking School) and the Currency School, see A. J. Schwartz, 'Banking School, Currency
School, Free Banking School', in *The New Palgrave Dictionary of Economics*, 1 (London:
Palgrave Macmillan, 2008), 353–58.
36   Currency School: D. Ricardo, *High price of bullion, a proof of the depreciation of
banknotes* (London: Murray, 1811), pp. 15–16.

Palmer, a leading advocate of Banking School type principles, when he was Governor of the Bank in the 1830s, was to buy foreign bills, which would be paid back in bullion, or to raise the Bank of England's minimum discount Rate (the Bank Rate), which raised interest rates generally in the country and attracted short-term bullion flows looking for high short-term returns. This method was based on his observations from 1833–36, when the self-balancing system described by the Currency School appeared not to work.[37]

Despite this experience, Peel had wanted to use the renewal of the Bank's Charter as an opportunity to reinforce his attempts to prevent undue fluctuations in prices, and to achieve that object he introduced a mathematical connection between the quantity of notes allowed to be in circulation and the amount of bullion in reserve.[38] The ability to issue notes in England was henceforth limited to the Bank of England, which was required to limit note issue according to the bullion they held. Other banks could not issue notes, and therefore, gradually, the issue of notes and the bullion reserve was to become centralised at the Bank.[39]

In fact, the Bank tried to compensate for the reduction of notes in circulation it was supposed to make whenever there was a bullion drain by reducing its reserve of notes.[40] This reserve was included in the 'notes in circulation' but was kept back to deal with fluctuations in demand. By running it down to very low levels the Bank could maintain the number of notes actually in circulation. However, the Bank was required by law to publish a summary of its accounts, weekly, and the drop in bullion reserves was very public, which tended to increase the demand for notes and credit just when they were short. After the April 1847 crisis, Horsley Palmer wrote to Joseph Henley, an MP, citing this requirement as the 'great blot which exists in the bill of 1844', and blaming it for the stopping of credit.[41] The letter ended up being forwarded to Russell as prime minister.[42] The ideas of the Currency School appeared to many to be failing to explain what was going on in October 1847 as the second crisis of that year reached its height. However, the ideas of the Banking School did not provide clearly laid out counter proposals.

37   Banking School: J. Horsley Palmer, *Causes and Consequences of the Pressure upon the money market* (London: Pelham Richardson, 1837), p. 6; *Committee of secrecy on Bank of England charter*, PP 1832–33 (722), pp. 52–53.

38   See C. Read, 'The Political Economy of Sir Robert Peel', in J. Hoppit, A.B. Leonard, D.J. Needham (eds.), *Money and Markets: Essays in Honour of Martin Daunton* (Woodbridge: Boydell Press, 2019), pp. 78–81.

39   K. Dowd (ed.), *The Experience of Free Banking* (London: Routledge, 1992), p. 33.

40   *Second Report from the Secret Committee of the House of Commons on Commercial Distress with minutes of evidence*, PP 1847–48 (584) Pt. I VIII.505, pp. 310–52.

41   Palmer to Henley, 15 May 1847, N.A., Russell papers, PRO 30/22/6C, ff. 290–93.

42   Ibid.; this letter is currently in the Russell Papers.

Both 'Schools' were loose groups of people with similar opinions and the varied individual views of their adherents caused confusion.[43] Russell was bemused by the variety of ideas and, looking for solutions at the height of the October crisis, wrote to Grey 'I wish you would lay your hands upon your pamphlet on the currency'.[44] Grey had published his pamphlet, *Thoughts on the Currency*, shortly after the Enquiry on the Banks of Issue of 1841 and now, after the crises of 1847, he sent Russell a copy.[45] From the panic in America in 1837 it drew the lesson that 'derangement' of the currency caused a 'real diminution in the productive power of the nation'.[46] In order to avoid such 'derangement' or periodic panics it suggested that the 'amount of [note] circulation ought not to be made in any degree dependent upon the state of the exchanges [balance of capital flows]'.[47] It also wished to 'put an end to the anomaly of allowing so important a function as that of issuing money to be exercised by any other hands than those of some responsible public authority'.[48] This would have put an end to the Bank of England's role in managing the currency because 'it ought not to be left to a trading corporation, of which the first object must naturally be its own profit, to regulate the currency of a great empire'.[49] He believed its commercial banking and currency functions should be fully separated, to avoid any conflict of interest, and that management of the latter should be put into the hands of currency commissioners appointed by the government.[50] In this respect Grey's plan went further in separation than the Currency School, but differed from ideas advocated by the likes of Wilson, who believed that private banks should be left to run the currency and that it should be kept away from politicians.[51]

The Currency School did not really recognise short-term bullion flows and their use to bring in bullion until the 1850s. They considered Bank Rate changes to be reinforcing the changes in the market. In contrast, the Banking School thought Bank Rate changes could be helpful or even essential, but they did not view them as desirable because they disturbed the tendency towards a natural balance of prices, bullion and interest rates. The solution for this problem

---

43 See Schwartz, 'Banking School, Currency School, Free Banking School'; note that both the adherents of the Banking School and the Free Banking School believed that banks should have the discretion and flexibility to issue whatever quantity of banknotes they desired, but that the Banking School was much more resigned to central banks and government intervention than the rigorously *laissez-faire* Free Banking School.
44 Russell to Grey, 15 October 1847, D.U.L., Earl Grey papers, GRE/B122/3/91.
45 Anon. (Third Earl Grey), *Thoughts on the Currency*.
46 Idem., p. 5.
47 Idem., p. 11.
48 Idem., p. 15.
49 Idem., p. 20.
50 Idem., p. 15.
51 J. Wilson, *Capital, Currency, and Banking* (London: The Economist, 1859), pp. 20, 197.

in Grey's pamphlet of 1842 was that bullion movements should not include coins and that the use of gold coins should be discouraged. This would tend to prevent panics because notes could not be exchanged for small amounts of gold.[52] Small amounts of gold from inexperienced investors could therefore not join together in a flow of short-term money abroad looking for advantage when higher interest rates were available outside the country. To this extent, the worries of the Banking School were acknowledged. This would restrict capital mobility and make the currency more stable. Also, the Commissioners who ran the currency scheme had to keep 50% bullion and 50% stock to fully back the note issue. This was the weak point for starting such a scheme in England as the capital for the bullion and stock had to be raised by the government from the beginning to start the scheme, whereas the Bank of England used bullion deposited by others, and not owned by the Bank, as part of their bullion reserve.

Under Grey's scheme bullion was owned by the Commissioners and could not be drained away by private investors when they withdrew their banking deposits as they could at the Bank of England. The Commissioners were not to be involved in commercial banking, which was to be carried out by private institutions. Although Grey was not an economist, he did have an experienced economist to help him from May 1848, when the undersecretary of state for war and the colonies, James Stephens was replaced with Herman Merivale.[53] Whereas Stephens had come from a legal background, Merivale had been the Professor of Political Economy at the University of Oxford from 1837 to 1842. His views were unorthodox in some respects, and although they grew out of conventional political economy, he came to heterodox conclusions about what policies governments should follow. In many ways they agreed with Grey's ideas. It is likely that the two reinforced each-others' theories.

Merivale's philosophy can be read in a series of lectures he published in 1841.[54] He subscribed to the idea that it was wrong that a colony 'should ever benefit a mother country by yielding it a "permanent tribute"' and that profits from a colony should be retained within it and used for the benefit of its people; the general population should be allowed to join a colony's elites and enjoy the success they had helped create.[55] These ideas agreed with some of the policy proposals of Grey and Edward Gibbon Wakefield, another colonial reformer, but he did question some of the latter's prejudices. Merivale was against slavery and accused the Bank of England of supporting it by helping

52   Anon. (Third Earl Grey), *Thoughts on the Currency*, p. 40.
53   J. C. Sainty (ed.), 'Appointments', *Office Holders in Modern Britain vol. 6: Colonial Office Officials 1794–1870* (London: University of London, 1976), pp. 8–32.
54   H. Merivale, *Lectures on Colonisation and the Colonies*, vol. 1 (London: Longman, 1841).
55   Idem., pp. 20, 26.

to bail out American banks.[56] He supported free trade and did so by arguing against Robert Torrens, a supporter of the Currency School, who, he said, had claimed a poor country could successfully improve its situation by tariffs.[57] However, there are signs of a willingness to accept theory from both Schools when Merivale recognises investment capital flows and 'the tide of evils which flow in along with a rapid influx of capital' (Banking School) and, as a consequence, a tendency for inflation (Currency School).[58] Grey may well have honed some of his currency ideas on the sharp intellect of Merivale; certainly his appointment of a professional economist who was likely to have ideas of his own went against previous Colonial Office practice of having a staff which mainly had 'no greater store of information or maturity of mind than usually belongs to a boy in the fifth form at Eton, Westminster or Rugby'.[59]

Grey had high hopes for his original ideas, but they were to be dashed on the rock of Russell's limited understanding. Russell replied within the day to Grey's pamphlet; 'I agree in much of what you say, but of course the passing of the Act of 1844 makes a great difference'.[60] In short, Russell was unwilling to go against the Currency School principles of note issue restriction as it would have alienated the Whigs' key allies in Parliament, the Peelites. To placate Grey, Russell suggested that a Committee should be appointed.[61] Wood, an adherent of the Bank Charter Act, firmly opposed Grey's arguments with his authority as chancellor of the exchequer.[62] The row was referred to Prince Albert, who was essentially acting as head of state in this period because Queen Victoria was pregnant. He ruled out Grey's suggestions and said that sterling banknotes may no longer be accepted by foreigners if his plans were carried out. He did agree, however, that 'the medium of exchange between different articles of trade, ought in no way to be allowed to become an article of trade itself'.[63] In other words, capital flows for investment rather than trade should be inhibited. When Grey complained of a lack of action to Russell, towards the end of November, Russell replied, 'I thought it had been understood that we were to move for a Committee on the Bank' and explained the political issues of retaining Peel, the main mover of the Act, on side, owing to the Whig government's lack of a Parliamentary majority.[64]

56   Idem., pp. 259–61, 295.
57   Idem., pp. 310, 306–07; also idem., vol. 2 (1842), p. 307.
58   Idem., vol. 2, p. 121.
59   E. T. Williams, 'The Colonial Office in the Thirties', *Australian Historical Studies*, 2:7 (1943), 141–60, at p. 144.
60   Russell to Grey, 16 October 1847, D.U.L., Earl Grey papers, GRE/B122/3/92.
61   Ibid.
62   Wood to Grey, 10 November 1847, D.U.L., Earl Grey papers, GRE/B105/5/18–19.
63   Albert to Grey, 23 November 1847, D.U.L., Earl Grey papers, GRE B75/3A/11 (original underline).
64   Russell to Grey, 26 November 1847, D.U.L., Earl Grey papers, GRE/B122/3/103.

Three Parliamentary Committees were eventually held on the issue. Two Committees were held in the House of Commons in 1848, the first dealing with England, the second mainly with Scotland and Ireland. The third one was held in the House of Lords. In the Commons, it was concluded that 'it is not expedient to make any alteration in the Bank Act of 1844'.[65] This concealed a substantial difference of opinion. When a vote was taken on the Resolution that it was agreed 'that in the opinion of this committee, the laws for regulating the issue of banknotes payable on demand aggravated the commercial distress in England in the year 1847' there were 11 ayes and 13 noes. The noes included Wood, Peel, Russell, Graham, and Richard Cobden. Amongst the ayes were Benjamin Disraeli, the future prime minister, Thomas Baring, the son of the chairman of Barings' Bank, Sir Francis Baring, the previous Whig chancellor of the exchequer, and Wilson.[66] The second Enquiry brushed aside the fears of Scottish and Irish witnesses on the basis of the first report: 'evidence has been given by some of the witnesses as to the effect both in Scotland and Ireland which they attribute to the Act of 1844, but as on this subject your committee have already stated their views, they do not think it necessary to offer any further observations thereupon'.[67] Only their comments on the 1845 Act were accepted, but these were not adverse because the restrictions on Scotland and Ireland in that Act were not onerous. The Committee in the Lords, by contrast, concluded 'that the Panic was materially aggravated by the operation of that Statute [the Act of 1844]', but this opinion was ignored by the government, as it was entitled to do in the absence of the agreement of the Commons.[68]

The Currency School's view and the Bank Charter Act of 1844 therefore became the orthodox stance on how the pound should be managed until Britain left the gold standard in 1931. Substantial portions of the 1844 Act, which grant the Bank of England its monopoly over the issue of banknotes in England and Wales, are still in force today.[69] In short, Grey's challenge to it within the United Kingdom failed. With it disappeared his attempt to circumvent the credit restrictions which stymied schemes to help Ireland during the famine, as described in the previous two chapters of this book. However, when a crisis arose in Mauritius in 1847, Grey was approached by those representing

65 *Reports from the Secret Committee of the House of Commons on Commercial Distress*, PP 1847–48 (395) VIII.1, VIII.379, p. vi.
66 Ibid.; the alignment of Grey's views and Wilson's vote on this issue suggests that their positions had some affinity. This inference explains why he turned to Wilson for advice when problems arose in Mauritius in 1847.
67 *Second Report from the Secret Committee of the House of Commons on Commercial Distress*, PP 1847–48 (584) microfiche number 51–52, p. ii.
68 *Report from the Secret Committee of the House of Lords on the causes of distress*, PP 1847–48 (565, 565-II), p. xlv.
69 'Bank Charter Act 1844', <http://www.legislation.gov.uk/ukpga/Vict/7-8/32> [accessed 29 February 2020].

Mauritius with a plea for urgent assistance, including a government-backed currency similar to his own recommendations. His request for a report on the matter from Wilson indicated that a famine was imminent because of financial collapse. Grey responded quickly with immediate policies to address most of the issues. The next section discusses how this came about and how Grey applied his ideas to Mauritius.

The Mauritian crisis

Mauritius was virtually a monoculture producing sugar from cane; all of the staple foods, mainly rice, eaten by its population of around 160,000 had to be imported from elsewhere.[70] During the financial crisis of 1847, four out of the five big London commercial houses that financed the Mauritian economy failed, along with many sugar estates and one of the island's two big banks as they struggled to find enough credit to continue.[71] The failures were caused by the stalling value of sugar production (Chart 6.1) that arose from the antici-pated falling price of sugar and the failure of the crop (by as much as 30% of expected production), which had likely become infected with gumming disease and moth borer.[72]

Rice prices had been high for several years, and a spike to their highest level in a decade in the middle of 1847 also contributed to the colony's terms of trade worsening considerably (Chart 6.2). Edward Chapman, co-owner of seven plantations and the commercial agent for 10 to 12 sugar estates, asserted that the colony's planters lost £195,000 on the 1847/48 sugar crop, a figure which, he claimed, rose to £480,000 if interest charges were included.[73] In 1846 Russell's government in London planned to equalise tariffs within five years for sugar imported into Britain, whether grown by free workers or by slaves. In response, Mauritian plantation owners attempted to recruit more immigrant workers and increase production to maintain their overall profits. However, in 1847, production did not increase, and the new workers faced starvation as plantations ceased to trade and sugar prices began to fall.

70   Griffiths, Huron, Carter, *Piastres to Polymer*, p. 67.
71   Allen, 'Maroonage and its Legacy in Mauritius and in the Colonial Plantation World', p. 148; Wilson, 'The Island of Mauritius', 17 October 1847, D.U.L., Earl Grey Papers, GRE/B145/D9; *The Times*, 25 October 1847, p. 3.
72   Rawson, 'Rapport fait par le Comité d'Agriculture de la Société Royale des Arts des Sciences de Maurice au Conseil de la Société sur une maladie du cannes', 9 October 1848, National Archives of Mauritius, HA/66/8.
73   *Second Report of the Select Committee on Sugar and Coffee Planting*, PP 1847–48 (137) XXIII, microfiche number 52.196–97, para. 3471, p. 3, cited in R. B. Allen, 'Capital, Illegal Slaves, Indentured Labourers and the Creation of a Sugar Plantation Economy in Mauritius, 1810–60', *Journal of Imperial and Commonwealth History*, 36:2 (2008), 151–70, at p. 158.

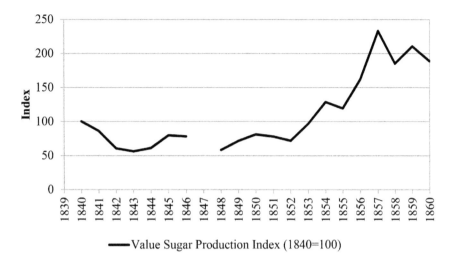

Chart 6.1. Index of total sugar production value (sugar production × price) in Mauritius, 1840 to 1860. Sugar production in 1847 did not rise and was up to 30% lower than expected. The 1847 figures were noted as unreliable because of the financial crisis, so are therefore not shown. *Sources:* O. Griffiths, J-M. Huron, M. Carter, *Piastres to Polymer* (Mauritius: Bioculture Press, 2018), p. 73, citing *Le Mauricien*, 7 April 1848; N.A., Mauritius Blue Books; *Progress of Sugar Trade*, PP 1884 (325) LXXIV.371, p. 26.

The plantation labourers, the poorest in society, were a mixture of former slaves, freed in 1835 following British legislation, and large numbers of imported Indian indentured labourers.[74] Since slavery had been abolished, there had been a number of attempts to start an indentured system. Between 1839 and 1842 it had been banned completely by the British government as akin to slavery and, as a result, the plantation owners had acquired a bad reputation in the British press. The lack of population became a critical issue for the sugar industry in the 1840s, and the plantation owners obtained permission from the British to restart an immigration scheme on the basis of a commitment to high standards such as free health care and rations, equal access to justice and encouraging immigrants to bring their families to help build a new society in Mauritius. The results were extensively monitored through the annual Treasury Blue Books.[75] However, the new immigrants, along with the existing population, were now threatened by famine after the harvest failure and financial crisis of 1847. All their staple food, rice, was imported by the plantation houses that were now bankrupt and unable to raise bills to pay for the food. Imminent

74   Griffiths, Huron, Carter, *Piastres to Polymer*, p. 67.
75   Mauritius Blue Books, N.A., Colonial Office papers, CO 172.

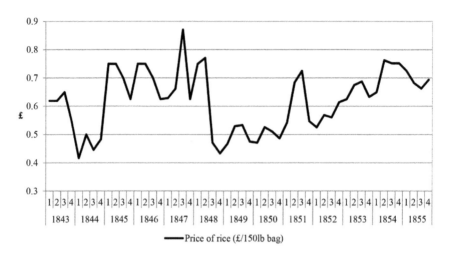

Chart 6.2. The price of rice in Mauritius by quarter, 1843 to 1855, in £/150lb bag.
Source: N.A., Mauritius Blue Books.

mass starvation threatened.[76] However, there is no 'Great Famine' of Mauritius because, in contrast to Ireland, the British government responded to the situation successfully.

The Times reported in October 1847 how the desire to import as much food as possible into England, where a shortage of grain had pushed up prices, had locked up funds from British traders, raised on credit, in sugar plantations in Mauritius. A crash in food prices in Britain and the second financial crisis of 1847 left them illiquid with unsellable property in Mauritius as collateral. *The Times* complained 'it is now sufficiently shown that the scarcity of money caused principally by the immense importations of provisions, and also by the failures in the corn trade, has occasioned the eruption of an old sore'; it blamed this on 'the way in which great houses, like Reid, Irving, and Co., Gower and Co., &c. carried on their business'. It considered that the problem arose from a desire to import as much produce into England as possible and that led to large advances being made to the planters in the West Indies and Mauritius on the security of property. When the planters became bankrupt this property came into the hands of the houses giving loans. Thus the defunct house of Reid, Irving, and Co. had more than £600,000 locked up in Mauritius plantations

---

76 Memorial from Barclay and Co. and others, 15 October 1847, and enclosures, *Correspondence with respect to the Condition of the Colony*, PP 1847–48 (61) XLIV.201, p. 258.

exclusively and A. A. Gower and Co. upwards of £200,000 in the same island.[77]
This overall picture is confirmed by documents in the Baring archive.[78]

Restarting commerce in Mauritius was therefore important, not only to feed the population in the future, but to speed recovery from the 1847 financial crisis in Britain. The problems were first raised by the 'Mauritius Association', an alliance of merchants and proprietors in Mauritius and traders in London, which took up matters concerning commerce with governments in both countries. At the time it was formed in October 1846 it was treated as a potentially troublesome source of insurrection, almost as if it was a tropical version of Ireland's Repeal Association, and its number of members was limited by Mauritius's Governor, W. M. Gomm.[79] Its polite persistence and constructive suggestions on how to overcome the problems of the island soon made negotiation with it by Grey and the Colonial Office not only acceptable, but desirable. On 15 October 1847 its London arm sent a memorial (a memorandum or petition) to Grey at the Colonial Office:

> The misfortunes which have so recently befallen Mauritius by the failure of so many houses extensively connected with it, renders it quite imperative on this association to claim your Lordship's immediate attention to two points.
> The first is the food of the people.
> The second is that of finance.[80]

The Association asked for the government to guarantee by means of a loan the continued supply of at least 30,000 bags of rice a month from Bengal – around three-quarters of the level of the island's normal food imports before the crisis – in order to ensure a continued supply of food 'as a precautionary measure against famine'.[81] The letter also petitioned for the plantation owners to obtain a loan from the funds held by the local government to continue the harvest of the current crop and to plant for the following year, 'not only to rescue the sugar that remains in the island, but also the crops of 1848/49'.[82] In addition, it also requested the issuance of a government paper currency in order to ease the credit situation, as the island had been cut off from its usual sources of finance because of 'the disorganization of commercial credit in England and

---

77   *The Times*, 25 October 1847, p. 8, supplement, from *Allgemeine Zeitung*.
78   Correspondence from Reid, Irving, and Co. to Barings, ING Baring Archives, HC3.62; failure of Reid, Irving, and Co., 20 September 1847, ING Baring Archives, HC17.30; valuation of Mauritius estates under Barings direction, ING Baring Archives, HC3.75.
79   Barclay and Irving (Agents for Mauritius) to Earl Grey, 16 October 1846, and enclosures, *Correspondence with respect to the Condition of the Colony*, PP 1847–48 (61) XLIV.201, pp. 1–2.
80   Idem., Memorial from Barclay and Co. and others, 15 October 1847, p. 258.
81   Ibid.
82   Ibid.

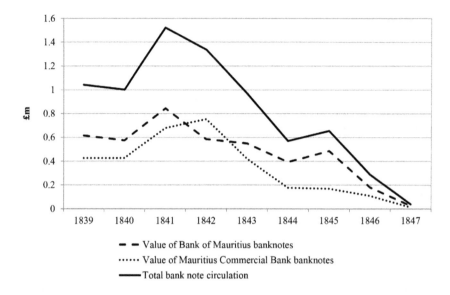

Chart 6.3. Banknote circulation in Mauritius, 1839 to 1847. *Source*: Griffiths, Huron, Carter, *Piastres to Polymer*, p. 73, citing *Le Mauricien*, 7 April 1848.

India'.[83] Since 1843 the existing banknote circulation had collapsed and the metallic coins had gradually drained away as, it was believed, they were turned into jewellery or taken abroad by migrants (see Chart 6.3).[84]

   On the same day he received the Association's memorial, Grey immediately consulted Wilson, the editor of *The Economist* and a newly elected Whig MP, on how to respond to the crisis in Mauritius, sending him a copy of his pamphlet on currency. Wilson is much scorned in many books about the Irish famine as an advocate for non-intervention in the face of harvest failure in Ireland.[85] However, in the case of Mauritius, he promptly recommended a course of government intervention as necessary to avoid famine. Wilson replied to Grey's letter the next day, saying of the pamphlet that although he could not see the principles as being a final settlement of the pound currency, 'I look upon it as affording the clearest explanation of those principles that I have yet met with – and I believe a currency so framed – would combine every possible advantage'.[86] He followed this up on 17 October 1847 with a discussion of the proposals for food, loans and currency to solve the island's main 'difficulties ... first the

83   Ibid.
84   Griffiths, Huron, Carter, *Piastres to Polymer*, p. 70.
85   See, for instance, Ó Gráda, *The Great Irish Famine*, pp. 44–45.
86   Wilson to Grey, 16 October 1847, D.U.L., Earl Grey papers, GRE/B132/11/4.

immediate supply of food and second, means of continuing the cultivation of the soil'.[87] Wilson's assessment was that owing to 'the peculiar circumstances of the labouring population ... and having no other means whatsoever but the sugar estates, the great proportion of which must be immediately suspended', some interference was justified, 'which might not be justifiable under ordinary circumstances'.[88] He went on to lay out a detailed plan for the founding of a paper currency, guaranteeing food and the restarting of cultivation on the basis of £150,000 provided by the home government (Britain) and secured on the value of existing and future crops.[89]

Why did Wilson respond so differently to the plight of Ireland compared to that of Mauritius? It would be tempting to see the comparison between the two as an example of Peter J. Cain and A. G. Hopkins's 'gentlemanly capitalism'.[90] It could be very easily argued that intervening in Ireland was against the City of London's interest (in that it contributed to severe financial crises that year), while intervening in Mauritius would have helped relieve the London finance houses that had over-lent to Mauritius. This might have had some influence. However, Wilson did not frame his arguments about the Irish famine and the crisis in Mauritius in terms of bailing out the City. Instead, he clearly and consistently grounded his suggestions in terms of how best to help the poor using economic theory. In Ireland he opposed the central government giving out food or the centralised public-works schemes organised by the Treasury because of worries about inefficiency, the imperfect information of central government and concerns about crowding out the private sector.[91] 'It is the duty of the owners of the Irish soil to provide for the Irish', he argued, and they should be helped in that by a local Poor Law organised by government.[92] The memorial of the Mauritius Association overcame these objections. The plantation owners explicitly promised to organise the relief efforts themselves, as well as to 'reimburse the drafts' for the imported food and the other assistance measures: 'the association does not ask for the present interference on the part of Her Majesty's Government with a view of relieving the colonists from the cost of

---

87   Wilson to Grey, 17 October 1847, D.U.L., Earl Grey papers, GRE/B132/11/5, enclosed plan B145/D9.
88   Idem., p. 2.
89   Idem., p.11.
90   For the background to this idea see P. J. Cain, A. G. Hopkins, 'Gentlemanly Capitalism and British Expansion Overseas, 1: The Old Colonial System, 1688–1850', *Economic History Review*, 39:4 (1986), 501–25; P. J. Cain, A. G. Hopkins, 'Gentlemanly Capitalism and British Expansion Overseas, 2: New Imperialism, 1850–1945', *Economic History Review*, 40:1 (1987), 1–26; P. J. Cain, A. G. Hopkins, *British Imperialism: Innovation and Expansion 1688–1914* (London: Longman, 1993).
91   *The Economist*, 21 March 1846.
92   Idem., 21 March 1846; idem., 3 October 1846.

such shipments'.[93] Wilson also thought there were other sources of employment in Ireland, such as would be created by the reclamation of wastelands and in Irish industry, but in Mauritius there were no other options owing to 'the entire absence of other resources on the Island [of Mauritius], besides their sugar plantations'.[94] Thus he argued 'there is a great risk that the island will be left without its necessary supplies'.[95]

The Colonial Office acted particularly fast to help Mauritius to meet 'the risk of famine'.[96] On 25 October 1847, just ten days after the receipt of the original memorial, Grey issued two formal Despatches (no. 91 and no. 92) directing the Governor to make advances to the planters out of the Government balances on the security of shipments of sugar.[97] These were not to exceed £0.15m, a very similar sum to the amount the Treasury was initially permitted to spend importing Indian corn into Ireland.[98] The Court of Directors of the East India Company also instructed the Presidency of Bengal to ensure that at least 30,000 bags of rice, the amount the Mauritius Association had requested, were imported into Mauritius each month.[99] Steps were taken to cut the charges associated with land transfers to ensure bankrupt sugar estates could be sold more quickly (which provides an interesting parallel to Ireland's Encumbered Estates Acts).[100] However, unlike Ireland, communication with Mauritius was slow and took place at the speed of a sailing ship. The Mauritius Association received a reply in the affirmative and the loan and importation of food was carried out, after the Despatches issued by Grey were received in Mauritius on 17 January 1848, while ensuring that the sugar crop on which the monies were secured were properly insured.[101] The instructions to the Bengal government had arrived more quickly, which had kept supplies of food flowing to Mauritius.

93   Memorial from Barclay and Co. and others, 15 October 1847, and enclosures, *Correspondence with respect to the Condition of the Colony*, PP 1847–48 (61) XLIV.201, p. 258.
94   Wilson, 'The Island of Mauritius', 17 October 1847, D.U.L., Earl Grey Papers, GRE/B145/D9, paper enclosed in letter Wilson to Grey, D.U.L., Earl Grey Papers, 17 October 1847, GRE/B132/11/5.
95   Ibid.
96   Grey to Gomm, Despatch no. 91 of 25 October 1847, *Correspondence with respect to the Condition of the Colony*, PP 1847–48 (61) XLIV.201, p. 255.
97   Grey to Gomm, Despatch no. 92 of 25 October 1847, idem., p. 259.
98   Ibid.
99   Grey to Gomm, Despatch no. 90 of 25 October 1847, idem., p. 255.
100   Grey to Gomm, Despatch no. 94 of 26 October 1847, idem., p. 261.
101   Gomm to Grey, 17 January 1848, *West India Colonies and Mauritius*, PP 1847–48 (399) XLV.75, p. 216; Baillie to Hawes, 26 October 1847, idem., p. 262; Hawes to Messrs Barclay Bros and Co., 29 October 1847, *Correspondence with respect to the Condition of the Colony*, PP 1846–47 (61) XLV.201, p. 263.

The Colonial Office also agreed that a government-backed colonial paper currency would be issued.[102] However, Grey had a number of battles to fight in order to get his currency scheme started. In particular, there were the Lords of the Treasury to keep happy. When he issued his Despatch no. 90, he gave the President of the Board of Control and the East India Company as his authority for ordering rice imports into Mauritius and for sanctioning a paper currency, which meant he could circumvent restrictions imposed by the Treasury. Wilson was to become one of the joint secretaries of the Board from 16 May 1848, a position commonly given to those with heterodox economic views. Wilson later stated that he was 'very doubtful' the Lords in the Treasury had concurred in Grey's 1847 currency scheme.[103] Grey's initial agreement with Wilson fell apart a little when it transpired that Wilson had not mentioned that he thought the scheme should be administered by private banks rather than Commissioners (in fact, this became one of the characteristic points of disagreement on policy between the Colonial Office and the Treasury). Grey found a compromise by appointing government Commissioners to run the system and hold specie, with private firms doing the administration. Grey insisted that the government undertake the issue of notes itself, to the exclusion of all private parties, through Commissioners bound to conduct the issues according to laid down rules, including to retain a specie reserve of 50% of note circulation to pay the notes on demand. The initial specie was a loan of £0.125m from the Mauritius Government.

Grey made it a condition of the entire measure that the two Banks in Mauritius at that time (the Mauritius Bank and the Commercial Bank) should resign the right of issue they possessed under their charters. Being led to believe they would not object to do so, and in a hurry to re-establish the economy, he had notes to the value of £0.275m printed in London and sent out to the colony.[104] However, the Mauritius Bank went out of business in February 1848 because of the financial crisis and the Commercial Bank refused to give up its note issuing powers.[105] So Ordinance no. 8 of 1848, intended to bring the paper currency into being, remained inoperative until March 1849 when Grey personally negotiated a revision of the scheme with the agent in England of the Commercial Bank and directed the new, and more co-operative Governor, Sir George Anderson, to submit the revised plan to the Mauritian Council and the Commercial Bank.[106] The remaining specie after the 50% reserve was to

102   Grey to Gomm, Despatch no. 90 of 25 October 1847, idem., p. 255.
103   Colonial Office confidential print, Wilson Report on Mauritius Currency, N.A., Colonial Office papers, CO 882/1 XVIII, ff. 309–20, p. 3.
104   Idem., pp. 2–3.
105   See correspondence, *West India Colonies and Mauritius*, PP 1847–48 (399) XLV.75, pp. 273–74.
106   Grey to Anderson, 22 March 1849, *Instructions to Sir G. Anderson*, PP 1849 (554) XXXVII.969, p. 1.

be invested in stock by the Commissioners, and the interest, only, paid to the Government instead of the principal (the original capital remained invested) being placed at the Government's disposal as in the original plan. The Lords of the Treasury were eventually won round, although initially Wood had objected, claiming he had consulted with Overstone, Norman and Arbuthnot, who had 'spent nearly a whole day on the subject' and had concluded that 'the best currency for our colonies ... is to allow the circulation of certain coins of neighbouring countries at fixed rates'.[107] This approach to the situation was not much help as this was already the scheme that had not worked in Mauritius and which the new currency was intended to fix.

At this time the government in London made the decision to base the currency on silver, rather than gold. This decision, in part, was made because much of Mauritius's trade (such as its rice imports) was with India, which was on a silver standard. This has been seen by many commentators as, in retrospect, being unwise because of the devaluation of silver against gold later in the century. Wilson also suggested another explanation: the decision may have been made to protect the interests of the Bank of England. 'It arose from a participation in a popular delusion that a gold circulation is more expensive than a silver one and from the apprehension, quite unfounded ..., of trenching upon the gold reserve of the Bank of England'.[108] This would have been a particular worry between 1847 and 1849, as its reserves were low and were vulnerable to bullion drains in that period.

In the end, Grey's plan was implemented by the Council's Paper Currency Ordinance no. 9 (1849). The coin in the local Mauritian Treasury, and some exchequer bills owned by the Mauritius Government, were to be transferred to the currency commissioners as the new currency's reserve. In exchange, the currency commissioners then returned an equal amount in notes to the Treasurer. The Government of Mauritius was then to lend £0.125m of these notes to the Commercial Bank at a low rate of interest, with that bank depositing an equal value of stock with the Government as security for the loan. The Commissioners retained the excess notes for the moment to cover expenses. At the same time the cash business of the Government, whether for receipt of revenue or payment of expenditure, was to cease at the Treasury and be conducted by the Bank with the new banknotes.[109] The original plan had contained an additional loan for the sugar industry of up to £0.15m to be secured on future crops, but this issue had already been dealt with by the time the currency scheme was implemented.[110] It should be noted that the act

107   Wood to Grey, 20 January 1849, D.U.L., Earl Grey papers, GRE/B105/5/45; see also O'Brien, *The Correspondence of Lord Overstone*, pp. 431–36, 442–47.
108   Colonial Office confidential print, N.A., Colonial Office papers, CO 882/1 XVIII, p. 17,
109   Idem., pp. 1–8.
110   *Correspondence with respect to the Condition of the Colony*, PP 1847–48 (61) XLIV.201, p. 257.

of restarting paper currency by issuing notes increased the money supply in the colony by, in effect, doubling the money backing the currency which now existed as notes and bullion and foreign securities. Because of the need for the currency to be backed by specie, the scheme contained some restrictions of the Currency School, but it also had some flexibility of liquidity because the income from the investments in foreign stocks could be used to purchase more specie if commerce demanded it. However, in the 1850s, once the crisis had passed, the Treasury in London, then represented by Wilson, attempted to restore the Mauritian system to private hands. A note added to Wilson's description of events, records that:

> The sequel was that nothing was done till 1858–59, when a long Treasury Minute was sent out to the Colony recommending the Legislative Council to abolish the Government notes and revive issues by the Chartered Joint Stock Banks. The Governor Sir W. Stevenson, who agreed with the Treasury, urged the Legislative Council to do as the Board recommended, but he obtained only one vote, that of the manager of the [new] Oriental Bank who happened to be in the Legislative Council and the rest of the council unanimously voted the continuance of the Government note currency on a reformed footing. The Treasury acquiesced in this. The old Rupee notes were withdrawn and new Notes issued expressed in pounds or shillings.[111]

The essential advantage of the currency-board system over that operated by the Bank of England was that the specie held to back notes was wholly owned by the board's commissioners and could only be withdrawn by note-holders. In contrast, the bullion in the Bank of England could be withdrawn by its depositors as well: in fact, they had a prior claim because the Bank would have had to stop if it could not pay out to its depositors. This super-charged the Mundell-Fleming trilemma when it came to Peel's three aims of a gold standard, free capital flows and low interest rates, as the balance of payment constraint became ultra-sensitive to international interest-rate fluctuations. By relaxing the link between note issue, interest rates and bank deposits withdrawn to become international capital flows, currency boards relieved some of the pressure. After the introduction of its currency-board system, Mauritius was thus often able to keep its interest rates lower than those prevailing in London (see Chart 6.6).

After a slow start, currency-board schemes spread throughout the British Empire and beyond. Mauritius is generally seen as the first currency board.[112] Prince Edward Island and New Zealand rejected them in the 1850s, but Wilson set up India's currency partially as a currency board in the 1860s and the Ceylon

111   Colonial Office confidential print, N.A., Colonial Office papers, CO 882/1 XVIII, f. 319; R. Chalmers, *Colonial Currency* (London: Eyre and Spottiswoode, 1893), p. 367.
112   K. Stukenbrock, *The Stability of Currency Boards* (Frankfurt am Main: Peter Lang AG, 2004), p. 61.

currency was taken over by commissioners of currency from private banks in 1884.[113] The Falklands set up similar systems in 1899, Bermuda in 1915, Gibraltar in 1927, the Irish Free State in 1928, and Hong Kong in 1983. In 1945 the number of currency-board-like systems reached over 45 globally.[114] Eventually even Britain nationalised its central bank in the 1940s, a 'tip of the hat' to the Mauritian model of government ownership, even though the Bank of England continued with a central-bank currency model.[115] The currency-board arrangements have generally been seen as a success (except for a notable failure in Argentina, which had a long history of financial problems under various currency systems). Kurt Schuler has shown by an analysis of 155 countries including over 99 per cent of the world's output that countries with currency boards performed better, judged by output growth, than those with central banks.[116] So even though Grey was unable to benefit Ireland during its famine with his innovation, the lesson learnt from 1847 can be said to have assisted many developing countries elsewhere in the world since.

Reform and modernisation in Mauritius

In addition to its immediate concerns about the food supply and the currency, the Mauritius Association highlighted other policy issues, which triggered a round of constructive economic reform and modernisation on the island. Economic changes in Ireland did not develop as the British government planned. Instead of increased employment, emigration and a loss of arable land to pasture occurred, outcomes that several historians of the Irish famine suggest were purposeful on the part of government. This section describes how economic and social reform was carried out in the immediate aftermath of the Mauritian crisis, contrasting the policies used there with those used for Ireland.

The Mauritius Association expressed its gratitude for the assistance given in respect of the food supply and currency in a memorial dated 28 October 1847, but raised further requests which were aimed at securing the future of the island as a trading and commercial base.[117] The Association also thanked Grey for his commitment to establishing a government colonial currency. With the

113   Chalmers, *Colonial Currency*, pp. 35–36.
114   Stukenbrock, *The Stability of Currency Boards*, p. 55.
115   S. H. Hanke, 'Exchange Rate Regimes and Capital Flows', *Annals of the American Academy of Political and Social Science*, 579:1 (2002), 87–105, at p. 89.
116   K. Schuler, 'Should Developing Countries Have Central Banks? Currency Quality and Monetary Systems in 155 Countries', *IEA Research Monograph* no. 52 (London: Institute of Economic Affairs, 1996), 1–126.
117   Mauritius Association to Grey, 28 October 1847, published in *Morning Chronicle*, 8 November 1847, p. 3.

setting up of a currency commission, Mauritius therefore had control of its own currency from 1849. This stands in contrast to Ireland where monetary policy was made by the Bank of England in London. The Bank of Ireland did issue its own banknotes, but it was more a commercial bank and did not function in any significant way as a central bank for Ireland. This situation was partly because the circulation of its notes rarely rose much above the initial amount which might be issued without being backed by bullion. The Association also thanked Grey for calling to the Governor's attention the high rates of taxes that were necessary to support what was considered an excessive establishment of administrators and civil servants, the civil list. Figures for the establishment were from then on included in the Blue Books and show a reduction from £403,901 in 1844 to £285,204 in 1853.[118] This reduction contrasts sharply with the excessive rises in local taxes in Ireland caused by the transfer of relief costs from the United Kingdom accounts to the Irish Poor Law as described in the previous chapter.

The Association then raised some further issues about the supply of free labour to keep Mauritian sugar production competitive against plantations using slave labour in Brazil and Cuba. The most important one was attracting 'Labour' and this had a long history behind it. For some time there had been requests to lift the limits imposed on immigration. Stung by the reputation of Mauritius that dated from the slavery era as a place where plantation workers were treated particularly badly, the Association had committed itself from October 1846 as 'prepared to promote by every practical means the material and moral improvement of the people who may be allowed to answer our invitation'.[119] The invitation was to the poorest inhabitants of India, because Mauritius's original population of former slaves either moved back to Africa after 1835 or set themselves up as middle-class artisans, no longer needing to work as labourers. Replacement workers were needed if Mauritian sugar plantations were to remain competitive against foreign competition and if the island was not to waste away in economic terms.

Yet there were deep-rooted problems with attracting workers to the island. Mauritius (then Île de France) was ceded to Britain under the Treaty of Paris in 1814, following the Napoleonic Wars. It was an important strategic point from which the naval and shipping route from Britain to India could be protected. The French developed the island, encouraging settlers to start agriculture, using a system of slave labour initiated under Dutch control. Escaped slaves (the maroons) hid in the Le Morne mountain and when Britain outlawed slavery an expedition was sent into the mountain to tell the slaves they were free. Local

118 Mauritius Blue Books, N.A., Colonial Office papers, CO 172/70 1844, p. 59; idem., CO 172/79 1853, p. 93.
119 Eight merchants and agents in Mauritius to Gomm, 19 October 1846, *Immigration of Labourers*, PP 1847 (325) XXXIX.115, p. 291.

tradition states that, because of a misunderstanding, many slaves jumped off
the mountain rather than, as they thought, be returned to slavery. Le Morne
is now a UNESCO World Heritage Site and on 1 February each year there is
a national holiday (Abolition Day) in Mauritius in memory of this event in
1835.[120] It was not surprising therefore that many freed slaves gradually left
Mauritius and the plantations became short of labour by the 1840s. There
were various schemes from the 1830s to start an apprenticeship scheme, but
these were outlawed by Britain as being suspiciously close to slavery, after a
popular campaign against them.[121] Immigration was allowed in 1843, when
Lord Stanley was war and colonial secretary, but Gomm, the Governor,
reported that this caused 'immoderate' immigration and had resulted in the
island being populated mainly by men without families, and the bounties
which were used to attract them exhausted public funds and diverted money
from public-works projects.[122]

   Grey was insistent that help for Mauritius was in exchange for the plantation
owners' commitment to material and moral improvement of the population
along English lines, but augmented with liberal ideas. He refused to answer a
petition on the subject of allowing immigration until proposed changes to an
Ordinance on the 'Rights and Duties of Servants and Masters' were altered
so that the Indian labourers should have economic encouragement to work
rather than be forced to work. In short, the previous semi-feudal system of
indentured labour would be reformed into a capitalist system, where work
was encouraged with cash rewards rather than the threat of punishment. In
Grey's own words:

> The original error to which all the objectionable provisions of the Ordinance
> are to be traced, is that it proceeds upon the principle of endeavouring by law
> to enforce upon the immigrants the due performance of the obligations to
> labour which they have contracted by accepting a free passage to the colony,
> instead of seeking to place them in a situation in which they might be acted
> upon by the same motives by which men are impelled to labour in countries in
> which industry flourishes. This I conceive to be a great mistake ... instead of
> encouraging the Indian labourers to enter, before they arrive at the Mauritius,
> into contracts to labour for several years for particular employers, and then
> by stringent regulations, to enforce the performance of these contracts ... the

120   Online at <https://www.worldheritagesite.org/list/Le+Morne> [accessed 19 November
2021].
121   *The Anti-Slavery Reporter*, 6 May 1840; J. Scoble, *Hill coolies: a brief exposure of
the deplorable conditions* ... (London: Harvey and Darton, 1840).
122   Stanley to Gomm, 27 July 1842, Approval of Ordinance appropriating annual sum
toward the immigration of free labourers, *Papers relative to emigration from the West coast
of Africa to the West Indies*, PP 1844 (530) XXXV.297, p. 163; Gomm to Grey, 2 November
1846, *Immigration of Labourers*, PP 1847 (325) XXXIX.115, p. 288.

true policy would be to adopt regulations of which the effect should be to make it the decided and obvious interest of the immigrants to work steadily for the same employers for a considerable time.[123]

To ensure that the plantation owners meant what they said and adhered to what was agreed, a particularly apt appointment was made. Macaulay (Trevelyan's relative) was appointed as the first manager of the new currency in Mauritius.[124] His father Zachary Macaulay, a Scottish statistician and one of the founders of London University, campaigned against slavery and indentured labour in Mauritius. The temporary suspension of indentured labour there in 1839 was due to his and his son's efforts. His presence in Mauritius must have been an implicit reminder: the landlords should co-operate with the relief effort, Grey's policies and the new currency, or they would have their supply of cheap labour cut off, and Mauritius would fade away as a viable plantation island.

In short, the threat hanging over the plantation owners was that they had to co-operate with the relief effort or face their entire socio-economic class disappearing, eliminating any risk of moral hazard on the part of the landlords. There was also the advantage that Macaulay's appointment would reassure anti-slavery opinion in Britain, as well as placate the Treasury in London. However, his immediate task was both challenging and mundane: to sign by hand the notes to be issued. Macaulay estimated he could sign 14,000 a week, engaging him for a total of 33 weeks without assistance.[125]

Comparing this situation with Ireland, Wood's policies forced work upon those receiving relief and forced the landlords to employ labourers or pay for them on the rates in a far less subtle manner. The overtly coercive nature of legislation in Ireland was a continual bone of contention there. Grey argued for more positive measures in Ireland like those in Mauritius such as 'giving an industrial character to the education of children'. He realised that the movement of labour in Ireland away from the poorest Poor Law Unions was seen as unhelpful but pointed out that if a viable economy was to be built, 'free circulation of labour ... is the first requisite for rendering labour productive'.[126] These ideas fell like seeds on stony ground because there was no like-minded authority to promote them. The development of the Mauritian community, by contrast, was recorded in the Blue Books returned annually to the Treasury in London. Not only economic measures were recorded, but data on population,

123   Grey to Gomm, 21 February 1847, *Immigration of Labourers*, PP 1847 (325) XXXIX.115, p. 297 refers to idem., Grey to Gomm, 29 September 1846, p. 143.
124   Colonial Office confidential print, Colonial Office papers, CO 882/1 XVIII, p. 2.
125   Macaulay to Gomm, 7 March 1848, National Archives of Mauritius, RA 956, ff. 314–15. Image of 1848 Currency Commissioners Banknote, 5 rupees, signed by C. Macaulay: see Lagesse, *150 Années de Jeunesse*, p. 38.
126   Grey to Russell, 18 December 1848, D.U.L., Earl Grey papers, GRE/B144/12.

immigration, health, the numbers of places of religious worship (with different religions treated equally), the numbers in education, employment, food in storage, food prices, wages for the different classes of employment, complaints, the state of hospitals and of prisons.

Ireland did not receive anything like the same attention to or recording of its social and economic state. Official-record collection of social and economic data in Ireland – where the emphasis was on one-off surveys and once-a-decade Censuses – was relatively worse than in Mauritius.[127] In Ireland civil registration of births, deaths and marriages was not obligatory for the whole community until 1864 (although marriages of Protestants and Jews had to be registered from 1845).[128] In contrast, all births, marriages and deaths were recorded in Mauritius long before the 1840s. Furthermore, there was official encouragement of immigration and interest in their welfare to reduce the number returning to their homeland. A Protector of Immigrants oversaw their fair treatment, and they were equal under the law with their employers. If they left early, they were noted as defaulters but in effect they could leave if they paid for their own passage and a fine. Contemporary descriptions of the standard of living in their place of origin suggest that the move to Mauritius would have brought many a better standard of living in spite of the lasting stigma associated with the arrangements; bounties were also offered to the prospective labourers as upfront payment for their work.[129]

These arrangements were, in effect, compensation to the Mauritian labourers, because the planters were eventually allowed to run an apprenticeship system which demanded a service of a minimum of five years in return for their travel costs to Mauritius. The plantation owners had petitioned concerning the duties charged on the export of sugar, as special low tariff rates favouring sugar imports from British colonies had recently been abolished. However, the change was not reversed because of the Russell government's free-trade policies, and so Mauritius was compensated by the apprenticeship system being legalised. As Ryan Saylor has convincingly shown, Mauritius attracted population and developed into one of Africa's most successful economies then and now because the island's main export industry was willing to work closely with colonial officials.[130] The contrast with Ireland, whose middle classes and landlords

---

127   There was official record keeping in Ireland, such as the Census of 1841, statistics about agricultural production collected in 1847 and Griffith's Valuation. These provide snapshots of the state of Ireland's population and economy, but do not provide runs of annual data that the Blue Books do for Mauritius.

128   For instance, this is noted in S. McAteer, B. Trainor, *Guide to Sources for Researching McAteer Families in Ireland* (Belfast: Ulster Historical Foundation, 2001), p. 11.

129   R. Neave of the Bengal Civil Service, *Note*, in *The Labour and Indian Immigration Question at Mauritius* (Mauritius, 1845) B.L., 8132, f.15, pp. 116–17, reprinted in *Simmonds Colonial Magazine and Foreign Miscellany*, vol. 6, September–December 1845, pp. 300–02.

130   Saylor, 'Probing the Historical Sources of the Mauritian Miracle', pp. 474–76.

developed an increasingly antagonistic relationship with the British government during the famine, is stark. Emigration and population loss continued for many decades after the famine in Ireland, while immigration and population gain accelerated after the crisis in Mauritius came to an end.

Tariffs on exporting sugar from Mauritius to Britain were another issue raised in the Association's letter of 28 October 1847. Not only was there the 'one pound sterling per ton duty on sugar' to the Mauritian government on sugar exported, but on entering Britain the same tariff was charged on sugar from the British colonies, grown using free labour, as on foreign sugar, grown using slave labour. As free labour was more expensive, the planters felt they had been duped into agreeing to the release of slaves on the false promise of a lower tariff for colonial goods, what became known as 'Imperial Preference'.[131] Peel had maintained the differential between slave and free grown sugar. However, when the Russell government came into power one of its rash moves towards free trade was to equalise, from 3 August 1846, the tariff on sugar whether it came from British colonies or the slave plantations of places such as Brazil and Cuba.[132] The reversal of this was the one request of the Mauritius Association which was not approved. Grey notes in his diary that at a meeting 'at Ld. John's' on 12 November 1847 it was resolved that sugar duties must remain the same 'and that we must do what we can to relieve the colonies in other ways'.[133] This decision enraged Lord Bentinck, a prominent protectionist and Conservative opposition leader, who had already attacked the government on their handling of the famine in Ireland. He issued many Select Enquiry reports gathering evidence on the treatment of the sugar and coffee producing colonies, culminating in a Committee report presented on 29 May 1848.[134]

Russell announced that the tariffs on sugar would remain on 16 June 1848, but there were a number of concessions.[135] The planters were allowed to engage immigrants on five-year contracts and once more use bounties to agents to attract immigrants, the duty on colonial rum was lowered and the distillation in the United Kingdom from sugar was permitted. In these ways it was hoped that increased sales to Britain would make up for the lack of preference in terms of price. The increased duties on colonial sugar were to be brought in gradually, in a similar way to Peel's introduction of free trade, over a period of five years. At the end of this time, Gladstone, as the new chancellor of the exchequer, said that any further relief from the abolition of preference for sugar from British

131   R. L. Schuyler, 'The Abolition of British Imperial Preference, 1846–60', *Political Science Quarterly*, 33:1 (1918), 77–92.

132   Sugar Act 9 & 10 Vict. c. 63; before this the tariff had been regularly reviewed: Sugar Acts 8 & 9 Vict. c. 5, 9 & 10 Vict. c.29, c. 43.

133   Grey's Journal, D.U.L., Earl Grey papers, GRE V/C3/13, p. 158.

134   *Hansard*, XCVI, 3 February 1848, cc. 7–79; *Eighth Report from the Select Committee on Sugar and Coffee Planting*, PP 1847–48 (361, 361-II) microfiche number 52.214–20.

135   *Hansard*, XCIX, 16 June 1848, cc. 730–41.

colonies was 'entirely impossible'.[136] The Mauritius Association did have more success in achieving a reduction in the Mauritian sugar export duty, which was reduced by two-thirds, but this was within the remit of Grey rather than Russell and Wood.[137] The British tariff had a marked detrimental effect on the success of Mauritian sugar exports and the wealth of the colony and can be compared with the effect on Ireland of Peel allowing the importation of foreign meats in 1842. This change had caused a sudden drop in pig prices in Ireland, where the ordinary agricultural labourer relied on selling the few pigs he kept to pay his rent.[138] The difference between the countries was that in Ireland, tariff changes weakened the peasantry class whose lifestyle was then swept away by the famine. However, Mauritius struggled through with the backing of a sound currency which was still able to provide the correct monetary environment to encourage loans for investment in the sugar-exporting industry.

Another further issue in the Association's letter was a request to Britain to negotiate peacefully with Madagascar. Formerly Mauritius had traded with Madagascar, but recently relations had been broken off between the islands and there had been a number of armed incursions by Madagascans into the island. Part of the issue was that Madagascar still ran a system of slavery whereas Mauritius did not. If slaves were introduced from Madagascar to Mauritius, even though they would become free, it was considered by Britain to 'promote a species of slave trade'.[139] In April 1848 Benjamin Hawes, undersecretary of state for the colonies, gave evidence to the Seventh Select Enquiry Report that 'there are communications going on, which I hope may lead to a restoration of peaceful and profitable relations between the Mauritius and Madagascar'.[140] An added pressure was fear of insurrection in Mauritius. *The Mauritian* newspaper had reported on unrest in Europe and on the withdrawal of labour by Lancashire cotton workers, and shortly afterwards, in November 1847, it published complaints that journals were being monitored and legislation was placing them under the control of the 'Police Correctionnelle!'[141]

Following Grey's wishes that the planters should produce a community that would encourage immigrant labourers to stay and build families and lives for themselves, the Association proposed that municipal institutions, in addition to the Mauritian government, should be set up. Towns should be granted charters of incorporation and sheriff's courts on the Scottish model should be set up

136   *Hansard*, CXXV, 18 April 1853, c. 1357.
137   R. Saylor, *State Building in Boom Times: Commodities and Coalitions in Latin America and Africa* (Oxford: OUP, 2014), p. 114.
138   C. Read, '"The Repeal Year" in Ireland: An Economic Reassessment', *Historical Journal*, 58:1 (2015), 111–35.
139   *Seventh Report from the Select Committee on Sugar and Coffee planting*, PP 1847–48 (245), microfiche number 52.210–14, p. 93.
140   Ibid.
141   *The Mauritian (Le Mauricien)*, National Library of Mauritius, 28 October, 17, 22 November 1847.

to deal with legal matters including property law. All these arrangements were put into place, and the Blue Books record the growing local authorities. These new and straightforward arrangements contrast sharply with the arrangements in Ireland where a clash of local administrations (counties, ancient baronies, new Poor Law Unions and differing parish areas for the different religions) inhibited the administrative organisation of relief in a timely manner. Mauritius developed a range of religious buildings for the different religions, and Catholic churches were funded by local government resources along with other religions. In Ireland there were proposals to pay Catholic priests, but arrangements were not approved by the Catholic Church. The results in the modern era are striking. While Mauritius has a reputation as 'a religiously plural society with freedom of religion granted under the constitution', assessed as a good thing because 'co-operation is an essential component of human life', Northern Irish society continues to be divided along denominational lines.[142] The support locally in Mauritius for these liberal ideas was shown by a disturbance in the Council meeting, reported in *Le Cerneen* on 29 December 1847, in which further civil rights were demanded, including the right for black people to hold administrative and judicial offices just like other British subjects, the demand for an elective council 'fitted to the elements composing our society', and trial by Jury. Therefore, it appeared that much of the island united behind the plans being put in place.

Another striking example of the strength of Mauritius's ability for social empathy was the donation made to Irish relief by Mauritius. The Irish and Scottish Relief Committee founded on 14 May 1847 at the Hotel d'Europe, just as the crisis was unfolding in Mauritius, had collected £3260 5s 3½d in donations by August (including around £100 from the Seychelles and Rodrigues) of which £3,220 was sent to the British Association for the Relief of Extreme Distress in the Remote Parishes of Ireland and Scotland.[143] The concern for Ireland was recorded in local newspapers and the volume of donations increased when news of the Irish loan crisis of that spring reached Mauritius. The Mauritius donation was higher than the £2,000 publicly donated by Queen Victoria and is one of the highest per capita donations of any colony in the British Empire for Irish relief. However, when the lowering of duty to encourage the importation of rum from Mauritius and the West Indies was discussed, with the intention of recompense for being 'brought to beggary and ruin', as Lord Bentinck put it, by the abolition of preferential duties, it was opposed by Irish MPs for partisan reasons.[144]

142   Shaver et al., 'The Boundaries of Trust: Cross-Religious and Cross-Ethnic Field Experiments in Mauritius', pp. 1, 4.
143   *Le Cerneen*, 17 August 1847; C. Kinealy, *Charity and the Great Hunger in Ireland: The Kindness of Strangers* (London: Bloomsbury, 2013), p. 215.
144   *Hansard*, C, 17 July 1848, cc. 534–61.

The long-term economic performance of Ireland and Mauritius

Mauritius had some tough economic challenges ahead, as did Ireland, and this section will analyse the robustness of its economy and compare it with that of Ireland. Although some historians point out that income per head grew faster in Ireland after the famine than in Great Britain, it was not Ireland but Mauritius that was able to use its increasing wealth to support a growing population.

First, the claim that the Mauritius currency was the first currency board and was, indeed, a representative of Grey's alternative currency scheme can be tested by checking whether the notes issued were backed 50% by bullion with the remainder backed by investments in foreign bills, as was the intention. This was a lot to ask, because the start-up period for the currency was very uneven as the currency in circulation started from zero and made inroads into the main circulation which was coinage. Chart 6.4 shows the total Commissioners of Currency notes in circulation (total notes) after 1848; the figures before are for previous note issues and show how these issues suddenly fell off, contributing to the general crisis.

As well as the specie held by the Commissioners of Currency, the figures for notes held in reserve are shown. These notes in reserve form part of the notes in circulation because they are available to be issued at any time. This situation is similar to the Bank of England but is frequently misunderstood. When the number of notes in reserve falls to a low level, the currency system is under pressure, as can be seen in 1855 for Mauritius in the lead up to the British financial crisis of 1857. The reaction by the Commissioners was to increase the specie held by the following year. Chart 6.5 applies the test of looking at the ratio of specie to total notes. It shows that the Commissioners held it close to the 0.5 required by Grey's scheme for the currency, through all the upheaval of startup. Mauritius held this closer to the required 0.5 than did the Bank of England. The Bank of England, of course, was working to a different system with 100% backing with bullion after an initial fiduciary allowance, but in effect the requirements were similar at that time. The Bank of England's figure for the ratio is low around 1855–57, showing the Bank did not have what was seen as sufficient bullion reserve, and after 1866 it increased its bullion ratio under pressure of commentators, such as *The Economist* and the Banking School, as can be seen from Chart 6.5. The remainder of the Mauritian notes in circulation, those in addition to the ones backed by gold, were covered by deposits made in the Calcutta Treasury (equivalent to Treasury bills), and records of the receipts exist in the British Library.[145]

---

145 Mauritius Commercial Bank, request of Governor that Agents of, be permitted to deposit securities in Calcutta Treasury, B. L., India Office records, IOR/Z/E/4/21/B93: receipts 1850–51, IOR/Z/E/4/23/F153: 1852–53, IOR/Z/E/4/24/C221: 1853–54, IOR/Z/E/4/26/F170: 1855.

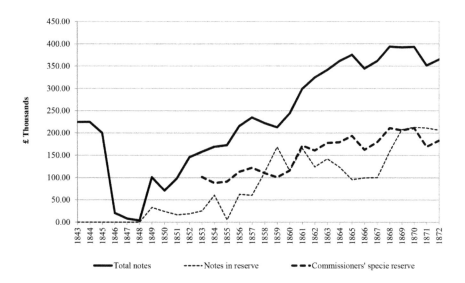

Chart 6.4. Total notes in circulation and reserve, total notes in reserve and specie held by the Commissioners of Currency in Mauritius, 1843 to 1872. *Source:* N.A., Mauritius Blue Books.

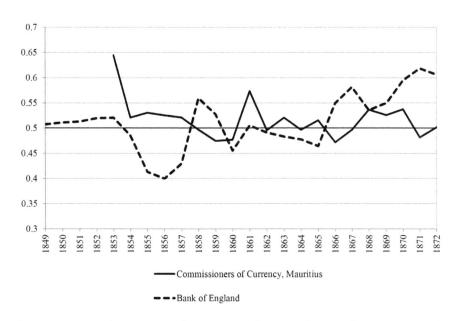

Chart 6.5. Ratio of specie to total notes in circulation and reserve for Mauritius and the Bank of England, 1849 to 1872. *Sources:* N.A., Mauritius Blue Books; BoE.A. Bank of England daily account books.

There was an important difference between the specie (in effect bullion) reserves in Mauritius and the Bank of England. In Mauritius, as part of Grey's scheme, the specie was owned by the Commissioners and built up with the interest on its other investments (which were mainly in India where interest rates were high). The Commissioners could not trade or speculate with it. In the Bank of England the 'reserve' was a mixture of bullion owned by the Bank and the deposits of other Banks and private citizens. Thus, the Bank of England had no direct control over outflows of bullion from its reserve. After controversy between adherents of the Banking and Currency Schools among its directors and governors, it fell into the habit of using a raised Bank Rate to attract bullion into the country and hopefully its reserve, by rule of thumb and compromise rather than by following any agreed theory. This came to be believed to cause unstable and high rates by some, as complained of later in the century by Inglis Palgrave and commented upon by George Clare.[146] The rates were high during financial crises when credit was in short supply, a policy which came to be supported by the Currency School, but a situation that Grey thought should have been avoided.

The whole point of Grey's scheme was to try and counteract this problem, which he identified many years before Palgrave and Clare. Remembering Mauritius did not have a reputation for stability or the size of the Bank of England, it is possible to look at interest rates in both places to see if there are signs of release from the retrictive mechanism under which the Bank of England and the Bank of Ireland, which was subservient to it, operated. Chart 6.6 shows the interest rate for bills on London (or England) for Ireland and Mauritius. These were the type of bills which merchants in both countries would have had to raise to export to Britain. It can be seen that after the introduction of Grey's currency scheme there are four phases of interest rates in Mauritius. Up to 1853 they are lower than for Ireland. Between 1853 and 1857 the rates follow Irish rates up to another crisis. After the end of colonial preference and the 1857 financial crisis, interest rates were similar to those of Ireland but slightly lower, and after the crisis of 1866 (during which Mauritius was swept by a malaria epidemic that killed a quarter of its population), interest rates were generally always lower than those in Ireland.[147]

It is perfectly consistent with Grey's intentions for his currency system that the commercial banks in Mauritius were able to offer low interest rates during and after the 1866 crisis. While the Bank Rate in the United Kingdom was 10%

---

146   R. H. I. Palgrave, *Bank Rate and the Money Market in England, France, Germany, Holland and Belgium 1844–1900* (London: John Murray, 1903), pp. 218–19; G. Clare, *A Money Market Primer and Key to the Exchanges* (London: Effingham Wilson, 1900), p. 100.
147   More details of the malarial-fever outbreak of 1864–68 are given in R. Boodhoo, *Health, Disease and Indian Immigrants in Nineteenth Century Mauritius* (Port Louis: A. Ghat Trust Fund, 2010), pp. 178–81. The peak mortality was in 1867.

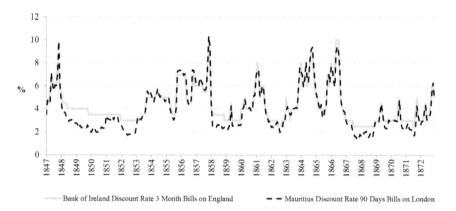

Chart 6.6. Interest rates (or nearest equivalent) for Mauritius and the Bank of Ireland, 1847 to 1873. *Sources:* calculated from N.A., Mauritius Blue Books; Bank of England, 'Three centuries of macroeconomic data' spreadsheet; F. G. Hall, *History of the Bank of Ireland*, (Dublin: Hodges, Figgis & Co., 1944) Appendix D, p. 381.

for fourteen weeks, rates in Mauritius varied between 8.98% and 8.91% for the monthly average. Mauritius's annual average for 1866 was 6.82%, similar to the United Kingdom.[148] By comparison in India, the Bank of Bengal charged a minimum of 9.147% on the annual average.[149] Generally colonies such as Mauritius and India would have been expected to have higher interest rates than in the United Kingdom, as capital was scarcer there than in Britain, so Mauritius did well in maintaining them at or below United Kingdom levels. Chart 6.4 shows that during the 1866 period the Commissioners were able to maintain credit by digging deeper into their note reserve, but without it approaching zero. The result of this ability to maintain reasonable interest rates and available credit was that trade was maintained and the general wealth of the colony was enhanced in comparison to Ireland. Richard Allen has highlighted the importance of cheap capital in the success of Mauritius's commercial life throughout the nineteenth century, and therefore this characteristic was an asset.[150]

Another reason for the introduction of the paper currency in Mauritius was to enable the labouring class to be paid with notes, and for this reason the

148 BoE.A., Bank of England daily account book, 1866; Mauritius Blue Books, N.A., Colonial Office papers, CO 172.
149 BoE.A., Bank of England daily account book, 1866; Mauritius Blue Books, N.A., Colonial Office papers, CO 172; G. P. S. Scutt, *History of the Bank of Bengal* (Calcutta: Bank of Bengal, 1904), p. 151.
150 Allen, *Slaves, Freedmen, and Indentured Labourers in Colonial Mauritius*, p. 22.

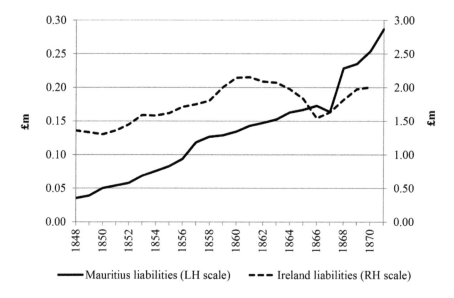

Chart 6.7. Government Savings Bank in Mauritius and savings banks in Ireland, total liabilities, 1848 to 1870. *Sources:* N.A., Mauritius Government Gazettes, CO/171; *Irish Savings Banks*, PP 1849 (344), 1852 (213), 1854 (245, 245-I), 1854-55 (493), 1857 Session 1 (128), 1857-58 (55), 1859 Session 2 (165, 165-I), 1860 (584), 1861 (470), 1862 (484), 1863 (531), 1864 (449), 1865 (439), 1866 (322), 1867 (403), 1867-68 (400), 1868-69 (277), 1870 (197), 1871 (252), 1872 (201).

notes were issued in rupees, with which the Indian workers would have been familiar. This eased transactions within the island and was an inhibition to the labourers leaving with large quantities of specie, which helped to reduce outward capital flows. In Ireland, before the famine, labourers saw very little cash, and what they did receive from the sale of a pig or from employment they spent in local shops.[151] Most of that cash was coin, and notes were not in favour; often cash was hidden by burying it, which reduced the impact of fractional-reserve banking. Conversely for the middle classes, notes were preferred and as a consequence the circulation of notes held up through the famine, during the time in which poor labourers left Ireland or died from the effects of the famine.[152] However, gold coin was used by the middle classes for transferring

---

151 W. N. Hancock, 'On the variations of the supply of silver coin in Ireland during the operations for the relief of distress 1846–47', *The Bankers' Magazine* 7:5 (1847), 340–48; also see *The Bankers' Magazine* 7:1 (1847), p. 18.
152 Circulation figures for issuing banks were published in the *Dublin Gazette*.

funds to America, although there is no data for exactly how much.[153] Irish banks tended to transfer bullion to London banks initially just for safe-keeping, but later in exchange for notes. The end result of these outflows was that Ireland did not have sufficient bullion to exchange with Great Britain to buy the industrial goods it required with the proceeds of an agricultural economy without decreasing their circulation. The balance of payments with Great Britain was not official, but this lack of bullion may explain why Ireland remained so poor in comparison. In contrast, greater credit availability in Mauritius helped to boost the economy, make investments, and secure food supplies. As Chart 6.2 shows, the beginnings of a sharp rise in the price of rice can be seen in the third quarter of 1847, but this is then moderated as credit facilities were put in place with India for rice to be exported to Mauritius.

The disparity between the economic resilience of Mauritius compared to Ireland becomes evident when the overall deposits (liabilities) for savings banks are compared. Chart 6.7 shows the different reactions to the global financial crisis of 1866 of Ireland and Mauritius. Ireland shows a levelling off of total savings as the crisis approaches and over a 25% fall from their peak during the crisis. In comparison, Mauritius shows only a small dip and a propensity for increased saving afterwards, in spite of a severe malaria epidemic. A good proportion of labourers held accounts in the Government Savings Bank, and the report of the bank always measured its achievement in this respect. Its performance was in spite of some setbacks and problems. After their five-year stay, a proportion of labourers tended to leave and take their money with them.[154] Reputational problems beset the bank when a teller dishonestly took money at the end of the 1850s and when it became clear that deposits were made on the basis of the gold equivalent but withdrawn in the silver equivalent, which caused a loss to be made when the price of silver fell relative to gold.[155] Yet despite all this, in 1861 the bank had £133,000 on loan for mortgages, and by the Second World War, it has been claimed, former indentured labourers from the Indian sub-continent, the once poorest of Mauritius's poor, had bought around 50 per cent of the cultivated land on the island with their wages.[156] The basis of the

153　L. Barrow, 'The Use of Money in Mid-Nineteenth Century Ireland', *Irish Quarterly Review*, 59:1 (1970), 81–88, at p. 82.

154　In 1865, 1,328 out of 7,049 depositors in the Government Savings Bank were Indian agricultural labourers. They held an average of £22 16s 6d in their accounts. *Mauritian Government Gazette 1866*, N.A., Colonial Office papers, CO 171/30.

155　*Mauritian Government Gazette 1856–60*, Government Saving Bank reports and results, N.A., Colonial Office papers, CO 171/20–4.

156　*Mauritian Government Gazette 1861*, N.A., Colonial Office papers, CO 171/25, p. 287; K. Hazareesingh, *Histoire des Indiens à l'Île Maurice* (Paris: Adrien Maisonneuve, 1973), p. 198.

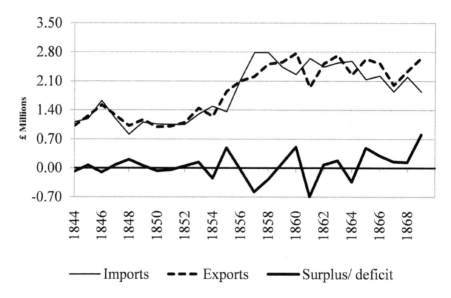

Chart 6.8. Trade figures for Mauritius, 1844 to 1869. *Source:* N.A., Mauritius Blue Books.

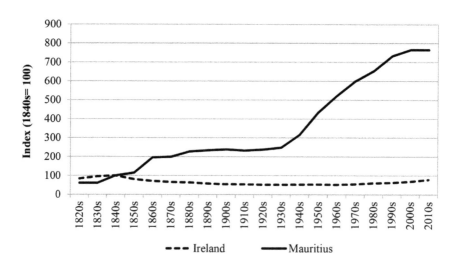

Chart 6.9. Census populations of Ireland and Mauritius from the 1820s to the 2010s. *Sources:* Central Statistics Office Ireland; NISRA; UN DESA; <https://statsmauritius.govmu.org/Pages/Statistics/By_Subject/Population/SB_Population.aspx> [accessed 15 February 2020].

accumulated wealth can be seen in the trade figures, which retained a healthy balance throughout the 1866 period (Chart 6.8).

More dramatic is the difference between the long-term trajectories of the population charts for the two countries (Chart 6.9) with Mauritius being far more successful at retaining and growing its population.

Third Earl Grey, Ireland, and Mauritius

Grey was convinced that the currency arrangements in the Bank Charter Act of 1844 were at the heart of the problem of being unable to raise loans in 1847 for Irish relief and assisted emigration schemes. At the worst point of the crisis, just before the Bank Charter Act of 1844 was suspended in the autumn of 1847, Grey put pressure on Wood to challenge the Governor of the Bank of England, who was proposing to severely limit the availability of credit.[157] However, the Governor stood firm on remaining within the terms of the Bank Charter Act. Grey suggested that the Governor's stance should be recorded, presumably with the implication that he would be held to account, but Wood demurred from doing this on the basis that 'he is strict beyond all fear and likely to carry things to an extreme the other way'.[158] Wood later publicly blamed the crises on the Bank of England but in ways which did not implicate the Bank Charter Act.[159] The liabilities of the Bank of England remained at a similar level from 1844 to 1847, but large deposits had accumulated in Scottish and London banks. Generally, these were seen as a sign of basic strength, but it was realised they could cause problems if, for instance, all the London banks developed problems at the same time.[160] The Banking School and Grey believed that if the commercial world had expanded, then the amount of currency available should be allowed to expand with it, so long as it was backed by bullion. However, the partial Currency School solution introduced by Peel limited notes, while allowing other types of money to expand. Therefore, the Banking School could blame the crisis on the legal restrictions on issuing notes, the reserves of which were run down nearly to the limits allowed, and the Currency School could blame the increase in deposits across the country, which was uncontrolled.

It was often stated at the time that the limits on credit did not affect Ireland, but this is not strictly the case. All Irish banks found themselves under pressure to provide coin, which was already scarce because of the increased amount needed for payments in small amounts for day labour on public-works schemes.

---

157   *Hansard*, XCV, 30 November 1847, cc. 396–98.
158   Wood to Russell, 8 October 1847, N.A., Russell papers, PRO 30/22/6F, ff. 168–69.
159   *Hansard*, XCV, 30 November 1847, cc. 383–84; idem., cc. 411–12.
160   Idem., c. 398.

The Bank of Ireland had made an arrangement with the other Irish banks to provide coin in times of shortage but still had to import £0.2m in coin from Britain in 1847 in order to meet their commitments.[161] When the works stopped, the silver was transferred back to the Bank of England.

The relative economic success of Mauritius encouraged Grey in his alternative plan for currency. It did not require interest rates to be raised by policymakers to retain bullion, instead leaving rates to be managed by the market, thereby increasing confidence in the new currency. The Bank of England was not in a position to change to this system because it did not have enough bullion. The so-called bullion reserve had many owners other than the Bank of England and interest rates were at the mercy of its fluctuations. So Ireland did not receive any benefits accruing from Grey's theories at the time. It is a reasonable assessment to say that Grey's ideas did assist Mauritius, especially when the outcome is compared to that in Ireland. It would not be correct to say that emigration schemes were held up solely because of Grey's *laissez-faire* leanings. His great fear was the spread of civil unrest in the colonies as a result of their opposition to Irish emigration.[162] His ingenuity went beyond conventional political economy to try and solve problems in ways which were effective and viable. His liberal leanings are more easily recognised in the social ideals that he supported in Mauritius, including its even-handed approach to the different religions on the island, all of which received financial contributions from the government.

It was, perhaps, the success of social improvements in Mauritius that later on encouraged him to argue for similar liberal policies to be used in Ireland. In March 1866 he called for a committee on the state of Ireland in Parliament, for which he recommended many ideas from Mauritius.[163] He began by describing the 'unsatisfactory state of Ireland' including its poor housing, poor methods of agriculture, limited trade and tendency for emigration in times of distress. He was 'convinced that Ireland ought to maintain in comfort a far larger population than it at present does'. He regarded emigration as 'losing that which ought to be precious' but 'unfortunately Ireland has long been distracted by political and religious animosity'. He was dismayed by the violence of the Fenians and the large amounts of money contributed by Irish immigrants in America to a fund 'established with the avowed object of overthrowing the Government they left at home'. He went through a list of legislation from Catholic Emancipation to the Encumbered Estates Act which had been brought in to try and resolve and recompense for matters, but pointed out that it was 'seventeen or eighteen years since all the measures for the improvement of Ireland which the Imperial Parliament has been able to devise have been in operation' and matters had

161   F. G. Hall, *History of the Bank of Ireland* (Dublin, Hodges, Figgis & Co., 1949), pp. 218–19.
162   Grey to Russell, 6 September 1848, N.A., Russell papers, PRO 30/22/7D, ff. 16–17.
163   *Hansard*, CLXXXII, 16 March 1866, cc. 358–418.

become worse not better. He thought it clear that Ireland was now not over taxed compared with the rest of the United Kingdom, and that land reform was not the solution. Although land law was 'confused, and required to be simplified and made clear', the best long-term solution was 'to leave landlord and tenant to settle their relations'. It was now disaffection more than poverty which discouraged investment and the development of prosperity. He had come to the conclusion, having excluded other matters, that the equal endowment of religions was 'at the root of the matter'; a policy that worked well in Mauritius was conspicuously absent in Ireland.

> Let me remind you that the Church property in Ireland formerly belonged to the Roman Catholic Church, and that when the people of England shook off their connection with Rome, though the Irish people adhered to the ancient faith, the Church property was transferred to the clergy of the conquering nation, while the Church of the majority was left without any endowment whatever. To make that injustice more galling, at a later period the Presbyterians, who were as much Dissenters as the Roman Catholics and far better able to provide for their own wants, received the assistance of Parliament towards the maintenance and spread of their own religion, while none was given to the Roman Catholics ... if we suppose that the Roman Catholics of Ireland have the feelings of other men, it is impossible that they should not be deeply impressed with the injustice to which they are subject of devoting all the national revenues which originally belonged to the Roman Catholic Church to the exclusive support of the rich minority, while the poor majority are left to their own resources.[164]

He proposed the solution was 'first, to establish religious equality; and next, to avoid, as far as possible, the disturbance of existing interests'. Russell answered Grey's proposal by refusing to spend money and preferring 'sound alterations of a quiet character'.[165] The motion to form a committee was refused, for once again, in the spring and summer of 1866, the Bank of England was experiencing persistent outflows from its bullion reserve despite frequent Bank Rate hikes; distraction by financial issues once again hurt Ireland's interests.[166]

Even so, Grey continued with his campaign to reform the currency system. He fell out with Wood seriously over the matter of currency in the colonies and this was most likely why he was not involved in future governments. To James Bruce, Earl of Elgin, he wrote in 1850, 'I have a long-standing controversy with the Treasury (i.e. in fact with C. Wood) on the whole subject of Colonial Currency which seems to me in a most unsatisfactory state'.[167] After James

164   Idem., cc. 367–68.
165   Idem., c. 416.
166   BoE.A., Bank of England daily account book 1866.
167   Grey to Elgin, 25 October 1850, quoted in A. G. Dougly (ed.), *Elgin Grey papers 1846–52*, vol. 2 (Ottowa: Patenaude, 1932), p. 723.

Wilson's death, he found a sympathetic ear in the form of Walter Bagehot, the replacement editor of *The Economist*.[168] By 1875 Bagehot was sending him the proofs of an article for *The Economist* on 'A Plan for a Government Paper Currency', with an opposing view featured in the following number.[169] Grey also published letters in *The Times*, but this was brought to a halt when their city editor, Arthur Crump, decided to 'suppress all currency controversy', according to Grey's nephew, Henry.[170]

Ireland therefore did not benefit from Grey's highly innovative and intelligent currency plans in the nineteenth century. They were overruled for use in the United Kingdom by Wood and Russell and were implemented mainly in the British Empire. Surprisingly, however, on gaining independence, the Irish Free State did adopt Grey's policy and ran a currency-board scheme from 1928 until the 1970s, when it was gradually faded out. The currency was backed 100% with the British pound and, for a new country's currency, benefitted from comparatively low and stable interest rates. However, independent Ireland did not make full use of this advantage owing to its self-imposed protectionist and balanced-budget policies.[171]

Would Ireland have been better off as a colony?

There are some major differences between the Mauritius crisis and the Irish famine. Mauritius had a population of approximately 160,000 and so was cheaper to keep afloat than an island with a population of over 8 million.[172] The speed, severity and length of the Irish famine were truly astonishing, even compared to Ireland's previous experiences of harvest failure.[173] Yet the situation in Mauritius also seemed desperate at the time with a population, some recently attracted to the island, which had no means of feeding itself

---

168   Bagehot to Grey, 3 December 1860, D.U.L., Earl Grey papers, GRE/B77/2/1.
169   Bagehot to Grey, 22 January 1875, D.U.L., Earl Grey papers, GRE/B77/2/16; *The Economist*, 27 February 1875, pp. 242–45; idem., 6 March 1875, pp. 270–72.
170   Henry Grey to Grey, 22 February 1886, D.U.L., Earl Grey papers, GRE/B90/1/93. Crump was later dismissed by *The Times* after receiving a cheap loan from the Bank of England: D. Kynaston (abridged D. Milner), *City of London: The History* (London: Chatto & Windus, 2012), p. 158.
171   P. Honohan, 'Currency Board or Central Bank? Lessons from the Irish Pound's Link with Sterling 1928–79', *Banca Nazionale del Lavoro Quarterly Review*, 50:200 (1997), 39–67, at pp. 52–53, 55.
172   For population figures, see Griffiths, Huron, Carter, *Piastres to Polymer*, p. 67 and T. A. Larcom, 'Observations on the Census of the Population of Ireland in 1841', *Journal of the Statistical Society of London*, 6:4 (December 1843), 323–51, at p. 324.
173   See P. M. Solar, 'The Great Famine Was No Ordinary Subsistence Crisis', in E. M. Crawford (ed.), *Famine: The Irish Experience 900–1900* (Edinburgh: John Donald, 1989), 112–31, at pp. 114–22.

or buying imported food. The Colonial Office and the Board of Control were able to raid the resources of the East India Company to help Mauritius (and other sugar colonies also suffering from financial difficulties in the West Indies), which the Treasury could not feasibly do to help Ireland. Nevertheless, otherwise, the similarities between Ireland and Mauritius are remarkable. Both were substantially Catholic and had populations of agricultural labourers that did not speak English. Both were monocultures, sugar for Mauritius and potatoes for Ireland, as far as food for the poorer classes went. The farming sectors of both were reliant on cheap labour. In the late 1840s both were hit by new crop diseases that slashed production, threatened rural labourers with famine and triggered collapses in banknote circulations, to the point where banknotes almost disappeared in Mauritius. The new diseases lowered crop yields well into the 1850s in both places.

So why was the outcome in Ireland truly catastrophic, whereas in Mauritius it ended up as a famine that never was? At first glance, it could be argued that Mauritius was treated better because it was in the interest of either the British Empire or the City of London for it to be so. The problem with that idea, however, is that the British government, in overall terms, used a very similar approach to relief policy in Ireland and Mauritius. A supply of money was allocated for relief raised by local taxes, after initial assistance by advances made by the Treasury in London, and local elites were charged with the responsibility of organising the relief.

There were two major differences, which led to these policies causing a disaster in Ireland and an economic 'miracle' in Mauritius. The first was the way in which the relief effort was funded. Whereas Mauritius's new currency arrangements, inspired by Grey's ideas, enabled Mauritian landowners to refinance themselves after the collapse of the island's financial system, the restrictions of the particular application of Currency School ideas in the Bank Charter Act of 1844 meant that the United Kingdom was not able to borrow to help Ireland without panicking financial markets. Ireland became trapped inside Britain's currency system, which would undergo crisis again in 1857 and 1866. Bank failures continued to be a problem in Ireland beyond Britain's last systemic banking crisis of the nineteenth century (in 1866).[174] In contrast, Mauritius became more resistant to such events. It built up a viable economy which could support a growing population and build an economy which could afford to pay its local taxes, quite the opposite to Ireland.

The second difference is the extent to which all levels of Mauritian society co-operated with each other and the British authorities in Port Louis and London. The Mauritius Association and the plantation owners had little option but to

---

174   For instance, the Munster Bank failure of 1886; see C. Ó Gráda, 'The Last Major Irish Bank Failure: Lessons for Today?', *University College Dublin Centre for Economic Research Working Paper Series* WP 10/38 (2010).

co-operate with the British government. If they did not, no apprenticeship schemes would have been allowed; the sugar industry would have then been destroyed by foreign competition and the island's population would most likely have faded away to next to nothing. In short, Mauritius would have become little more than a military base.[175] The condition attached to British assistance for Mauritius was that the plantation owners had to build a society attractive enough for those immigrating to bring their families and settle permanently. Their social conditions were monitored extensively in detail in the Treasury Blue Books.

By contrast, Ireland descended into class war during the famine between the poor, who blamed the landlords for their plight, and the landlords, who often did as much as they could to avoid paying for poor relief.[176] The famine did nothing to bring together classes or religions in Ireland and the reporting of the limited attacks on tradespeople worsened the atmosphere.[177] Middle-class nationalist journalists in Ireland undermined the case for further assistance by attacking the British government for providing famine relief for the Irish poor. *The Nation* thundered, for instance, 'let us have no begging appeals to England – no gathering eleemosynary help, to be distributed for the use of paupers – no feeding of our people with alms and as mendicants' by a 'foreign parliament – ignorant, vain, headlong, insolent and selfish'.[178] Yet nationalist opinion provided no constructive or coherent demand for a different policy.[179] Their position became one of hypocrisy given later nationalist accusations that the British government was, in retrospect, not generous enough. Such attacks did real damage to the willingness of politicians later on during the famine to find further ways of helping Ireland.[180] Their rudeness compared unfavourably with the politeness of the Mauritius Association, particularly in its requests for assistance in 1847: 'having thus placed these important facts as they stand before your Lordship, the Association feels assured they will receive that mature consideration they merit'.[181]

The accusation that Ireland was treated like a colony during the famine goes deep and has been made as long ago as the event itself.[182] Over the past

175   The Chagos Islands were evacuated after being demanded by the United States as a military base after the Second World War.
176   Extensively documented in *Poor Law Inspectors: entry book of their replies to a Treasury Circular on Unemployment*, January 1848, N.A., Treasury papers, T 64/400.
177   *Pictorial Times*, 25 April 1846, p. 260; *Hansard*, CLXXXII, 16 March 1866, cc. 361–63.
178   P. Bew, *The Politics of Enmity 1789–2006* (Oxford: OUP, 2007), pp. 177–78, citing *The Nation*, 8 November 1845.
179   M. Daly, *The Famine in Ireland* (Dundalk: Dundalgan Press for the Dublin Historical Association, 1986), pp. 115, 123.
180   Grey to Russell, 6 September 1848, N.A., Russell papers, PRO 30/22/7D, ff. 16–17.
181   Mauritius Association to Grey, 28 August 1847, *Correspondence with respect to the Condition of the Colony*, PP 1847–48 (61) XLIV.201, p. 252.
182   N. Canny, *Making Ireland British, 1580–1650* (Oxford: OUP, 2001); K. Kenny, 'Ireland in the Empire', in K. Kenny (ed.), *Ireland and the British Empire* (Oxford: OUP,

decade the 'colonial' nature of the British response to the crisis has been once again emphasised by anti-revisionist historians.[183] Yet membership of the United Kingdom came with its responsibilities for its elites as well as its benefits. Although both islands were treated in a broadly similar way, more was expected of the longstanding elites of Ireland, which was now part of the United Kingdom, than those of Mauritius as a recently acquired formal colony.[184] Mauritius therefore found it easier to live up to expectations, whereas Ireland's elites constantly disappointed. It is not surprising therefore to find contemporary opinion of the view that Ireland would have been better off as a colony. As John Stuart Mill, who worked for the East India Company during the crises in Ireland and Mauritius, argued in 1868, the problem with integration into the United Kingdom was that 'Englishmen are not always incapable of shaking off insular prejudices, and governing another country according to its wants, and not according to common English habits and notions'.[185] In contrast to a policy of full integration with Great Britain (for Ireland), more policy flexibility was available for formal colonies, which did not need to follow exactly what was implemented in Great Britain. For example, Mill suggested, 'India is now governed ... with a full perception and recognition of its differences from England. What has been done for India has now to be done for Ireland'.[186] Most importantly, while Ireland was forced to be part of the United Kingdom's monetary policy in the 1840s, this was not true of Mauritius and other places in the Empire, as they were encouraged to create currency systems that diverged from policy in London.

The British response to the Mauritian crisis should raise serious questions about the direction of anti-revisionist literature on the famine. If Britain's response to the Irish famine was driven by imperial prejudice, why was

---

2004), 90–122; Kinealy, 'Was Ireland a Colony?'; D. Lloyd, 'After History: Historicism and Irish Postcolonial Studies', in C. Carroll, P. King (eds.), *Ireland and Postcolonial Theory* (Notre Dame: University Press, 2003), 46–62, at pp. 48–49; R. Ingelbien, 'Irish Studies, the Postcolonial Paradigm and the Comparative Mandate', in J. P. Byrne, P. Kirwan, M. O'Sullivan (eds.), *Affecting Irishness: Negotiating Cultural Identity within and beyond the Nation* (Bern: Peter Lang, 2009), 21–41; T. Foley, M. O'Connor, *Ireland and Empire: Colonies, Culture, and Empire* (Dublin: Irish Academic Press, 2006).

183   See, for instance, Nally, *Human Encumbrances: Political Violence and the Great Irish Famine*; Nally, 'The Colonial Dimensions of the Great Irish Famine'; W. J. Smyth, 'The Longue Durée – Imperial Britain and Colonial Ireland'.

184   Ireland could be considered more colonist than colony when compared to Mauritius because two governors of Mauritius were Irish: Sir Galbraith Lowry Cole (1823–28) and Sir John Pope Hennessy (1882–89). Also, the Third Earl Grey wrote to Bessborough that he was willing to placate Daniel O'Connell by giving appointments to Irish lawyers in the colonies; Grey to Bessborough, 7 September 1846, D.U.L., Earl Grey papers, GRE/B78/2B/24.

185   J. S. Mill, *England and Ireland* (London: Longmans, 1868), pp. 22–23. India received its pseudo-Currency Board in 1861, issuing notes in rupees.

186   Ibid.

Mauritius, which was actually a colony, treated in a more appropriate manner with a better outcome than Ireland, which was an integral part of the United Kingdom? If an obsession with combatting moral hazard was responsible for the failure of British policy in Ireland, why did British policy work better in Mauritius, where the imposition of liberal social attitudes was carried out more rigorously? Was it that the threat towards the Mauritian landlords – if they did not act 'morally' and assist with the relief effort, the indentured labour and the sugar-based economic system over which they presided would end – was a much more effective way of achieving co-operation than the greater tolerance to elites in Ireland? Why did the policy suggestions of those opposed to the method of intervention in Ireland work so well in Mauritius? Whatever the answer to these questions, the critics of the Russell government's currency policies, inside and outside the Cabinet, need to be taken more seriously by historians. For when they were in control of a famine relief effort, their ideas really did work, unlike the Currency School's, which contributed to a disaster in Ireland.

The British state's success in Mauritius and failure in Ireland had long-term consequences for their histories. In Ireland the perception that Britain did not do enough during the famine fuelled demands for separation later in the century, which eventually led to independence in the form of the Irish Free State in 1922. In contrast, the academic literature increasingly suggests that, despite the restrictions of the apprenticeship system, the modern Mauritian economic 'miracle' had colonial foundations. The close co-operation between Mauritius's main export industry, sugar, and colonial administrators, that was pioneered by the Mauritius Association and the Colonial Office in the 1840s, has been cited as a source of that success.[187] Mauritius's post-colonial disputes with Britain largely date from events in the later twentieth century, such as the separation from Mauritius of the Chagos Islands in 1965 and the subsequent forced deportation of its population, rather than its Victorian past.

It can be seen clearly in present-day Ireland and Mauritius that they have developed different attitudes towards their relationships with Great Britain in the nineteenth century. When Ireland became an independent republic in 1949, it removed the large statue of Queen Victoria that stood outside its government buildings. Mauritius became a republic in 1992, albeit one that still uses Britain's Privy Council as its highest court of appeal. However, its statue of Queen Victoria was allowed to remain outside Government House in Port Louis, where it stands to this day.

187   Saylor, 'Probing the Historical Sources of the Mauritian Miracle: Sugar Exporters and State Building in Colonial Mauritius', p. 476.

Conclusion:
Britain's biggest economic-policy failure

Behold this place, of a terrible mystery the witne[ss],
Advance! but a secret horror thrills my heart.
These cloisters, these graves, cause my heart
To beat involuntary with horror.
I perceive this redoubted talisman
Who is to bestow upon me
Great power and immortality.

> Robert the Devil, in Eugène Scribe and Germain Delavigne's
> *Robert le Diable: An Opera in Five Acts* [1831] (version playing
> at the Haymarket Theatre in London in May 1847).[1]

Many of the illustrations used throughout this book are cartoons published in London that ridicule the policy responses of British politicians to the problems they faced in the 1840s. That may, at first, seem an odd choice for a book about the Irish famine. Nevertheless, they show that the British press was always as willing to criticise and denigrate their own political leaders as much as they were those of the Irish, if not more so. Altogether, the cartoons suggest a significant level of contemporary unease in London with the direction of British economic policy, which was often seen as being carried out in a way bordering on the farcical.

The Irish famine was, and is, no laughing matter. Between 1841 and 1851, as Nusteling has put it, 'nearly 4 million of the original population of about 8.3 million had definitively emigrated or unexpectedly died' in Ireland.[2] Those circumstances changed the course of the history of Ireland as well as that of the United Kingdom. The cartoons reinforce the message of this book: that British governments launched a set of untried and untested economic policies in the 1840s, many of which were intended to help Ireland through

---

1   A. E. Scribe, G. Delavigne, *Robert-le-Diable, an opera in five acts: With an easy translation, line for line with the French* (London: H. N. Millar, 1847), p. 49 (spelling modernised).
2   H. P. H. Nusteling, 'How Many Irish Potato Famine Deaths?: Towards Coherence of the Evidence', *Historical Methods*, 42:2 (2009), 57–80, at p. 74.

"ROBERT THE ━━━━━━━" PARALYSING JOHN BULL WITH HIS MYSTIC BRANCH.

Figure 7.1. 'Robert the -----', *Punch*, 29 May 1847, pp. 221–22. The cartoon refers to the performance in London of Giacomo Meyerbeer's opera *Robert le diable*.

significant intervention in its economy during the famine, yet most of which badly backfired. That government policy failed to save as many lives in Ireland as was intended has been shown to have been as much the result of the failure of government intervention as it was a story of *laissez-faire*.

Perhaps no cartoon published during the famine encapsulates this book's description of British economic policy as well as the one that appears on the cover.[3] Only caricature would have got away with the serious point it makes; a normal newspaper article laying out similar accusations may well have been considered libellous at the time. It is a satire of current events in 1847 based on an opera scene that is hard to imagine being performed on stage in Victorian Britain. Yet performed it was, and frequently, in the 1830s and 1840s. In the third act of Giacomo Meyerbeer's opera *Robert le diable*, the devil summons zombie nuns, who rise from their tombs in the ruined cloister of Sainte-Rosalie, a nunnery. He asks them to dance, while praising the pleasures of drinking, gambling and lust. Their task is to seduce Robert ('with your charms do him

3   *Punch*, 29 May 1847, pp. 221–22.

assail') – and force the hero (a character loosely based on Robert, Duke of Normandy, the father of King William the Conqueror) to accept a magic talisman.[4] Their abbess orders the ghosts to waltz, 'Ye once daughters of heaven! Now of hell! Listen to my order supreme!'[5] After being kissed by one of them, bewildered by love, he picks up the talisman, a magic branch, which he hopes will bestow on him 'great power and immortality' with its power to paralyse its victims.[6]

The Italian version of the opera opened at Her Majesty's Theatre on 4 May 1847, just a few weeks after the Irish loan crisis, to an audience which included the Royal Family and the composer Felix Mendelssohn.[7] The reviewer of the first night in *The Times* recorded 'that we never witnessed such a scene of enthusiasm as that displayed last night' by the audience in applauding the performance.[8]

It is therefore unsurprising that a few weeks later, on 29 May 1847, *Punch* magazine used the opera, fresh on Londoners' minds, to satirise the recent economic crisis, also much on people's minds.[9] What was being attacked was Sir Robert Peel's currency policy, based on Lord Overstone's theories, which were held partially responsible for the financial panics of 1847 and for causing the Russell government's plans for the financing of the relief efforts in Ireland to fail. Yet Peel clung to these principles for the rest of his life, despite criticism at the time. The cartoon depicts Peel as 'Robert the devil' – the last part of that phrase blanked out, probably to avoid libel – paralysing John Bull into thinking that he is bankrupt, a situation symbolised by out-turned pockets. Robert uses his magic branch – labelled 'Bank Charter', referring to Peel's Act of 1844, to work the spell.[10] John Bull, a longstanding representation in caricature of taxpayers and the British fiscal state, is shown to be stunned into inaction even though Peel is standing in front of £9m of gold, a sum that Thomas Tooke later noted was equal to the bullion reserves of the Bank of England at the worst point of the crises of 1847.[11] The publication of this depiction of the crisis in such a popular satirical magazine suggests that the influence of Peel's economic

4   Scribe, Delavigne, *Robert-le-Diable*, p. 47.
5   Idem., p. 47.
6   Idem., p. 49.
7   Her Majesty's Theatre, *Roberto il Diavolo: Robert the Devil an Opera in Four Acts* (London: Her Majesty's Theatre, May 1847); *Tallis's Dramatic Magazine and General Theatrical & Musical Review* (London and New York: John Tallis and Company, 1850), p. 6; W. A. Lampadius, W. L. Gage, (trans.), *Life of Felix Mendelssohn Bartholdy: From the German of W. A. Lampadius, with Supplementary Sketches by Julius Benedict and Others* (London: William Reeves, 1876), p. 243.
8   *The Times*, 5 May 1847, p. 5.
9   *Punch*, 29 May 1847, pp. 221–22.
10 Ibid.
11 For the development of John Bull as a caricature of taxpayers and the British fiscal state, see T. L. Hunt, *Defining John Bull: Political Caricature and National Identity in Late*

policies, most notably the Bank Charter Act, in stunning Britain into inaction during the Irish loan crisis was well appreciated at the time.

When the strength of allegiance by Peel and Sir Charles Wood to the Bank Charter Act is understood, it provides an answer to the vexed question of why Victorian politicians seemingly stood by and let Ireland suffer during the famine. Why did starvation, death and emigration devastate an island which was part of the world's wealthiest economy?[12] Part of the answer is that the depth and speed of the famine was astonishing. Most importantly, it completely swamped any agility ministers might have had in adapting British economic policy to Irish needs. The financial impasse that the Bank Charter Act had created explains the policy of retrenchment which held sway in 1847, during a Parliamentary session which has otherwise been called 'a high-water mark of State intervention'.[13] The same reason – economic policy – explains why the Russell government seemed to stand by while so many of its citizens starved or died in Ireland, when, today, it is noted for its contribution to the development of human-rights law, and to the politics of humanitarianism adopted by the Liberals later in the century.[14] The viewpoint from Britain in terms of economic policy provides a stunning contrast to the one from suffering Ireland which has developed into folk memory and legend. Yet both are compatible and equally valid descriptions of the disaster.[15]

Sir Robert Peel, the politician, and Robert the devil, the opera character, also share another startling similarity, as inferred by the *Punch* cartoon.[16] Both hoped for 'great power and immortality', Robert the devil with his 'magic branch' from the nuns' tomb and Sir Robert with the legislation enacting his currency plans as part of his macroeconomic policies, which were intended to grasp the reins of economic fate from Providence.[17] Peel wanted historians to remember his economic legacy in glowing terms, not the emerging protest about the 1844 Act. As Richard Gaunt, a biographer of Peel, has described

Georgian England (Abingdon: Routledge, 2017); T. Tooke, *History of Prices*, vol. 4 (London: Longmans, 1848), p. 332.

12   R. Haines, *Charles Trevelyan and the Great Irish Famine* (Dublin: Four Courts Press, 2004), p. 542.

13   P. Mandler, *Aristocratic Government in the Age of Reform: Whig and Liberal 1830–52* (Oxford: OUP, 1990), pp. 251–52.

14   R. Huzzey, 'Review: *The Slave Trade and the Origin of International Human Rights Law*, J. Martinez', *Journal for Maritime Research*, 14:2 (2012), 139–141; idem., *Freedom Burning: Anti-Slavery and Empire in Victorian Britain* (New York: Cornell University Press, 2012), p. 145; see E. F. Biagini, *British Democracy and Irish Nationalism 1876–1906* (Cambridge: CUP, 2007), p. 39.

15   For an authoritative analysis of folk memories see C. Ó Gráda, *Black '47 and Beyond: The Great Irish Famine in History, Economy and Memory* (Cambridge: CUP, 1989), Chapter 6.

16   *Punch*, 29 May 1847, pp. 221–22.

17   Scribe, , Delavigne, *Robert-le-Diable*, p. 49.

with great insight, 'Peel did not merely hope for his reward in heaven – but in history'.¹⁸ His interest in what posterity would say about him is perhaps only matched by two other British prime ministers: Winston Churchill and Tony Blair.¹⁹ After Peel's early and untimely death in 1850 – a result of a fall from his horse on Constitution Hill in London – his followers edited and published his memoirs and private correspondence to define his legacy as a pragmatist, using his U-turns over Catholic Emancipation in 1829 and the Corn Laws in 1846 as the chief policy exemplars.²⁰ As a result of the Peelites' efforts, he came to be seen by historians as both the progenitor of Gladstonian Liberalism as well as the founder of the modern Conservative Party.²¹ Discussion of the Bank Charter Act was repressed. The interpretation of Peel as the 'chief architect' of the mid-Victorian 'age of stability', in stark contrast to the revolutions of continental Europe, laid out in the twentieth century by Norman Gash, has dominated the historical literature on this subject in recent decades.²² This mirrored Peel's presentation of his own policies as an attempt to provide a stable platform for economic expansion.²³

The argument of this book is that this historical assessment of Peel's policies – one carefully crafted by the man himself – has drawn attention away from their immediate effect in Ireland. Peel pioneered a set of economic policies – that historians would later call 'sound finance' and which inspired the later parsimony of Gladstonian finance at the Treasury – that provided the framework under which economic policy operated in the United Kingdom until 1931.²⁴ This combination of economic policies that Peel implemented and Wood sustained in the 1840s, and the arguably incorrect assumptions upon

18   R. A. Gaunt, *Sir Robert Peel: The Life and Legacy* (London: I. B. Tauris & Co., 2010), pp. 160, 201.
19   Idem., p. 201, citing D. Reynolds, *In Command of History: Churchill Fighting and Writing the Second World War* (London: Penguin, 2004).
20   R. Peel, *Memoirs by the Right Honourable Sir Robert Peel*, vol. 1, vols. 2/3, ed. Earl Stanhope, E. Cardwell (London: John Murray, 1856–57); C. S. Parker, *Sir Robert Peel from his Private Papers*, 3 vols. (London: John Murray, 1891–99).
21   Parker, *Sir Robert Peel from his Private Papers*; D. Hurd, *Robert Peel: A Biography* (London: Phoenix, 2007).
22   N. Gash, *Sir Robert Peel: The Life of Sir Robert Peel after 1830* (London: Longman, 1972), p. 714.
23   A. Hall, *The Opinions of Sir Robert Peel* (London: Arthur Hall, 1850), pp. 477–78.
24   For the link between the Irish loan crisis of 1847 and Gladstonian parsimony see J. Morley, *The Life of William Ewart Gladstone* (Cambridge: CUP, 2011), p. 651 and J. Tomlinson, *Problems of British Economic Policy, 1870–1945* (Abingdon: Routledge, 2006), pp. 46–47; see also for more general background about the importance and duration of Peel's economic-policy regime change, C. Read, 'The Political Economy of Sir Robert Peel', in J. Hoppit, A.B. Leonard, D.J. Needham (eds.), *Money and Markets: Essays in Honour of Martin Daunton* (Woodbridge: Boydell Press, 2019), 71–89.

which it was based, should shoulder a great share of the blame for the failure of the Russell government's relief policies in Ireland.

For many historians already, the role of *laissez-faire* has been an altogether insufficient explanation of the failure of the Russell government's relief policies in Ireland.[25] The response of the British government to the famine involved unprecedented intervention in the Irish economy, on a scale unimaginable before the crisis. The public sector dominated the funding of relief efforts, with approximately £10m coming from Treasury loans and grants, £9m from landlords from Poor Law rates and works schemes and just £1–2m donated by private charitable subscriptions.[26] In its first year of office, in 1846/47, the Russell government massively expanded Peel's relief efforts, spending four times as much Treasury money on relief in Ireland in its first nine months in office as Peel's did in its final year. Charles Wood, Russell's chancellor of the exchequer, whose influence loomed large in Irish policy, was certainly not wrong when he commented that 'so much was never done for any country by another in the history of the world' in that period of the famine.[27] 'The people starved, in spite of the enormous national expenditure', as one astounded observer, George Poulett Scrope, put it.[28] Even after the crises of 1847, when the Treasury could no longer borrow without panicking markets, the hand of government intervention reached into rural Ireland. Taxation was squeezed out of the Irish economy to pay for relief until the 'pips' of Irish landlords and large farmers 'squeaked'. Local taxation soared in Ireland from around 2% of GDP in 1845 to a record-breaking 5% of GDP in 1848.[29] By 1849, in 62 Poor Law Unions, rates reached over 10 shillings in the pound, with one charging 34 shillings 3 ¼ d in the pound – or a tax rate on property of over 170%.[30] Wood intended the

---

25   Robert Montague suspected that the role of *laissez-faire* and political economy had been exaggerated in accounts of the failure of the Russell government's relief policies, but his conclusions were never fully published; see R. J. Montague, 'Relief and Reconstruction in Ireland 1845–49', Oxford University, unpublished DPhil dissertation (1977), p. ii.

26   Figures cited by Robin Haines in 2004; see Haines, *Charles Trevelyan and the Great Irish Famine*, p. 2.

27   Wood to Russell, 9 April 1848, N.A., Russell papers, PRO 30/22/7B/87, ff. 249–52.

28   G. P. Scrope, *The Irish Relief Measures, Past and Future* (London: James Ridgway, 1848), p. 55.

29   For tax data sources see note to Chart 5.3.

30   Combined poundage for Poor Law, cess and annuity for government loan to Poor Law Unions: *Treasury minutes June 1850 prescribing arrangements for repayment of advances to Poor Law unions in Ireland – Report of Poor Law Commissioners in Ireland, December 1851*, PP 1852 (19) XLVII.113, pp. 13–15. Rates collected and not collected: *Return of Financial state of unions in Ireland at time of appointment of paid Guardians: Reports and Resolutions relating to the management of unions under paid Guardians*, PP 1850 (251) L.109, pp. 4–5. Valuation: *Rate in-aid (Ireland) An account of all sums levied and issued* ..., PP 1851 (554) XLIX.513.

legislation to be deliberately coercive when it came to Ireland's upper classes: 'employ the people at wages or you will have to keep them by rates' in the Poor Law system.[31] That was not a policy of *laissez-faire, laissez-passer*, but quite the opposite: an attempt unprecedented in scale in Irish history to redistribute entitlements from the rich to the poor. It was so great in scale that it broke capitalism in many parts of Ireland, encouraging emigration, disinvestment and capital flight.[32] Wood was not lying outright when he told Russell in 1846 that, 'You must not think that I am insensible to the state of Ireland or the necessity of Government interference to an extraordinary degree'.[33] The sort of 'Government interference' that the government pursued was not necessarily the best sort for combatting the humanitarian disaster unfolding in Ireland in retrospect, but it was well intended and was carried out against contemporary *laissez-faire* inhibitions.

Neither does the influence of contemporary ideas of 'liberal political economy', as a monolithic entity, provide a full explanation of the Russell government's failure in Ireland.[34] That is because, as far as matters of currency, banking and how governments should respond to financial crises went, it was no longer a single, coherent ideology.[35] The 1840s marked the height of the civil war within political economy between advocates of the Currency School and the Banking School. Of the two, the Currency School was the greater opponent of *laissez-faire*, with its supporters advocating the strict and rigid regulation of banknote issuance, intervention in the currency market to maintain the fixed value of currency and even the full nationalisation of the central bank by government.[36] It was the ideas of the Currency School, embodied in the Bank Charter Act of 1844, which did much to influence the economic policies that Peel and Wood pursued in the 1840s.[37] As the cartoon of John Bull and Robert the Devil that *Punch* published on 29 May 1847 suggests, it is these economic policies that did so much to stun Britain into thinking it was nearly

---

31   Wood to Bessborough, N.A., Russell papers, PRO 30/22/5 F, f. 248.

32   C. Read, 'Taxation and the Economics of Nationalism in 1840s Ireland', in D. Kanter, P. Walsh (eds.), *Taxation, Politics, and Protest in Ireland, 1662–2016* (Basingstoke: Macmillan, 2019), 199–225, at pp. 214–19.

33   Wood to Russell, 16 October 1846, N.A., Russell papers, PRO 30/22/5D, ff. 214–15.

34   P. Gray, 'A Policy Disaster: How British Famine Relief Measures Failed to Quell the Devastation of the Famine', RTÉ online at <https://www.rte.ie/history/famine-ireland/2020/1123/1180004-a-policy-to-disaster-british-famine-relief-measures> [accessed 31 May 2021].

35   A. J. Schwartz, 'Banking School, Currency School, Free Banking School', in *The New Palgrave Dictionary of Economics*, 1 (London: Palgrave Macmillan, 2008), 353–58.

36   See, for instance, D. Ricardo, *The high price of bullion* (London: Murray, 1811) and idem., *Plan for the Establishment of a National Bank* (London: Murray, 1824).

37   R. J. Moore, *Sir Charles Wood's Indian Policy, 1853–66* (Manchester: MUP, 1966), pp. 5–6.

bankrupt during the crises of that year.[38] Most importantly, it should be noted that not all political economists – or even advocates of *laissez-faire* ideas – agreed with these policies, the Banking School being a particularly notable group of objectors.

Peel and Wood's new economic-policy regime was, at best, a great experiment and a big leap into the dark. Many of the ideas it was based on, including the theories of the Currency School, were new and untested, and the government did not have ready access to all the data needed to fully understand their effect. As a result, these economic policies produced an institutional framework, which, combined with the state of international markets in 1847, meant the Treasury struggled to adequately fund Peel and Wood's policies in Ireland without panicking markets. The failure of British-government relief policy thus stemmed from the failure of British economic policy, which had increasingly baneful consequences for Ireland after 1847.

The main conclusions of this book

Chapter 1 introduced the background to the political and economic scene in 1840s Britain. It introduced Overstone, an influential and wealthy banker, as the principal driver of the economic theories behind Peel's Bank Charter Act of 1844. Overstone's main aim was banking stability as opposed to the social stability that was desired by Peel. By linking the number of banknotes with the bullion reserve of the Bank of England that could be drained by its depositors, his system magnified any pressure on its bullion reserves and on the availability of credit in the economy more widely, but this defect was partly due to the way in which the Act was implemented. The United Kingdom's political and electoral history leading up to the 1840s shows why it did not have a government with the level of political capital necessary to take control of policy, or inspire co-operation to the extent necessary to save more lives in the famine. Providentialism – which in its traditional Calvinist form was falling out of fashion in Great Britain – was a manner of speaking and was often used as an excuse for financial failings.

Chapter 2 examined the motives of Peel in designing the new economic-policy regime of the 1840s. Peel, in 1846, certainly intended to help Ireland during the famine. More than that, he intended to aid the interests of a wide range of social groups across the United Kingdom, making the lives of the labouring classes more comfortable, while protecting the upper classes from class war. Peel developed a whole new economic-policy regime: a fixed-exchange rate with a controlled banknote supply (the Banking Acts of 1844 and 1845),

38 *Punch*, 29 May 1847, pp. 221–22.

freer trade and capital flows (achieved with tariff reductions in 1842 and 1846), and low interest rates and balanced budgets to help pay off the debts incurred during the Napoleonic Wars. He did not see himself as a *laissez-faire* or providential ideologue.[39] He thought he was following a middle course between *laissez-faire*, free trade and free banking on the one side and intervention, protection, and banknote regulation on the other. He researched and worked out how to implement the changes himself, in an effort to become the master of economic forces. However, in hindsight, Peel's economic knowledge was much more limited than he thought. The combination of policies Peel chose increased the vulnerability of Britain's financial system to crisis and the risk that it could lose either control over the value of its currency or control over monetary policy, when faced with a trade deficit. Overstone's currency regime made the loss of control over monetary policy and the pressure on credit more directly linked with bullion flows, internal and external. While Peel may have thought he was acting for the best of reasons, Overstone acted for what can be considered self-serving reasons for the banking community. Yet Peel's overall policy regime was probably more to blame than Overstone's particular currency policies.

Chapters 3 and 4 showed how the combination of Peel's economic-policy choices constrained the ability of the British government to fund relief efforts after 1845. The intellectual descendants of the Banking School and the Currency School would produce different explanations of exactly how those policies contributed to causing the financial crises of 1847. Those economists who acknowledge the Mundell-Fleming trilemma would suggest it was the combination of three policies he chose, and Wood sustained. They understand that the 1844 Bank Charter Act made the effect of the Mundell-Fleming policies stronger. Because it counted both depositors' gold and gold owned by the bank against the note issue, international drains which required the note issue to be reduced became more likely whenever depositors moved their bullion abroad.[40] The currency and commercial departments of the Bank had not really been separated. In turn, fluctuations in interest rates were triggered more easily as the Bank tried to attract bullion back into the country away from high rates in other countries. The Mundell-Fleming model assumes that interest-rate parity between countries operates due to arbitrage, and the 1844 Act encouraged that mechanism. In contrast, adherents of the price-specie flow mechanism may prefer to emphasise the impact of increased food imports, but the effect on relief policy was much the same.

But the link between the April crisis and the sudden speed at which relief was cut in its aftermath is undeniable. The financial crisis matches the changes in policy over Irish relief spending to the day in 1847, unlike other explanations

39 *Hansard*, XXCI, 2 July 1845, c. 1427.
40 Compare with the Horsley Palmer rule which is based on 'Total Liabilities' (Notes issued + Deposits).

for the policy change, which do not correlate closely at all. The October crisis made Wood's abandonment of any further loans, and therefore Treasury advances for Ireland, permanent. Russell's Cabinet explored other ways of sustaining Treasury funding of Irish relief, for instance by raising the income tax or restricting convertibility to enable more borrowing. However, these ideas failed to gain traction in 1847–48 as a result of the weakness of the minority Russell government in Parliament against opposition from the Peelites and the Irish Repealers.

Chapter 5 explored the failure of the Russell government's relief policies to save more lives after 1847. No longer able to advance the funds needed for relief in Ireland through central government borrowing after the financial crises of 1847, the Russell government was forced to find a new way of financing relief efforts. It did so by placing it off-balance sheet, onto that of the Irish Poor Law Unions, and forcing them to fund it from redistributive taxation on Irish property owners. This was very similar to Amartya Sen's theories in the twentieth century about redistributing entitlements during famines. This chapter concluded that Ireland's tax base was too small and its economy too undeveloped to fund the levels of relief needed to reduce excess mortality. It has been shown that the later levels of emigration show a similar pattern to local taxes, as excessive tax rates of 170% or more on property income encouraged the flight of human and financial capital abroad. A study of Kilworth, for which Census records remain, has given a glimpse of a possible scenario of population movement in which some of the poor replaced the middle-classes as they emigrated to America. The dismantling of these redistributive policies in 1853, and the consequent fall in tax rates, caused a parallel collapse in the numbers leaving Ireland for America with a lag consistent with the start. Not only did the redistribution cause emigration but it led to a disaffected community in America with an antagonistic attitude to Britain. This link helps to explain why the Irish diaspora in America became more viciously nationalist than other *emigrée* communities, providing an enthusiastic audience for nationalist interpretations of the famine ever since. Many of the migrants felt that they were forced to leave Ireland because they were taxed out of their homeland by the British government.

Many at the time blamed Peel's Bank Charter Act of 1844 for the fact that Britain was, in economic terms, paralysed as the Irish famine worsened, and were determined to explore financial reforms that would avoid the same problems in the future. The most prominent of these was Earl Grey, the colonial secretary. Chapter 6 explored his alternative policies for the United Kingdom and the success of their implementation in Mauritius. His ideas for reform of the currency, influenced in part by the ideas of the Banking School before the famine, were blocked by Peel and the Peelites in Parliament. However, when a severe harvest failure, a severe banking crisis and the risk of famine threatened Mauritius in 1847, he lost no opportunities in implementing a version of his scheme there. The same overall approach to relief policy was applied in both Ireland and Mauritius: central government should provide a source of funding for relief and allow local organisation to administer and distribute it. The difference was that the Bank Charter Act of 1844 restricted credit during the crises of 1847, making it harder for the Treasury to borrow for Ireland, while Grey's less-rigid policies were more successful at refinancing the bankrupt Mauritian economy. Grey's currency-board system lessened the risk to the Mauritian financial system of specie drains and rising interest rates abroad. All the specie backing the banknotes was owned by the Commissioners and could only be called on by note holders. Depositors could not send it out of the country, as unlike the Bank of England, the currency board had no deposits; a situation that reduced fluctuations in bullion reserves and interest rates. It should be noted that, in effect, control of rates by the Commissioners had been given up and placed in the hands of the commercial banks where it was controlled only by market forces. But the system worked. Mauritius's subsequent prosperity suggests that, alongside the financing of relief policies and local co-operation with the relief effort, the key issue that determined its success had been low and stable interest rates for future investment and development by companies and individuals.

Even so, the reader may ask, did the government use the financial problems and crises of the era as an excuse for pursuing a policy of *laissez-faire* in Ireland that was their real aim? Were the financial problems simply an excuse for letting famine policy drift? The trouble is that such propositions are not based on logic. It is quite clear, particularly in Trevelyan's and Earl Grey's public pronouncements and private correspondence, that the *laissez-faire* explanation is the main one given in publicly published documents, while the financial problems and crises of the era are the issues mostly discussed in private letters. Therefore, it is the *laissez-faire* explanations that are the ones being used to hide the government's financial failings, not the other way around. There is no point in keeping your 'excuse' private and publishing reality. Unfortunately, historians, along with civil servants in later famines in India, have understandably been taken in by the government's *laissez-faire* cover story.[41]

Commentators who have blamed the cutting of relief funding mainly on *laissez-faire*, as described in Chapter 3, have fallen for the confidence trick that

---

41   In the Indian famine of 1866, local officials were punished for using *laissez-faire* policy, which they had read about in *The Irish Crisis* and had erroneously concluded was an established government attitude but was actually considered highly inappropriate by senior ministers at home. Yet Overstone was still trying to push such policies for use in India in 1874: Secretary Board of Revenue Calcutta to Commissioner of Cuttack, 1 February 1866 in *Papers and Correspondence relative to the famine in Bengal and Orissa Pt. II* PP 1867 (335) LI.1, 403, 641, p. 234; *East India (Madras and Orissa) Famine*, PP 1867 (490) Vol. LII.173, for example, p. 221.

was deliberately intended by Overstone and the British government. Problems with the stability of the currency and of the banking system set up by the Bank Charter Act of 1844 were hidden in the belief that this would help raise market confidence and make the issue go away. They were covered up by the fictional reassurance that *laissez-faire* ideas had won through. To the ideologues of the Currency School in the City of London – including Lord Overstone, the guiltiest of the lot – the reputation of the currency was all important, more of a concern than the suffering poor in Ireland. The publishing of Trevelyan's *The Irish Crisis* in 1848 under his name, but influenced by Overstone's views from the start, was intended to show that the threat to financial affairs and the currency caused by the famine was over.[42] The first *Edinburgh Review* article was originally intended by the editor to be written by Overstone to serve this purpose, but he backed out. Trevelyan, the substitute author, added an especially positive emphasis on the Treasury's relief efforts in Ireland (which became the main reason for republication), in part to distract from problems in the City, but also to defend his own personal record and advance his career.[43] Chapter 5 showed that both Peel and Russell, far from being non-interventionists, considered many other ideas for helping Ireland and intended to continue to be highly proactive. But most of their schemes foundered on financial problems and upon objections from the Treasury and the City of London. As a result, eye-watering-ly high rates for Poor Relief, the Rate-in-aid and the encumbered-estates reforms continued after the British Association, and even the Quakers, whose voluntary relief activities are often praised by historians for their generosity, had halted their charitable efforts. It was Overstone's British Association that gave up as soon as possible, far more than the politicians and the government.

Peel: the chief architect of an age of instability?

Despite Peel's successful attempts at managing his own legacy, the research that this book presents has challenged the interpretation of Peel as the chief architect of stability, as least as far as Ireland goes in the 1840s. The history of Peel's economic policies and the famine is a tale of failure and unintended consequences. Peel and Wood appeared to genuinely believe that lower prices, achieved through their economic-policy choices would help the lower classes of the entire British Isles, including Ireland. These policies, they hoped, would provide cheaper food for the lower classes, as well as increased employment,

---

42   '"The crisis" referred not only to the dire emergency caused by the failure of the potato crop, but to the accompanying crisis in exchequer funding'; see Haines, *Charles Trevelyan and the Great Irish Famine*, p. 406.
43   Idem., p. 326.

and would help relieve the famines and slumps witnessed in the 1840s; but the policies made the situation worse causing the financial crises of 1847. Those crises made geographical transfers of relief money from Britain to Ireland increasingly difficult and provoked the failure of redistributive policies to transfer enough entitlements to the poor to sustain them after 1847. The reader must make the final judgement for themselves as to whether Peel and Wood are more to blame than Overstone, the difference being whether the road to hell was paved with good intentions by those in power, or with gold by those who were only advising them.

Peel thought the Bank Charter Act of 1844 would increase financial stability, whereas its application in fact helped to create the crises of 1847 because of apprehension in the City by bankers and investors such as Overstone about the effect of the Irish loan in the context of the new rules on currency. This is an important point because the underlying economic problem in Ireland during the famine was a lack of finance and monetary resources to lure food supplies from abroad. This problem could have been ameliorated by relief spending by the British state assisting all classes. However, such an option was unavailable because of Peel and Wood's economic-policy agenda, which discouraged further loans being raised. Despite that consequence, they persistently clung to their self-imposed rules, which encased policymakers in a 'golden cage', with monetary policy ruled by bullion flows.[44] Mortality levels, caused by inappropriate relief policies during the rest of the famine, were therefore exacerbated by the inability of policymakers to understand how the British and Irish economies functioned.

This lack of economic flexibility and understanding was partly the result of Britain's early industrialisation. There was no consensus in political economy about how currencies should be regulated, and financial crises ameliorated or avoided in a newly industrialised economy, for Peel and other policymakers to fall back on. The debate on these issues between advocates of the Currency School and its critics would continue to rage for decades ahead. Peel's reforms – an attempt to find middle ground between advocates of free trade and protection, as well as between the Banking and Currency Schools – was at best a great untried experiment. It is thus difficult to quibble with the conclusions of the first scholarly historian (and eyewitness) of the Irish famine, John O'Rourke, that, 'to have met the Potato Famine with anything like complete success, would have been a Herculean task for any government. The total failure of the food of a nation was ... a fact new in history'.[45] The government's lack of economic knowledge about how to deal with the scale of the harvest failures, and the subsequent financial panics, that hit the United Kingdom between 1846–47 also

44   'A golden cage does not feed the bird', *Italian proverb*.
45   J. O'Rourke, *The History of the Great Irish Famine of 1847* (London: James Duffy, 1875), pp. 196–97.

contributed to the scale of the humanitarian disaster. In O'Rourke's words, 'no machinery existed extensive enough to neutralize its effects, nor was there extant any plan upon which such machinery could be modelled. ... Great allowance must be therefore made for the shortcomings of the Government, in a crisis so new and so terrible'.[46]

Some scholarship about the history of famines has recently begun to de-emphasise the role of ideology in worsening these disasters, in favour of a focus on poor quality institutions and a lack of economic knowledge as the key factors. For instance, as Tirthankar Roy has recently argued about India, the limitations of knowledge available and the 'fiscal capacity of the state' do as much, if not more, to shape official responses to harvest failures as ideology or malice.[47] The evidence presented in this book suggests that the Irish famine should be added as another example where the outcome was shaped by fiscal constraints and poor economic knowledge.

Some historians have pointed out that the Treasury managed to find £69.5m for the Crimean War of 1854–56, compared with around £10 million from central-government funds for the Irish famine.[48] However, this comparison ignores the contrasting economic contexts during these periods. The failure of the potato crop around the United Kingdom after 1845, coupled with rising prices for imported food and raw cotton, created a trade deficit and a shortage of bullion at the Bank of England.[49] In the 1850s, by contrast, the United Kingdom had built up a trade surplus and the Bank of England had raised its bullion reserves to over £22m.[50] Government borrowing, in sterling banknotes, on a fixed-exchange rate with free capital flows, to pay for imports – whether for food as Irish relief in the 1840s or for war materiel in the 1850s – was thus substantially easier during the Crimean War than the Irish famine. The governments during the Crimean War also commanded large majorities in Parliament that could be easily coerced into supporting the raising of taxes. During the war, the income-tax rate was raised from 6d in the pound to 1s 4d in the pound; indirect taxation was increased too.[51] In contrast, during the

46   Ibid.

47   T. Roy, 'Were Indian Famines "Natural" or "Manmade"?', *LSE Economic History Working Papers*, 243/2016 (2016), 1–24, at p. 5.

48   O'Rourke, *The History of the Great Irish Famine of 1847*, p. 324; C. Ó Gráda, *The Great Irish Famine* (Cambridge: CUP, 1995), p. 49; J. Mokyr, *Why Ireland Starved: A Quantitative and Analytical History of the Irish Economy, 1800–1850* (London: George Allen & Unwin, 1983), p. 291.

49   C. Read, 'Laissez-faire, the Irish Famine and British Financial Crisis', *Economic History Review* 69:2 (2016), 411–34, at pp. 420–23.

50   Haines, *Charles Trevelyan and the Great Irish Famine*, p. 77; Bank of England, daily account book 1852, June–August weekly totals.

51   O. Anderson, 'Loans versus Taxes: British Financial Policy in the Crimean War', *Economic History Review*, 16:2 (1963), 314–27, at p. 318.

Irish famine, the Whig minority government struggled to get taxes renewed, let alone increased. Even Irish MPs, who held the balance of power between Whigs and Conservatives, tended to oppose higher taxes to pay for famine relief.[52] In a Parliamentary system designed to hold large majorities to account, the result was fiscal gridlock.

Therefore, political misjudgement and instability also played a role in the crisis, in addition to economic problems. How did the United Kingdom end up with such a weak minority government after 1846 that behaved less like a purposeful Leviathan and more like a beached whale that struggled to fulfil its basic task of passing legislation through Parliament? The answer is that Peel's decision to repeal the Corn Laws and thereby split his party in 1846 should be seen as catastrophic for Ireland. This unleashed a period of instability in British politics such that between 1841 and 1868 only one government managed to maintain a majority throughout an entire Parliament.[53] The initial demand-side relief policies implemented by Peel's strong and unified Cabinet were relatively successful at minimising excess-mortality levels. However, Peel came to believe that by repealing the Corn Laws by means of a policy of gradualism, economic and political instability caused by immediate repeal could be avoided. In addition, any possible working-class revolt that might be generated by refusing all attempts at reform would be defused.[54]

The result in 1846 was the exact opposite. Instead of holding his party together, the issue split the Conservatives in two. The new Whig government temporarily suspended the Corn Laws in 1847, anyway, and in Peel's view exacerbated the financial instability. The Conservatives' split also resulted in a hung Parliament in which the new government failed to find a majority to raise taxes in order to continue funding his generous relief policies. Attempts at borrowing threatened the credit market and the commercial enterprises that relied on it, causing disagreement over currency policy. Other policies that could have raised funds for Irish relief, such as raising the income tax or reducing convertibility to enable more borrowing, lacked enough support in Parliament because of the political games being played by the Peelites and Irish Repealers. This increased the fiscal burden on Poor Law Unions in Ireland, which lacked sufficient nutritional knowledge and the ability to raise enough money to fully relieve the shortfall of entitlements to food that the Irish famine produced. The result was Irish depopulation, not only through the death and emigration of the Irish poor, but also the flight of human and financial capital of the wealthier classes away from high taxation.

---

52   See, for instance, D. Kanter, 'The Politics of Irish Taxation, 1842–53', *English Historical Review*, 127:528 (2012), 1121–55, at pp. 1132–33.
53   I. St. John, *Disraeli and the Art of Victorian Politics* (London: Anthem Press, 2010), p. 39.
54   Read, 'The Political Economy of Sir Robert Peel', p. 88.

The issue of income tax is intimately connected with the issue of famine-relief funding. The exemption of Ireland from Britain's income tax in 1842 meant that the United Kingdom of Great Britain and Ireland was not a complete fiscal union. This decision contributed to the popular feeling in Great Britain that Irish property should pay for Irish poverty, as Wood firmly told Russell was the attitude in Parliament.[55] British taxpayers felt that they had already done their bit, while Irish landlords had not because of the lack of an income tax in Ireland. After 1847 the will to increase income tax to pay for more assistance to Ireland was lacking because the self-interest of the Irish upper and merchant middle classes, not British economic policy, was seen as responsible for Ireland's problems.[56] Furthermore, as some British MPs pointed out in early 1848, the taxpayers of English industrial towns and cities already felt they were doing their part by keeping destitute Irish migrants fleeing the famine on the English poor rate.[57] Some modern colonial and geo-economic theory is still, in essence, occupied with disputing the historic accusation that the Irish rich were culpable for the disaster, made by the British electorate and its representatives at the time. There was certainly much evidence then for them to point to: Repeal and Irish members opposed 'any proposals likely to cost Irish landowners money', including an income tax.[58] Without an Irish income tax, ministers were unable to raise the British rate to pay for increased relief spending.[59] Perhaps the only firm conclusion that can be drawn from this story is that no-one liked paying income tax.

The decisive role that political crisis played in the late 1840s is illustrated by the British response to the next harvest failure on the scale of the Great Famine in 1879. This occurred during the life of the next majority Conservative government (1874–80), led by Benjamin Disraeli. However, in contrast to the 1840s, high levels of excess-mortality were avoided principally because of the prompt deployment by Disraeli's ministers of relief policies similar to Peel's, funded by advancing loans to Ireland.[60] This was possible, in part, because the government had been able to use its Parliamentary majority to raise income tax from 2d to 5d in the pound and to borrow from previously accumulated

55   Wood to Russell, 9 April 1848, N.A., Russell papers, PRO 30/22/7B/87, ff. 249–52; see Chapter 5.
56   J. S. Donnelly Jr., '"Irish Property Must Pay for Irish Poverty": British Public Opinion and the Great Irish Famine', in C. Morash, R. Hayes (eds.), *Fearful Realities: New Perspectives on the Famine* (Blackrock: Irish Academic Press, 1996), 60–76, at pp. 62–65; C. Kinealy, *This Great Calamity: The Irish Famine, 1842–52* (Dublin: Gill and Macmillan, 1994), p. 345.
57   *Hansard*, XCVII, 29 February 1848, cc. 34–35.
58   Kanter, 'The Politics of Irish Taxation, 1842–53', pp. 1125, 1132.
59   Ibid.
60   *Correspondence relative to Measures for Relief of Distress in Ireland, 1879–80*, PP 1880 (c.2483, c.2506) LXII.157, 187, pp. 7–15 (2483), pp. 6–7 (2506).

funds.[61] The severity of the Irish famine should therefore not only be seen simply in terms of Amartya Sen's entitlements thesis or Alex de Waal's health crises, but also as an unintended consequence of political instability and uncertainty across the United Kingdom, of the sort Martin Ravallion stresses as a casual factor for famine in his research.[62]

In short, the severity of the Irish famine was caused by the failure of central government intervention on a catastrophic scale. The worst economic crisis in the modern history of the British Isles was not worsened by malicious action, nor even a lack of action, but instead by a series of well-intentioned economic-policy interventions that failed because of a lack of political judgement and economic understanding, principally on the part of Peel. The economic, financial and political institutions of the United Kingdom fell woefully short of the responsibilities that harvest failures in Ireland between 1845 and 1853 placed on them. Yet, the record of more successful responses by the British government to other harvest failures both earlier and later in the same century suggests that bad luck also had a role to play.[63] As Peter Solar has shown, the famine consisted of extraordinarily severe and repeated crop failures of more than half of average yields, which lasted much longer than other famines at home and abroad.[64] For this immense disaster, even by the standard of Irish potato failures, to occur in a decade when Peel launched an experimental new economic-policy regime was bad luck indeed. It weakened British financial institutions, and his repeal of the Corn Laws sparked a generation of political instability by destroying the established party system. John Mitchel famously argued that 'the Almighty, indeed, sent the potato blight, but the English created the famine', an accusation much repeated by Irish nationalists ever since.[65] Yet it was in fact bad luck that brought together at one time a harvest failure of such depth and length in Ireland, the zenith of Peel's ambitions for economic-policy reform, and a severe outbreak of political instability in Britain. No British politician intended or anticipated that such a severe, long-lasting and ferocious blight would hit Ireland at a moment in time when British economic and political institutions were least able to cope with the fiscal demands imposed upon them.

61   Ibid.; J. Wormell (ed.), *National Debt in Britain, 1850–1930*, vol. 5 (London: Routledge, 1999), p. 170.
62   M. Ravallion, *Markets and Famines* (Oxford: OUP, 1987), p. 20.
63   See, for instance, L. Kennedy, P. M. Solar, 'The Famine that Wasn't? 1799–1801 in Ireland', QUCEH Working Paper Series, no. 2019-06 (2019), 1–33.
64   P. M. Solar, 'The Great Famine Was No Ordinary Subsistence Crisis', in E. M. Crawford (ed.), *Famine: The Irish Experience 900–1900* (Edinburgh: John Donald, 1989), 112–31.
65   J. Mitchel, *The Last Conquest of Ireland (Perhaps)* [1861], P. Maume (ed.), (Dublin: University College Dublin Press, 2005), p. 219.

Epilogue: pushing beyond disciplinary boundaries

The research presented in this book has shown that it is impossible to understand the British government's relief policies in Ireland, or why they did not save as many lives as intended, simply through a political or cultural approach to the Great Famine alone. It is impossible to fully understand the reasons and motivations behind the U-turn in policy in 1847 without an understanding of the economics at work behind the financial panics of that year. Moreover, it is impossible to comprehend these economic forces without an appreciation of what was going on in food and currency markets across the world at this point in time. Neither is it possible to comprehend why so many people in Ireland continued to die even when food supplies were available and local funding for relief was available without help from the history of science. Not only was a lack of economic knowledge by policymakers a problem, a lack of understanding of modern nutritional science meant that they did not address the problems involved with substituting Indian corn for potatoes as Ireland's staple food.

Furthermore, it is impossible to understand the ideological forces at play over both British monetary policy and the issue of financing Irish relief without an appreciation of the civil war in British political economy that was underway between the Currency School and the Banking School of economic thought. The relative success of more heterodox approaches in reaction to harvest failure and financial crisis in Mauritius suggested that contemporary criticism of British monetary policy and relief policy in Ireland by Banking School thinkers should be taken more seriously by modern scholarship. The fact that economists and historians for generations have dismissed the importance or seriousness of the financial panics of 1847 and their impact on Irish relief policy, because an economist in 1950 erroneously believed the Bank of England had an additional bullion reserve, shows the attention that economic historians should pay to archival detail and representing what actually happened at the time accurately.[66] The new insights offered in this book are not intended as any kind of excuse for Britain's actions, but as an important step in understanding how natural disasters, economic-policy regimes and financial crises interact, to help inform scholars and policymakers in the future.

The methods and ideas used here to reach new conclusions about British financial crises and the Irish famine of the 1840s should be extended to other periods of nineteenth- and twentieth-century history. First, as this book has shown, to understand political history properly requires not only a grasp of social history but a proper understanding of economics as well. The focus

---

66   C. N. Ward-Perkins, 'The Commercial Crisis 1847', *Oxford Economic Papers* 2:1 (1950), 75–94, at p. 89.

by historians on the repeal of the Corn Laws in 1846 is one good example. Although, politically, this event destroyed Peel's original Conservative Party and shattered the established British party system, in economic terms, as quantitative economic historians have shown, 1846 marked neither the beginning nor the end of Britain's progress towards free trade in grain.[67] The obsession with this one piece of legislation has obscured how the broader move towards free trade from the 1820s onwards interacted with the Bank Charter Act of 1844. It was all these legislative changes *together* that formed the new economic-policy regime that more or less lasted until 1931 in the United Kingdom. This book has excavated from the archives what this policy-regime change meant for Ireland in the 1840s and 1850s, but much more research into the long-term impact of Peel's political economy on mid and late Victorian Britain's politics, economic development and financial stability needs to be undertaken.

Second, this book highlights the importance of addressing the history of economic policy in an interdisciplinary way that is not afraid to borrow from the history of science or to use quantitative methods where necessary and appropriate. As quantitative economic historians remind us, the Repeal of the Corn Laws was not an event but a decades-long process. A wider methodological approach points up to political historians that they should not assume that events were the wishes of policymakers just by the fact that they happened. More often, the intentions behind their policies were very different from their actual impact. Policymakers, for instance, thought Indian corn was a good nutritional substitute for potatoes; modern medical science now tells us this was not the case. Historians need to acknowledge more fully that the limited understanding and knowledge of policymakers hampered their efforts to develop effective responses to crises, rather than blaming all their policy errors on ideology. This point is of particular importance for writing the history of famines elsewhere in the British Empire. Unintended outcomes and government failure may have played at least as much of a role as *laissez-faire*, for example, during Indian famines. An embarrassment of incompetence, chaos, and confusion may provide a better explanation for policy failures than ideology alone. As this book has shown, the Russell government's response to events around the British Empire was shaped as much by the anarchic battle between government departments following different agendas – namely between Wood at the Treasury and Grey at the Colonial Office – as by any single guiding ideology.[68]

---

67 P. Sharp, '1846 and All That: The Rise and Fall of British Wheat Protection in the Nineteenth Century', *University of Copenhagen Department of Economics Discussion Papers*, 06-14 (2006), 1–27, at p. 23.

68 This reality is why books about Victorian famines that focus too much on a single ideology are so unconvincing; for instance M. Davis, *Late Victorian Holocausts* (Brooklyn, NY: Verso, 2000).

Third, viewing events through a narrow geographical lens does not produce a full understanding of historical events. The world in the nineteenth century was going through a process of globalisation. The economies and financial markets of various countries and regions around the world were becoming increasingly inter-connected. So British and Irish histories, even when describing events in these countries, need to be considered in a global context. They need to recognise and investigate the growing inter-connections between economic events around the world, not simply make comparisons. The Irish famine provides a case in point. To understand the failure of British relief policy in Ireland requires an understanding of what was happening in London's money markets and commodity markets. To understand what was happening in London's markets requires an understanding of what was going on in markets in Europe, America and even Mauritius in the middle of the Indian Ocean. Indeed, to understand why famine-relief policy failed in Ireland requires an understanding of why it seemed to work in Mauritius. In the wise words of the late Christopher Bayly, 'all historians are world historians now, though many have not yet realised it'.[69] That applies as much to historians of the Irish famine as it does to those of any other event in the past.

69   C. S. Bayly, *The Birth of the Modern World 1780–1914* (Oxford: Blackwell, 2004), pp. 468–69.

Bibliography

Manuscript Primary Sources

Bank of England Archive
Daily account books 1840s.
Court of directors' minutes 1840s.

Bedfordshire and Luton Archives and Records Service, Bedford
Earl de Grey 'Journal of a month's tour' (L31/114/2–3).
Lady de Grey's papers (L30/18/70).
Lucas Archive collection (L30).
'Irish Diary of the Earl de Grey' [1844] (L31/114/17–21).
Transcript of 'Memoirs of the Earl de Grey' [1859] (CRT/190/45/2).
Transcript of 'Earl de Grey's History of Wrest Park to his daughter Anne'
    [1846] (CRT/190/45/2).

Bodleian Library, University of Oxford
Papers of George William Frederick Villiers, 4th Earl of Clarendon, 1820–70
    (MSS Clar.).
Trevelyan Letter Books (microfilm 1186–95).

British Library, St Pancras, London
Gladstone papers (Add. MS. 44358–44371).
Graham papers (Add. MS. 79619–79641).
India Office: political and secret department records (IOR/Z).
Peel papers (Add. MS. 40225–40546).
Ripon papers (Add. MS. 40863).

Cambridge University Library
Graham papers (MF MS. 32–36).
Hickleton papers (MF MS. 1489–1523).

Durham University Library
Third Earl Grey papers and journals (GRE).

ING Baring Archives, London
Ericksen, Irish Loan, Trevelyan letters (HC 3).
Reid, Irving, and Co. (HC 3.62, HC 17.30, HC 3.75).

Lancashire Record Office, Preston
Stanley Irish estate papers (DDK/1701–1712).

Liverpool Record Office, Central Library, Liverpool
Papers of Edward Smith, 12th Earl of Derby (920 DER 12).
Papers of Edward Smith, 13th Earl of Derby (920 DER 13).
Papers of Edward Smith, 14th Earl of Derby (920 DER 14).

The National Archives of Ireland, Dublin
1851 Census records (M4685 and 999/643).
Relief Commission papers (RLFC).

The National Archives, Kew
Confidential prints (CO 882).
Home Office papers (HO/43).
Mauritius, despatches (CO 167).
Mauritius, government Gazettes (CO 171).
Mauritius, Treasury Blue Books (CO 172).
Russell papers (PRO 30/22).
Treasury: Blue Books (T/14).
Treasury: Trevelyan papers (T/64).
War Office papers (WO/63).

The National Archives, Mauritius
Government records (HA/66).

National Library of Ireland, Dublin
British Relief Association, minutes (MS 2022).
Monteagle papers (MSS 13, 397).

National Library of Wales, Aberystwyth
Nassau Senior papers (series C, D, and E).

National Museums, Liverpool Maritime Archives and Library
Customs, Liverpool, bills of entry (C/BE/LIVERPOOL).

Public Record Office of Northern Ireland, Belfast
Caledon papers (D2433).

Robinson Library, University of Newcastle
Trevelyan private letter books (GB186/CET).

Royal Archives, Windsor Castle, Berkshire
Queen Victoria's papers (RA D15).
Microfilm 95709/5.

Southampton University (Hartley) Library
Broadlands manuscripts, Palmerston papers (GC/RU).
Wellington papers (WP/1–WP/2/104/1–19).

Surrey History Centre
Goulburn papers (304, 714).

University College Dublin Archives
Papers of Daniel O'Connell (P12/5–P12/7/57).

Wren Library, Trinity College, Cambridge
Macaulay papers (MAC).

Printed Primary Sources

United Kingdom Statutory Instruments and Publications and other official publications

Published official documents

Census of Ireland 1851, General Report; Part V tables of deaths (Dublin: HMSO, 1856).
Census of Ireland for the year 1861, Area, population and number of houses, Ireland (Dublin: HMSO, 1863).
Hansard reports.
Papers relating to proceedings for the relief of distress and state of the Unions and Workhouses in Ireland, fifth series (Dublin: Poor Law Commission Office, 1848).
Poor Law Unions and Electoral Divisions: reports of the Commissioners for inquiring into the number and boundaries of Poor Law Unions and Electoral Divisions in Ireland, nos. 1–14, HMSO, 1849–50.
Report from Her Majesty's Commissioners of Inquiry into the state of the law and practice in respect to the occupation of land in Ireland (Dublin: Her Majesty's Stationery Office, 1845).

Report on Bengal, Famine Inquiry Commission, India (New Delhi: Government of India, 1945).

Report of the Commissioners appointed to take the Census of Ireland for the Year 1841 (Dublin: Alexander Thom, 1843).

Statutes of the United Kingdom of Great Britain and Ireland 1847 (London: Her Majesty's Printers, 1847).

Statutes of the United Kingdom of Great Britain and Ireland 1848 (London: Her Majesty's Printers, 1848).

Statutes of the United Kingdom of Great Britain and Ireland 1849 (London: Her Majesty's Printers, 1849).

Parliamentary papers

Note: references to Parliamentary papers *are given as: session year, (paper no.), volume in Roman numerals,* manuscript *number of first page within volume. Footnote references to specific pages refer to the* printed *page number within the document.*

Irish Savings Banks, series. 1849 (344) XXX.403, 1852 (213) (213-I) XXVIII.597, 671, 1854 (245) (245-I), 1854–55 (493) XXX.649,1857 Session 1 (128) VIII.109, 1857–58 (55) L.265, 1859 Session 2 (165) (165-I) XV.581, 671, 1860 (584) XL.339, 1861 (470) XXXV.305, 1862 (484) XXXI.299, 1863 (531) XXXI.289, 1864 (449) XXXIV.213, 1865 (439) XXXI.291, 1866 (322) XL.329, 1867 (403) XL.407, 1867–68 (400) XLI.363, 1868–69 (277) LVI.371, 1870 (197) XLI.603, 1871 (252) XXXVII.563, 1872 (201) XXXVI.471.

1832–33 (722) VI.1. *Committee of secrecy on Bank of England charter.*

1837–38 (207) XLVI.377. *Presentments (Ireland.) Grand jury presentments. Abstracts of the accounts of presentments made by the grand juries of the several counties, cities and towns in Ireland (pursuant to act 49 Geo. III. c. 84, s. 31, and 4 Geo. IV. c. 33, s. 18), in the year 1837.*

1837–38 (479) microfiche number 41.139–40. *Minutes of the 1837–38 Select Committee on the Poor Law, 42nd Report, Minutes of Evidence.*

1839 (104) XLVII.573. *Presentments (Ireland.) Grand jury presentments. Abstracts of the accounts of presentments made by the grand juries of the several counties, cities and towns in Ireland (pursuant to act 49 Geo. III. c. 84, s. 31, and 4 Geo. IV. c. 33, s. 18), in the year 1838.*

1840 (41) XLVIII.211. *Presentments (Ireland) Grand jury presentments. Abstracts of the accounts of presentments made by the grand juries of the several counties, cities and towns in Ireland (pursuant to act 49 Geo. III. c. 84, s. 31, and 4 Geo. IV. c. 33, s. 18), in the year 1839.*

1840 (602) IV.1. *Report from the Select Committee on Banks of Issue; with the minutes of evidence, appendix, and index.*

1841 Session 1 (143) XXVII.265. *Presentments (Ireland.) Grand jury presentments. Abstracts of the accounts of presentments made by the grand juries of the several counties, cities and towns in Ireland (pursuant to act 49 Geo. III. c. 84. s. 31, and 4 Geo. IV. c. 33, s. 18), in the year 1840.*

1841 Session 1 (366) V.1. *First report of the Select Committee on banks of issue.*

1841 Session 1 (410) V.5. *Second report of Select Committee on banks of issue.*

1842 (567) XXV.55. *Report of the Colonial Land and Emigration Commissioners.*

1842 (577) XXVI.441. *Return of Grants or Loans of Public Money in Aid of Distressed in Great Britain, 1825–42.*

1843 (459) LI.319. *Correspondence of Lord-Lieutenant of Ireland.*

1844 (530) XXXV.297. *Papers relative to emigration from the West coast of Africa to the West Indies.*

1845 (435) XLVI.68. *Wheat &c. An Account of the Quantities of Wheat, Barley, Oats, Wheat Flour, and Oatmeal, imported into Great Britain from Ireland, in the years 1842, 1843 and 1844; distinguishing the quantities in each year.*

1845 (630) XLVI.683. *An account of the quantities of wheat, barley, oats, wheat, flour, and oatmeal, imported into Great Britain from Ireland, in the years 1842, 1843 and 1844; also, from the 5th day of January 1845 to the 5th day of July 1845.*

1846 (28) XXXVII.33. *Copy of the report of Dr Playfair and of Mr Lindley on the present state of the Irish potato crop, and on the prospect of approaching scarcity, dated 15th November 1845.*

1846 (33) XXXVII.35. *Potato crop. Extract of a report of the commissioners of inquiry into matters connected with the failure of the potato crop.*

1846 (735) XXXVII.41. *Correspondence explanatory of the measures adopted by Her Majesty's Government for the relief of distress arising from the failure of the potato crop in Ireland.*

1847 (32) LIX.493. *An account of ... the Number of Cattle, Sheep and Swine imported into Great Britain from Ireland in 1846.*

1847 (51) LVI.279. *Indian meal sold through government stations.*

1847 (325) XXXIX.115. *Immigration of Labourers.*

1847 (737) (737-II) VI.1. *Report of the Select Committee of the House of Lords on Colonisation from Ireland.*

1847 (761) LI.1. *Correspondence relating to the measures adopted for the relief of distress in Ireland from July 1846 to January 1847 (Commissariat Series).*

1847 (764) L.1. *Correspondence relating to the measures adopted for the relief of distress in Ireland from July 1846 to January 1847 (Board of Works Series).*

1847 (799) XVII.19. *Distress (Ireland) First Report of Relief Commissioners.*

1847 (819) XVII.75. *Distress (Ireland) Second Report of Relief Commissioners.*

1847 (834) (860) XVII.589, 603. *Report of the Commissioners of Public Works (Ireland).*

1847 (836) XVII.103. *Distress (Ireland) Third Report of Relief Commissioners.*

1847 (852) LXX.99. *Letter from the Secretary of State for Foreign Affairs to Her Majesty's minister at Washington, acknowledging the donation in food and money by the citizens of the United States of America, for the relief of the famine in Ireland.*

1847 (859) XVII.143. *Distress (Ireland) Fourth Report of Relief Commissioners.*

1847–48 (61) XLIV.201. *Correspondence with respect to the Condition of the Colony.*

1847–48 (93) LIV.1. *Return of Freight paid by Government on Donations of Food from America, for Relief of Poor of Ireland and Scotland.*

1847–48 (196) XXXIX.571. *Stock and annuities transferred.*

1847–48 (245) microfiche number 52.210–14. *Seventh Report from the Select Committee on Sugar and Coffee planting.*

1847–48 (361, 361-II) microfiche number 52.214–20. *Eighth Report from the Select Committee on Sugar and Coffee Planting.*

1847–48 (395) VIII Pt.I.1, VIII Pt.II.1, 379. *Report from the Secret Committee of the House of Commons appointed to enquire into the causes of the distress which has for some time prevailed amongst the commercial classes, and how far it has been affected by the laws for regulating the issue of banknotes payable on demand. Together with the minutes of evidence, and an appendix.*

1847–48 (399) XLV.75. *West India Colonies and Mauritius.*

1847–48 (415) XVII.1. *Report of the Select Committee of the House of Lords on Colonisation from Ireland.*

1847–48 (454) XXXIX.153. *Return of Number and Amount of Exchequer Bills issued, June 1847–48.*

1847–48 (461) VII.1. *Report from the Select Committee on Agricultural Customs, together with the minutes of evidence, and index.*

1847–48 (565) (565-II) VIII Pt. iii.1, 537. *Supplemental Reports from the Secret Committee of the House of Lords on Commercial Distress; incl. Appendix.*

1847–48 (584) Pt. I VIII.505. *Second Report from the Secret Committee of the House of Commons on Commercial Distress with minutes of evidence.*

1847–48 (923) LVII.1. *Returns of agricultural produce in Ireland in the year 1847.*

1847–48 (983) XXXVII.213. *Commissioners of Public Works (Ireland) Sixteenth Report.*

1847–48 (1000) LVII.109. *Returns of agricultural produce in Ireland in the year 1847 Pt. II – Stock.*

1849 (170) XV.325. *Fifth Report from the Select Committee on Poor Laws (Ireland).*

1849 (194) XV.347. *Select Committee on Poor Laws (Ireland), seventh report.*

1849 (365) XVI.543. *Select Committee of House of Lords to inquire into Operation of Irish Poor Law, Fourth Report, Minutes of Evidence.*

1849 (554) XXXVII.969. *Instructions to Sir G. Anderson.*

1849 (588) L.403. *Grain, flour, &c. Returns of the quantity of grain and flour of all sorts imported into Ireland, from 1st January 1839 to 1st January 1849;*

of grain and flour and other agricultural produce imported from Ireland into Great Britain; of grain, flour and live stock imported into Great Britain and Ireland from foreign countries and colonies; and of British and Irish manufactures exported to those countries; also of the number of emigrants from Great Britain and Ireland.

1849 (1047) XXIII.725. *Final Report from the Board of Public Works, Ireland.*

1849 (1116) XLIX.1. *Returns of Agricultural Produce in Ireland.*

1850 (251) L.109. *Return of Financial state of unions in Ireland at time of appointment of paid Guardians: Reports and Resolutions relating to the management of unions under paid Guardians.*

1850 (460) LII.287. *Price of Wheat.*

1851 (62) XXXI.159. *Public Income and Expenditure: Return of the net Income and Expenditure of the United Kingdom, for the several years ending 5th April 1842–50, respectively.*

1851 (554) XLIX.513. *Rate-in-aid (Ireland) An account of all sums levied and issued.*

1852 (19) XLVII.113. *Treasury minutes June 1850 prescribing arrangements for repayment of advances to Poor Law unions in Ireland- Report of Poor Law Commissioners in Ireland, December 1851.*

1852 (20) XLVII.409. *Presentments Grand jury presentments (Ireland). Abstract of accounts of presentments made by the grand juries of the several counties, cities, and towns in Ireland, in the year 1850--(pursuant to acts 49 Geo. 3, c. 84, s. 31, and 4 Geo. 4, c.33, s.18).*

1852 (152) XLVII.413. *Presentments Grand jury presentments (Ireland). Abstract of accounts of presentments made by the grand juries of the several counties, cities, and towns in Ireland, in the year 1851--(pursuant to acts 49 Geo. 3, c. 84, s. 31, and 4 Geo. 4, c.33, s.18).*

1852 (319) XLV.51. *Poor rate. Return of the gross amount of sums levied under the head of poor rate in England and Wales, in each year, from 1830 to 1851, and in Scotland and Ireland, from 1840 to 1851, stated in pounds sterling, and in quarters of wheat taken at the annual average of the quarter of wheat in money.*

1852 (373) XLVI.357. *Comparative View of Census of Ireland, 1841–51.*

1852 (1466-I) LII.1. *Tables of the Revenue, Population, Commerce &c. of the United Kingdom and its Dependencies Part XX 1850.*

1852–53 (366) XCIV.573. *Presentments Grand jury presentments (Ireland). Abstract of accounts of presentments made by the grand juries of the several counties, cities, and towns in Ireland, in the year 1852--(pursuant to acts 49 Geo. 3, c. 84, s. 31, and 4 Geo. 4, c. 33, s. 18).*

1854 (207) LVIII.367. *Presentments Grand jury presentments (Ireland). Abstract of accounts of presentments made by the grand juries of the several counties, cities, and towns in Ireland, in the year 1853--(pursuant to acts 49 Geo 3, c. 84, s. 31, and 4 Geo. 4, c. 33, s. 18).*

1854 (300) LV.751. *Return of Irish Poor brought to Ports of Liverpool, Glasgow, Bristol, Swansea, Neath, Cardiff, and Newport from the coast of Ireland.*

1854 (346) LXV.529. *Indian corn, &c. Return of the quantities of Indian corn, millet seed, and dari imported into the United Kingdom in each year since 1840, showing the ports at which it has been entered for consumption, and the quantities in each year at each port.*

1854 (396) XVII.1. *Select Committee on Poor Removal Minutes of Evidence.*

1856 (2087-I) XXXIX.261, (2087-II) XXX.1. *Census of Ireland 1851.*

1857 (220) (220-1) Pt. I, X Pt.II.1. *Report from the Select Committee on Bank Acts.*

1857 Session 2 (288) XLII.447. *Returns from each Poor Law Union in Ireland. 1845–55.*

1861 (402) XXXIV.139. *Public income and expenditure. Return of the total income of each year from 1829 to 1860–61 inclusive, as estimated in the budget, and of the actual income received; the total expenditure so estimated, and the actual expenditure; the surplus or deficiency so estimated, and the actual surplus or deficiency; the Exchequer balance at the commencement of each year; and the increase or decrease of that balance at the close of the year; the balance of money raised by the creation of debt or of money applied to the reduction of debt; and the excess of advances or repayments; together with the date of each budget; also the estimated income and expenditure for the year 1861–62.*

1864 (341) XXXIV.395. *Transfer of stock … England to Ireland.*

1864 (538) L.185. *County rates, &c. charges. Return for each year of all charges formerly paid out of county rates, but now paid out of the public taxes, from the year 1849 inclusive to the present time, in England and Scotland; similar return for Ireland; also, return of the sums paid for poor rates in Ireland, in each of the years since the year 1844 inclusive; &c.*

1867 (335) LI.1 *Papers and Correspondence relative to the famine in Bengal and Orissa Pt. II.*

1870 (C 156) XXXVI.1. *Report of the Irish Poor Law Commissioners 1870.*

1878 (69-I). *Return of the name of every member of the lower house of Parliament, microfiche no 84.478-85 Pt. II.*

1880 (c.2483, c.2506) LXII.157, 187. *Correspondence relative to Measures for Relief of Distress in Ireland.*

Newspapers
British Library, Colindale (St Pancras after March 2014)

Bell's Life in London
Blackburn Standard
Dublin Evening Herald
Dublin Gazette
Enniskillen Chronicle & Erne Packet (*Fermanagh Mail* after 1849)
Fermanagh Mail

Galway Vindicator and Connaught Advertiser
Huddersfield and Halifax Express
Kerry Evening Post
Kilkenny Journal
Liverpool Mercury
Liverpool Telegraph and Shipping Gazette
Lloyd's Weekly Newspaper
London Gazette
Londonderry Sentinel
Londonderry Standard
Mayo Constitution
Meath Herald
Morning Chronicle
Nenagh Guardian
Pictorial Times
Reynold's Newspaper
Telegraph or Connaught Ranger
The Anti-Slavery Reporter
The Bankers' Magazine
The Champion or Sligo News
The Colerain Chronicle
The Companion
The (Cork) Constitution or Cork Advertiser
The Cork Examiner
The Drogheda Argus and Leinster Journal
The Economist
The Irish Times
The Lady's Newspaper
The Limerick Reporter
The Newry Commercial Telegraph
The Tralee Chronicle
The Tyrawly Herald
Tipperary Constitution
Tipperary Free Press
United Irishman
Waterford Mail
Western Star

British Newspapers (& Periodicals) 1800–1900 Online

Cleave's London Satirist and Gazette of Variety
Daily News
Freeman's Journal
The Era
The Penny Satirist
Punch

Cambridge University Library
Journal of Agriculture

Illustrated London News Historical Archive 1842–2003
Illustrated London News (London)

Irish Newspaper Archives Online
The Nation

The National Archives, Kew
Herapath's Journal and Railway Magazine
Le Cerneen
Le Mauricien (The Mauritian)

National Library of Ireland, Dublin
Athlone Sentinel
Belfast Chronicle
Belfast Commercial Chronicle
Belfast Newsletter
Dublin Gazette
Dublin Weekly Register
The Citizen
The Nation
The Newry Commercial Telegraph
The Southern Citizen

National Library of Mauritius
Le Cerneen
Le Mauricien (The Mauritian)

National Library of Scotland
Punch

Princeton University Library
The Money Bag

The Spectator Archive
The Spectator

Times Online Archives
The Times

United States Library of Congress: Online Historic Newspapers
New York Daily Tribune

Miscellaneous
Boston Globe
Geelong Advertiser and Intelligencer
The Irish Examiner

Printed Books, Pamphlets and Reports
A member of the Committee of the Church of Scotland, *The Church Considered* (Edinburgh: William Whyte, 1835).
[Anon.] (Third Earl Grey), *Thoughts on the Currency* (London: Ridgeway, 1842).
[Anon.], *The Bank Charter Act in the Crisis of 1847* (London: Richardson Bros., 1854).
Arbuthnot, H., *The Journal of Mrs. Arbuthnot, 1820–1832*, F. Bamford, G. Wellesley (eds.) (London: Macmillan, 1950).
Bagehot, W., *The Works and Life of Walter Bagehot*, R. Barrington (ed.), vol. 3 of 9 (London: Longmans, 1915).
Baring, A., *Financial and Commercial Crisis Considered* (London: John Murray, 1847).
Barrington, E. I., *The Servant of All: Pages from the family, social, and political life of my father James Wilson: Twenty Years of mid-Victorian life*, vol. 1 (London: Longmans, 1927).
Benson, A. C., Esher, Viscount (eds.), *The Letters of Queen Victoria, vol. 1, 1837–43: A Selection from her Majesty's Correspondence Between the Years 1837 and 1861* (London: John Murray, 1908).
British Relief Association, *Report of the British Relief Association for the Relief of Extreme Distress in Ireland and Scotland* (London: Richard Clay, 1849).
Burdett, H. C., *Burdett's Official Intelligence*, vol. 12 (London: Burdett, 1894).
Butt, I., 'The Famine in the Land: What has been Done, and What is to be Done?' *Dublin University Magazine*, 29:172 (1847), 501–40.
Copleston, E., *A letter to the Right Hon. Robert Peel on the Pernicious effects of a variable standard of value* (London: John Murray, 1819).
——, *An Enquiry into the doctrines of necessity and predestination: in four discourses preached before the University of Oxford* (Oxford: John Murray, 1821).
——, *A Second Letter to the Right Hon. Robert Peel* (Oxford: John Murray, 1819).
Curran, J. O., 'Observations on scurvy as it has lately appeared throughout Ireland, and in several parts of Great Britain', *The Dublin Quarterly Journal of Medical Science*, 4:1 (1847), 83–134.

Daunt O'Neill, W. J., *Ireland and her Agitators* (Dublin: J. Browne, 1845).

Dodd, C. R., *The Peerage, Baronetage, and Knightage, of Great Britain and Ireland* (London: Whittaker & Co., 1846).

Dougly, A. G. (ed.), *Elgin Grey papers 1846–52*, vol. 2 (Ottowa: Patenaude, 1932).

Earl Grey (Third), *Colonial Policy of Lord John Russell's Administration* (London: Bentley, 1853).

Evans, D. M., *The Commercial Crisis, 1847–48: being facts and figures* (London: Letts, Son and Steer, 1849).

Fullarton, J., *On the Regulation of Currencies* (London: John Murray, 1844).

Greville, C., *The Greville Memoirs* (London: Longmans, 1885); Strachey, L., Fulford, R. (eds.), *The Greville Memoirs, 1814–1860*, 8 vols. (London: Macmillan, 1938).

Hall, A., *The Opinions of Sir Robert Peel* (London: Arthur Hall, 1850).

Hall, S. C., *Ireland: Its Scenery, Character etc.* (London: How & Parsons/ Jeremiah How, 1841–3).

Hancock, W. N., *Is there really a want of capital in Ireland?* (Dublin: Dublin Statistical Society, 1850).

——, 'On the variations of the supply of silver coin in Ireland during the operations for the relief of distress 1846–47', *The Bankers' Magazine* 7:5 (1847), 340–48.

——, *The Law of poor removals and chargeability in England, Scotland and Ireland, with suggestions for assimilation and amendment: A paper read before the Statistical and Social Inquiry Society of Ireland, 23rd May, 1871; with suggestions on Poor Laws in a letter from Dr. Hancock* (Dublin: R. Webb, 1871).

——, *Three Lectures on the questions should the principles of political economy be disregarded at the present crisis? and if not, how can they be applied to the discovery of methods of relief?* (Dublin: Hodges and Smith, 1847).

Her Majesty's Theatre, *Roberto il Diavolo: Robert the Devil an Opera in Four Acts* (London: Her Majesty's Theatre, May 1847).

Hubbard, J. G., *A letter to Sir Charles Wood on the monetary pressure and commercial distress of 1847* (London: Longman, 1848).

Huskisson, W., *The question concerning the depreciation of our currency stated and examined* (London: J. Murray, 1810).

Inglis, H. D., 'Travels in the Tyrol', *Tait's Edinburgh Magazine*, 3:15 (June 1833), 287–98.

Jennings, L. (ed.), *The Croker Papers: The Correspondence and Diaries of the Late Right Honourable John Wilson Croker* (Cambridge: CUP, 2012).

Labrousse, E., Romano, R., Dreyfus, F-G., *Le Prix du Froment en France, 1726–1913* (Paris: S.E.V.P.E.N., 1970).

Lalor, J., 'Observations on the late epidemic fever', *Dublin Quarterly Journal of Medical Science*, 5 (1848), 12–30.

Lalor, J. F., *To the Landowners of Ireland, Tenakill, Abbeyleix, April 19*[th] (1847).

Larcom, T. A., 'Observations on the Census of the Population of Ireland in 1841', *Journal of the Statistical Society of London*, 6:4 (December 1843), 323–51.

Macaulay, T. B., *Letters of Thomas Babington Macaulay*, ed. T. Pinney, vol. 2 (Cambridge: CUP, 1974–81).

Malthus, T. R., *An Essay on the Principle of Population, or a View of its Past and Present Effects on Human Happiness: With an Inquiry into Our Prospects Respecting the Future Removal or Mitigation of the Evils which it Occasions* (Cambridge: CUP, 1992), (1798 edition), (1826 edition).

—, *An Investigation of the Cause of the Present High Price of Provisions* (London: J. Johnson, 1800).

—, [attributed] 'Newenham and others on the state of Ireland', *Edinburgh Review*, 12:24 (July 1808), 336–55 (review of T. Newenham, *Progress and Magnitude of the Population of Ireland* [London: Baldwin, 1805]).

Melville, L. (ed.), *The Huskisson Papers* (London: Constable, 1931).

Merivale, H., *Lectures on Colonisation and the Colonies*, vols. 1–2 (London: Longman, 1841, 1842).

Mill, J. S., *England and Ireland* (London: Longmans, 1868).

—, *Collected Works of John Stuart Mill*, ed. J. M. Robson (Toronto: University of Toronto Press, 1984).

Mitchel, J., *An apology for the British Government in Ireland* (Dublin: O'Donoghue; Gill & Son, 1905).

—, *The Last Conquest of Ireland (Perhaps)* [1861], ed. and introduction P. Maume (Dublin: University College Dublin Press, 2005).

—, *The History of Ireland: From the Treaty of Limerick to the Present Time*, vol. 2 (London: James Duffy, 1869).

Morren, C., *Instructiones populaires sur les moyens de combattre et de'truire la maladie actuelle des pommes de terre* (Paris : Oret, 1845).

Neave R., Note in *The Labour and Indian Immigration Question at Mauritius. (Report of the Committee appointed for the purpose of inquiring into the causes of the insufficiency of the labouring population.)* B.L. 8132, f.15.

Northcote, S. H., *Twenty years of financial policy* (London: Saunders, Otley, and Co., 1862).

Northcote, S. H., Trevelyan C. E., *Report on the Organisation of the Permanent Civil Service* (London: Eyre and Spottiswoode, 1854).

O'Brien, D. P., *The Correspondence of Lord Overstone*, vols. 1–3 (Cambridge: CUP, 1971).

O'Brien, W. P., *The Great Famine in Ireland: And a Retrospect of the Fifty Years 1845–95; with a Sketch of the Present Condition and Future Prospects of the Congested Districts* (London: Downey and Company, 1896).

O'Brien, W. S., *Principles of Government*, vol. 2 (Boston: P. Donahoe, 1856).

O'Connell, D., *The Life and Times of Daniel O'Connell, M.P.: With the Beauties of His Principal Speeches* (Dublin: James McCormick, 1846).

——, *The Correspondence of Daniel O'Connell*, ed. M. R. O'Connell, vols. 1–3 (Shannon: Irish University Press, 1972–4).

O'Rourke, J., *The History of the Great Irish Famine of 1847* (London: James Duffy, 1875), also third edition (1902).

Palmer, J. H., *Causes and Consequences of the Pressure upon the money market* (London: Pelham Richardson, 1837).

Parker, C. S., *Sir Robert Peel from his private papers*, vols. 1–3 (London: John Murray, 1891–99).

Peel, R., *An inaugural address delivered by the Right Hon. Sir Robert Peel, Bart., M.P., president of the Tamworth Library and Reading Room, on Tuesday, 19th January 1841* (London: James Bain, 1841).

——, *Financial Statement of Sir R. Peel in the House of Commons, March 11, 1842* (London: William Edward Painter, 1842).

——, *Memoirs by the Right Honourable Sir Robert Peel*, vol. 1, vols. 2/3, ed. Earl Stanhope and E. Cardwell (London: John Murray, 1856–7).

——, *Speeches of the late Sir Robert Peel Bart*, vol. 4, 1842–50 (London: Routledge, 1853).

——, *Tamworth Election: speech of Sir Robert Peel, June 28, 1841* (London: John Ollivier, 1841).

——, *The Manifesto by Robert Peel MP, British Prime Minister, addressed to the electors of the borough of Tamworth but intended for a national readership*, published on 18 December 1834.

Price, B., *Currency and Banking* (New York: Appleton, 1876).

Price, R., 'An Appeal to the Public', in J. R. McCulloch (ed.), *A Select Collection of Scarce and Valuable Tracts ... on the National Debt* (London: published privately Lord Overstone, 1857).

Ricardo, D., *An Essay on the Influence of a low Price of Corn on the Profits of Stock: showing the inexpediency of restrictions on importation; with remarks on Mr Malthus's two last publications, 'An inquiry into the nature and progress of rent' and 'The grounds of an opinion on the policy of restricting the importation of foreign corn'* (London: Murray, 1815).

——, *On the Principles of Political Economy and Taxation* (London: Murray, 1821).

——, *Plan for the Establishment of a National Bank* (London: Murray, 1824).

——, *The high price of Bullion* (London: Murray, 1811).

——, *The Works and Correspondence of David Ricardo* [1817 edition], vol. 1 (Cambridge: CUP, 1951).

Scoble, J., *Hill coolies: a brief exposure of the deplorable conditions ...* (London: Harvey and Darton, 1840).

Scribe A. E., Delavigne, G., *Robert-le-Diable, an opera in five acts: With an easy translation, line for line with the French* (London: H. N. Millar, 1847).

Scrope, G. P., *The Irish Relief Measures, Past and Future* (London: James Ridgway, 1848).

Scutt, G. P. S., *History of the Bank of Bengal* (Calcutta: Bank of Bengal, 1904).

Senior, N., *Four Introductory Lectures on Political Economy* (London: Longman, 1852).

——, 'Proposals for Extending the Irish Poor Law', *Edinburgh Review*, 84:372 (October 1846), 267–314.

Sigerson, G., *Report of the Medical Commission of the Mansion House Committee* (Dublin: Browne and Nolan, 1881).

Slater's Commercial Directory of Ireland (Manchester: I. Slater, 1846, 1856, 1870).

Smith, A., *An Inquiry into the Nature and Causes of the Wealth of Nations* [1776] (Oxford: OUP, 1993) (London: Methuen, 1961).

Stanley, W., *Commentaries on Ireland* (Dublin: R. Milliken and Son, 1833).

Strickland, H. E., Melville, A. G., *The Dodo and Its Kindred; or the History, Affinities, and Osteology of the Dodo, Solitaire, and Other Extinct Birds of the Islands Mauritius, Rodriguez, and Bourbon* (London: Reeve, Benham and Reeve, 1848).

Tableau décennal du commerce de la France avec ses colonies et les puissances étrangères 1847/56 pt. 1 (Paris, 1856).

Tallis's Dramatic Magazine and General Theatrical & Musical Review (London and New York: John Tallis and Company, 1850).

Thackeray, W. M., *The Irish Sketch Book* (London: Chapman Hall, 1845).

Thom's Irish Almanac and Official Directory for the Year 1845 (Dublin: Alexander Thom).

Thom's Irish Almanac and Directory for the Year 1848 (Dublin: Alexander Thom).

Thom's Irish Amanac and Dublin Directory, 1851 (Dublin: Alexander Thom).

Thom's Irish Amanac and Dublin Directory, 1853 (Dublin: Alexander Thom).

Thursfield, J. R., *Peel* (London: Macmillan, 1891).

Tooke, T., *An Inquiry into the currency principle* (London: Longmans, 1844).

——, *Bank Charter Act of 1844, its principles and operation* (London: Longman &c, 1856).

——, *History of Prices*, vols. 3–5 (London: Longman, 1840–57).

——, *On the Bank Charter Act of 1844* (London: Longman, 1856).

Trevelyan, C. E., *Statement of Sir C. E. Trevelyan of the Circumstances connected with his Recall from India* (London: Longman, 1860).

——, 'The Irish Crisis', *Edinburgh Review*, 87:175 (January 1848), 229–320.

——, *The Irish Crisis* (London: Longman, 1848).

Twain, M., *The Writings of Mark Twain vol. 6: Following the equator: a journey around the world*, part 2 (New York: Harper, 1899).

Urlin, E. D., 'The History and Statistics of the Irish Incumbered Estates Court', *Journal of the Statistical Society of London*, 44:2 (1881), 203–34.

Walpole, S., *Life of Lord John Russell*, vol. 2 (London: Longmans, 1889).

Wakefield, E. G., *View of the art of colonisation* (London: J. Parker, 1849).

Wellesley, G. (ed.), *Wellington and His Friends* (London: Macmillan, 1965).

Wilson, J., *Capital, Currency, and Banking* (London: The Economist, 1847).

——, *Fluctuations of Currency, Commerce and Manufactures; referrable to the Corn Laws* (London: Orme, Brown, Green and Longmans, 1840).

——, *Influences of the Corn Laws, as affecting all classes of the community, and particularly the Landed Interests* (London: Orme, Brown, Green and Longmans, 1840).

Databases

Bank of England

Three centuries of macroeconomic data spreadsheet and subsequent *A millenium of macroeconmic data*

Bank of England balance sheet weekly 1844–2006, online through <https://www.bankofengland.co.uk/statistics/research-datasets> [address correct at 1 December 2021].

Census populations

Central Statistics Office Ireland online at < https://www.cso.ie/en/census/censusthroughhistory/> [accessed 15 February 2020].

Statistics Mauritius, online at <https://statsmauritius.govmu.org/Pages/Statistics/By_Subject/Population/SB_Population.aspx> [accessed 15 February 2020].

Secondary Sources

Allen, R. B., 'Capital, Illegal Slaves, Indentured Labourers and the Creation of a Sugar Plantation Economy in Mauritius, 1810–60', *Journal of Imperial and Commonwealth History*, 36:2 (2008), 151–70.

——, 'Maroonage and its Legacy in Mauritius and in the Colonial Plantation World', *Outre-mers: revue d'histoire*, 89:366–67 (2008), 131–52.

——, *Slaves, Freedmen, and Indentured Labourers in Colonial Mauritius* (Cambridge: CUP, 1999).

Anbinder, T., 'Moving beyond "Rags to Riches": New York's Irish Famine Immigrants and their Surprising Savings Accounts', *Journal of American History*, 99:3 (2012), 741–70.

Anderson, O., 'Loans versus Taxes: British Financial Policy in the Crimean War', *Economic History Review*, 16:2 (1963), 314–27.

Andersson, F.N.G., Lennard, J., 'Irish GDP between the Famine and the First World War: Estimates Based on a Dynamic Factor Model', *European Review of Economic History*, 23:1 (2019), 50–71.

Antoine, R., Hayward, A. C., 'The Gumming-Disease Problem in the Western Indian Ocean Area', *Proceedings of the International Society of Sugar Cane Technologists*, 11:1 (1962), 789–94.

Ashton, T. S., *Economic Fluctuations in England, 1700–1800* (Oxford: OUP, 1959).

Baines, D., 'Review: *Why Ireland Starved* by J. Mokyr', *Economica*, 52:208 (1985), 524–26.

Barrett, C. B., 'Food Aid as Part of a Coherent Strategy to Advance Food Security Objectives', ESA Working Paper No. 06-09 (September 2006).

Barrow, L., 'The Use of Money in Mid-Nineteenth Century Ireland', *Irish Quarterly Review*, 59:1 (1970), 81–88.

Bartlett, T., *Ireland: A History* (Cambridge: CUP, 2010).

Bayly, C. A., 'Ireland, India and the Empire: 1780–1914', *Transactions of the Royal Historical Society*, series 6, 10 (2000), 377–97.

Beales, D., *From Castlereagh to Gladstone 1815–1885* (London: Sphere Books, 1971).

Beaumont, J., Montgomery, J., 'The Great Irish Famine: Identifying Starvation in the Tissues of Victims Using Stable Isotope Analysis of Bone and Incremental Dentine Collagen', *PLoS ONE*, 11:8 (2016), 469–90.

Bebbington, D., *The Mind of Gladstone: Religion, Homer and Politics* (Oxford, OUP, 2004).

Becsi, Z., 'The Shifty Laffer curve', *Federal Reserve Bank of Atlanta Economic Review* (Q3 2000) 53–64.

Bernanke, B., James, H., 'The Gold Standard, Deflation and Financial Crisis in the Great Depression: An International Comparison', in R. G. Hubbard (ed.), *Financial Markets and Financial Crises* (Chicago: Chicago University Press, 1991), 33–68.

Bernstein, G. L., 'Liberals, the Irish Famine and the Role of the State', *Irish Historical Studies*, 29 (1995), 513–36.

Bevant, Y. (ed.), *La grande famine en Irlande (1845–50): histoire et représentations d'un désastre humanitaire* (Rennes: PUR, 2014).

Bew, P., *Ireland: The Politics of Enmity, 1789–2006* (Oxford: OUP, 2007).

Biagini, E. F., *British Democracy and Irish Nationalism 1876–1906* (Cambridge: CUP, 2007).

——, *Gladstone* (New York: St. Martin's Press, 2000).

——, Daly, M. E. (eds.), *The Cambridge Social History of Modern Ireland* (Cambridge: CUP, 2017).

Bidelux, R., Jeffries, I., *A History of Eastern Europe: Crisis and Change* (London: Routledge, 1998).

Bigelow, G., *Fiction, Famine and the Rise of Economics in Victorian Britain and Ireland* (Cambridge: CUP, 2003).

Black, R. D. C., *Economic Thought and the Irish Question 1817–1870* (Cambridge: CUP, 1960).

Blake, R., *The Conservative Party from Peel to Churchill* (London: Eyre & Spottiswoode, 1970).

Boodhoo, R., *Health, Disease and Indian Immigrants in Nineteenth Century Mauritius* (Port Louis: A. Ghat Trust Fund, 2010).

Boot, H. M., *The Commercial Crisis of 1847* (Hull: Hull University Press, 1984).

Bordo, M. D., 'Monetary Policy Co-operation/Coordination and Global Financial Crises in Historical Perspective', *Open Econ Rev* (2021) paper given at 'From Bretton Woods to 2008 and Beyond: Global Monetary Governance', Brussels, Belgium, 18 September 2020.

——, White, E., 'A Tale of Two Currencies: British and French Finance during the Napoleonic Wars', *Journal of Economic History*, 51:2 (1991), 303–16.

Bourke, C. D., Berkley, J. A., Prendergast, A. J., 'Immune Dysfunction as a Cause and Consequence of Malnutrition', *Trends in Immunology*, 37:6 (2016), 386–98.

Bourke, P. M. A., 'The Extent of the Potato Crop in Ireland at the Time of the Famine', *JSSISI*, 10:3 (1959/60), 1–35.

——, 'The Irish Grain Trade, 1839–48', *Irish Historical Studies*, 20:78 (1976), 156–69.

——, *'A Visitation of God'? The Potato and the Great Famine* (Dublin: Lilliput Press, 1993).

Boylan, T., Foley, T., *Political Economy and Colonial Ireland: The Propagation and Ideological Functions of Economic Discourse in the Nineteenth Century* (London: Routledge, 2005).

Boyle, P. P., Ó Gráda, C., 'Fertility Trends, Excess Mortality, and the Great Irish Famine', *Demography*, 23:4 (1986), 543–62.

Bradshaw, B., 'Nationalism in Historical Scholarship in Modern Ireland', *Irish Historical Studies*, 26:104 (1994), 329–51.

Brady, C. (ed.), *Interpreting Irish History: The Debate on Historical Revisionism, 1938–1994* (Dublin: Irish Academic Press, 1994).

Brebner, J. B., 'Laissez Faire and State Intervention in Nineteenth-Century Britain', *Journal of Economic History*, 8:S1 (1948), 59–73.

Brenton, B. P., 'Pellagra and Nutrition Policy: Lessons from the Great Irish Famine to the New South Africa', *Nutritional Anthropology*, 22:1 (1998), 1–11.

Broadberry, S., Wallis, J., 'Growing, Shrinking and Long Run Economic Performance: Historical Perspectives on Economic Development', *Competitive Advantage in the Global Economy Series*, 65 (2017), 1–5.

Broderick, E., 'The Famine in Waterford as Reported in Local Newspapers', in D. Cowman, D. Brady (eds.), *The Famine in Waterford, 1845–50* (Dublin: Geography Publications, 1995), 153–213.

Brown, L., *The Board of Trade and the Free-Trade Movement 1830–42* (Oxford: OUP, 1958).

Bruner, R. F., Miller, S., *The Financial Crisis of 1847* (Charlottesville, VA: Darden Business Publishing, 2019).

Burroughs, P., 'Grey, Henry George, third Earl Grey (1802–1894), Politician', *Oxford Dictionary of National Biography* (Oxford: OUP, 2004), online at <https://www.oxforddnb.com/view/10.1093/ref:odnb/9780198614128.001.0001/odnb-9780198614128-e-11540> [accessed 26 February 2020].

Cain, P. J., Hopkins, A. G., *British Imperialism: Innovation and Expansion 1688–1914* (London: Longman, 1993).

——, 'Gentlemanly Capitalism and British Expansion Overseas, 1: The Old Colonial System, 1688–1850', *Economic History Review*, 39:4 (1986), 501–25.

——, 'Gentlemanly Capitalism and British Expansion Overseas, 2: New Imperialism, 1850–1945', *Economic History Review*, 40:1 (1987), 1–26.

Caldwell, J. C., Caldwell, P., 'Famine in Africa: A Global Perspective', in E. Van De Walle, G. Pison, M. Sala-Diakandam (eds.), *Mortality and Society in Sub-Saharan Africa* (Oxford: OUP, 1992), 367–90.

Campbell, G., 'Government Policy during the British Railway Mania and the 1847 Commercial Crisis', in N. Dimsdale, A. Hotson (eds.), *British Financial Crises since 1825* (Oxford: OUP, 2014), 59–68.

——, 'Two Bubbles and a Crisis: Britain in the 1840s', *Cliometric Society ASSA Session* (2011).

Cannadine, D., *G. M. Trevelyan: A Life in History* (London: Harper Collins, 1992).

Canny, N., *Making Ireland British, 1580–1650* (Oxford: OUP, 2001).

Carpenter, K. J., 'The Relationship of Pellagra to Corn and the Low Availability of Niacin in Cereals', in J. Mauron (ed.), 'Nutritional Adequacy, Nutrient Availability and Needs', *Experientia Supplementum*, 44 (Birkhäuser: Basel, 1983), 197–222.

Carter, M., 'The Transition from Slave to Indentured Labour in Mauritus', *Slavery and Abolition*, 14:1 (1993), 114–30.

Chadwick, O., *Secularisation of the European Mind in the Nineteenth Century* (Cambridge: CUP, 1975).

Chalmers, R., *Colonial Currency* (London: Eyre and Spottiswoode, 1893).

Chuffart, T., Dell'Eva, C., 'Did Carry Trades Hamper Quantitative Easing Effectiveness in Japan?', *35th International Symposium on Money, Banking and Finance*, paper (2018).

Clare, G., *The ABC of the Foreign Exchanges* (London: MacMillan, 1911).

——, *A Money Market Primer and Key to the Exchanges* (London: Effingham Wilson, 1900).

Clark, J. C. D., 'Providence, Predestination and Progress: or, Did the Enlightenment Fail?', *Albion*, 35:4 (2003), 559–89.

Clarke, A., 'Edwards, Robert Walter Dudley (1909–1988), Historian', *Oxford Dictionary of National Biography* (Oxford: OUP, 2004), online at <https:// www.oxforddnb.com/view/10.1093/ref:odnb/9780198614128.001.0001/ odnb-9780198614128-e-54049> [accessed 8 March 2020].

Clarkson, L. A., 'The Writing of Irish Economic and Social History since 1968', *Economic History Review*, 33:1 (1980), 100–11.

——, Crawford, E. M., *Feast and Famine: A History of Food and Nutrition in Ireland 1500–1920* (Oxford: OUP, 2001).

Clay, K., Schmick, E., Troesken, W., 'The Rise and Fall of Pellagra in the American South', *Journal of Economic History*, 79:1 (2019), 32–62.

Cohn, R. L., 'Nativism and the End of the Mass Migration of the 1840s and 1850s', *Journal of Economic History*, 60:2 (2000), 361–83.

Colley, L., *Britons: Forging the Nation* (London: Yale University Press, 2005).

Comerford, R. V., 'O'Connell, Daniel (1775–1847)', *Oxford Dictionary of National Biography* (Oxford: OUP, 2009), online at <http://www.oxforddnb. com/view/article/20501> [accessed 17 July 2010].

Connell, K., *The Population of Ireland 1700–1845* (Oxford: OUP, 1975).

Coogan, T. P., *The Famine Plot* (London: Palgrave Macmillan, 2012).

Cook, R., 'The General Nutritional Problems of Africa', *African Affairs* 65 (1966), 329–40.

Corporaal, M., Gray, P. (eds.), *The Great Irish Famine and Social Class: Conflicts, Responsibilities, Representations* (Oxford: Peter Lang, 2019).

Cousens, S. H., 'Regional Death Rates in Ireland during the Great Famine, from 1846 to 1851', *Population Studies*, 14:1 (1960), 55–74.

Crabb, M. K., 'An Epidemic of Pride: Pellagra and the Culture of the American South', *Anthropologica*, 34:1 (1992), 89–103.

Craig, F. W. S., Railings, C., Thrasher, M., *British Electoral Facts 1832–1999* (Abingdon: Routledge, 2018).

Crawford, E. M., 'Dearth, Diet, and Disease in Ireland, 1850: A Case Study of Nutritional Deficiency', *Medical History*, 28:2 (1984), 151–61.

——, 'Food and Famine', in C. Póirtéir (ed.), *The Great Irish Famine* (Cork: Mercier Press, 1995), 60–73.

—— (ed.), *Famine: The Irish Experience, 900–1900* (Edinburgh: J. Donald, 1989).

Creighton, M., *Memoir of Sir George Grey* (London: Longmans, 1901).

Crossman, V., Gray, P. (eds.), *Poverty and Welfare in Ireland 1838–1948* (Dublin: Irish Academic Press, 2011).

Crotty, R. D., *Irish Agricultural Production: Its Volume and Structure* (Cork: Cork University Press, 1966).

Cullen, L. M., *An Economic History of Ireland since 1660* (London: B. T. Batsford, 1972; 2nd edition 1987).

——, 'Irish Economic History: Fact and Myth', in L. M. Cullen (ed.), *The Formation of the Irish Economy* (Cork: Mercier Press, 1969), 113–24.

——, 'Irish History without the Potato', *Past & Present* 40:1 (1968), 72–83.

Curtis, R. H., *The History of the Royal Irish Constabulary* (Dublin: McGlashan & Gill, 1871).

Daly, M. E., *The Famine in Ireland* (Dundalk: Dundalgan Press for the Dublin Historical Association, 1986).

——, 'Historians and the Famine: A Beleaguered Species?', *Irish Historical Studies*, 30:120 (1997), 591–601.

Darwen, L., MacRaild, D., Gurrin, B., Kennedy, L., '"Unhappy and Wretched Creatures": Charity, Poor Relief and Pauper Removal in Britain and Ireland during the Great Famine', *English Historical Review*, 134:568 (2019), 589–619.

Daugherty, M. R., 'The Currency-Banking Controversy', *Southern Economic Journal*, 9 (1942), 140–55 and 9 (1943), 241–51.

Daunton, M. J., *Trusting Leviathan: The Politics of Taxation in Britain, 1799–1914* (Cambridge: CUP, 2007).

Davidson, L., 'Can Money Be Neutral Even in the Long Run? Chartalism vs. Monetarism', in L. Davidson (ed.), *Uncertainty, International Money, Employment and Theory* (London: Palgrave Macmillan, 1999), 196–210.

Davis, L. E., Hughes, J. R. T., 'A Dollar-Sterling Exchange, 1803–1895', *Economic History Review*, 13: 1 (1960), 52–78

Davis, M., *Late Victorian Holocausts* (Brooklyn, NY: Verso, 2000).

Delaney, E., *The Curse of Reason: The Great Irish Famine* (Dublin: Gill & Macmillan, 2012).

——, Suibhne, B. M. (eds.), *Ireland's Great Famine and Popular Politics* (New York: Routledge, 2015).

de Nie, M., *The Eternal Paddy: Irish Identity and the British Press, 1798–1882* (Madison, WI: University of Wisconsin Press, 2004).

——, 'The Famine, Irish Identity, and the British Press', *Irish Studies Review*, 6:1 (1998), 27–35.

Devine, T. M., *The Great Highland Famine* (Edinburgh: J. Donald, 2004).

——, 'Why the Highlands Did not Starve: Ireland and Highlands Scotland during the Potato Famine', in S. J. Connolly, R. A. Houston, R. J. Morris (eds.), *Conflict, Identity and Economic Development in Ireland and Scotland 1600–1939* (Preston: Carnegie, 1995), 77–88.

de Waal, A., 'A Reassessment of Entitlement Theory in the Light of Recent Famines in Africa', *Luca d'Agliano (Turin) and Queen Elizabeth House (Oxford) Development Studies Working Papers* no. 4 (1988) and *Development and Change*, 21:3 (1990), 469–90.

——, 'Famine Mortality, a Case Study of Darfur, Sudan 1984–85', *Population Studies*, 43:1 (1989), 5–24.

Dickson, D., Roebuck, P., 'Editorial', *Irish Economic and Social History*, 1:1 (1974), 5.

Donnelly, J. S., 'The Great Famine: Its Interpreters, Old and New', *History Ireland*, 1:3 (1993), 27–33.

—, *The Great Irish Potato Famine* (Stroud: The History Press, 2001).

Doran, Á., 'A Poor Inquiry: Poverty and Living Standards in Pre-Famine Ireland', *Queens' University Centre for Economic History Working Paper* 21-01 (2021).

Dornbusch, R., Frenkel, J. A., 'The Gold Standard and the Bank of England in the Crisis of 1847', in M. D. Bordo, A. J. Schwartz (eds.), *A Retrospective on the Classical Gold Standard 1821–1931* (Chicago: University of Chicago Press, 1984), 233–76.

Dowd, K. (ed.), *The Experience of Free Banking* (London: Routledge, 1992).

Doyle, D. N., 'Review: Cohesion and Diversity in the Irish Diaspora', *Irish Historical Studies*, 39:123 (1999), 411–34.

Dunn, N. R., 'The Castle, the Custom House, and the Cabinet: Administration and Policy in Famine Ireland, 1845–49', University of Oxford, unpublished DPhil thesis (2008).

Eastwood, D., 'Peel and the Tory Party Reconsidered', *History Today*, 4:3 (1992), 27–33.

—, '"Recasting our Lot": Peel, the Nation, and the Politics of Interest', in L. Brockliss, D. Eastwood (eds.), *A Union of Multiple Identities: The British Isles, c.1750–c.1850* (Manchester: MUP, 1997), 29–43.

Edwards, R. D., *Daniel O'Connell and his Times* (London: Thames and Hudson, 1975).

—, Williams, T. D. (eds.), *The Great Famine: Studies in Irish History 1845–52* (Dublin: Browne and Nowlan, 1956).

Eichengreen, B., *Golden Fetters: The Gold Standard and the Great Depression, 1919–1939* (Oxford: OUP, 1995).

Eicher, C. K., 'Facing Up to Africa's Food Crisis', *Foreign Affairs*, 61:1 (1982), 151–74.

Ejrnes, M., Persson K. G., Rich, S., 'Feeding the British: Convergence and Market Efficiency in the Nineteenth Century Grain Trade', *Economic History Review*, 61:S1 (2008), S140–S171.

Eltis, W., 'Lord Overstone and the Establishment of British Nineteenth-Century Monetary Orthodoxy', *University of Oxford Discussion Papers in Economic and Social History* 42 (2001).

English, R., *Irish Freedom: The History of Nationalism in Ireland* (London: Macmillan, 2006).

Erickson, A. B., 'Edward T. Cardwell: Peelite', *Transactions of the American Philosophical Society*, ns 49 pt. 2 (1959), 1–107.

Ernst, R. J., *Immigrant Life in New York City 1825–63* (New York: Columbia University Press, 1949).

Evans, E. J., *Sir Robert Peel: Statesmanship, Power and Party* (London: Routledge, 1991).

Fairlie, S., 'The Corn Laws and British Wheat Production: 1829–1876', *Economic History Review*, 22:1 (1969), 88–116.

——, 'The Nineteenth-Century Corn Law Reconsidered', *Economic History Review*, 18:3 (1965), 562–75.

Ferguson, N., *The House of Rothschild, vol. 1: Money's Prophets, 1798–1848* (Harmondsworth: Penguin, 1999).

Fessha, F., Nam, N. H. T., 'Is it Time to Let Go, the Best Loser System in Mauritius', *Afrika Focus*, 28:1 (2015), 63–79.

Fetter, F. W., *Development of British Monetary Orthodoxy 1797–1875* (Fairfield, NJ: Kelley, 1978).

Fleming, J. M., 'Domestic Financial Policies under Fixed and under Floating Exchange Rates,' *IMF Staff Papers*, 9 (1962), 369–79.

Flinn, M. W. (ed.), *Scottish Population History from the 17th Century to the 1930s* (Cambridge: CUP, 1977).

Fogel, R. W., 'Second Thoughts on the European Escape from Hunger: Famine, Chronic Malnutrition and Mortality Rates', in S. R. Osmani (ed.), *Nutrition and Poverty* (Oxford: Clarendon Press, 1992), 244–86.

Foley, T., O'Connor, M., *Ireland and Empire: Colonies, Culture, and Empire* (Dublin: Irish Academic Press, 2006).

Forker, M., 'The Use of the "Cartoonist's Armoury" in Manipulating Public Opinion: Anti-Irish Imagery in 19th Century British and American Periodicals', *Journal of Irish Studies*, 27:1 (2012), 58–71.

Foster, R. F., *Modern Ireland 1600–1972* (London: Penguin, 1989).

——, 'The Problems of Writing Irish History', *History Today*, 34:1 (1984), 27–30.

——, Gray, P., 'Interview: Our Man at Oxford', *History Ireland*, 1:3 (1993), 9–12.

Fotheringham, A. S., Kelly, M. H., Treacy, C., NCG Online Atlas Portal (2011), online at <http://ncg.nuim.ie/historical-atlas> [accessed 30 July 2014].

Fotheringham, A. S., Kelly, M. H., Charlton, M., 'The Demographic Impacts of the Irish Famine: Towards a Greater Geographical Understanding', *Transactions of the Institute of British Geographers*, 38:2 (2013), 221–37.

Frame, I., 'Between the "Bank Screw" and "Affording Assistance": Rules, Standards and the Bank Charter Act of 1844', *Modern Law Review*, 83:1 (2019), 64–90.

Fraser, D., 'Voluntaryism and West Riding Politics in the Mid-Nineteenth Century', *Northern History*, 13:1 (1977), 199–231.

Freeman, T. W., *Pre-Famine Ireland: A Study in Historical Geography* (Manchester: MUP, 1957).

Friedman, M., 'Quantity Theory of Money', in *The New Palgrave Dictionary of Economics*, 6 (London: Palgrave Macmillan, 2008), 793–815.

Gambles, A., *Protection and Politics: Conservative Economic Discourse, 1815–52* (London/Woodbridge: the Boydell Press in association with the Royal Historical Society, 1999).

Garner, E., *To Die by Inches: The Famine in North East Cork* (Fermoy: EIGSE Books, 1988).

Gash, N., *Mr Secretary Peel: The Life of Sir Robert Peel to 1830* (London: Longman, 1961).

——, 'Peel and the Party System 1830–50', *Transactions of the Royal Historical Society*, 5th series, 1 (1951), 47–69.

——, 'Review: *Correspondence of Lord Overstone* by D. P. O'Brien', *The English Historical Review*, 88:34 (1973), 395–98.

——, *Sir Robert Peel: The Life of Sir Robert Peel after 1830* (London: Longman, 1972).

Gaunt, R. A., *Sir Robert Peel: The Life and Legacy* (London: I. B. Tauris & Co., 2010).

——, 'Peel's Other Repeal: The Test and Corporation Acts, 1828', *Parliamentary History*, 33:1 (2014), 243–62.

Geber, J., Murphy, E., 'Scurvy in the Great Irish Famine', *American Journal of Physical Anthropology*, 148:4 (2012), 512–24.

Geoghegan, P. M., *Liberator: The Life and Death of Daniel O'Connell 1830–1847* (Dublin: Gill & Macmillan, 2010).

Ghosh, P., Goldman, L. (eds.), *Politics and Culture in Victorian Britain: Essays in Memory of Colin Matthew* (Oxford: OUP, 2006).

Gilley, S., Swift, R. (eds.), *The Irish in the Victorian City* (Beckenham: Croom Helm, 1985).

Gillissen, C., 'Charles Trevelyan, John Mitchel and the Historiography of the Great Famine', *Revue française de civilisation britannique*, 19:2 (2014), 195–212.

——, *Une relation unique: les relations irlando-britanniques de 1921 à 2001* (Caen: Presses universitaires de Caen, 2013).

Gonner, C. K., 'Ricardo and his Critics', *Quarterly Journal of Economics*, 4:3 (1890), 276–90.

Goodbody, R., 'The Quakers and the Famine', *History Ireland*, 6:1 (1998), 28–29.

Goodhart, C., 'Monetary Regimes: Then and Now', in S. Dow et al. (eds.), *Money, Method and Contemporary Post-Keynesian Economics* (London: Edward Elgar, 2018), 1–11.

——, 'The Bank of England, 1694–2017', in R. Edvinsson, T. Jacobson, D. Waldenström (eds.), *Sveriges Riksbank and the History of Central Banking Studies in Macroeconomic History* (Cambridge: CUP, 2018), 143–71.

——, Jensen, M., 'Currency School versus Banking School: An Ongoing Confrontation', LSE Research Online Documents on Economics 64068, LSE Library (2015) online at <https://EconPapers.repec.org/RePEc:ehl:lserod:64068> [accessed 12 January 2020].

Goodspeed, T. B. 'Microcredit and Adjustment to Environmental Shock: Evidence from the Great Famine in Ireland', *University of Oxford Working Paper* (2014). Also *Journal of Development Economics*, 121:S1 (2016), 258–77.

Götz, N., Brewis G., Werther, S., *Humanitarianism in the Modern World: The Moral Economy of Famine Relief* (Cambridge: CUP, 2020).

Graham, A. H., 'The Lichfield House Compact', *Irish Historical Studies*, 12:47 (1961), 209–25.

Grant, J., 'The Great Famine and the Poor Law in Ulster: The Rate-in-aid Issue of 1849', *Irish Historical Studies*, 27:105 (1990), 30–47.

Gray, P., 'A Policy Disaster: How British Famine Relief Measures Failed to Quell the Devastation of the Famine', RTÉ, online at <https://www.rte.ie/history/famine-ireland/2020/1123/1180004-a-policy-to-disaster-british-famine-relief-measures> [accessed 31 May 2021].

——, *Famine, Land and Politics: British Government and Irish Society 1843–50* (Dublin: Irish Academic Press, 1999).

——, 'Ideology and the Famine', in C. Póirtéir (ed.), *The Great Irish Famine* (Cork: Mercier Press, 1995), 86–103.

——, 'Irish Social Thought and the Relief of Poverty, 1847–80', *Transactions of the Royal Historical Society*, 20 (2010), 141–56.

——, 'National Humiliation and the Great Hunger: Fast and Famine in 1847', *Irish Historical Studies*, 32:126 (2000), 193–216.

——, 'Polemic without Plausibility', *The Irish Times*, 19 January 2013, online at <https://www.irishtimes.com/culture/books/polemic-without-plausibility-1.963743> [accessed 29 March 2021].

——, 'Potatoes and Providence: British Government Responses to the Great Famine', *Bullán*, 1:1 (1994), 75–90.

——, 'Review: The Great Irish Famine', *History Ireland*, 10:1 (2002), 49–52.

——, '"The Great British Famine of 1845–50"? Ireland, the UK and Peripherality in Famine Relief and Philanthropy', in D. Curran, L. Luciuk, A. Newby (eds.), *Famines in European Economic History: The Last Great European Famines Reconsidered* (London: Routledge, 2015), 83–96.

——, 'The Great Famine, 1845–1850', in T. Bartlett, J. Kelly (eds.), *The Cambridge History of Ireland*, 3 (Cambridge: CUP, 2018), 639–65.

——, *The Irish Famine* (New York: Abrams, 1995).

——, 'The Irish Poor Law and the Great Famine', IEHC Session 123 (2006), 1–17, online at <http://www.helsinki.fi/iehc2006/papers3/Gray.pdf> [accessed 27 February 2014].

——, 'The Making of Mid-Victorian Ireland: Political Economy and the Memory of the Great Famine', in P. Gray (ed.), *Victoria's Ireland?* (Dublin: Four Courts Press, 2004), 151–66.

——, O. Purdue, *The Irish Lord Lieutenancy* (Dublin: University College Dublin Press, 2012).

Green, E. R. R., 'Agriculture', in R. D. Edwards, T. D. Williams (eds.), *The Great Famine: Studies in Irish History 1845–52* (Dublin: Browne and Nolan, 1956), 89–128.

Gregory, T. E., Henderson, A., *The Westminster Bank through a Century* (London: OUP, 1936).

Griffiths, O., Huron, J-M., Carter, M., *Piastres to Polymer* (Mauritius: Bioculture Press, 2018).

Grigg, D., 'Farm Size in England and Wales from Early Victorian Times to the Present', *Agricultural History Review*, 35:2 (1987), 179–89.

——, *Population Growth and Agrarian Change: An Historical Perspective* (Cambridge: CUP, 1980).

Grimley, M., 'The Religion of Englishness: Puritanism, Providentialism, and "National Character", 1918–1945', *Journal of British Studies*, 46:4 (2007), 884–906.

Haines, R., *Charles Trevelyan and the Great Irish Famine* (Dublin: Four Courts Press, 2004).

——, *Emigration and the Labouring Poor: Australian Recruitment in Britain and Ireland, 1831–60* (London: Palgrave Macmillan, 1997).

——, 'Trevelyan, Sir Charles Edward (1807–86)', *Dictionary of Irish Biography* (October 2009), online at < https://www.dib.ie/biography/trevelyan-sir-charles-edward-a8647> [accessed 21 January 2021].

Hall, F. G., *History of the Bank of Ireland* (Dublin, Hodges, Figgis & Co., 1949).

Hanke, S. H., 'Exchange Rate Regimes and Capital Flows', *Annals of the American Academy of Political and Social Science*, 579:1 (2002), 87–107.

Hart, J., 'Sir Charles Trevelyan at the Treasury', *English Historical Review*, 75:294 (1960), 92–110.

Hartigan, R., 'Review: *Human Encumbrances: Political Violence and the Great Irish Famine*', *Irish Geography*, 45:3 (2012), 292–94.

Hazarreesingh, K., *Histoire des Indiens à l'Île Maurice* (Paris: Adrien Maisonneuve, 1973).

Hennessy, P., *Whitehall* (London: Secker & Warburg, 1989).

Hidrobo, M., Hoddinott, J., Peterman, A., Margolies, A., Moreira, V., 'Cash, Food, or Vouchers? Evidence from a Randomised Experiment in Northern Ecuador', *Journal of Development Economics*, 107(C) (2014), 144–56.

Hilton, B., *A Mad, Bad, and Dangerous People? England 1783–1846* (Oxford: OUP, 2006).

——, *Cash, Corn, Commerce: The Economic Policies of the Tory Governments 1815–1830* (Oxford: OUP, 1977).

——, *The Age of Atonement: The Influence of Evangelicalism on Social and Economic Thought, 1795–1865* (Oxford: OUP, 1988).

——, 'Peel: A Reappraisal', *Historical Journal*, 22:3 (1979), 585–614.

——, 'The Ripening of Robert Peel', in M. Bentley (ed.), *Essays in British History Presented to Maurice Cowling* (Cambridge: CUP, 1993), 63–84.

——, 'Whiggery, Religion and Social Reform: The Case of Lord Morpeth', *Historical Journal*, 37:4 (1994), 829–59.

Hobsbawm, E. J., *Labouring Men: Studies in the History of Labour* (London, 1964).

——,Wrigley, C., *Industry and Empire: From 1750 to the Present Day* (New York: The New Press, 1999).

Honohan, P., 'Currency Board or Central Bank? Lessons from the Irish Pound's Link with Sterling 1928–79', *Banca Nazionale del Lavoro Quarterly Review*, 50:200 (1997), 39–67.

Hoppen, K. T., *Elections, Politics, and Society in Ireland 1832–1885* (Oxford: OUP, 1984).

Horsefield, J. K., 'The Origins of the Bank Charter Act, 1844', *Economica*, NS 11:44 (1944), 180–89.

Hourihan, K., 'The Cities and Towns of Ireland', in J. Crowley, W. J. Smyth, M. Murphy (eds.), *Atlas of the Great Famine, 1845–52* (Cork: Cork University Press, 2012), 228–39.

Howe, A., *Free Trade and Liberal England 1846–1946* (Oxford: OUP, 1997).

Hughes, J. R. T., 'The Commercial Crisis of 1857', *Oxford Economic Papers*, 8:2 (1956), 194–222.

Hunt, T. L., *Defining John Bull: Political Caricature and National Identity in Late Georgian England* (Abingdon: Routledge, 2017).

Hurd, D., *Robert Peel: A Biography* (London: Phoenix, 2007).

Hutch, R. K., *The Radical Lord Radnor: The Public Life of Viscount Folkestone, Third Earl of Radnor (1779–1869)* (Minneapolis: University of Minnesota Press, 1977).

Huzzey, R., *Freedom Burning: Anti-Slavery and Empire in Victorian Britain* (New York: Cornell University Press, 2012).

——, 'Review: *The Slave Trade and the Origin of International Human Rights Law*', *Journal for Maritime Research*, 14:2 (2012), 139–41.

Ingelbien, R., 'Irish Studies, the Postcolonial Paradigm and the Comparative Mandate', in J. P. Byrne, P. Kirwan, M. O'Sullivan (eds.), *Affecting Irishness: Negotiating Cultural Identity within and beyond the Nation* (Bern: Peter Lang, 2009), 21–41.

Institute for Economics & Peace, *Global Peace Index 2019: Measuring Peace in a Complex World* (Sydney: Institute for Economics & Peace, 2019).

Irwin, D. A., 'Political Economy and Peel's Repeal of the Corn Laws', *Economics and Politics*, 1:1 (1989), 41–59.

——, Chepeliev, M. G., 'The Economic Consequences of Sir Robert Peel', *NBER Working Paper* no. 28142 (2021), 1–33.

Jappah, J. V., Smith, D. T., 'State Sponsored Famine: Conceptualizing Politically
    Induced Famine as a Crime against Humanity', *Journal of International and
    Global Studies*, 4:1 (2012), 17–31.
Jenkins, B., *Irish Nationalism and the British State* (Montreal: McGill-Queen's
    University Press, 2006).
——, *Henry Goulburn 1784–1856: A Political Biography* (Liverpool: Liverpool
    University Press, 1996).
Jenkins, T. A., *Sir Robert Peel* (New York: St Martin's Press, 1999).
Jones, W. D., *Prosperity Robinson: The Life of Viscount Goderich 1782–1859*
    (London: Macmillan, 1967).
Jordan, D., 'The Famine and its Aftermath in County Mayo', in C. Morash, R.
    Hayes (eds.), *Fearful Realities: New Perspectives on the Famine* (Blackrock,
    Irish Academic Press: 1996), 35–48.
Jowitt, J.A., 'Parliamentary Politics in Halifax, 1832–1847', *Northern History*,
    12 (1976), 172–201.
Kanter, D., 'The Politics of Irish Taxation, 1842–53', *English Historical Review*,
    127:528 (2012), 1121–55.
——, 'Post-Famine Politics, 1850–1879', in T. Bartlett, J. Kelly (eds.), *The
    Cambridge History of Ireland* (Cambridge: CUP, 2018), 688–715.
Katona, G., *Psychological Economics* (New York: Elsevier, 1975).
Katona, P., Katona-Apte, J., 'The Interaction between Nutrition and Infection',
    Clinical Infectious Diseases, 46:10 (2008), 1582–88.
Kee, R., *Ireland: A History, New Edition* (London: Abacus, 2008).
——, *The Green Flag: A History of Irish Nationalism* (London: Penguin,
    2000).
Kelly, J., 'Coping with Crisis: The Response to the Famine of 1740', *Eighteenth
    Century Ireland*, 27 (2012), 99–122.
——, *Food Rioting in Ireland in the Eighteenth and Nineteenth Centuries: The
    'Moral Economy' and the Irish Crowd* (Dublin: Four Courts Press, 2017).
Kennedy, L., *Colonialism, Religion and Nationalism in Ireland* (Belfast: The
    Institute of Irish Studies, 1997).
——, 'The Cost of Living in Ireland 1698–1998', *Historical National Accounting
    Group paper* (January 2002).
——, *Unhappy the Land: The Most Oppressed People Ever, the Irish?* (Sallins:
    Merrion Press, 2015).
Kennedy, L., Ell, P. S., Crawford, E. M., Clarkson, L. A., *Mapping the Great
    Irish Famine* (Dublin: Four Courts Press, 1999).
Kennedy, L., Solar, P. M., 'Market and Price Fluctuations in England and
    Ireland, 1785–1913', paper presented at *Trinity College Dublin* (2011).
——, 'Markets and Price Fluctuations in England and Ireland, 1785–1913', in
    R. J. Van der Spek, J. L. van Zanden, B. van Leeuwen (eds.), *A History
    of Market Performance: From Ancient Babylonia to the Modern World*
    (London: Routledge, 2015), 287–307.

——, 'The Famine that Wasn't? 1799–1801 in Ireland', QUCEH Working Paper Series, No. 2019-06 (2019), 1–33.

Kenny, K., 'Ireland in the Empire', in K. Kenny (ed.), *Ireland and the British Empire* (Oxford: OUP, 2004), 90–122.

Kiernan, B., 'From Irish Famine to Congo Reform: Nineteenth-Century Roots of International Human Rights Law and Activism', in R. Provost, P. Akhavan (eds.), *Confronting Genocide* (London: Springer, 2011), 13–44.

Killeen, J., *The Fairy Tales of Oscar Wilde* (Farnham: Ashgate, 2013).

Kindleberger, C. P., *Manias, Panics, and Crashes: A History of Financial Crises* (London: Macmillan, 1978) (New York: Wiley, 2005).

Kinealy, C., 'Beyond Revisionism: Reassessing the Irish Famine', *History Ireland* 3:4 (1995), 28–34.

——, '"Brethren in Bondage": Chartists, O'Connellites, Young Irelanders and the 1848 Uprising', in F. Lane, D. Ó Drisceoil (eds.), *Politics and the Irish Working Class, 1830–1945* (London: Palgrave Macmillan, 2005), 87–111.

——, 'The British Relief Association and the Great Famine in Ireland', *Revue Française de Civilisation Britanique*, 19:2 (2014), 49–66.

——, *Charity and the Great Hunger in Ireland: The Kindness of Strangers* (London: Bloomsbury Academic Press, 2013).

——, *A Death-Dealing Famine: The Great Hunger in Ireland* (London: Pluto Press, 1997).

——, 'Food Exports from Ireland 1846–47', *History Ireland*, 5:1 (1997), 32–36.

——, *The Great Irish Famine: Impact, Ideology and Rebellion* (New York: Palgrave, 2002).

——, 'Peel, Rotten Potatoes and Providence', in A. Marrison (ed.), *Free Trade and its Reception 1815–1960: Freedom and Trade: vol. 1* (London: Routledge, 1998), 50–62.

——, 'Potatoes, Providence and Philanthropy: The Role of Private Charity during the Irish Famine', in P. O'Sullivan (ed.), *The Irish Worldwide: vol. 6: The Meaning of the Famine* (London: Leicester University Press, 1997), 140–71.

——, *Repeal and Revolution: 1848 in Ireland* (Manchester: MUP, 2009).

——, *This Great Calamity: The Irish Famine, 1845–52* (Dublin: Gill and Macmillan, 1994).

——, 'Was Ireland a Colony?' in T. McDonough (ed.), *Was Ireland a Colony? Economics, Politics and Culture in Nineteenth-Century Ireland* (Dublin: Irish Academic Press, 2005), 48–65.

Kingdon, R. M., 'Laissez-Faire or Government Control: A Problem for John Wesley', *Church History*, 26 (1957), 342–54.

Kinzer, B. L., *England's Disgrace: J. S. Mill and the Irish Question* (Toronto: University and Toronto Press, 2001).

Kissane, N. *The Irish Famine: A Documentary History* (Dublin: National Library of Ireland, 1995).

Knobel, D. T., '"Celtic Exodus": The Famine Irish, Ethnic Stereotypes, and the Cultivation of American Racial Nationalism', 2:November *Radharc* (2001), 3–25.

Kollewe J., Farrell, S., 'UK Bonds that Financed First World War to Be Redeemed 100 Years Later: Treasury's Redemption Scheme Stretches All the Way Back to Napoleonic and Crimean Wars and Irish Potato Famine', *The Guardian*, 31 October 2014, online at <http://www.theguardian.com/business/2014/oct/31/uk-first-world-war-bonds-redeemed> [accessed 5 November 2014].

Kynaston, D. (abridged D. Milner), *City of London: The History* (London: Chatto & Windus, 2012).

——, *Till Times Last Sand: A History of the Bank of England* (London: Bloomsbury, 2020).

Laffer, A., 'The Laffer Curve: Past, Present and Future', *Backgrounder*, Heritage Foundation, 1 June 2004, 1–16.

Lagesse, M., *150 Années de Jeunesse* (Port Louis: Caravelle, 1988).

Lane, P. G., 'The Management of Estates by Financial Corporations in Ireland after the Famine', *Studia Hibernica*, 14 (1974), 67–89.

Latham, M. C., *Human Nutrition in the Developing World* (Rome: Food and Agriculture Organisation of the United Nations, 1997).

Lebow, R. N., *White Britain and Black Ireland: The Influence of Stereotypes on Colonial Policy* (Philadelphia: Institute for the Study of Human Issues, 1976).

Lentz, E., Barrett, C. B., Hoddinott, J., 'Food Aid and Dependency: Implications for Emergency Food Security Assessments', *International Food Policy Research Institute Discussion Paper* no. 12:2 (2005).

Lewy, G., 'Can there Be Genocide without the Intent to Commit Genocide?' *Journal of Genocide Research*, 9:4 (2007), 661–74.

Lindert, P. H., 'Poor Relief before the Welfare State: Britain versus the Continent, 1780–1880', *European Review of Economic History*, 2:2 (1998), 101–40.

Lloyd, D., 'After History: Historicism and Irish Postcolonial Studies', in C. Carroll, P. King (eds.), *Ireland and Postcolonial Theory* (Cork: Cork University Press, 2003), 46–62.

Lyons, J. S., Cain, L. P., Williamson, S. H. (eds.), *Reflections on the Cliometrics Revolution* (Abingdon: Routledge, 2008).

Macaulay, A., 'William Crolly, Archbishop of Armagh 1835–49', *Seanchas Ardmhacha: Journal of the Armagh Diocesan Historical Society*, 14:1 (1990), 1–19.

——, *William Crolly: Archbishop of Armagh, 1835–49* (Dublin: Four Courts Press, 1994).

MacDonagh, O., *Early Victorian Government 1830–1870* (London: Holmes & Meier, 1977).

——, *States of Mind: A study of Anglo-Irish Conflict, 1780–1980* (London: Harper Collins, 1983).

——, 'The Irish Famine Emigration to the United States and the British Colonies during the Famine', in R. D. Edwards, T. D. Williams (eds.), *The Great*

Famine: Studies in Irish History 1845–52 (Dublin: Browne & Nolan, 1956), 319–90.

MacIntyre, A., *The Liberator: Daniel O'Connell and the Irish Party 1830–1847* (London: Hamish Hamilton, 1965).

Mandler, P., *Aristocratic Government in the Age of Reform: Whig and Liberal 1830–52* (Oxford: OUP, 1990).

Martinez, J. S., *The Slave Trade and the Origins of International Human Rights Law* (Oxford: OUP, 2012).

Masterson, J., *County Cork, Ireland, a Collection of 1851 Census Records* (Baltimore: Genealogical Publishing Co., 2004).

Matthew, H. C. G., 'Disraeli, Gladstone, and the Politics of Mid-Victorian Budgets', *Historical Journal*, 22:3 (1979), 615–43.

——, *Gladstone 1809–1874* (Oxford: OUP, 1991).

The Mauritius Commercial Bank, 1838–1963 (Port Louis: Mauritius Commercial Bank, 1964).

McArthur, W. P. 'Medical History of the Famine', in R. D. Edwards, T. D. Williams (eds.), *The Great Famine: Studies in Irish History 1845–52* (Dublin: Browne & Nolan, 1956), 263–315.

McAteer, S., Trainor, B., *Guide to Sources for Researching McAteer Families in Ireland* (Belfast: Ulster Historical Foundation, 2001).

McCaffrey, L. J., *Daniel O'Connell and the Repeal Year* (Lexington: University of Kentucky Press, 1966).

McComas, K. A., Besley, J. C., Steinhardt, J., 'Factors Influencing U.S. Consumer Support for Genetic Modification to Prevent Crop Disease', *Appetite*, 78 (2014), 8–14.

McGowan, M., 'Famine, Facts and Fabrication: An Examination of Diaries from the Irish Famine Migration to Canada', *The Canadian Journal of Irish Studies*, 33:2 (2007), 48–55.

McGuire, J., 'T. Desmond Williams (1921–87)', *Irish Historical Studies*, 26:101 (1988), 3–7.

McHugh, R. J., 'The Famine in Irish Oral Tradition', in R. D. Edwards, T. D. Williams (eds.), *The Great Famine: Studies in Irish History 1845–52* (Dublin: Browne & Nolan, 1956), 391–436.

McLaughlin, E., 'Microfinance Institutions in Nineteenth Century Ireland', unpublished PhD thesis, Maynooth: National University of Ireland (2010).

——, 'Philanthropy, Fraud and Failure: Microfinance in the Great Famine', University of Edinburgh, unpublished paper (2014).

——, '"Profligacy in the Encouragement of Thrift": Savings Banks in Ireland, 1817–1914', *Business History*, 56:4 (2014), 569–91.

McMahon, R., *Homicide in Pre-Famine and Famine Ireland* (Oxford: OUP, 2013).

Merk, F., 'British Government Propaganda and the Oregon Treaty', *American Historical Review*, 40:1 (1934), 38–62.

——, 'The British Corn Crisis of 1845–46 and the Oregon Treaty', *Agricultural History*, 8:3 (1934), 95–123.

Miller, I., 'The Chemistry of Famine: Nutritional Controversies and the Irish Famine, c.1845–47', *Medical History*, 56:4 (2012), 444–62.

Miller, K., *Emigrants and Exiles: Ireland and the Exodus to North America* (Oxford: OUP, 1985).

Mitchell, B. R., *British Historical Statistics* (Cambridge: CUP, 1988).

Mokyr, J., 'The Deadly Fungus: An Econometric Investigation into the Short-Term Demographic Impact of the Irish Famine', *Discussion Paper, Northwestern University*, no. 333 (1978), 1–75.

——, 'Irish History with the Potato', *Irish Economic and Social History*, 8:1 (1981), 8–29.

——, 'Reply to Peter Solar', *Irish Economic and Social History*, 11:1 (1984), 116–21.

——, *Why Ireland Starved: A Quantitative and Analytical History of the Irish Economy, 1800–1850* (London: George Allen & Unwin, 1983).

——, Ó Gráda, C., 'Height and Health in the United Kingdom 1815–1860: Evidence from the East India Company Army', *Explorations in Economic History*, 33:2 (1996), 141–68.

Montague, R. J., 'Relief and Reconstruction in Ireland 1845–49: A Study of Public Policy during the Great Famine', University of Oxford, unpublished DPhil dissertation (1977).

Moore, R. J., *Sir Charles Wood's Indian Policy 1853–66* (Manchester: MUP, 1966).

Moran, G., *Sending Out Ireland's Poor* (Dublin: Four Court's Press, 2004).

——, '"Shovelling Out the Paupers": The Irish Poor Law and Emigration during the Great Famine', in C. Reilly (ed.), *The Famine Irish: Emigration and the Great Hunger* (Dublin: The History Press, 2016), 22–40.

Morgan, E. V., 'Railway Investment, Bank of England Policy and Interest Rates, 1844–48', *Economic History* 4:15 (1940), 329–40.

Morley, J., *The Life of William Ewart Gladstone* (Cambridge: CUP, 2011).

Müller, O., Krawinkel, M., 'Malnutrition and Health in Developing Countries', *Canadian Medical Association Journal*, 173:3 (2005), 279–86.

Mundell, R. A., *International Economics* (New York: Macmillan, 1968).

Nally, D. P., 'The Colonial Dimensions of the Great Irish Famine' in J. Crowley et al. (eds.), *Atlas of the Great Irish Famine, 1845–52* (Cork: Cork University Press, 2012), 64–74.

——, *Human Encumbrances: Political Violence and the Great Irish Famine* (Notre Dame: The University of Notre Dame Press, 2011).

Narciso, G., Severgnini, B., 'The Deep Roots of Rebellion: Evidence from the Irish Revolution', *Trinity Economics Papers* 2216 (2017), online at <http://eh.net/eha/wp-content/uploads/2018/06/Narciso.pdf> [accessed 30 January 2020].

Neal, F., *Black '47: Britain and the Famine Irish* (Basingstoke: Palgrave Macmillan, 1997), (Liverpool: Newsham Press, 2003).
——, 'The Foundations of the Irish Settlement in Newcastle upon Tyne: The Evidence in the 1851 Census', *Immigrants and Minorities*, 18:2–3 (1999), 71–93.
Needham, D., 'Covid-19 and the UK National Debt in Historical Context', History & Policy paper, 22 April 2020, online at <http://www.history-andpolicy.org/policy-papers/papers/covid-19-and-the-uk-national-debt-in-historical-context> [accessed 29 April 2020].
Newbould, I., 'Sir Robert Peel and the Conservative Party, 1832–1841: A Study in Failure?', *English Historical Review*, 98:387 (1983), 529–57.
Nicholson, A., *Annals of the Famine in Ireland* (Dublin: Lilliput Press, 1998).
Nicholson, W., *Microeconomic Theory* (Hinsdale: Dryden Press, 1978).
Nockles, P. B., 'Church or Protestant Sect? The Church of Ireland, High Churchmanship, and the Oxford Movement, 1822–1869', *Historical Journal*, 41:2 (1998), 457–93.
——, 'Continuity and Change in Anglican High Churchmanship in Britain, 1792–1850', University of Oxford, unpublished DPhil dissertation (1982).
——, *The Oxford Movement in Context: Anglican High Churchmanship, 1760–1857* (Cambridge: CUP, 1994).
Norgate, G. L. G., 'Somerville, William Meredyth, First Baron Athlumney, and First Baron Meredyth (1802–1873)', revised Sinéad Agnew, *Oxford Dictionary of National Biography* (Oxford: OUP, 2004), online at <http://www.oxforddnb.com/view/article/26028> [accessed 31 Oct 2012].
North, D. C., 'International Capital Flows and the Development of the American West', *Journal of Economic History*, 16:4 (1956), 493–505.
Nowlan, K. B., 'The Political Background', in R. D. Edwards, T. D. Williams (eds.), *The Great Famine: Studies in Irish History 1845–52* (Dublin: Browne & Nolan, 1956), 131–206.
Nusteling, H. P. H., 'How Many Irish Potato Famine Deaths?: Towards Coherence of the Evidence', *Historical Methods*, 42:2 (2009), 57–80.
O'Brien, D. P., *Foundations of Monetary Economics, vol. 4: The Currency School* (London: Routledge, 1994).
——, idem., *vol. 5: The Banking School* (London: Routledge, 1993).
——, idem., *vol. 6: Monetary Non-Conformists* (London: Routledge, 1994).
O'Brien, G. (George), *The Economic History of Ireland from the Union to the Famine* (London: Longman, 1921).
O'Brien, G. (Gerard), 'Workhouse Management in Pre-Famine Ireland', *Proceedings of the Royal Irish Academy*, 86:C (1986), 113–34.
Obstfeld, M., 'International Macroeconomics: Beyond the Mundell-Fleming Model', *NBER Working Paper*, no. 8369 (2001), 1–56.

——, Shambaugh, J., Taylor A., 'The Trilemma in History: Tradeoffs among Exchange Rates, Monetary Policies and Capital Mobility', *Review of Economics and Statistics*, 87:3 (2005), 423–38.

Ó Cathaoir, B., *Famine Diary* (Dublin: Irish Academic Press, 1999).

Ó Cioséin, N., 'Was there "Silence" about the Famine?' *Irish Studies Review*, 4:13 (1995-96), 7–10.

O'Connor, J., *The Workhouses of Ireland* (Dublin: Anvil Books, 1995).

Odlyzko, A., 'Collective Hallucinations and Inefficient Markets: The British Railway Mania of the 1840s' (2010), online at <http://www.dtc.umn.edu/~odlyzko> [accessed 23 November 2011].

——, 'Supplementary Material for Economically Irrational Pricing of 19th Century British Government Bonds' (2015), online at <http://www.dtc.umn.edu/~odlyzko> [accessed 22 February 2020].

Officer, L. H., *Between the Dollar-Sterling Gold Points: Exchange Rates, Parity and Market Behaviour* (Cambridge: CUP, 1996).

Ó Gráda, C., *A Rocky Road: The Irish Economy since the 1920s* (Manchester: MUP, 1997).

——, *Black '47 and Beyond: The Great Irish Famine in History, Economy and Memory* (Princeton: Princeton University Press, 1999).

——, *Eating People Is Wrong, and Other Essays on Famine, its Past, and its Future* (Princeton, NJ: Princeton University Press, 2015).

——, 'Famine in Ireland, 1300–1900', *UCD Centre for Economic Research Working Paper Series* WP15/13 (2015), 1–34.

——, *Ireland: A New Economic History 1780–1939* (Oxford: OUP, 1994).

——, *Ireland before and after the Famine* (Manchester: MUP, 1993) second edition, note: similar editions of this book have different page numbering.

——, 'Making History in Ireland in the 1940s and 1950s: The Saga of the Great Famine', *The Irish Review (Cork)*, no. 12 (Spring-Summer, 1992), 87–107.

——, 'Markets and Famines in Pre-Industrial Europe', *Journal of Interdisciplinary History*, 36:2 (2005), 143–66.

——, 'School Attendance and Literacy before the Famine: A Simple Baronial Analysis', *UCD Centre for Economic Research Working Paper Series* WP10/22 (2010).

——, *The Great Irish Famine* (Basingstoke: Macmillan, 1989).

——, *The Great Irish Famine* (Cambridge: CUP, 1995).

——, 'The Heights of Clonmel Prisoners 1845–49: Some Dietary Implications', *Irish Economic and Social History* 18:1 (1991), 38–47.

——, 'The Last Major Irish Bank Failure: Lessons for Today?' *University College Dublin Centre for Economic Research Working Paper Series* WP 10/38 (2010).

——, 'The Next World and the New World: Relief, Migration, and the Great Irish Famine', *Journal of Economic History*, 79:2 (June 2019), 319–55.

——, Guinnane, T. W., 'The Workhouses and Irish Famine Mortality', in T. Dyson, C. Ó Gráda (eds.), *Famine Demography* (Oxford: OUP, 2002), 44–64.

——, O'Rourke, K. H., 'Migration as Disaster Relief: Lessons from the Great Irish Famine', *European Review of Economic History*, 1:1 (1997), 3–25.

O'Herlihy, T., *The Famine, 1845–47: A Survey of its Ravages and Causes* (Drogheda: Drogheda Independent Co., 1947).

Ohlmeyer J., 'Eastward Enterprises: Colonial Ireland, Colonial India', *Past and Present*, 240:1 (2018), 83–118.

O'Mahony, C., Thompson, V. (eds.), *Poverty to Promise: The Monteagle Emigrants 1838–58* (Darlinghurst, N.S.W.: Crossing Press, 1994).

Ó Murchadha, C., *Figures in a Famine Landscape* (London: Bloomsbury, 2016).

——, *The Great Famine: Ireland's Agony 1845–52* (London: Continuum Books, 2011).

O'Neill, P. D., 'Memory and John Mitchel's Appropriation of the Slave Narrative', *Atlantic Studies*, 11:3 (2014), 321–43.

Oppermann, M., 'Views of Peel', *Journal of Liberal History*, issue 80 (2013), 48–49.

O'Rourke, K. H., 'Did the Great Irish Famine Matter?' *Journal of Economic History*, 51:1 (1991), 1–22.

——, 'The European Grain Invasion, 1870–1913', *Journal of Economic History*, 57:4 (1997), 775–801.

Palgrave, R. H. I., *Bank Rate and the Money Market in England, France, Germany, Holland, and Belgium 1844–1900* (London: John Murray, 1903).

Parry, J., *The Rise and Fall of Liberal Government in Victorian Britain* (New Haven: Yale University Press, 1993).

Persson, K., *Grain Markets in Europe, 1500–1900: Integration and Deregulation* (Cambridge: CUP, 1998).

——, 'Law of One Price', EH.Net Encyclopedia, ed. R. Whaples, 10 February 2008, online at <http://eh.net/encyclopedia/the-law-of-one-price/> [accessed 15 July 2014].

Phillips, J. A., Wetherell, C., 'The Great Reform Act of 1832 and the Political Modernisation of England', *American Historical Review*, 100:2 (1995), 411–36.

Porter, B., *The Absent-Minded Imperialists: Empire, Society, and Culture in Britain* (Oxford: OUP, 2004).

Prest, J. M., *Lord John Russell* (London: Macmillan, 1972).

Preston, M. 'We Cannot but Regret the Delay: Reflections on the Writings of the North Dublin Union Guardians during the Famine', in D. A. Valone (ed.), *Ireland's Great Hunger*, vol. 2 (Lanham: University Press of America, 2009–10), 21–38.

Purdue, O., 'Poverty and Power: The Irish Poor Law in a N. Antrim Town 1861–1921', *Irish Historical Studies*, 37:148 (2011), 567–83.

Quinn, J., 'Southern Citizen: John Mitchel, the Confederacy and Slavery', *History Ireland*, 15:3 (2007), 30–5.

Ravallion, M., *Markets and Famines* (Oxford: OUP, 1987).

Read, C., 'De Grey [née Cole], Henrietta Frances, Countess de Grey (1784–1848)', *Dictionary of Irish Biography* (January 2014), online at <https://www.dib.ie/biography/de-grey-henrietta-frances-a9548> [accessed 21 January 2021].

——, 'The Economics of Food Subsidies: Feeding Expectations', *The Economist*, 22 February 2014.

——, 'Ireland and the Perils of Fixed-Exchange Rates', History & Policy paper, 20 February 2015, online at <http://www.historyandpolicy.org/policy-papers/papers/ireland-and-the-perils-of-fixed-exchange-rates> [accessed 25 March 2016].

——, 'The Irish Famine and Unusual Market Behaviour in Cork', *Irish Economic and Social History*, 44:1 (2017), 3–18.

——, 'Laissez-faire, the Irish Famine and British Financial Crisis', *Economic History Review*, 69:2 (2015), 411–34.

——, 'Peel, De Grey and Irish Policy 1841–44', *History*, 99:334 (2014), 1–18.

——, 'The Political Economy of Sir Robert Peel', in J. Hoppit, A. B. Leonard, D. J. Needham (eds.), *Money and Markets: Essays in Honour of Martin Daunton* (Woodbridge: Boydell Press, 2019), 71–89.

——, '"The Repeal Year" in Ireland: An Economic Reassessment', *Historical Journal*, 58:1 (2015), 111–35.

——, 'Review: David P. Nally, *Human Encumbrances: Political Violence and the Great Famine*', *Irish Economic and Social History*, 39:1 (2012), 155–57.

——, 'Taxation and the Economics of Nationalism in 1840s Ireland', in D. Kanter, P. Walsh (eds.), *Taxation, Politics, and Protest in Ireland, 1662–2016* (Basingstoke: Macmillan, 2019), 199–225.

Read, D., *Peel and the Victorians* (Oxford: Basil Blackwell, 1987).

Reed, M., 'Loyd, Samuel Jones, Baron Overstone (1796–1883)', *Oxford Dictionary of National Biography* (Oxford: OUP, 2004), online at <http://www.oxforddnb.com/view/article/17115> [accessed 26 December 2013].

Reid, S. J., *Lord John Russell* (London: Sampson Low, Marston & Co., 1895).

Reynolds, D., *In Command of History: Churchill Fighting and Writing the Second World War* (London: Penguin, 2004).

Rock, H., 'Quakerism Understood in Relation to Calvinism: The Theology of George Fox', *Scottish Journal of Theology*, 70:3 (2017), 333–47.

Rostow, W. W., *British Economy in the Nineteenth Century* (Oxford: OUP, 1948).

Roy, T., 'Were Indian Famines "Natural" or "Manmade"?', *LSE Economic History Working Papers* no. 243/2016 (2016), 1–24.

Royal Swedish Academy of Sciences, 'Press Release: The Bank of Sweden Prize in Economic Sciences in Memory of Alfred Nobel, 1999, to Professor Robert A. Mundell', 13 October 1999, online at <http://www.nobelprize.

org/nobel_prizes/economic-sciences/laureates/1999/press.html> [accessed 4 April 2016].

St. John, I., *Disraeli and the Art of Victorian Politics* (London: Anthem Press, 2010).

Sainty, J. C. (ed.), 'Appointments', *Office Holders in Modern Britain vol. 6: Colonial Office Officials 1794–1870* (London: University of London, 1976).

——, *Peerage Creations* (Chichester: Wiley-Blackwell, 2008).

Saylor, R., 'Probing the Historical Sources of the Mauritian Miracle: Sugar Exporters and State Building in Colonial Mauritius', *Review of African Political Economy*, 39:133 (2012), 465–78.

——, *State Building in Boom Times: Commodities and Coalitions in Latin America and Africa* (Oxford: OUP, 2014).

Schama, S., *A History of Britain vol. 3: The Fate of Empire 1776–2000* (London: BBC Worldwide, 2002).

Scherer, P., *Lord John Russell: A Biography* (Selinsgrove: Susquehanna University Press, 1999).

Schonhardt-Bailey, C., *From the Corn Laws to Free Trade: Interests, Ideas, and Institutions in Historical Perspective* (London: MIT Press, 2006).

Schuler, K., 'Should Developing Countries Have Central Banks? Currency Quality and Monetary Systems in 155 Countries', *IEA research monograph* no. 52 (London: Institute of Economic Affairs, 1996), 1–126.

Schuyler, R. L., 'The Abolition of British Imperial Preference, 1846–60', *Political Science Quarterly*, 33 (1918), 77–92.

Schwartz, A. J., 'Banking School, Currency School, Free Banking School', in *The New Palgrave Dictionary of Economics*, 1 (London: Palgrave Macmillan, 2008), 353–58.

Scutt, G. P. S., *History of the Bank of Bengal* (Calcutta: Bank of Bengal, 1904).

Sen, A., *Poverty and Famines: An Essay on Entitlement and Deprivation* (Oxford: OUP, 1981).

Shapiro, B., Sibthorpe, D., Rambaut, A., Austin, J., Wragg, G. M., Bininda-Emonds, O. R. P., Lee, P. L. M., Cooper, A., 'Flight of the Dodo', *Science*, 295:5560 (2002), 1683.

Sharp, P., '1846 and All That: The Rise and Fall of British Wheat Protection in the Nineteenth Century', *University of Copenhagen Department of Economics Discussion Papers*, 06-14 (2006), 1–27.

——, '1846 and All That: The Rise and Fall of British Wheat Protection in the Nineteenth Century', *Agricultural History Review*, 58:1 (2010), 76–94.

Shaver, J. H., et al., 'The Boundaries of Trust: Cross-Religious and Cross-Ethnic Field Experiments in Mauritius', *Evolutionary Psychology*, 16:4 (2018), 1–15.

Sheriff, A., Teelock, V., Wahab, S., Peerthum, S., *Transition from Slavery in Zanzibar and Mauritius* (Dakar: Council for the Development of Social Science Research in Africa, 2016).

Smith, E. A., 'Grey, Charles, Second Earl Grey (1764–1845), Prime Minister', *Oxford Dictionary of National Biography* (Oxford: OUP, 2004), online at <https://www.oxforddnb.com/view/10.1093/ref:odnb/9780198614128.001.0001/odnb-9780198614128-e-11526> [accessed 26 February 2020].

——, *Reform or Revolution? A Diary of Reform in England, 1830–32* (Stroud: Sutton, 1992).

Smith, N., *Wrest Park* (London: English Heritage, 1995).

Smyth, W. J., 'The Longue Durée', in J. Crowley et al. (eds.), *Atlas of the Great Irish Famine, 1845–52* (Cork: Cork University Press, 2012), 46–63.

——, 'The Roles of Cities and Towns during the Great Famine', in J. Crowley et al. (eds.), *Atlas of the Great Irish Famine, 1845–52* (Cork: Cork University Press, 2012), 240–52.

Solar, P. M., 'Occupation, Poverty and Social Class in Pre-Famine Ireland, 1740–1850', in E. F. Biagini, M. E. Daly (eds.), *The Cambridge Social History of Modern Ireland* (Cambridge: CUP, 2017), 25–37.

——, 'The Great Famine Was No Ordinary Subsistence Crisis', in E. M. Crawford (ed.), *Famine: The Irish Experience 900–1900* (Edinburgh: John Donald, 1989), 112–31.

——, 'The Irish Butter Trade in the Nineteenth Century', *Studia Hibernica*, no. 25 (1990), 134–61.

——, 'Why Ireland Starved: A Critical Review of the Econometric Results', *Irish Economic and Social History*, 11:1 (1984), 107–15.

——, Why Ireland Starved and the Big Issues in Pre-Famine Irish Economic History, *Irish Economic and Social History*, 42:1 (1998), 62–75.

——, Smith, M. T., 'Background Migration: The Irish (and Other Strangers) in Mid-Victorian Hertfordshire', *Local Population Studies*, no. 82 (2009), 44–62.

Solomou, S. N., *Themes in Macroeconomic History: The UK Economy 1919–39* (Cambridge: CUP, 1996).

Solow, B. L., *The Land Question and the Irish Economy, 1870–1903* (Cambridge, MA: Harvard University Press, 1971).

Spring, D., 'Aristocracy, Social Structure and Religion in the Early Victorian Period', *Victorian Studies*, 6:3 (1963), 263–80.

Steele, D., 'Baring, Francis Thornhill, First Baron Northbrook (1796–1866)', *Oxford Dictionary of National Biography* (Oxford: OUP, 2004), online at <http://www.oxforddnb.com/view/article/1383> [accessed 4 December 2011].

Steele, G. R., *Monetarism and the Demise of Keynesian Economics* (London: Palgrave Macmillan, 1989).

Stewart, R., *Party and Politics, 1830–52* (New York: Macmillan, 1989).

——, *The Politics of Protectionism: Lord Derby and the Protectionist Party 1841–52* (Cambridge: CUP, 1971).

Stukenbrock, K., *The Stability of Currency Boards* (Frankfurt am Main: Peter Lang AG, 2004), online at <http://library.oapen.org/handle/20.500.12657/26710> [accessed 17 November 2021].

Swift, R., Gilley, S. (eds.), *The Irish in Britain 1815–1939* (London: Pinter Publishers, 1989).

Taylor, A. J. P., 'Genocide: A Review of *The Great Hunger* by Cecil Woodham-Smith (1962)', in A. J. P. Taylor, *Essays in English History* (Harmondsworth: Penguin, 1976), 73–79.

Thompson, E. P., 'The Moral Economy of the English Crowd in the Eighteenth Century', *Past & Present*, 50:1 (1971), 76–136.

Tóibín C., 'Erasures: Colm Tóibín on the Great Irish Famine', *London Review of Books*, 20:15 (30 July 1998), online at <https://www.lrb.co.uk/the-paper/v20/n15/colm-toibin/erasures> [accessed 17 November 2021].

——, Ferriter, D., *The Irish Famine: A Documentary* (New York: St. Martin's Press, 2001).

Tomlinson, J., *Problems of British Economic Policy, 1870–1945* (Abingdon: Routledge, 2006).

Trabant M., Uhlig, H., 'How do Laffer Curves Differ across Countries?' in A. Alesina, F. Giavazzi (eds.), *Fiscal Policy after the Financial Crisis* (Cambridge MA: NBER Books, 2013), 11–49.

——, 'How Far Are We from the Slippery Slope? The Laffer Curve Revisited', *NBER Working Paper* no. 15434 (2009 revised 2011).

Trevelyan, L., *A Very British Family: The Trevelyans and their World* (London: I.B. Tauris, 2006).

Vanhaute, E., '"So Worthy an Example to Ireland". The Subsistence and Industrial Crisis of 1845–1850 in Flanders', in C. Ó Gráda, R. F. J. Paping, E. Vanhaute (eds.), *When the Potato Failed. Causes and Effects of the 'Last' European Subsistence Crisis, 1845–50* (Turnhout: Brepols, 2007), 123–48.

Vanhaute, E., Paping, R. F. J., Ó Gráda, C., 'The European Subsistence Crisis of 1845–1850: A Comparative Perspective', in C. Ó Gráda, R. F. J. Paping, E. Vanhaute (eds.), *When the Potato Failed. Causes and Effects of the 'Last' European Subsistence Crisis, 1845–50* (Turnhout: Brepols, 2007), 15–40.

Vaughan, W. E., *Landlords and Tenants in Ireland 1848–1904* (Dublin: Dundalgan Press, 1984).

Verdier, D., 'Between Party and Faction', in C. Schonhardt-Bailey (ed.), *The Rise of Free Trade*, vol. 4 (London: Routledge, 1997), 309–40.

Verdone, H., 'Sectarianism in Belfast during Ireland's Great Famine, c.1847–50', University of Cambridge, unpublished MPhil thesis (2021).

von Ranke, L., *The Theory and Practice of History: Edited with an Introduction by Georg G. Iggers* (Abingdon: Routledge, 2010).

Walker, B. M., 'Missed Opportunities and Political Failures: The Great Famine General Election of 1847', *History Ireland*, 17:5 (2009), 27–30.

—— (ed.), *Parliamentary Election Results in Ireland, 1801–1922* (Dublin: Royal Irish Academy, 1978).

——, 'Politicians, Elections and Catastrophe: The General Election of 1847', *Irish Political Studies*, 22:1 (2007), 1–34.

——, 'Villain, Victim or Prophet? Lady Gregory, Sir William Gregory and the Great Irish Famine', paper presented at the Cambridge Seminar in Modern Irish History (30 October 2013); 'Villain, Victim or Prophet? William Gregory and the Great Famine', *Irish Historical Studies* 38:152 (2013), 579–99.

Ward, J. M., 'The Colonial Policy of Lord John Russell's Administration', *Historical Studies, Australia and New Zealand*, 9:35 (1960), 244–62.

Ward, J. T., *Sir James Graham* (London: Macmillan, 1967).

Ward-Perkins, C. N., 'The Commercial Crisis 1847', *Oxford Economic Papers*, 2:1 (1950), 75–94.

——, 'Review', *Economica*, 16:64 (1949), 384–87.

Watkins, S. C., Menken, J., 'Famine in Historical Perspective', *Population Development Review*, 11:4 (1985), 647–75.

Webb, P., Stordalen, G. A., Singh, S., Wijesinha-Bettoni, R., Shetty, P., Lartey, A., 'Hunger and Malnutrition in the 21st Century', *British Medical Journal*, 361:k2238 (2018).

Williams, C. D., 'Kwashiorkor: A Nutritional Disease of Children Associated with a Maize Diet', *Nutrition Reviews*, 31:11 (1973), 350–51, originally: 'Kwashiorkor, a Nutritional Disease Associated with a Maize Diet', *Lancet*, no. 224 (1935), 1151–52.

Williams, D., *The Rebecca Riots: A Study in Agrarian Discontent* (Cardiff: University of Wales Press, 1955).

Williams, E. T., 'The Colonial Office in the Thirties', *Australian and New Zealand Historical Studies*, 2:7 (1943), 141–60.

Williamson, J. G., 'The Impact of the Corn Laws Just Prior to Repeal', *Explorations in Economic History*, 27:2 (1990), 123–56.

Woodham-Smith, C., *The Great Hunger: Ireland 1845–49* (London: Hamish Hamilton, 1962) (London: Penguin Books, 1991).

World Food Programme, 'Building Resilience, Protecting Livelihoods and Reducing Malnutrition of Refugees, Returnees and other Vulnerable People', Paper WFP/EB.2/2014/8-B/4.

Wormell, J. (ed.), *National Debt in Britain, 1850–1930*, vol. 5 (London: Routledge, 1999).

Zant, W., 'How Is the Liberalization of Food Markets Progressing? Market Integration and Transaction Costs in Subsistence Economies', *World Bank Policy Research Working Paper*, no. 6331 (2013).

Zastoupil, L., 'Moral Government: J. S. Mill on Ireland', *Historical Journal*, 26:3 (1983), 707–17.

Zimmermann, G.-D., *Songs of Irish Rebellion: Political Street Ballads and Rebel Songs, 1780–1900* (Dublin: Allen Figgis, 1967).

Index

PEOPLE, MARKETS, GOODS:
ECONOMIES AND SOCIETIES IN HISTORY

ISSN: 2051-7467

PREVIOUS TITLES

1. *Landlords and Tenants in Britain, 1440–1660:*
Tawney's Agrarian Problem *Revisited*,
edited by Jane Whittle, 2013

2. *Child Workers and Industrial Health in Britain, 1780–1850*,
Peter Kirby, 2013

3. *Publishing Business in Eighteenth-Century England*,
James Raven, 2014

4. *The First Century of Welfare:*
Poverty and Poor Relief in Lancashire, 1620–1730,
Jonathan Healey, 2014

5. *Population, Welfare and Economic Change in Britain 1290–1834*,
edited by Chris Briggs, Peter Kitson and S. J. Thompson, 2014

6. *Crises in Economic and Social History: A Comparative Perspective*,
edited by A. T. Brown, Andy Burn and Rob Doherty, 2015

7. *Slavery Hinterland: Transatlantic Slavery and*
Continental Europe, 1680–1850,
edited by Felix Brahm and Eve Rosenhaft, 2016

8. *Almshouses in Early Modern England: Charitable Housing in the Mixed*
Economy of Welfare, 1550–1725,
Angela Nicholls, 2017

9. *People, Places and Business Cultures:*
Essays in Honour of Francesca Carnevali,
edited by Paolo Di Martino, Andrew Popp and Peter Scott, 2017

10. *Cameralism in Practice: State Administration*
and Economy in Early Modern Europe,
edited by Marten Seppel and Keith Tribe, 2017